From Donington to Dov[...]

The History of Rock at Donington Park

By

Ian Carroll

It has been an amazing journey producing this book, from cloudy Plymouth to rainy Holland to bright and sunny Donington Park, there has not been a dull moment in the last 9 years of writing this book, a book of blood, sweat & beers, many many beers……

After writing the Official Book of the Reading Festival it was time to make a start on the book of my other 'favourite' festival Donington Monsters of Rock - and as it is now – Download, the greatest rock festival the world has ever seen.

This book features over 300 interviews from major mega stars to small bands, to artists who are sadly no longer with us – included is an interview with the legend that was (and still is) Ronnie James Dio, who phoned me at home a week before he cancelled his last UK tour due to cancer, this is possibly one of his last interviews that he completed.

This book was a nightmare to produce, with publishers picking it up and dropping it due to the 'current book climate' and Live Nation being messed around by them as much as I was – though without the help of Andy, John & Stuart, I would not be where I am with this book today. I would also like to thank the journalist who sent me a couple interviews and the legendary Bailey Brothers who I did a few interviews with from when they were the DJ's, hosting the main stage and spinning discs between bands, great guys and still going!

Finally, thanks to all the 'festival attendees' who were interviewed for experiences over the years, they were great additions to the book.

So, the book is finally out as a Kindle published book which is the way forward for new releases, though I don't rule out a printed copy in the future if another suitable publisher comes along.

Ladies and Gentleman, welcome to Donington Park

Dedicated to Raine, Nathan, Josh & Rex, the coolest little family that anyone could ever wish for

Introduction

If in deed it was true that Robert Johnson 'sold his soul to the Devil' in order to master the guitar and perform the most amazing blues music, then something similar must have occurred in Leicestershire in 1980 and every year since at the site of the Donington racetrack.

Selling their souls to the Devil in exchange for a weekend of Rock & Metal; thousands of similarly minded fans make the annual pilgrimage to Donington, for a weekend of every style of rock music available.

Donington has become the Mecca for 'metal heads' the world over, with people attending from as far afield as Australia for their annual fix of all that is best in the world of rock music.

From the initial Monsters Of Rock in the shadow of the Dunlop tyre to Download Festivals magnificent 'on form' show in 2009, nothing it appears can stop the metal beast from tearing up the countryside and laying waste to the ears of the thousands of punters in attendance.

With classic performances over the years from rocks giants such as AC/DC, Iron Maiden, Metallica and Kiss to the 'new school' of rock in the form of bands like Slipknot, Linkin Park, System of a Down and My Chemical Romance, the festival grows in stature and cult status each year.

The hallowed grounds of Donington Park are where most bands want to play and where most fans want to see them play. It's now developed into more than just a festival; it's an event, a gathering of similar minded people with a need to belong. A 'rock & metal brotherhood' where a feeling of 'family' and camaraderie is second to none. From the close knit community of the Official Download forums to the 'feel good factor' in the campsites, Download is now the place to be as a 'musical rite of passage' for thousands of people all over the world and with the increase in capacity, this extended family of rock is extending just that little bit more each year.

My first attendance at Donington was for Monsters Of Rock in 1983. I was there to see Whitesnake the most, with a dash of Twisted Sister and a sprinkling of Dio; with the rest of the line-up working well as an aperitif.

Living in Plymouth I had to travel over night each year, leaving Devon by coach at around midnight and eventually arriving at Donington at round 6am. It was usually cold, foggy and a place with nothing to do but drink, until the gates opened at around lunchtime. So after six hours or so of solid drinking, peeing in the woods and getting bored, it was down to the front of the 'bowl shaped' arena for a day of rocking out.

Every year that I attended Monsters Of Rock there were many 'stand out' moments; Motley Crue's first appearance in '84, Magnum's extremely British opening slot in '85, Metallica's debut also in '85, Cinderella playing in torrential rain in '87, Guns N' Roses over popular set in '88, Metallica's first headline slot in '95 and Kiss in full make up at the last Monsters Of Rock in '96; all classic sets and greatly appreciated by the fans, who heaved a great sigh when MOR died in '96, only to be re-born as Download Festival in 2003.

Download Festival has carried on the tradition that Monsters Of Rock had already established; amazing bands, fantastic times and best line-ups ever for a rock festival. Who could forget Metallica's secret set in '03 and their returning the following year without Lars and still pulling it off, Billy Idol returning to the UK to headline the 2nd stage in '05, Metallica playing

'Master Of Puppets' in its entirety in '06, Iron Maiden proving they were still the best British metal band in '07, Kiss proving they were still a massive festival band (with all the trimmings) in '08, the debut of the reformed Faith No More in '09 and the mighty return of Def Leppard 23 years since the last appearance to headline the final scorching day in '09. Again all amazing performances and thousands of other also; from the fourth to the mainstage the variety and choice of who to see and who not to see has never been better, but lets not mention the 'clashes'.

If you speak to any rock & metal bands in the world and ask 'which festival do you want to play at' their answer will always be the same, 'Donington'; ask the question to any rock fan 'which festival is the best one every year' and you get the same immediate reply 'Donington' (or Download depending on your age).

The festival has steadily developed into a weekend that now lasts nearly a full year. The Forums are teaming with peoples memories of that years festival from the day after it's all over up to about September. From September to January the forums are chock full of speculation about the following year's line-up and from January to June there is mass hysteria about the confirmed artists, about who's playing, who's not playing and those dreaded 'clashes', where a classic band that someone wants to watch on the mainstage clashes with a Norwegian Black Metal band that they want to watch on the 3rd stage, this frustration of course all gets directed at Andy Copping, because it's his fault. As we all must know, the booking of bands, on the scale that the festival has now reached, must be a real headache for Andy and of course there are going to be some clashes; but that's festivals for you and no one should be to blame.

With the increase in metal and rock festivals in Europe, such as Wacken Open Air, Hellfest, Sweden Rock, Graspop and of course now the European versions of Sonisphere, Download has still continued to flourish, building on it's success year after year and is still the dominant festival of its kind.

Over the next 25 chapters you will get a feel for the festival (if you have never been before), will be able to reminisce (if you have been to the festivals over the years) and you will get a full insight into the festival from not only the bands point of view, but also the fans and the organisers perspectives.

So, welcome to the Official Book of the Donington & Download Festivals and in the words of the Bailey Brothers:

'Rock Not Pop Metalheads!!!'

(Ian Carroll Author)
Forward by Mr Lars Ulrich, all the way from Brazil to my kitchen

"It's THE hallowed ground.

Over the 30 years, some of the best 'metal moments' have happened there; starting off with Rainbow and up through the AC/DC's and the Maiden's and the Whitesnake's and everybody else.
You could probably parallel the history of Donington to the history of rock.
Who's hot, who's was in, who was out, who moved up, who fell from grace; there's certainly a correlation between writing the history of Donington to writing the history of hard rock and metal.
To have been present six and a half times, it's certainly awesome to be part of the history of something that I am extremely proud of and I really, really sincerely hope that Metallica will come back and play it again."
Lars Ulrich (Metallica – Drums)

1980
Rainbow,
Judas Priest, Scorpions, April Wine, Saxon, Riot, Touch, Neal Kaye

August 16th 1980, a date that should be firmly noted in all diaries as a day of rock music celebrations; the day that the 'rock' was firmly embedded at Donington.

Prior to the inaugural festival in 1980, the only place that you could see rock & metal bands in the open, in the summer, was at Reading Festival. Though in the late '70's, Reading had strayed away slightly from rock music and had been covering New Romantic bands and up and coming new indie/punk bands such as the Police, Patti Smith and the Jam; the launch of a new music festival for 'out and out' rock fans was just was the doctor ordered. Situated 'slap bang' in the middle of England, Donington Park racetrack seemed like the ideal location for a festival, equidistant to all travelling rock fans.

Organised by promoter Paul Loasby and Maurice Jones of MCP, they had the task of putting on what would become the longest running rock & metal festival in the UK.

The first years line-up was a 'who's who' of rock giants, from Germany's finest Scorpions to Birmingham's 'Metal Gods' Judas Priest to the magnificent headliners Rainbow, who still featured two members of Deep Purple *and were quite the draw on the day. This show was to be the last Rainbow performance for both Graham Bonnet and Cozy Powell; Bonnet left to pursue a solo career and then joining the Michael Schenker Group, Cozy Powell leaving to become drummer for Bonnet's solo project, then MSG and finally a full time member of Whitesnake, where he would return to Donington in 1983, again in a headline slot.*

Added to this line up were Riot and Touch from New York and April Wine from Canada.

Touch had the honour bestowed on them of being the first ever band to play at the MOR Festival and the first band to play at Donington and certainly not the last! Saxon were also on the bill, as part of the NWOBHM (New Wave Of British Heavy Metal). This was their first appearance and it had such an affect on them that they even wrote a song dedicated to their experience of the festival, 'And the Bands Played On'; this would not be their last performance at the festival.

One of the most bizarre moments of the festival was when a member of Touch, the opening act swallowed a bee onstage.

The Rainbow performance, or part of it, was broadcast by the BBC late at night, to the joy of rock fans everywhere With an approximate attendance of 35,000 the festival, with a bargain ticket price of £7.50, was deemed a success, which paved the way for all future Monsters Of Rock festivals.

"I remember it being the best show that I had ever been on because, for one reason all my family were there and it was the first time they had ever seen the band play live. My Mum and Dad weren't really 'hard rock' fans, but they saw the show and they were just blown away.

It was a special treat for me and it was a very sad day at the same time because Cozy left and I was about to leave the same day too, but when he did leave it changed the whole

atmosphere of the band, so later on I actually left myself. It was a great day and I will never forget it, ever.
I didn't think it was particularly one of the best shows we played musically, but there was something about it. The might have been a few rough edges here and there from everybody, but the crowd was fantastic and it went very well. I remember it being a very long day.
I remember walking around in the afternoon a little bit, but we didn't really hang around the place very much at all.
We didn't get out of that place until about six the next morning, because there were so many people walking on the road, going wherever they were going.
We got back to the hotel in Leicester and said goodbye to Cozy until he got into his car and drove away."
Graham Bonnet (Rainbow – Vocals)

"Playing at the Monsters of Rock Festival in Donington after Reading was vastly different for us - being that PRIEST in 1980 were no longer rookies - if anything we were the front runners of metal in the UK!!
 That's why Donington being all out rock and metal was the ultimate gig at the time for us!! It was the one we just had to play.
I can remember feeling immensely proud to be up there banging my head with thousands of metal heads in sync with us!! Donington attracted the cream of metal bands from all over the world. And I am sure I can speak for all of the bands and all of the fans when I say that there should be a Donington every single weekend!!"
K.K. Downing (Judas Priest – Guitar)

"I do remember it was a special moment for us in time. I remember it was great to play with the Scorpions and Saxon and Rainbow as well. It was just a great festival line-up and I have very fond memories of it."
What does stick in my mind was that we had some serious pyrotechnics to let off and for some reason we weren't allowed to, I don't know why it was. They were serious fireworks and they were in 3 foot tubes and we had to set them off were car

batteries. As we didn't set them off, we shared them out between us.
We saved them until bonfire night and dished them out and we all had an incredible firework display. I remember I lived in a little village in Staffordshire; I let mine off and the police arrived within 10 minutes because they thought someone had let bombs off and it was pretty spectacular and the loudest noise I'd ever heard."
Glenn Tipton (Judas Priest – Guitar)

"Thinking about Donington, it was not only an amazing bill, in 1980 there were bands like Judas Priest, Rainbow, etc., it was also a very memorable moment, with five Germans racing (on their way to the stage) round the legendary Donington Speedway in the wrong direction. Can you imagine the expression on the face of our driver / Tour manager Bob Adcock (Liverpool) facing a bunch of motorbikes coming at high speed towards us around the corner. Well, the Scorpions survived."
Scorpions

"I forget exactly the year we were there but it was in the early '80's. 1982 I think. The day we were there was sunny and dry. The first dry day of Donington that year. The grounds were soaked. Soft, sticky mud everywhere backstage and out front. The backstage crew had put straw down on the ground to try and soak up the moisture but with the grass turning to mud, the straw just added to the problem and footwear was caked with straw and mud to the point of making everyone's feet look huge!
We were all issued rubber boots or Wellingtons as I think the British call them.
I brought mine home to Canada and used them for many years. Must be the Scot in me.
The dressing rooms were quite some distance from the stage and we were driven there by kamikaze young drivers.
The road to the stage was dirt and rather bumpy and those mad shuttle pilots choose to go as fast as possible.
We almost threw our driver out and drove ourselves. It was

that bad!
Rainbow was the headliner that day. I wasn't a fan as much as I am today. It was Cosy Powell's last show with them.
I wish I had stayed to watch him and Ritchie Blackmore. I know I missed something special.
Everyone backstage and out front was in dressed in black except us. At that time we were wearing red and white and all our Marshall amps were red with white grill cloth. Did we stick out in an embarrassing way? Yes! We played our songs to a very wet crowd of mud men. Not all, but enough to remember it that way.
Our big hit at the time in the USA and Canada was a love ballad called "Just Between You and Me". To me that worked in North America but not that day. It was a Heavy Metal crowd and we looked like a damn pop band. I remember feeling a tad out of place playing that tune.
We had some heavy songs that rocked like "Crash and Burn" "Before the Dawn", "Sign of the Gypsy Queen', but in England we were billed as a Heavy Metal band compared to the USA and Canada where we were known as a Hard Rock Band. England took their metal seriously!
It might have been me feeling out of our element that day or it might have been it was just Rainbow's day, but I never really came away with good memories of our performance at Donington.
If it came to do it again, I would in a flash, but without the red and white which was gone the next year anyway.
I'm glad I was part of Donington's long history."
Brian Greenway (April Wine – Guitar/Vocals)

"The first time was fantastic. Obviously it was the first major metal festival in England, maybe Europe actually, but definitely in Britain.
We were one of the rising stars then of the '80's metal scene and they asked us to play it. We'd had a very big album released previously, 'Wheels Of Steel', so it was great walking onstage in front of 60,000 people that all knew the songs; that was a new thing for us, we'd never experienced that before.

I think it really broke us bigger, because we weren't the same as other bands on there. We were looked on as a 'newer rising act' and bands like Rainbow, Judas Priest and Scorpions were established acts.
It was really great; it was a special festival where the audience wanted to see everybody."
I went for a ride on Rob Halfords Harley-Davidson around the track, he didn't know though!
We watched all the bands because then it was different; the festival was in the field and the dressing rooms were in the pit lane. There wasn't much down at the stage actually.
Our agent booked all the bands and we were earmarked to become big. We came on in the afternoon, which isn't always a good thing, but the reviews were actually really good for us 'we should have been on later', 'they stole the show' and all that sort of silliness, but we really enjoyed it"
Biff Byford (Saxon -Vocals)

"In 1980 it was announced to us that we had been booked for Donington a new festival; this was a good year for us as 'Wheels Of Steel' and two singles both did great and we were selling out everywhere,
When we arrived, the dressing rooms were miles from backstage so we settled into our room. We had a balcony overlooking the courtyard below and Judas Priest was doing a photo shoot in full metal regalia with Rob looking like a 'Metal God'. A few weeks before we had done a 7 week tour with them and Top Of The Pops so we went down to say hi and noticed a few people from other bands snickering at Rob in his gear; but they had the smile wiped off their faces when Priest hit the stage.
Fortunately the set from Saxon was preserved on audio and listening to a new version recently (09) mastered at Abbey Road by EMI, it's easy to see why this is the penultimate Saxon line up of the 5 original members with Pete Gill hammering the drums relentlessly and I in true Metal tradition destroyed my Stratocaster in 'Machine Gun'.
All the bands and liggers used a shuttle bus to the back stage area and I sat opposite to Joe Elliot who was sporting black

and white trousers striped he was going down to catch our set as at that point he had not seen us or us them and were both curious to see the competition (but he was just a guest).
The roar of the crowd when we hit the stage was unforgettable and when Gilly and Dobby were playing the sing back part in 'Bap Shoo Ap' the beat from just two was like a steam hammer and I remember thinking 'this is Metal Woodstock. After our set I was going to watch the Scorpions when a Mercedes pulled up right behind the stage and the window came down. I heard Graham and it was Ritchie Blackmore shouting me over and he spoke as though we were old friends he said we did a great set and he also said I cannot tell you have a handicap (like Tony Iommi I have a finger end missing). He told me he had seen Hendrix at the Isle Of White Festival ten years before and he signed my program 'To Graham' which I still have to day. We chatted a while and he wished me well and off he went to his private room, but I had never spoke to him before.

At this time we did not know that Donington, the first one, would become the iconic festival it has become or that the following years it would become the most famous metal gig of all. It was only when we met people like Lars, Dimebag and Motley Crue; they all asked about 'wow what was the first Donington like?' and it was great to tell the story to so many musicians and fans."
Graham Oliver (Saxon – Guitar)

"Well, while things were brewing in the States with our singles "When The Spirit Moves You" and "Don't You Know What Love Is" our manager Bruce Payne got us on a tour with Rainbow and we were off to Europe to open up. Quite memorable being on tour with the guitar player of my favorite band "Deep Purple" to say the very least.
One show, Monsters of Rock Live At Donington, turned out to be more than we could have ever imagined. We arrived on a rainy, muddy day at the huge race track to open up the show which featured Rainbow, Judas Priest, Scorpions, Riot and April Wine. Without knowing it at the time, we became the first band ever to play at Monsters of Rock Festival.

There was a sea of faces (60,000 people I was told)...almost as far as we could see...and I remembered what someone said...if you can get the front 5,000 people, you are good to go. I think it went really well, though no sound check...anyway, the audience responded great, though they had never heard of us before, mainly we focused on performing the songs properly. Tapes I've

heard since, we sound spot on...the harmonies, etc. though it's hard to resist playing the songs a tad faster when the adrenalin is rushing thru you...

What was interesting was, the mayhem that followed with all the other bands, we were fortunate to have been set up and ready to go (e.g. bass drum mic on the bass drum and guitar mic on the guitar, rather than on something else) because changing mics and channels, etc. through the day was a great challenge for the crew. This definitely helped when it came to mixing the "live" LP that was released.

When I got off stage there was quite a commotion, rumours that our bass guitar player had maybe possibly swallowed a bee. That event seems to have overshadowed the entire day, the music, the two years of striving to get to that stage, kind of surreal really...and it was a good lesson to us.

Anyway "Don't You Know What Love Is" became #1 on the Melody Maker

chart and there was Doug on the front page of Melody Maker holding the plastic cup from which he says he may have swallowed the bee. Is this Spinal

Tap, or what?

We ended up using the live performance on a live CD of the show and, to his credit, Roger Glover, who produced the LP, wouldn't let us overdub or change the originally recorded tape...an honest moment... though we would have loved to have added our 30 part harmonies and walls of keyboards (I only have two hands and this was before sequencing, samples and all that).when I heard the CD I saw other bands hadn't quite been as "reserved" in their approach, but it was cool and sounded OK.

Anyway, proud to have done it, proud to have been there, look back at it with a huge smile on my face...would love to do it

again...loved the time, the vibe, the musicianship, the values...all good stuff..."
Mark Mangold (Touch – Keyboards / Vocals)

"The funny thing about Donington was that when I was with Motorhead and Doug Smith Management, he was trying to put something on at Donington but Maurice Jones from MCP nipped in behind him and got the rights to Donington, so we were there right at the beginning, but that was why we did Port Vale. We were going to play Donington!"
Fast Eddie Clarke (Motorhead - Guitar)

"I was present at Cozy Powell's final gig with Rainbow, spending time with him in the afternoon, meeting Ritchie Blackmore for the first time, I was sorry to see CP leaving the band, I always thought that Rainbow were one of the metal bands, and CP was a vital ingredient of the band."
Bernie Marsden (Whitesnake – Guitar)

"The first one that I went to was the first one that was headlined by Rainbow in 1980.
I was actually just out in the audience; I went with Sean Harris and Colin Kimberley the bass player.
It was a good gig and we particularly enjoyed Rainbow as that was who we had mainly gone to see and Judas Priest were on. Priest were good on the day and I remember them doing 'You Don't Have To Be Old To Be Wise'."
Brian Tatler (Diamond Head – Guitar)

"I remember very vividly as a kid, looking at the Donington posters and thinking one day I will play that (the year that Rainbow headlined in particular) I think Judas priest played that year also."
Myke Gray (Skin – Guitar)

"We feel privileged to be a part of the history of the Donington Monsters Of Rock festival.
We were there at the very first Monsters Of Rock in 1980. We thought we had a great vantage point looking down over the

crowd underneath a Union Jack with Sheffield proudly painted across it. The view was great but the sound was awful. Half the music just disappeared up a cow's arse a mile down the road due to a swirling wind. It was like watching a video out of sync (The gig not the cow's arse).
Saxon were good, so were the Scorpions, but Rainbow was fuckin' awesome. Graham Bonnet looked like he had just come from a wedding party but what a voice.
You have to applaud Paul Loadsby (promoter) who was brave enough to stick his arse on the line to give us Rock and Metal fans a festival we could finally call our own. Helped out by another legend in the rock promoter circus Maurice Jones of MCP (Midland Concert Promotions)."
The Bailey Brothers (Mick & Dez Donington Comperes)

"The first ever 'Monsters of Rock' at Castle Donington, was to be my first ever experience of a gig, and to be honest, as a naïve 16 yr old, I don't remember that much of the actual performances, it was the experience as a whole.
The red double decker bus ride from Broadmarsh Bus station to the venue, buzzing with anticipation. The sight of the gathering crowd outside the gates. Once inside, I was blown away by the sea of people, the stalls, the plethora of colours, the smells (some very suspect!!!!) and the mud bath! I vividly recall a group of fans skidding and sliding up and down the field, left of stage, to uproars, and ovations, plastered from head to toe in sludge.
It was a day where I heard the sentence "OK you bad ass M. F's..." more times than I care to mention....And the portaloo experience, which I'd rather forget.....the queues, my fear of getting lost........oh, and Rainbow, a classic performance of 'Since you've Been Gone'.
Fond, fond memories."
Jane Bartley (Plymouth)

"I attended all 15 of the 'Monsters of Rock' festivals at Castle Donington.
I am probably fortunate that I was at the right age at the time of the first festival (17 years old) to be able to go on to attend

all the festivals. In fact (although a little sad in hindsight) during the 80s it was my highlight of the year each year.
I would organise the tickets, the transport (5 of us in a Ford Cortina in 1980 to 20 of us in two transit vans in '87 and '88), the banners & flagpoles (these became more ambitious every year with flags and flashing lights etc being added each year, some people actually used our flagpoles as meeting points), and of course……..the beer. Over the years the rules for which containers you could use for carrying your beer in changed from using virtually whatever you liked to not being able to use anything at all, but the daftest idea was probably when you could use a 2-litre bottle as long as the top and neck had been cut off, this made it almost impossible to carry when full.
Most people would probably say that spending all day in a mostly muddy (Donington was famed for its mud way before Glastonbury) field with up to 100 thousand denim and leather clad rockers listening to a sometimes inaudible racket was their version of Hell, but to me it has given me some of the greatest memories of my life and I am proud to claim that I attended them all and loved every minute of it.
In 1980 I had never attended an outdoor festival before, so my excitement was at fever pitch during the preceding week, especially as my all-time hero (still is to this day) Ritchie Blackmore would be headlining. There were all sorts of rumours about Blackmore playing a major solo on top of the speaker stacks way above the stage (as it happened this didn't take place due to some mechanical lift failure apparently).
My very first view of Donington (and my earliest memory) was as we approached the entrances from the car park I could see the merchandise stalls from afar with the Rainbow 'Down to Earth' knitted scarves pinned to the top of the marquees. I had missed out on one of these scarves from the tour earlier in the year, so my wallet was honed into buying one as soon as we got in. I still have it today (along with all the festival t-shirts and programmes from every year).

I also recall that there was a Greenpeace stall, selling 'what else' but 'Rainbow Warrior' t-shirts. There was also an official Rainbow fan club stall on site.
Musically the highlight of the day (and probably of any day) was the way Rainbow segued 'Since You Been Gone' into 'Somewhere Over The Rainbow' and then straight into 'Stargazer' (my favourite song ever)….even though Graham Bonnet did mess the words up a bit. Cozy Powell's '1812 overture' drum solo went off with its usual bang and Blackmore's (stage managed) setting fire to a speaker stack during his guitar onslaught finale were other fond memories of the headlining act.
I remember getting into a queue for a burger approx 20 minutes prior to Judas Priests' set and still being stood in the same place in the queue some one and a half hours later after they had left the stage. I think the stallholder must have been a Priest fan.
To me Scorpions were playing as well as they ever did at that time in their career (prior to the MTV-friendly version we got a few years later) and their set was as faultless as ever (I saw them 3 times during 1980). I recall 'Pictured Life' being a particular favourite of mine at the time.
Saxon were also on a roll on the back of their nationwide 'Wheels of Steel' tour. They went down very well.
Of the other bands I can only really remember April Wine being ok.
The weather on the day was fine, but the preceding fortnight continuous rain had made the site a mudbath.
The toilets were appalling!!!"
Paul Hartshorn (Chesterfield)

"I have to admit I don't remember a whole lot about the bands as this was my first festival and I was just caught up in the atmosphere of the whole thing. However, this is what I can remember.
Saxon, who were the first band I ever saw live, were at their peak and put in a decent set, including their 2 biggest hits 'Wheels of Steel' and '(747) Strangers in the Night' fronted by my neighbour from Barnsley Pete 'Biff' Byford. I remember

Biff lived in a 2-up 2-down terrace house at the time but rode the biggest motorbike I'd ever seen which must have been worth as much as the house.
Speaking of motorbikes, there was a huge roar from the crowd when Rob Halford took to the stage on a Harley although if memory serves there was some confusion at first as Halford had changed his hair colour/style for the gig and for a few seconds some people were in a panic that Halford had been replaced by someone else. Scorpions were as brilliant as they've always been in the dozen or so times I've seen them.
Klaus Mein's 'Hello Donning Castle' was classic Klaus. Rainbow were awesome instrumentally but Rick Astley look-a-like Graham Bonnet's voice could never match Dio's live.
Blackmore was his usual tease, giving little snippets of classic Purple/Rainbow songs, so when he started playing 'Stargazer' we all thought we'd just get a few bars as he'd always said it was too complicated a song to reproduce live. When we realised they were ACTUALLY GOING TO PLAY 'STARGAZER' the whole placed erupted! It still brings chills to my spine 30 years later.
I was on such a high from the whole day that I didn't care that I was caked in mud, we missed our last bus home, had to sleep under a tree by a river which I fell into in the middle of the night and then spend the early hours of Sunday morning wandering around Derby to find a launderette to dry my clothes. It was one of those days that I'm privileged to say that 'I was there'."
Tony Nixon (Plymouth)

"The best experience I ever had at Donington park was at the first ever Monsters of rock Saturday 16th August 1980. Back then I was 18 and it was my first ever festival.
I attended it with my good friend Robert Tosh, who sadly isn't with us anymore. RIP. He was 24 and decided to take me with him to Donington. I remember every detail of the experience we started by getting the overnight Liverpool boat on the Thursday in order to be there for Friday, we then got the train to Crewe, and then travelled from Crewe to Derby. We dropped our stuff off at the Redsetters guest house and went

off to buy our Monsters of Rock tickets. (Which I still have, it's proudly framed and hung on the wall as its one of my most prized possessions). I can still remember that the ticket only cost us £7.50 each, which is unreal considering the bands we got to see live.

On the Saturday we got the bus into Donington Park, it was a sunny day, but the fields were covered in muck, but that didn't matter we just couldn't wait to see all the bands on stage. I always thought it was amazing how between each bands performance instead of having music playing in the background they had DJ Neal Kay playing.

Throughout the performances of the bands that played there, there are a couple of moments that will always stand out to me.

Saxon on stage playing '747' and 'Wheels Of Steel', the crowd went nuts.

Rob Halford walking out on stage dressed head to toe in leather and studs milking the crowd, and then cracking his whip straight into the intro song and KK Downing, ripping away on his flying V guitar to 'Sinner'.

One of the main highlights was definitely when the main headliner RAINBOW were to appear on stage, their intro music soared through the sound system, and as soon as they appeared on stage I was lifted about 30-40ft forward because of the surge of the crowd and ended up at the very front of the stage, I couldn't believe I was so close to these rock n roll legends.

From then I attended Donington until 1984, then travelled back again in 2008 and 2009 for Download. I'm now 48 and still a loud and proud metal head."

John Dickson (Belfast)

1981
AC/DC,
Whitesnake, Blue Oyster Cult, Slade, Blackfoot, More, Tommy Vance DJ

Back for another year and another amazing line-up. With AC/DC making their first headline appearance at Donington the festival was bound to be a success. Coming off the commercial triumph that was 'Back In Black', several songs from the album littered the set, including 'You Shook Me All Night Long', 'Hells Bells' and the albums title track. Now with Brian Johnson, accepted by all the fans, at the helm on vocals, after Bon Scott's death in 1980, AC/DC were slowly becoming one of the most popular and biggest rock bands in the world. They remain the band that is most linked with the Donington festivals from the beginnings of MOR to Download; 2010 will be their 4th slot at the festival, a joint record for Donington headline appearances equalled by Iron Maiden. Whitesnake were in the special guest spot and they were becoming bigger with each release. They had recently brought out the 'Come an' Get It' album, hitting the UK album charts and spawning the singles 'Don't Break My Heart Again' and 'Would I Lie To You'.
Elsewhere on the bill Blue Oyster Cult weren't having a good day and as Joe Bouchard put it *'it was probably the worst show in BOC history'*; drummer fired in the

morning, poor sound and Eric Bloom going crazy on his plaque (read on for his account of the day).

Slade played before BOC with toilet rolls in large quantities being thrown into the crowd from the stage and vice versa. Noddy and the boys were at the time having a 'second wind' due to their successful slot at Reading Festival the previous year, where they were last minute replacements for Ozzy Osbourne. Unfortunately Slade played during the worst rain of what ended up being a somewhat wet day.

Blackfoot played their brand of Southern Rock, with Rickey Medlocke on lead vocals and guitar; Medlocke now plays guitar for the ultimate Southern Rock band Lynyrd Skynryd.

The opening slot this time was given to More, another band that had been added to the ever increasing category of NWOBHM bands, flooding venues up and down the UK at the time. Laurie Mansworth, lead guitarist of More, went on to manage Roadstar who opened the 2006 Monsters Of Rock festival at the Milton Keynes Bowl; Roadstar have now transformed into Heaven's Basement.

Another year was over, a very wet year and the first to feature the Radio One DJ Tommy Vance as the shows compere; Tommy hosted the Friday night Rock Show on Radio One from 1978 to 1993. 'TV On The Radio' was the new voice of Monsters of Rock at Donington for the next 5 years.

"The first one I worked was with AC/DC in 1981, which was as cracker."
David Coverdale (Whitesnake – Vocals)

"I have very fond memories of Donington. I played in 1981, as I am sure you are aware on the AC/DC bill. I regard the show as the most memorable of festival gigs, even though we were not headliners.   On the day we felt very pleased to say the least, the crowd were amazing and

*I felt that our recent return from the USA had been very personal from the vast UK audience. Backstage I remember one thing very clearly. Those US people from Blue Oyster Cult deemed that they were "disrespected" on the bill, and took great pleasure smashing their memento mounted posters from Maurice Jones the promoter, Maurice had made one for each member of every band, a nice gesture, I still have mine. The BOC guys said they were making their point, but the only people that saw their act were other members of bands on the bill, of whom all just looked at one another and shrugged, "Americans".... On stage I personally remember looking out from the stage and realizing the crowd was as big in width as it was in length, and that shook me a little, word has it that 140,000 could have been there that day, well I believe it.
I continued a friendship with Rick Medlocke, now in Lynryd Skynyrd, he was in Blackfoot when I first encountered him at a radio station in Nottingham the night before."*
Bernie Marsden (Whitesnake – Guitar)

*"1981 was BOC's only Donington appearance, part of a larger tour of the UK, having played in Dunstable, W. Runton and London a few days before.
The headliner was AC/DC, an act that had opened for BOC in the USA previously but was now undeniably a bigger band. My memories of this day haven't faded much since it was the same day our drummer was let go, but that's another story. The drum roadie, Rick Downey, drummed his first 'real' show with us...quite a first gig, in front of 70,000 people. If you're running the often-used photo of me jumping on the festival plaque, that would tell a lot, but not the whole story. Of course, I don't have the same perspective as the AC/DC folks (and by the way, I love AC/DC's music, great band) but as I recall there was some bad blood on their part about some slight when they opened for us somewhere in the USA, not getting all our lighting system or something like that. (It's quite standard practice that the headliner doesn't allow the opening act to have the entire lighting system at their disposal, i.e. when we opened for Alice Cooper (a legend who should be in*

the R&R Hall of Fame) we got some lights, not all, but that's quite normal and we didn't cop an attitude about it).
I showed up at Donington and was told straight off that AC/DC's folks weren't allowing us to use a motorcycle on stage (a gag that I often did in those days). Ok...so right away things were stirring. We finally get into our set and after a few songs our soundman uses his talkback from the mixing desk telling us to play 'Reaper' immediately and get off...the sound system wasn't working for us and no one could hear a thing we were doing. I immediately thought 'sandbag'...an oft-used term for the headliner's sound people ruining the sound of opening acts, like only using half the system or worse. Hard to believe, but this was stuff that would happen on occasion, not unknown.
It was a tough day...first our drummer was fired in the morning, the attitude I received upon arriving at the grounds, then sounding terrible in front of a festival with 10's of thousands of fans.
To take out my frustration I took the plaque given to all the band members and laid it across a rock and stomped on it. Impetuous youth, perhaps :) Our sound man George Geranios can tell the sound story on his own and his perspective is an important part of the whole festival.
Nowadays, I love playing the UK, always did except for that one unfortunate afternoon 26 years ago."
Eric Bloom (Blue Oyster Cult – Vocals/Guitar/Keyboards)

"It was not the best show for us. There has been much discussion of that concert with fans on the web.
It seems it all started as a tiff we had with AC/DC's management when they denied letting us use of pyro and our motorcycle onstage. With that rumbling behind the scenes and the replacement of our drummer the day before the show, and the sabotaged sound system, it was probably the worst show in BOC history."
Joe Bouchard (Blue Oyster Cult – Bass)

"In 1981 the Castle Donington music fest featured the bands More, Blackfoot, Slade, Blue Oyster Cult, Whitesnake and

AC/DC. The weeks leading up to this appearance had been stressful for the Oysters. Serious internal problems had developed between Albert Bouchard and other band members. They ostensibly revolved around Albert's choice of travelling mate, a young lady who was not his current wife. Band wives in the party were incensed. Tensions were high. Albert and his paramour travelled separately and he was late for two shows. He was summarily fired just before the band was to play the main event on this English run: the massive Donington show. Up to 60,000 are expected to attend. Rick Downey (the lighting designer) had stepped in earlier in the week when Albert was late. He was now tapped to do the show rather than have the band suffer a humiliating cancellation. Given the subsequent events, perhaps a cancellation would have been better. At the time, however, we thought we had found a clever solution for the sudden departure of the band's drummer on the eve of this hugely important English festival.

Bands would come to Donington Park a day before the actual concert. The first day was for sound and equipment checks. Various wrinkles were ironed, stage space was allocated, and input lists were checked and implemented. Ideally all the bands were given a chance to play a song or two through the sound system. Settings for monitors and front-of-house could be logged for recall the next day so that the band techs were not starting "cold."

The sound contractor for this festival was Malcolm Hill. Hill Audio was a well-known native company based in Hollingbourne, UK in the great Tradition of the Times the company was named after, owned and run by Malcolm Hill. Malcolm and his employees designed and purpose-built a great deal of the equipment in his own shop. Speaker cabinets, power amplifiers and mixing consoles were all custom made and proprietary.

We arrived the day before for our sound check and set up the gear. I ambled out to the mix position and begin to set input levels. I remember trying to reset Joe Bouchard's bass direct level at the console. For some reason I did not have enough range on the channel's input attenuator. I was surprised when

I was informed that the console had only a limited range of adjustment and a call had to be made back to the stage to set another level control there. This, I felt, was a less than ideal system but a lot of Hill's gear was like this. The speakers themselves were a custom one-box design with several new elements. This show was to be the debut of this new design. A wall of these untried boxes flanked each side of the stage.

I remember that despite my unfamiliarity with the console the sound check went OK. The system, though not thrilling, was adequate. There certainly was enough of it up there to make a big noise. However, those who play Donington as support soon learn not to count their decibels before they hatch.

The day arrives. We in the Cult Camp were in a state. It was Rick Downey's first huge show. The audience was quite large, something like 60K. It was, of course, a miserable day of overcast skies and intermittent rain. There was schism regarding our use of the motorcycle gag. AC/DC said we couldn't do the motorcycle thing because they are doing the motorcycle thing. The situation (I learned later) got heated. There were bad vibes in the air.

I, however, must perform my hour or so of work so I trudged dutifully to the front of house position. I don't really remember exactly when I went out. It may have been during Blackfoot's set. I know I was there for the entirety of Slade's set. At some point it was evident that something was wrong with the system. Things did not sound good. Things did not sound right. It was not simply 'operator error.' In the old days the only real qualification for getting work as a live sound mixer was having the job. Power was (and still is) put in the hands of fools. "Hey, my brother-in-law once owned a stereo. He can be our sound guy!" This was not that. This mix was OK, the system itself sounded wrong.

I remember distinctly, I was standing in back of the mix riser and a fellow emerged from the vast mass of soggy humanity. He was quite upset.

He got my attention and said, "Is Blue Oyster Cult going to sound this bad?"

I said, "I hope not." Optimism, however, was fleeing.

Toward the end of Slade's set the sound simply disappeared.

Noddy, the lead singer, realized something had gone wrong. I remember that he launched into something obviously quite familiar to the assembled horde and, surprisingly, got most of the audience singing along! Perhaps it was their BIG HIT. I think it was their last song.

It was now the Cult's turn. There was much consternation during the set change. No one seemed to know exactly what the problem with the system was, but we all knew there was a problem. We started the set and there was very little volume available. The sound check settings produced an anaemic squeak from the huge mass of boxes flanking the stage. At some point during the set I looked up to see Malcolm Hill himself crawling around the stage right stack at a great height, ears into boxes. I was told not to try to turn the system up, but the band is inaudible. I try anyway and as I push the main faders up, the system volume decreases even more! Things are upside down, and I would be upside down if I tried that again, so said my minders at the front of house. At one point during this farce I got on the talkback mike between songs and told the band to simply leave the stage. Maybe they could come back out when things were sorted. If they continued without acknowledging the problem then our Donington appearance would be shot. They do not do this and our Donington appearance is shot. The Band finishes with a flourish and…….there is nothing. No response from the audience. Sixty-thousand metal fans stand sullen and silent. It is, as they say, an oil painting out there.

As interesting as the actual performance was, some of the later developments were fascinating. Jake Berry, AC/DC's production manager took on the role of damage control for the band and Malcolm Hill and apparently told the assembled press that I blew up the system. As you can see from this account,

the system was already in deep trouble well before B.O.C.'s set. Let us consider the essence of the definition of "blow up." It is to destroy and hence render <u>inoperable</u>. By most accounts the system was fully operational by AC/DC's set. It was rendered inoperable by a basic power distribution problem, a mobile recording truck had apparently been hooked up improperly and the main system had "dropped a leg." In laypersons terms, the system was running on inadequate and unbalanced power. This fact did not alter Berry's spin, as senseless at it was on closer inspection. Year's later, when he was with Whitesnake and I was with Anthrax, he bent my then girlfriend's ear at a show in the US, describing me as a bad guy, a representative of Satan, and who knows what else. Tell the same lie often enough and it becomes the truth.

The Band survived this debacle to move on to other debacles in other large venues: dare I say Pasadena Rose Bowl with Journey or shows in Germany with Whitesnake (where our own sound company "sandbagged" us). These "festivals" always bring out the knife sharpeners. I believe the band bled for a long time in the UK due to this. But in the end it isn't useful to discuss who was at "fault." It was a big, complicated show and something went wrong. There was an error and, unfortunately the audience didn't get all the show they paid for."

George Geranios (Blue Oyster Cult – Sound Engineer)

"I went as a guest to all the other Doningtons and was at the side of the stage for AC/DC the following year and the fire works at the end were awesome.

By this time we had wrote 'And The Bands Played On' all about Donington '80. I came up with a riff Quinny the chorus and Dobby, Biff AND Gilly did the words; a team effort which proved to be a top twenty hit rising to 12 and we performed our tribute to Donington on Top Of The Pops."

Graham Oliver (Saxon – Guitar)

"I first went to Castle Donington in 1981, aged 15, and 5 foot nothing, with my older brother.

We somehow got separated while in line at the fried chicken stand between Blackfoot and Slade. The rest of the day I spent alone in a crowd of 30,000 metalheads. My innocence hid the fact they were mostly drunk or stoned. Never once did I feel I didn't belong or was in any danger. I was ok; I still had enough sandwiches and pop to last me.

Not that I could see, but soon there would be, live onstage, 2 of the bands which had turned my life around and given it meaning, Whitesnake and AC/DC. All the songs I knew word for word and would scream the lyrics without seemingly being heard over the deafening PA.
Fireworks over, I turned and headed for the Goodyear Tyre. Near the top of the hill I saw the familiar patched combat jacket of my older brother. I ran up to him.
"What did you think?"
"Fucking amazing!"
Floyd London (The Almighty – Bass)

"My first Donington experience was when I was a teenager in '81 when it was AC/DC and Whitesnake.
Whitesnake were on their 'Come and Get It' album and it was awesome and all the bands that played were excellent. I just remember it so well and it was one of my first festival experiences and I was just hooked."
Pete Spiby **(Black Spiders – Vocals / Guitar)**

"Monsters Of Rock was the highlight of our year. We worked it for 11 years right through the glory days of Whitesnake, Iron Maiden, AC/DC, ZZ Top, Kiss and Ozzy. All the heavy metal bands that meant anything played Donington...the names are legendary now – Guns N Roses, Metallica, Bon Jovi, David Lee Roth, Dio, Aerosmith, Uriah Heep, Anvil, Motley Crue, Twisted Sister, Wasp... too many to recount.
Donington was fun. It was always the same team meeting up at the Priesthouse Hotel under the watchful eye of Maurice Jones. There was a great feeling of camaraderie, we understood the job in hand and even if we never had time to chat on the day, a snatched encounter in catering at most, we'd always have a drink or three back at the hotel later and regale our highlights. I remember one memorable festival where Maurice had had some bad news and wanted to talk, I sat up till 4am just listening, the least I could do for an old friend."
Judy Totton (Monsters Of Rock PR)

"Just 12 months before people were saying it was over for AC/DC after the death of their vocalist Bon Scott but the 'Back In Black' album catapulted AC/DC to worthy headline status. For sheer energy and balls to the wall simple effective rock 'n 'roll they are hard to beat.
One of the surprises on the day was Slade. They were really entertaining and went down a storm."
The Bailey Brothers (Mick & Dez Donington Comperes)

"After a few initial rumours about who was to headline the second festival (Rush, Kiss, Black Sabbath), it was announced that AC/DC would be the main band with Whitesnake as special guests.
Our entourage more than doubled this year (5 in 1980 to 12 in 1981), including a couple of girlfriends. We travelled down in a transit van. This was to become our normal form of transit for the next decade or so.
For me, the band of the day title was taken from under AC/DC's nose by the mighty blues rock of Whitesnake. Coverdale and co were one of the best live bands around in the early eighties.
AC/DC were let down by over-long gaps between songs. Also, apart from 'THE' Bell, their stage show was a bit sparse. Their shows at later Doningtons were much better.
Blue Oyster Cult had a 'very' bad day at the office.
Slade were a breath of fresh air on a wet Saturday afternoon. I can't recall whether it was footballs or toilet rolls (or both) that they threw into the crowd, but I do remember Noddy Holder proclaiming that the rain was 'pissing' in from the (AC/DC)Bell hung from a crane high above the stage. Great fun.
Blackfoot were also in the form of their life in August 1981. 'Good Morning' and 'Wishing Well' going down a storm, but the piece de resistance was 'Highway Song' (a song almost, but not quite as good as Lynryd Skynyrd 'Freebird')."
Paul Hartshorn (Chesterfield)

1982
Status Quo,
Gillan, Saxon, Hawkwind, Uriah Heep, Anvil, Tommy Vance

This year was an all British affair with the exception of the Canadian opening act Anvil.

Anvil were heavily influential on the up and coming 'Thrash Metal' scene which has since been covered in great depth in their successful movie 'ANVIL: The Story of Anvil'; Metallica, Anthrax and Slayer all cite Anvil as a big influence on their careers. Not a hugely popular opener as they were mostly unknown at the time and so had a lot of 'stuff' thrown at them, but would increase in popularity when they were on the bill for the following years Reading Festival.

Two stalwarts of the 'prog rock' scene were also included in the shape of Hawkwind (not a usual MOR band) and Uriah Heep who were gradually evolving into a classic British rock band.

Saxon, now more popular than on their previous appearance, had leap frogged up the bill to sit in the 3rd place slot which in previous years had been held by Scorpions and BOC, both major league players; this showed how Saxon were now contenders. There latest album 'Denim And Leather' included the hits 'Princess of the Night' and 'And The Bands Played On', the latter reaching the top 20 in the UK.

Gillan were in the second place spot this year, now featuring new guitarist Janick Gers (the former White Spirit guitarist) who had replaced Bernie Torme the previous year; Janick Gers is now one of the three guitarists in Iron Maiden and has been since 1990. Gillan at the time were extremely popular, with Top Of The Pops appearances and chart hit singles, but this was not to last as Ian Gillan (ex Deep Purple vocalist) split the band the same year and left to record the 'Born Again' album with Black Sabbath, who headlined the 'final' Reading Festival in 1983.

Headliners Status Quo were regulars at Reading Festival over the 70's, but this was their only appearance at MOR, perhaps they weren't heavy enough? Quo churned out the hits and the denim and leather clad punters lapped it up and for a change the weather stayed fairly dry.

Third year in a row and still great line-ups, how long could this go on for? A long time as the bill was getting better each year and the amount of 'big' American was due to increase as the festival started to become well known overseas.

Ticket prices had now risen to £10 in advance or £11 on the day and Tommy Vance was still playing records between bands and introducing the acts on the stage.

"Saxon was onstage as we pulled up and it was a mudfest. People were throwing mud and bottles of piss at the stage. Someone had taught him how to speak to an audience and they finished a number and Biff was saying 'let's calm down, we are Saxon and we don't need all this'. He eventually got them calmed down and he said 'now what we are going to do is our new single and we want you all to go fucking potty' and it all started up all over again. We were 'side-splitting' in our car, watching the entire goings on."
Ian Gillan (Gillan - Vocals)

"The second time we played was great, but not as special as the first one.

A lot of people around the world, we'd just come back from Japan, are interested in the first Donington, especially the younger journalists."
Biff Byford (Saxon -Vocals)

"One year later we were on tour with Rainbow and we were asked to play Donington again and this made Saxon the 'First band to play it TWICE'.
We were in Texas on Thursday with Rainbow, left Friday to fly to UK and arrived Saturday morning in Gatwick, where a private plane took us to East midlands airport. Before we landed the pilot took us over the crowd as the first band was playing. We landed though totally knackered and we were all bronzed with Texas tans.
But the gig was not as good as the first due to a combination of things plus the Quo's crew were very unhelpful to put it politely.
I remember talking to Gary Bardon and Mr Schenker in the drinks tent then we were taken to hotel for an early flight back to the USA and Sunday night we headlined the NY Palladium with Frank Marino as Support; that was a tough schedule for any one but we rose to the challenge and did a great set."
Graham Oliver (Saxon – Guitar)

"The bill for Donington Monsters of Rock in 1982 was Anvil, Uriah Heep, Hawkwind, Saxon, Gillan and Status Quo. Donington for Uriah Heep was fantastic.
We took to the stage after Anvil a Canadian band that were very glam rock and were pelted with mud and abuse so taking to the stage after that reaction we were very unsure of how the audience would react. Also we had not played in the UK for quite a while and thought that we had been forgotten.
We did not need to worry as the roar from the crowd as we took the stage was fantastic. I clearly remember having a small tuning problem with my Les Paul Guitar and at the end of the show on the crescendo I rubbed the guitar up and down the scaffolding that was holding the P/A and broke off the headstock. I was so high on adrenaline that it did not matter.

It was a brilliant day and one festival that I will always remember from the many we have played over the years."
Mick Box (Uriah Heep – Guitar)

"I have very vivid memories of my first festival!!! It was probably one of the most meaningful yet troubling experiences in my entire career.
Playing first was frightful....to say the least. They were still plugging in speaker cabinets when we began our set. Our live show was very stressful but OK.
My memories or at least the ones I want to have are of the backstage. It was an extravaganza of rock stars, playing there or otherwise. I had the opportunity to have been friends with Howard Johnston from Kerrang! Magazine and he began introducing me to various people to my complete amazement. Some such people were Gary Barden, the ex singer of the Michael Schenker Group, who a week later ended up playing with Michael at the Reading Festival. Other guys like Dee Snider or old acquaintances like the guys from the Diodes an old punk band from Canada. It was very exciting for me.
I remember the photographers came to take pictures of us at our trailer and I distinctly remember our producer Chris Tsangarides and John Sykes being inside the trailer laughing as I was making all kinds of dog noises as they took the photos of us standing outside the trailer. I also remember some very funny moments as I watched Saxon playing from the VIP section. I noticed Lee Kerslake (Heep drummer) quite buzzed out and a fan asked him for his autograph and he quickly said hold this and he swished his glass of beer all over the guy!!! I was shocked and so was the fan!!! But in the end they were shaking hands and laughing about it.
Another great person I met there was Lord Philip Harvey. He was many of the rock stars personal friends at that time. We ended up doing quite a bit of partying with him during our stay in the U.K. in 82 and 83."
Lips (Anvil – Vocals/Guitar)

"There's a few never forgetting memories from that moment in time.

Ya sure I remember, at like 10..am in the morning being backstage and going out up to the stage to see what it was gonna be all about, only to walk at the side stage area and look first out at the ocean of people and thinking to myself 'Fuck I've never seen so many people up this earlier waiting for a show to start', (there was at that time already over 30.000 head bangers and then turning my eyes towards the stage and being in total shock, being that the stage was totally covered in fresh ripped up grass all over it, and tons of wet mud everywhere on the stage and the backline. And nobody at all was bothering about any of it, to stop it or clean anything. At this moment I thought, this is gonna be more than just another gig. Like, are we even gonna be able to start never mind finish? It was totally fuck from anything I had ever seen to that point.

Right from the start of the set to the end, there was endless amounts of shit flying non-stop...was simply next to retarded to perform under those conditions, let alone plastic bottles half full with fresh warm just filled urine, being tossed per second spaying anything and everything within it's reach...ya how could anyone forget all that.

Remember though watching and finally getting to see bands like Uriah Heep and Saxon. Was up lifting.....but spent most of the time getting stoned smoking hash and real enjoying getting away from home (Canada).

Robb Reiner (Anvil – Drums)

"We can remember Saxon getting more than a fair share of crap thrown at them on stage.
Vocalist Biff Byford stopped the band playing and said:
"If you don't stop throwing we ain't gonna play anymore, calm down"
Status Quo were always the Monsters of Boogie. If you didn't have a denim waist coat and a pair of white trainers where we lived you weren't a rock fan."

The Bailey Brothers (Mick & Dez Donington Comperes)

"Our job started maybe six months before the event, building up to it and then arranging photo calls and supervising interviews and TV crews on the day. We were fielding requests right up to the last minute with Kerrang! always managing to talk their way into passes for every member of their staff...20 and counting. The thing about Donington was it attracted press from all over the world so we frequently had to put the photographers in relays in the pit. Getting them in was easy, getting them out much harder, particularly if they only had two songs each. My assistant Carmine, who came back to work Donington for me even after she'd left my company, was a dab hand at that. We marched 'em in and we marched 'em out. And there was always the inevitable photographer who just turned up from France with no pass (I'd usually let them shoot the photo calls even if we couldn't give them photo pit access)."

Judy Totton (Monsters Of Rock PR)

"I don't think that 1982 was one of the best years in the history of Donington.
The main problem for the headliners Status Quo was the sound. Rolled down in front of the speaker stacks either side of the stage were two massive reproductions of (I think) the 'Just Supposin' album cover, whether this caused the sound problems I don't know, but none of the other bands on the bill suffered the same fate. After about an hour of 'Quo we decided to make our way home. This was the first of only two times that I left early. Because we only live approx 30 minutes from Donington we even managed to get back to the local for a pint.
Therefore the band of the day was probably Gillan, just edging out Saxon. The highlights of Gillan's set were a new song called 'Bluesy Blue Sea' and a 'new' old song called 'Black Night'. Also I remember Janick Gers emblazoned all in white climbing up the speakers during his solo spot.
The best of Saxon's set was the song that they had written about their appearance at the 1980 Donington show '….And The Bands Played On'.
The best merchandise of the day was the Uriah Heep red 'Abominog' t-shirts."

Paul Hartshorn (Chesterfield)

1983
Whitesnake,
Meat Loaf, ZZ Top, Twisted Sister, Dio, Diamond Head, Tommy Vance

From 1983 the world of rock and metal music sat up and definitely started to take notice of the Monsters Of Rock festival. For the 4th years festival, the line-up included four bands from the USA and two British bands.

This was the second appearance of Whitesnake, but this time they were on the top of the pile; another British band gets to headline Donington and what better than the 'bluesy rock' of Mr Coverdale and co. The line-up of Whitesnake had changed radically; out were Ian Paice, Bernie Marsden and Neil Murray and their replacements were Cozy Powell, Mel Galley and Colin Hodgkinson. The Whitesnake video 'Whitesnake Commandos : Donington '83' was released on video the same year, covering most of the headline performance; with a camouflaged theme running from the programme and t-shirts to Cozy wearing a camouflaged t-shirt and Mel Galley in a khaki coloured jumpsuit on the day. A stand out moment was the Cozy Powell drum solo to the '1812 Overture' and '633 Squadron' theme accompanied by helicopters with searchlights and the crying women during 'Ain't No Love In The Heart Of The City'. Whitesnake would be a considerably different breed of band when they made their return in 1990.

Diamond Head were the opening band on the day and the favourites of Lars Ulrich played 'Am I Evil' as their opening track; Metallica would later cover this song and make it a staple of their live shows. Merv Goldsworthy played on bass at this time, prior to leaving to join British AOR legends FM.

One of the most anticipated sets of the day was from Dio. Ronnie James Dio had played in Rainbow and most recently Black Sabbath, before leaving them in 1982. This performance by Dio was one of his first shows with his new band, featuring Jimmy Bain on bass (ex Rainbow), Vivien Campbell on guitar (ex Sweet Savage; after Dio he joined Whitesnake and is currently in Def Leppard) and Vinnie Appice on drums (ex Black Sabbath, now with Heaven & Hell); basically a rock supergroup in the vein of Rainbow and Whitesnake. The 'Holy Diver' album had just been released and so the set was heavily based around this with a couple of Rainbow and Black Sabbath songs thrown into the mix.

If any band was going to get stuff thrown at them it was Twisted Sister; looking like a bunch of builders dressed in fluorescent clothes and makeup they were an obvious target and get things thrown at them they did. The audience 'lobbed' everything at the band that they could, but they didn't expect the kind of reaction that they got from Dee Snider (lead singer). Dee invited anyone who was throwing stuff to come up on stage for a fight, of course there were no takers and they won the crowd over.

ZZ Top were on a new high, with massive success in the UK with the album 'Eliminator' that had been released that year in March. One of the most popular bands of the day and the first of three appearances at the festival.

Meatloaf came and went and again had a vast amount of items thrown at him; not a popular choice with the metal masses, but a good filler before Whitesnake.

It was quite a sunny day and unlike other Doningtons there was no mud bath! Tommy Vance yet again provided the banter and in between bands music.

"We played in '83 with Cozy and we shot the video for 'Whitesnake Commandos" also with Mel Galley, God bless his soul; God bless both of them. They're all good memories, all positive, playing at home isn't it."
David Coverdale (Whitesnake – Vocals)

"I remember it being a spectacular event and something we were really proud to take part in, especially since it just after the release of our first album so it was a very special time to present it to an audience, especially a British audience, which was very cool.
Having known the guys from Whitesnake for a long time it was nice to see them again of course and it was the first place that I met the guy who would become our drummer for ten years and that was Simon Wright.
It was the first time that I met Simon and he had just gotten the gig with AC/DC, he was only 18 years old at the time and I knew his wife, she came over and introduced me to Simon and I loved him from the off, what a great kid, just the best. Here was a guy who had played with some other bands, but had never really played with anything of that scale and suddenly he was thrust into the fore of one of the biggest bands on the face of the earth. He handled it so well, he was in awe of them, and he was just a regular person, so that was one of the things that I remember the most of Donington.
It was one of our first gigs; I think that we had played a couple of shows before then, I think we had done some small American tour of some kind and then came over to Britain, so it was our first time in Europe for us.
There was some mud thrown on the first show and it hit a lot of people, but they didn't throw any mud at us and being that we were second on the bill we should have been a good target; those people certainly respected what I had done before with Sabbath and Rainbow, so they gave me the same kind of respect that I always give them."
Ronnie James Dio (Dio – Vocals)

"We came to Donington and now we've had hit records out. Out of 40,000 people, 90% loved us, but 10% of the crowd can throw a lot of shite.
So we were up there and we were getting bottles and shit flying all over the place and we got to a break and I thought I'd call them out again and I said 'YOU MUTHA FUCKERS, MEET ME AT THE SIDE OF THE STAGE', but they had already heard that one at Reading so they went 'YAAAAAAAA!!!!!!'
So we did another song and we were ducking pebbles and bottles.
So, I said 'Have we got any friends here? Do you know what, if I was out there and my friend was onstage and someone was throwing things at him I would BEAT THE PISS OUT OF THAT MUTHA FUCKER?' So I then said 'if you're my friends then kick this Mutha fucker's ass and if he's too big, get a whole bunch of you and bring him down to the ground.'
We started the next song and it was like Altamont with the Rolling Stones, you could see fights all over the audience. There were people beating people down, awesome!
Meatloaf was on the bill and he was just fuckin' drunk off his ass. I'm not going to get into the conversation that we had, but he passed the 'baton of rock' to me, I didn't ask him for it, but apparently he had it! But, he went out onstage and he was shit faced and he was getting angry at all the shit being thrown. He walked to the edge of the stage and said 'ARE YOU MUTHA FUCKERS THROWING STUFF, C'MON'. They buried that sad fuck!
I saw Meatloaf outlined in litre plastic bottles! I was at the side of the stage and I said 'NO', and he staggered back and the bottles fell to the ground.
How drunk have you got to be to tell an English crowd to throw shit at me?"
Dee Snider (Twisted Sister – Vocals)

"We'd already known about Reading and knew that Donington was more of a heavy rock show, so we knew that people who came to see lighter acts wouldn't be pissed off, because there

were some heavy bands on the bill, us, ZZ Top, Whitesnake and Meat Loaf, back when he was really popular.
I remember we went over great, the show itself was spectacular, there were about 70,000 people there, and I remember thinking 'wow that was different to Reading'. Everybody loved it and we didn't get anything thrown at us, but Meatloaf?
He said 'Alright, if you think you can throw shit, go for it!' When you tell people to go for it, they threw everything and the kitchen sink at him! Fucking mud pies! They threw toilet paper. It got so bad at the end of his set that while ZZ Top's road crew were changing over, they were so afraid to come out that they were using cymbals as shields! They were holding the cymbals and they were going 'BING BING BING'.
It was a lot of fun."

Jay Jay French (Twisted Sister – Guitar)

"One funny thing that sticks in my mind was that there were portable bathrooms where there hook them up to a water supply and it looks like a regular bathroom, even though it's on wheels.
The bathroom had about four or five stalls in it and regular urinals, but they were just for people in the bands. There were Dio, ZZ Top, Meatloaf, Whitesnake and us. I was sitting in the bathroom on 'the ole throne' and then I heard someone come in and sit next to me and I said 'who's that next to me?' and he said 'it's Jon Lord' and I was like 'how are you doing?' I was there having a conversation with Jon Lord of Deep Purple on the toilet!! They could probably have sold those stalls for a fortune after the festival, after all the famous bands had come in and dropped a load. So, we finished our conversation and I left, never having even spoke to him face to face. But I actually saw him half hour later and I did say that we'd just had a pretty interesting conversation, which was a very funny thing.
When Meatloaf went on stage, Bob Kulick was playing with him at the time, sporting his bald head, which was way ahead of the times. Meatloaf came on stage and said 'do you wanna throw something' and he was nearly buried in the stuff!

I always remember that Whitesnake headlined and that they had helicopters, I won't forget that! They were definitely making a point that they were headlining."
Eddie Ojeda (Twisted Sister – Guitar/Backing Vocals)

"I don't drink and I don't do drugs, but I still don't remember that much.
We went on during the daylight, which was tough for us as we're used to going on in a dark club or dark hall, to go on in the sunlight it was a bit weird for us.
It was a great show; it was such a good feeling for us, because you don't have 'big shows' like that in the US. It was so new for us and a great feeling. We were up and coming and everyone like us, except for some of those in other bands. They were like 'what are these fuckin' idiots doing?'
It was a phenomenal experience and I remember we stayed for the whole night. I remember seeing ZZ Top and Cozy Powell with Whitesnake and his drum solo with the helicopter; it was a great festival and a lot of fun."
Mark 'The Animal' Mendoza (Twisted Sister – Bass)

"It was a really big deal to us, as it was probably this biggest gig that we had done to that date, about 35,000 people or so we'd been told.
It's always hard opening a show and we'd been told that it was difficult, but we were just glad to get away with not going down badly and getting bottled off.
I do remember Meatloaf getting bottled at that gig.
There was a lot of mud going onto the stage. They were throwing chunks of mud at the band if they didn't like them.
One the things that made it difficult for us was that we had just come out of making our 3rd album 'Canterbury', which had been a difficult album to make. We had introduced a keyboard player and we also had a new drummer and bass player, so we were all still finding our feet. This gig was the first that the keyboard player had done with us, his name was Bob, so that must have been a bit of a shock to him, straight to Donington for you first gig!

Things seemed to go ok but it wasn't our finest; at least we didn't die a death.
I remember briefly meeting people backstage like Whitesnake, but not ZZ Top, they kept themselves to themselves in their portakabin.
I do remember that there was a big argument between Meatloaf and Dee Snider and they came into our dressing room so that they could have the argument. There was a big row and I think that they wanted to keep out of the way of their band members, so that they could let off steam at each other and that was quite interesting to hear the two of them, two scary Americans going at each other, face to face.
I did get nervous going to the gig, I can remember someone drove us there and each time you saw signs for Donington, my heart would go as we were getting closer. It's not far from where I live, it's probably only an hour or an hour and a halfs drive. We had to leave at some ridiculous time as we were first on at one o'clock in the afternoon, so we were told that we needed to be there for eleven.
I just remember it being a nerve wracking gig and I was worried about how we would be received and I think someone had organised, through the fan club, a banner competition. If you designed your banner and we picked the best one, you'd win a signed album. So there was maybe a dozen big banners in the audience with Diamond Head on and the logo and that was quite exciting to look at and see the support."
Brian Tatler (Diamond Head – Guitar)

"I did Donington with AC/DC and Twisted Sister.
It was a remarkable festival and a great place to play at, always great promoters."
Phil Carson (Ex head of Atlantic records)

"The following year I was a guest and I will never forget I was talking to David Coverdale and Ian Paice when a drunk barged in to hospitality area and shouted to David 'Is it true Tommy Bolin was a Junkie?' Now Tommy was David's close friend and band mate who tragically died at a young age and David went white with fury and I had to restrain him before he

took the guys head off and security dragged the asshole away."
Graham Oliver (Saxon – Guitar)

"I also went to the Whitesnake headliner show with ZZ Top, I remember being slightly disappointed that Whitesnake played most of the same set I had played with Ian Paice and Neil Murray when the original band folded, but it was a good show and the crowd   loved it, and they are the important people at all festivals."
Bernie Marsden (Whitesnake – Guitar)

"I went to Donington to '83 in response to the Dio 'Holy Diver' album coming out. It was Diamond Head, Dio, Twisted Sister, Meatloaf, ZZ Top and Whitesnake. The weird thing was that we ended up touring with ZZ Top."
Toby Jepson (Little Angels - Vocals)

"Twisted Sister didn't come to the Monsters of Rock to be taken seriously AND THEY WEREN'T!"
The Bailey Brothers (Mick & Dez Donington Comperes)

"From what had been a relatively disappointing year (1982), we now came to a year that I still recall as one of the best days ever…topped off by a magnificent version of 'Mistreated' by Whitesnake………when Coverdale announced that this would 'probably be the last time he would ever play this song' you just knew it was gonna be something special. In fact the overall Whitesnake performance is still my favourite of all the headlining acts over the years. 'Here I go again' was also brilliant, especially Coverdale's singing at the start. Visually the highlight was Cozy Powell's drum solo, which now incorporated the '633 Squadron' music as well as the '1812 Overture'. During the '633 Squadron' section the festival site was 'dive-bombed' by light aircraft (helicopters I think). There was over £50,000 worth of pyrotechnics used during the Whitesnake set. Magnificent.
But Whitesnake were not the only band on form on the day.

ZZ Top were riding on the back of their 'Eliminator' album and received favourable comments all round. One memory I have of their set was when a naked female started dancing to 'Gimme All Your Lovin' just in front of our base camp. This performance was supported by appreciative jeering from all the males in the vicinity.
Twisted Sister's Dee Snider probably gave the best introduction to a song ever at Donington......... "This next song's a bit slow for Twisted Sister......but its f*****g mean". The song in question was 'Destroyer' from their 'Under The Blade' album.
Apart from Whitesnake, my other favourite band of the day was DIO. The band was playing their very first ever live show (apart from a couple of warm-ups). The soon to be classic album 'Holy Diver' had just been released. Their set included a mixture of songs from this album plus various Rainbow and Black Sabbath classics including 'Stargazer', 'Heaven and Hell' etc.
The biggest disappointment of the day was Diamond Head. I had expected them to perform better than they did.
I remember the weather being good this year."
Paul Hartshorn (Chesterfield)

1984
AC/DC,
Van Halen, Ozzy Osbourne, Gary Moore, Y&T, Accept, Motley Crue, Tommy Vance

Back for its 5th Anniversary and for what most fans have agreed was the best line-up of all of the Monsters Of Rock Festivals from 1980 to 1996.
With AC/DC back for their 2nd headline appearance at the festival, you couldn't want for a more popular band to be topping the bill.
With the 'Flick Of The Switch' album released the year before, AC/DC slotted 'Guns For Hire' and the title track into the set alongside many favourites, now all considered classics; for the encore of 'For Those About To Rock' there was the accompaniment of the now famous cannons.
Special guests on the day didn't come any bigger than Van Halen. Massive in the USA and making a rare UK appearance, British fans were treated to a selection of greatest hits and some from their latest album, the record breaking '1984'; the last to feature David Lee Roth who left shortly after to be replaced by Sammy Hagar. Songs played on the day from '1984' included 'Panama', 'Hot For Teacher', 'House Of Pain' and the song that Van Halen are internationally recognised for 'Jump'.
DLR high kicked his way through the performance and told 'tall tales' between songs, Eddie Van Halen played

the most intricate and complicated guitar seen at Donington so far, Alex Van Halen playing the largest drum kit in Donington history and Michael Anthony, well he played solid and perfunctory bass.

Also on the bill was Ozzy Osbourne whose band at the time featured another guitar legend, Jake E. Lee; Lee was a former member of Mickey Ratt which went on to become the platinum selling Ratt, he was also an early member of Dio. Lee was the permanent replacement for Randy Rhoads who had died in tragic plane crash with Ozzy's tour bus; Brad Gillis of Night Ranger had played with Ozzy but was not considered a permanent member.

Gary Moore played his way through a short blues / metal package and showed his guitar skills to all; his set was incredibly loud.

Y&T from the USA and Accept were also appearing on the day, but most people and press were in attendance to see the UK debut of Motley Crue. Having just released the 'Shout At The Devil' album, the Crue were starting to make a name for themselves and not just for their music. Known for the wild times and wild hair, Motley Crue's performance on the day was short, but drew a massive crowd; this would be the first of their four performances to date at Donington.

For the first time in MOR history, there were bars selling actual alcohol inside the venue!!! The annoying problem for most people was that the bars were only open for usual British bar times, these being 11:30am to 2pm and then re-opening from 6pm to 9pm, bizarre compared to the alcohol on sale at Download now, from open to close. You were still able to bring in your own alcohol if dispensed into the appropriate containers.

Highlights of the show and interviews were also featured on BBC2 on 'The Old Grey Whistle Test'.

"It was us Van Halen, Y&T, Accept and more and it was just incredible and it was the biggest show that I had played up until then and to play it in England with all my family and there!

There was the 'bigness' of the set, the production, all that was going on and the trucks and the buses and everything, my family were all blown away.
They remember me just bashing my drums in my bedroom and then suddenly I'm playing in front of 80,000 people. That was definitely my best moment so far; there have been others, but that was England and it stood out as being really important.
Simon Wright (AC/DC – Drums)

"We consider ourselves fortunate to have played probably the best Monsters of Rock lineup in the history of the festival. Still to this day people tell us that Castle Donington MOR 1984 was the best lineup the festival ever had. Every band on that bill we were either good friends with or had played shows with. It was cool to see them all and experience such a monumental day together.
Of course one thing that will never escape my memories of that show was being bombarded by the punters throwing bottles of piss on stage. When we'd previously supported AC/DC on tour for two months, they warned us that every band who opens for AC/DC gets stuff thrown at them and gets booed off the stage. The AC/DC band and crew were shocked when audiences everywhere never once threw anything at Y&T, but in actual fact, gave us encores almost every night. Same with The Reading festival; heard we would be pelted - never happened. We knew it was the norm for that to happen, but having bottles of piss hit my guitar and splatter up on my body while performing was a real downer. Yeah, we realized they did that with every band, but it sucked anyway and makes you feel like a moving target." **Dave Meniketti (Y&T – Guitar / Vocals)**

"I remember our bus driver told Castle Donington security that he had AC/DC in the bus. So Y&T got escorted by police motorcade through the festival grounds to backstage. We felt rather important for a few minutes there. Don't get me started on the piss bottles! I was so angry after our set that I punched out the window in our dressing room. But, when I

think back to the ridiculous clothes we were wearing that day-- I guess we deserved it. Motley Crue was staying at our hotel, hanging in the bar. The first thing Tommy Lee said was, "Where can I get some flesh." I said, "Good luck, dude, we're in England...The punters here are all dudes".
We knew all the bands on the bill that day and it was great fun to catch up with everyone backstage. But AC/DC was the only band that didn't fraternize; they stayed cloistered in their little dressing room trailer. So I barged in and said hello to all of them before they went on stage. All the other bands were fired up and partying, but these guys just sat there as if they were about to go to the gas chamber. It was strange. Maybe they feared the piss bottles!" **Phil Kennemore (Y&T – Bass)**

"I will never forget when we played the "Monsters Of Rock" festival at
Donington back in 1984.
We just came back from a very long U.S. tour and it was our first concert in
Europe after having the worldwide success with the "Balls To The Wall"
album. And the success stayed on.
We were the second band on stage but the reception was that of at least a co-headliner. Everybody was singing along every song we played and so that festival (together with the other two "Monsters Of Rock" festivals in Germany that same year) became our breakthrough in Europe.
But there were strange things happening as well. During the gig we saw
something big flying onto the stage and when we looked closer, it was a
horse head (a real one - believe me). Also, somebody threw an apple on
stage which hit Wolf's guitar so hard, that the neck pick-up was shot
through the guitar's backside.
But hey - that's rock'n'roll - and I still have great memories about the gig in Donington."

Stefan Kaufmann (Accept – Drums)

"Saw Eddie Van Halen, standing with Gary Moore on the side of the stage, Gary was in shock, Eddie was just about the best at the time I think! Met Dave Lee Roth and Steve Vai for the first time at Donington." **Bernie Marsden (Whitesnake – Guitar)**

"I remember going to the '84 one, especially to see Van Halen. I remember shaking hands backstage with Eddie Van Halen who was one of my heroes."
Brian Tatler (Diamond Head – Guitar)

*"The first one I went to was AC/DC, Van Halen & Ozzy Osbourne.
I was lucky enough to have a backstage pass and met Eddie Van Halen & Jake E Lee, my absolute hero at the time."*
Myke Gray (Skin – Guitar)

*"Seeing Van Halen with Diamond Dave Lee Roth again should have been the ultimate experience but Dave seemed to think we gave a toss about his experience with a tart in a hotel room that must have took him 5 minutes to tell the story.
Then we get the obligatory drum and bass solo.
Ok, Eddie's piece was worth witnessing in the flesh, but add up the waffle and all the solos and we could have had another shit load of songs.
It turned out to be their final show with DLR and as huge VH fans we just wanted to hear the songs."*
The Bailey Brothers (Mick & Dez Donington Comperes)

"My first Monsters of Rock was 1984, AC/DC and Van Halen; I joined MCP that year."
Stuart Galbraith (ex – Donington Organiser)

"We had our own portakabin in the guest area which became a bit of a haven for many of the snappers. We also had our regular local press turn up year in year out, many bringing us little presents; it was like a Christmas club. I remember

Maurice being horrified one year to find we'd been burning incense to create a chill out factor – he didn't think it was heavy enough at all. The local media were always very supportive and there was a tradition in the early days of as many of the acts as possible going into Radio Trent on the Friday night to record a round table. Even the headliners would take part if they could. That just wouldn't happen now. It was hosted by a DJ called Graham (who came to a very sad end)."

Judy Totton (Monsters Of Rock PR

"This was my first year and it featured an absolute barnstormer of a lineup (many, myself included consider this the best MOR lineup). I travelled down via a concert coach company with 1 friend who I managed to lose within 45 minutes of entering the arena.

On entering the arena I was absolutely struck dumb by the sheer size of the crowd, the arena and the monster of a stage. As we positioned ourselves stage left Motley Crue hit the stage, they performed a quick energetic set and managed to dodge most of the missiles heading their way, the throwing of empty and piss filled bottles was already a tradition and the openers usually got more than their fair share purely for being the first band up.

Next up were German band Accept who seemed to fair better on the bottle front and also seemed to go down reasonably well, however, I was never a fan of Udo's squawking vocals so I spent most of their set drinking and chatting to some Italians in front of us.

After a short break Y&T were up; this was the first band of the day that I really wanted to see and they did not disappoint, I surged forward and secured a decent spot to headbang my way through their set, frantically during the fantastic 'Forever'. If I remember correctly some bloke dressed as the robot from the cover of their latest album 'In Rock We Trust' wondered onto the stage at one point.

From then on the day got better and better, next up was Gary Moore, who at the time was doing really well over here and had several hits that were circulating the airwaves, he played like the true axe hero he was, however, I cannot for the life of me remember who else was in his band at the time or what the set list consisted of, I think that the beer was starting to take hold of my senses.

Four bands in and a bladder full of beer and it was time to experience my first festival toilets, they did not disappoint and were as dirty and smelly as I had been reliably informed they would be. On the way back into the crowd it was noticeable that the mixture of sun and alcohol was having an effect on many as there were scores of people who were sleeping/ passed out littering the grass near the back, to this day, this is something that has never changed, some people do not seem to manage past the first band before they adopt this position and are then usually covered in crap from their friends or drawn/ painted on.

Near the front the crowd was starting to condense as Ozzy hit the stage, he stormed through an impressive rat arsed set which concluded with him emotionally receiving a gold disk on stage from the late, great Tommy Vance for his latest album 'Bark At The Moon'.

Next up were special guests Van Halen who I would witness four more times in the future but they were never as good as they were on this day in their original lineup. I stormed to the front and went berserk whilst they played hit after hit from their back catalogue and the current masterpiece '1984' which of course included the rather radio friendly 'Jump'. At one point David Lee Roth informed us that he was going to buy us all a beer; he was always a master of bullshit but I do not know whether or not anyone tried it on at the bar, I had visions of scores of people queued up requesting a beer on Dave's tab, I could imagine the response that they would get from the staff! By this time the bottle fights had reached fever pitch, but it was now not just bottles being slung about it was anything loose, I just managed to dodge a hail of half full yoghurt pots, all of which hit the bloke in front of me, he was absolutely covered but too pissed by then to actually care.

Van Halen finished and it took me some considerable time to get out of the crowd for another trek to the submerged latrines, it was my first time in such a dense crowd and I must admit, I

got a wee bit panicky trying to push my way through the masses. At the back of the arena a strange naked cricket match was going on? The rules did not appear to follow the game to the letter but at least ten merry revellers were having fun participating, I wondered if 'cock before wicket' would be considered as out?   As dusk descended it was not long before that day's headliner- the mighty AC/DC burst on to the stage surrounded by masses of lights and easily that day's best and loudest sound. I was transfixed by Angus and his continual motion and boundless energy, from the second they hit the stage he just kept going and did not stop till the end.
I was not the greatest fan of their recorded material at that time but they won me over big time that night, amongst my favourite tunes they played were 'Highway to Hell', 'Whole Lotta Rosie', 'Back In Black', 'Hells Bells' (complete with full size bell being twatted by Brian J), 'T.N.T.' and 'For Those About to Rock' (complete with canon firing finale). For my first time experiencing a festival headline set DC definitely lived up to my expectations.

And that was it, after a rather cool firework display the show was over and it was time to find the blasted coach, which took ages mainly because several hundred other coaches had arrived after us so it was like finding a needle in a haystack. Still, about 50 mins later I was re-united with the coach and friend that I had lost at the beginning of the show, he never went again, I don't think he got on with the sheer size of the crowd, however, that was the beginning of my love affair with Donington Park, one that continues to this day."
Roger Moore (Glinton, Peterborough)

"What a scorcher…….the weather was red hot. I even got sunburn.
The day's line up wasn't too bad either. Most people would probably look back on the 1984 show as having the best line up of all.
AC/DC performed much better than in 1981 and rolled out the cannons for the Donington crowd for the first time. 'For Those

About To Rock' was televised on 'The Old Grey Whistle Test' a few weeks later.

I wasn't a big Van Halen fan prior to the event, but I got carried away with all the hype and decided to give them a closer look. Venturing down to the front for the first time in 5 years. I really enjoyed their set….even Michael Anthony's bass solo (he rolled around the stage with his bass clutched to his chest if my memory serves me well). When I made my way back up to the rest of our troupe they all said that they had been disappointed with Van Halen. Maybe the performance didn't carry too well towards the back of the crowd, but from my vantage point (approx 6 rows from the front) they were very good.

I remember Ozzy performing with his usual 'craziness' and also receiving a Gold Disc during his set.

I recall Gary Moore resurrecting 'Parisienne Walkways' for the day (I think he had previously dropped the song from his usual set list). His set comprised of the usual mixture of rockers and ballads.

I enjoyed Y&T. I still like to give their 'Meanstreak' album a spin every once in a while.

Neither Motley Crue nor Accept ever really did anything for me, although I do remember a big surge to the front when Motley Crue came on stage about half hour earlier than advertised.

The event T-shirt had pictures of gravestones on the back, each one showing the line up from previous Doningtons….a neat idea I thought (I still have mine, in fact I still have all the event T-shirts and programmes)."

Paul Hartshorn (Chesterfield)

1985
ZZ Top,
Marillion, Bon Jovi, Metallica, Ratt, Magnum, Tommy Vance

The bill this year was a bill of two halves. Three bands making their debut and only Donington performances and three bands who would return again, two in headline slots.

Openers Magnum were at the time unsigned, but they were head hunted by a talent scout from the Polydor labels German office. Having just released 'On A Story Tellers Night' in the UK on FM Records, Polydor had picked up on this and come to watch their performance at Donington, signing them in the backstage area.

Next up were Ratt; raised in LA like Motley Crue and of the similar 'hair metal' contingent which included Poison, who were yet to make their Donington debut. Ratt were already big news in the States with 'Round And Round' already an MTV hit. Lead guitarist Robbin Crosby sadly died from AIDS in 2002 at the age of 42; his guitar dexterity on the day was very popular.

Marillion made their only appearance at MOR in the special guest spot on the day, which seemed a little out of place for a 'prog rock' band at a rock and metal festival; although an exceptional band, could they have been described as a 'Monster of Rock'. At the time Marillion were riding high on the success of their chart singles 'Garden Party', 'Punch and Judy', 'Assassing' and their biggest hit then and which they haven't topped since, the passionate, yet heart-rending, 'Kayleigh'.

Bon Jovi were making their debut at Donington, only to return 2 years later as triumphant headliners. Their album '7800° Fahrenheit' had been released four months before and so was already a favourite with their adoring fans; tracks included from it on the day featured were 'Only Lonely', 'In And Out Of Love' and the rousing 'Tokyo Road' as their opener.

Making their first appearance, the band with the record for the most shows at Donington were Metallica. Playing mid afternoon with original bass player Cliff Burton, they were like nothing else at the festival and were more fitting with Download Festival now; Burton was die in a coach crash only 13 months later in Sweden on the 'Master Of Puppets' tour.

Metallica were targets for bottles on the day, but were targets for adoration from that point on; their first headline show at MOR was in 1995, but they also played in '87 & '91, rising up the bill each time.

ZZ Top were 'topping' the bill this year and would not return until 2009, then in the 3rd place slot.

Playing a greatest hits set, packed full of tracks from 'Eliminator' and their illustrious back catalogue. ZZ Top would release their 10th album 'Afterburner' 2 months later, but surprisingly no tracks from the album were played on the day. What did make an appearance was the ZZ Top car, the red 1933 Ford 3-window coupé Hot Rod from their videos, suspended above the crowd from a helicopter.

Great sunny weather for the whole festival and the dulcet tones of Tommy Vance again throughout the day.

"Growing up as a fan of music and metal, clutching my copies of Sounds and Kerrang! on a weekly basis, as I grew up through the eighties, getting to see Metallica's name on a

Donington poster in 1985 was obviously a pretty big deal. We were bright eyed and completely star struck and we were so psyched to come in there and be a part of that whole thing. We went on that first year early in the afternoon; this was back then and whenever we played festivals it would always be with rental gear and half the issues were 'would the gear function?' We wouldn't get to the gear until we were actually at the site, so you never really knew what you were walking into.

It was early in the afternoon and we were ready to go out there and just throwdown as hard as we could. The main memory and the story that has become folklore from that gig was that there was a pigs head thrown up onto the stage. We were playing and it was back in the day when there was a lot of mud throwing, bottles of piss and all that type of stuff, which we had been warned about and took no offence to, as it was all part of the fun and games; but when the old pigs head ended up on stage, I remember the look on Cliff Burton's face was one of surprise and 'that they really go a step further here!' It's all true!!

It was a fun day and our first foray into British 'mega festivals'. It was certainly the first time that anybody playing our type of music was introduced to an audience that was that big and varied in it's make up.

It was a very varied line-up and we were obviously proud to represent, the kind of music that we were representing and it certainly was the first time that an audience of that kind of cross section of rock fans, were introduced to us, or a band of our ilk.

We must have made some impact because I remember I saw Marillion about a month later, they were playing in Copenhagen where we were recording 'Master Of Puppets' and I went to see them as I was quite a big Marillion fan actually. I remember at one point Fish was talking and introducing the band, with a bit of stage banter. All of a sudden he started talking about 'we're not like some of these new bands that you run into at the festivals playing this horrible noisy stuff' and then Marillion, lo and behold, went into their attempt at 30 seconds of 'speed metal'. I'm not sure if they were aware that I was in the audience, but it was quite funny

and there was a smile on my little Danish face because we must have made some kind of impact on the other bands. The festival was certainly a fun day and there was a great 'piss up' back at the hotel that was a couple of miles from the site where a bunch of the other bands were playing. Some of the guys from Ratt were hanging out and some of the guys from Venom came up and we had a lot of fun."
Lars Ulrich (Metallica – Drums)

"It was a really hot typical summer's afternoon and Donington was quite a day in the History of Marillion. It was one of those occasions that put us in books as being a good festival band. We played just before ZZ Top and really rocked the audience so much so that when the ZZ Top car was flown over the stadium I don't think that many of the crowed actually saw it and realised the significance of (ZZ Top arriving).
We didn't get to see ZZ Top as they had their own enclosure inside the enclosure INSIDE the back stage area. My guess is they were not wanting to be disturbed.
We were in the band area which was pretty secure with Bon Jovi and the others. I don't remember much socializing going on except with the Magnum boys as we new them quite well and they were and still are good blokes I imagine although I haven't seen any of them for years.
Bon Jovi looked the part and played a good set as far as I remember, but we were more focussed on our own show than anything else My Wife Fiona was there with me and enjoyed herself along with the other Wags.
Interestingly we played just before Bon Jovi at Rock In Rio back in the early 90's and they put their heads round the door and wished us good luck having remembered us from those earlier years."
Pete Trewavas (Marillion – Bass)

"To be Honest I was trippin' a little before we played because I was on the sides of the stage watching the other bands play before our set and I was seeing plastic one gallon milk jugs full of piss being chucked up at the stage and all over each other in the crowd.

And I was thinking, if I get hit in the fucking head with a jug of piss I'm gonna lose it.
What did come flying onstage was even more shocking, some stooge cut the head off a pig and threw the head on stage......Ummm, was that 1985? Ummm no it was 1578 that's right!!
Unbelievable gigs there. I had heard that while Ozzy was on that another part of the pig flew up there and all they could tell was that it was a female....
Hello Cleveland!"
Bobby Blotzer (Ratt – Drums)

"We had a German record executive, come over from Germany; he had approached us and had heard the 'On A Storytellers Night' album. A DJ gave him the album and said to him 'you should sign this band'; he then contacted us and said that he wanted to put the album out on the Polydor label, who he worked for.
So I can remember that we went on stage at Donington and I turned around and I could see this German guy, he was called Michael Göhler and he had come to see us play live.
So we played, I don't remember much about the playing part, but our manager then came up to us backstage and said that Michael wanted to sign us to Polydor. That was obviously the start of things for the band; he signed us and helped us a lot over the years.
I watched ZZ Top and I watched Marillion from out front. I remember also being interviewed in a caravan with a guy from Ratt; but I didn't even remember seeing Metallica, they were in their infancy then. I can remember Jon Bon Jovi walking around, but I didn't actually see them play."
Tony Clarkin (Magnum – Guitar)

"That was the day that we signed a major deal with Polydor, a lovely German guy called Michael **Göhler** and he loved us so much that he got us to sign on the dotted line.
Only a few things were thrown, so we were very lucky."
Bob Catley (Magnum – Vocals)

"I remember that we had to stop on the motorway on the way there for the police to form a cavalcade and escort us in there. I do remember a piece of mud hit my mixing desk, I'd love to thank the guy who did that."
Mark Stanway (Magnum – Keyboards)

"My first great experience at Donington was the first time I ever went. I was watching Ratt play and a mysterious and very cute girl stood beside me and asked which member of Ratt was my favourite. Knowing nothing about Ratt I chose the guitarist who looked like Joe Perry, whereupon she called me a star and gave me a blowjob. My first groupie and the best blowjob I ever got. All thanks to a rather dreadful hair metal band from Los Angeles." **Ginger (The Wildhearts – Vocals/Guitar)**

"I went in '85 and Metallica were 'fucking awesome'; although at that time I was a proper 'Ratt head'. I was into all those bands from LA like Ratt and Motley Crue."
Pete Spiby **(Black Spiders – Vocals / Guitar)**

"ZZ Top thought flying their car over Donington would be impressive.
We saw Pink Floyd at Main Road Manchester. During the show a man in a hospital bed appeared on a large video screen above the band on stage. He took off through the ward and out of a window, seconds later a full size bed flow over the length of the football ground with a man in it and crashed right into the video screen.
Now that's impressive!"
The Bailey Brothers (Mick & Dez Donington Comperes)

"I first became aware of some... thing called "Monsters Of Rock" around 83/84. I wasn't really into metal at the time - I was more hard rock (Queen, Magnum, and ZZ Top) and prog (Genesis, Jethro Tull, Marillion) then, so didn't really bother much with the likes of Ozzy, AC/DC, The Scorpions, Motorhead etc. But I'd seen the t-shirts at gigs and the posters in HMV & Kerrang!

In 85 ZZ Top, Marillion & Magnum were all on the bill for that years event. I'd attended my first festival - the infamous 1984 Nostel Priory festival - already and felt ready at the age of 18 for more. There was a company in Leeds called "Cavendish Travel" who did travel & tickets to events all over the country so my girlfriend of the time and myself went to their seedy little office, handed over the money (£12.50 I think, and about a tenner for the coach) and retreated tickets in hand.

The night before, I listened to the Friday Rock Show as DJ Tommy Vance was doing a run down of the bands on the bill that year. Three of the bands I knew well, but Ratt, Metallica and Bon Jovi were very much unknowns at the time. I wasn't impressed with the Metallica track they played – 'Seek And Destroy' How cheesey. But the other two seemed ok.

Saturday morning dawned, and we headed into Leeds to catch the coach. The tannoy system announced the bay to go to catch the bus to the "Donington Pop Concert" and we tutted at National Express's ignorance of musical genres (as you tended to do at that age). The journey down the M1 was uneventful, but when we pulled off at the last services before getting there (Toddington) there seemed to be long hair and denim everywhere. It started getting exciting.

Getting off the coach into a sea of patches, studs, leather and denim we were swept along to the entrance with a very palpable buzz. Through the gate and into the arena. That's when the "Donington moment" hit me. A sea of every kind of rocker and metalhead you can imagine. The Dunlop Bridge to one side, burger vans and a bar to the other and an incline down to the stage which towered over everything. Nostell Priory was a sedate afternoon at a village fete in comparison. It seemed a heaving mass of people. Bottles (some empty, some not) seemed to orbit over our heads. I remember one time, later in the day when I'd managed to force my way as far as the sound desk a bottle landing on my back, wedged between me and some guy behind me and glugging its contents down the back of my German army jacket. I never wanted to know what was inside.

To start with we found a spot where we could enjoy the distant site of Magnum (no screens that year I seem to remember) rattle off what seemed to be a very brief 30 minute set.
Ratt were quite a disappointment from that distance, but Metallica were quite a revelation. Far from being the clichéd meathead fodder I was expecting, I found myself getting into their energy.
Bon Jovi showed all the promise they'd later come to fulfill - ready for the Arena stage, Jon Bon Jovi climbing the speaker stacks.
About this time we started to press forward as my favorite band - Marillion - were about to come on. They were pretty big at the time and really not a Monsters Of Rock type of band but as always they blew me away. It was the first time I'd seen Fish perform without his trademark makeup. There's a picture of Fish kneeling on the stage in Mick Walls "Market Square Heroes" Biography and my face is clearly visible in the crowd.
Then came the wait for the headliners. I moved out of the crush a bit at this stage, and the crowd roared in appreciation as the ZZ Top "Eliminator" car was flown suspended from a helicopter over the crowd - not something you'd get away with now! Their set was fairly unremarkable and a retread of the one I'd seen a couple of years earlier, so the day ended on a bit of an anticlimax. Spirits were high on the way home but I little realised the impact that day had had on me.
As I said earlier, I wasn't much into metal then. But I think that day changed me. I particularly think Metallica changed me. It didn't happen overnight, and it was a few years till I returned but it was to be another major day in my life."

Phil Hull (Download Forum Administrator)

"The first concert I went to was Monsters of Rock 1985.
The sun blazed down all day, the beer was wet and the burgers luke warm, but the music...well, that was a feast to behold!
Bon Jovi had just released 'Slippery When Wet' and their set was full of
sing along songs EVERYONE knew.

Metallica were a relatively unheard of band at the time but after that day and the performance they gave it was obvious to everyone they were going to be BIG! Sorry, did I say big... I meant ABSOLUTELY FUCKIN HUGE!!
To top the day off the 'Eliminator' car was suspended beneath a helicopter
and flown over the stage prior to ZZ Top Rockin the Castle!
So, a 250 mile drive home after my first festival with the sights and
sounds still buzzing my senses. Only 364 days to go till I get to do it
again...Hell Yeah
This year will be my 8th visit to the sacred home of Rock and 25 years
since my first and for the 4th year my wife and kids will be with me...and
my parents said I'd grow out of it!!!"
Doug Rae (Hawick, Scotland)

"Although on paper the line up looked relatively weak compared to the previous two years, some of the performances were excellent.
ZZ Top had returned to headline this year. Earlier in the (sunny) day their 'Eliminator' car had been flown over the site suspended beneath a helicopter. Several thousand plastic bottles being propelled skywards was quite a sight. The played a good solid headlining set.
I didn't really get Marillion at the time, but like me the previous year, some of the gang went down to the front and came back raving about the performance (most reviews backed this up over the following days….shows how much I know).
Bon Jovi were a fairly new name at the time, their meteoric rise to mega stardom was still a year away. Their performance was brilliant. One member of our gang (a Donington virgin at the time) even predicted that this band would headline within two years…….how right they were.
Definitely a contender for band of the day.

It would take me another 5 or 6 years before I took any notice of Metallica (or any thrash style bands), so it would be unfair for me to pass comment at this stage.
Magnum on the other hand was a band I was looking forward to seeing. The album 'On a Storyteller's Night' was one of my favourites at the time. Even though they were first band on they didn't disappoint. It would another 5 years before a band would challenge them for the title of best opening band. One image I remember is Bob Catley being hit in the crotch with a clump of (accurately thrown) mud. He was wearing very pale jeans which made it stand out even more.
Another warm day."
Paul Hartshorn (Chesterfield)

1986
Ozzy Osbourne,
Scorpions, Def Leppard, Motorhead, Bad News, Warlock, Tommy Vance

The rain was back and so was another 'Monsters Of Rock', now into its 7th year and increasing in status each year.

Warlock were up first, fronted by the current poster girl for the 'rock & metal brigade', Dorothy Pesch; at the time she could barely speak any English at the time, but that didn't hinder her and her band from getting the show off to a fine start.

Next on was the controversial choice of the day Bad News. A comedy band formed from the actors in 'The Young Ones' (Mayall, Planer, Edmondson and Richardson), the whole show was filmed to be used as part of the 'Comic Strip Presents' series, entitled 'More Bad News'. Bad News were seen by most of the crowd as a waste of bill space that could have been given to a 'real' band.

Motorhead made their debut at the festival and Lemmy stopped the show when someone fired a rocket at the stage, but carried on again after no one took up his offer to come on stage for a fight; Motorhead are booked in 2010 for their 4th appearance.

There can be only one reason that Donington 1986 sticks in people's memories and that was because of the victorious return to live performance of Rick Allen the drummer with Def Leppard. Allen had been in a severe car crash where his left arm had been torn off on New Years Eve in 1984. Now able to drum one handed, with a specially adapted kit which could involve more footwork, he returned to playing (after a few warm up shows) at probably one of the biggest shows that Def Leppard had done at the time.

Def Leppard received great applause and Rick Allen achieved a standing ovation.

Scorpions were back for their 2nd appearance, six years after their first one and the second German band on the bill for the day. Scorpions were at the high point of their career at the time and were well justified in their 'special guest' slot.

'Love At First Sting' in 1984 had seen them reach #6 in the USA and #17 in the UK and tracks from the album featured heavily in the set including 'Bad Boys Running Wild', 'Big City Nights' and the crowd pleaser 'Rock You Like A Hurricane'.

The 4th British headliner came in the shape of Ozzy Osbourne, back after a two year absence and now looking very much part of the 'hair metal' revolution that was taking place at the time in the UK and especially America. Lowered to the stage on a flamboyant golden throne, Ozzy was certainly perceived as the 'Prince of Darkness'. Wearing what looked like a diamante dressing gown, Ozzy belted out the hits and several new tracks from his latest album 'Ultimate Sin' including the single 'Shot In The Dark', which summed up the style of the whole album.

So, another festival ended and so did the appearances by Tommy Vance. Sadly no more Thomas 'The' Vance at Donington, apparently due to some article that he had written. So another British institution was gone and the following year Donington would see another radical change, no British bands and a bill that was known as 'The American Year'.

"We came back for another show in 1986 with Ozzy and Def Leppard.
Looking back, those shows were among the most exciting and unforgettable gigs in the 80's.
Donington Rocks!"
Scorpions

"My first experience of Donington was in '86; it was Rick Allen our drummers first big gig after his awful accident where he lost his arm. We had done 'warm ups' where we'd been playing in Ballybunion and other places in Ireland in the middle of nowhere. We had two drummers out; we had Rick Allen and just to play it safe, as he was playing electronic drums which were quite new back then, we had another drummer Jeff Rich, but he couldn't make one of the shows, so Rick played and he was great.
So we got to Donington and it was really emotional, because it was England. We'd never really been accepted as a major band in England, I think because we had such huge success in America and everyone got a little bit pissed off for whatever reasons. But they loved it because Rick had overcome his accident and it was amazing. It was a big deal, for us that one minute he had two arms and we take all that for granted and then he came back and it was huge, as he was doing such an unusual thing, playing drums in a rock band, but now you can't even hear a difference. Back then he was still learning and learning how to be a person again, which was really cool.
It kind of overshadowed everything and I remember Joe introducing Rick; everyone stood up and it was really emotional, there were people crying, but it worked out.
I also remember the weather wasn't great."
Phil Collen (Def Leppard – Guitar)

"It was the biggest gig we'd ever done and was about 100,000 people.

When we went up the stairs to the stage, I could hardly walk as my knees were shaking and it was so overwhelming. I remember the fans were going crazy and they were very supportive. The fans were so good to us and there was such a good atmosphere. My heart was beating; I thought I was going to have a heart attack as my adrenalin was so high!
We didn't have a long set, but we gave it our all and I was the first female to play on that stage!
The catwalk out to the people in the crowd was so long and I was so happy.
It was also the first time that I talked to Lemmy and he said 'hey let's go and see Ozzy Osborne', I said to him that I didn't have the right pass. Then someone was walking towards us and he said 'excuse me' and ripped the pass off the guy. He said 'that's mine' and he replied 'it's hers now' and we then walked arm in arm to watch Ozzy Osborne.
I couldn't speak English back then, so our conversations were a little limited.
I watched every band on the day and it was the first time that I got to see the Scorpions, even though I'm from Germany!
Everyone was so proud of Def Leppard's drummer as it was his first gig since his accident and they were amazing.
Somebody threw a firecracker at Motorhead and Lemmy was so pissed off that he walked off stage and then came back and said that if anyone did that again, they wouldn't come back on.
For us it opened so many doors. After the concert we had our first US release
; all the record company people had come to watch.
It was one of the most important gigs of our life, which we didn't know at the time, but afterwards we went off and toured Europe with Judas Priest, who were my favourite.
It was phenomenal. It was just an honour to play there with our heroes."
Dorothy Pesch (Warlock – Vocals)

"I loved Monsters of Rock; from when I was 14-16 it was great leaving the village of Cheddar in Somerset, getting on a coach with loads of 'metallers' and it was awesome, lush, just being with a bunch of other people of a similar ilk.

*The festival was wicked because it was full of people all pretty much looking the same; being part of a massive gang.
There were bottles of piss being thrown and it was really hardcore."*
Jack Bessant (Reef – Bass)

*"The first time I came to Donington was in 1986 when I was 12.
It was the ultimate show; Ozzy got lowered down onto the stage in a giant chair, it was amazing and fantastic, imagine being that age and seeing all that, it was incredible.
I also came in '87, '88, '90 and '91 as well."*
Richie Edwards (Stone Gods – Vocals/Guitar)

*"Having attended as fans over the years it was cool to have reached a stage in our career where we were invited as guests. It was a shock to realize that if you wanted to see the bands perform it was on a small TV monitor.
It was cool to hang out with so many old mates and a good place to make new contacts but if you think the Bailey's are watching Def Leppard on a piss pot TV screen, think again! We would often just piss off into the audience to watch the bands then leg it back stage.
A slice of world history was made during the 86 MOR. We ran into Def Leppard and were talking to Rick Allan and his mum who looked more nervous than he did. Rick was playing his first official gig since losing his arm in a car accident. Def Leppard made a triumphant return and when Joe Elliot turned around and said" Rick Allen on the drums" Rick got a standing ovation from the entire Donington audience. Rick's mum kindly gave the Bailey's a photo of him up on stage that day. It was also the day that we helped launch Metal Hammer magazine in the UK. We handed out thousands of flyers to the legion of metal heads attending on the day and gave it our seal of approval.
Bad News robbed an artiste of a slot on the bill and were what you would expect, a joke.
The Scorpions were, as always, energetic, entertaining and as tight as a ducks arse. We met Ozzy Osbourne back stage and*

he looked scary. He had way too much black mascara on and looked out of it. Somehow he still managed to get his arse on stage and do what Ozzy does best. Mick is never shy of organizing a photo shoot so pulled Ozzy, Brian May and Phil Collen of Def Leppard together for a mug shot."
The Bailey Brothers (Mick & Dez Donington Comperes)

"I started running the site in 1986, I was the site manager. I ran it from 1986, right through to 1996."
Stuart Galbraith (ex – Donington Organiser)

"Record companies would do their best to get a part of it, out vying each other with tents backstage and "extras" (giveaways, girls in army uniform, helicopters etc)....and of course other stars would turn up just to support their friends on the bill. Brian May came to support Bad News - and got stopped at the gate. Bad News were a controversial addition to the bill – they were pretty scared beforehand, probably quite rightly too, 72,500 bone fide rock fans were a tough audience to play to."
Judy Totton (Monsters Of Rock PR)

"This was my third visit to MOR, 1985 had been good but nowhere near as good as 84, however, that was largely down to the lineup for me, I could not stand ZZTop so their lacklustre (boring to be honest) headliner performance marred my day. '86 was a different kettle of fish altogether; I loved most of the lineup so this one was always going to live up to expectations.
The weather was hit and miss all day but the atmosphere was great as usual, Donington has always retained its friendly and good humoured atmosphere and there has always been a sense of togetherness, this is not something that I have felt at most of the other festivals that I have attended.
First band on were Warlock who were fronted by the pin-up rock chick favourite of the day, Doro Pesch. The band faired well and played a crowd pleasing set without getting too many missiles chucked in their direction, these of course were saved for the next band.........Bad News.

Bad News was the fake band consisting of members of the 'Comic Strip Presents', Ade Edmonson, Rick Mayall, Peter Richardson and Nigel Planer. They came on to a rapturous bottling which did not let up until they left about half hour later. I don't think that the crowd appreciated having the piss taken out of them, although this was a great success on TV and we all loved it, this simply did not work as well live. The band stumbled their way through about three songs and spent the rest of the time getting us to shout 'Fuck Off' and other profanities at them, this was later edited and formed part of the More Bad News. I for one was not that bothered by them and found it quite amusing that some people in the crowd were getting so worked up, however, I could not wait for some real music to begin again.

Motorhead were next on and got the crowd going quickly with heavy as fuck tracks like opener 'Iron Fist' newish track 'Killed by Death' and of course 'Ace of Spades'. All was going well until some dick threw a lit flare on to the stage! Lemmy quickly stopped the set and went mental, threatening to kick the shit out of the culprit if they dared to come on stage and face up to their wrongdoing. This interruption fortunately did not last long or spoil my enjoyment of the set. As they neared the end of their set a Bomber flew over the crowd, this obviously was not a coincidence and had been planned to great effect, I was impressed anyway.

During the interval I saw this bloke walking towards us carrying a vast tray of beers, so many in fact that he was having trouble getting his arms around them, he got to within two metres of us when a huge missile (which I think was a half full five litre cordial type container) came out of the sky and hit his tray. He lost the lot and went crazy, he started to rant and rave about the bastard bottler taking his soul or something along those lines, he then burst into tears and fell to the ground and started to pound the chip and urine covered grass with his fists, this was the one and only time I have witnessed anyone crying at Donington (but not the last time that I would witness a tray of drinks getting knocked out of someone's grasp.

Despite the rain that that had just started, I was really looking forward to the next band, Def Leppard, I was a huge fan of 'Pyromania' which I had played to death for at least a year, this was my first change to see them after their lengthy hiatus caused by the never ending recording of 'Hysteria' and also because of Rick Allen's terrible car accident. I was not disappointed, a huge crowd of us sang and bounced along to every track, we particularly went mental during 'Photograph'. During this track our colleague Teapot decided to try his hand at crowd surfing; we were about half way back and just stood and gazed in amazement as he was thrown into the air getting nearer and nearer the front until he disappeared into the security pit at the front of stage. We did not see him again until the very end of the gig.
Def Leppard came and conquered, and I did not think it could get any better until that is the Scorpions hit the stage. At that point in time Scorpions were another of my favourite bands and I expected them to put in a tight performance, but Christ, they were absolutely fantastic.
They stormed the stage with so much energy and enthusiasm it was impossible not to get won over, highlights for me were 'Blackout', 'Big City Nights', 'The Zoo', 'Bad Boys Running Wild' and closing track 'Cant Get Enough' which of course included their patented human pyramid routine. That was easily one of the best and tightest sets I have ever witnessed at any festival and makes me smile just thinking about it - Rudy and the boys done good.
After Scorps we finally found the other half of our group that had wondered off for a piss three hour ago and of course spent a few minutes reminiscing about the Scorps and Leps sets. One of the biggest problems with festivals in those days was finding people when they got lost, no matter how hard you tried to use a flag or the legendary pizza bus as a point of reference, it was virtually impossible finding people in the mass of denim and leather, we all looked so similar. This of course is not a problem nowadays, the invention of the mobile phone has ensured that no matter where you get lost or how stupid you are, and you can always find your friends again (unless they don't want to be found).

Another staple at Donington (and other fests) is the dusk tradition of the good old bonfire! In good weather many people turn up in just a T-Shirt forgetting the fact that by sundown they will start to feel the chill no matter how much alcohol they have consumed. This of course requires action and this is when people's minds turn to nice toasty camp fires. They say that there are three elements to fire: fuel, oxygen and ignition, all of these are readily available at any outdoor show. Oxygen is obviously everywhere, fuel has been thrown about all day and is readily available in bottle or cardboard form covering every inch of ground and last but not least we have ignition, which is in abundance via lighters which of course have been used throughout the day to light cigarettes and other slightly less legal variants and will also be used later to hold aloft during a headliner ballad."
Roger Moore (Glinton, Peterborough)

"It was 1986 and off me and my friends went to Donington after going to the M.O.R .party at the Derby Rockhouse the night before with the Bailey Bros as the house dj's I was a little worse for wear, but being cheered up by winning a Phonogram promo cap I was looking forward to the day ahead.
Having watched Warlock, Bad News and the return of the mighty Leps, I decided to go and meet up with my friends Nick and rich.
They came down waving two backstage passes I could not believe it, just been backstage but there's not really any one there they said, how did you get them I asked. Seen these lads with 2 passes and we said give us your passes mate and true enough they did.
I was gob smacked Rich said if you want them you and Ribs go in while we watch Motorhead so off we went in; could not believe it backstage at Donington! I was like a kid in a sweet shop in we walked not many people about so we decided to sample the backstage beer, after one or two I was rubbing my eyes and in strolls Doro and Niko from Warlock, I thought I'd had one to many.

So I made haste and got her to sign my tour book, awesome, had a chat with them and they made there way to the bar , then I turned round and I could not believe my eyes return of the thunder god Mr Rick Allen after wetting myself I calmed myself down and made an approach ,
'Rick can you sign my program' I said and give him the book He said 'you will have to hold it for me', I felt about two inches tall ,giving a one armed man a program and a pen at the same time how does he hold it ..
He saw the funny side and signed my book and we had a good chat. I then returned to watch Scorpions and told the lads of my experience not to say I had the piss taken out of me all night,
But what the hell I had an amazing day long live the Leps....."
Jamie Taylor (Belper, Derbyshire)

"In comparison, 1986 was overcast and very cold. This contributed to the fact that our gang was depleted this year, with only half a dozen or so attending.
Ozzy put on a great show, being lowered to the stage on a giant throne. Even though the weather wasn't great, the sound was very good. I think he was introduced on stage by Tommy Vance (but it could have been Jonathon King).
Once again I decided to venture to the front of the stage, this time to watch Scorpions who very rarely disappoint. I was rewarded by capturing one of Hermann Rarebell's (used) drumsticks at the end of the set. This is still in my possession. The highlight of Motorhead's set was the fly over by a bomber aircraft. The low point being Lemmy's bad mood and predicting (wrongly) how Motorhead would headline the following year's festival.
Def Leppard's set was predictably emotional, as it was the return of Rick Allen following his car crash. But alas they have never been my cup of tea, so beyond the curiosity factor I didn't pay them too much attention.
Why was Bad News (a TV spoof band) put on the bill above Warlock (a bona fide rock group)? Fair enough, Warlock weren't the greatest band in the world but they had their moments and of course……they had Doro. Probably the best

photo in any of the Donington programmes was the one of Doro in leather trousers with a red crotch.
A day of mixed performances, fortunately Ozzy was on tiptop form."
Paul Hartshorn (Chesterfield)

1987
Bon Jovi,
Dio, Metallica, Anthrax, WASP, Cinderella, The Bailey Brothers

Monsters Of Rock '87 was unlike any other year; all of the line-up was made up of bands from the USA.

Glam metal and thrash were the flavours of the day with classic sets from most bands concerned.

Opening band, in the torrential rain, was Cinderella from Philadelphia. Already popular thanks to the constant video play for the single 'Shake Me' and the fact that their album 'Night Songs' was released almost a year to the day before they played at the festival and so was well known amongst the rock fraternity.

W.A.S.P. were also making their debut, but they would return in five years, but nothing would compare to their 'shock rock' show in 1987. With a large wooden wardrobe on stage as the main prop and a topless woman inside as the other prop, Blackie Lawless of W.A.S.P. proceeded to torture her and cut her throat with a large machete; Alice Cooper style theatrics gone mad!!!

The music was excellent, culling tracks from the 'W.A.S.P.' and 'The Last Command' albums, plus the anthem 'Animal (Fuck Like A Beast), which had made them so popular, in a bad way, with the PMRC led by Tipper Gore in the States.

Next was a double dose of thrash; Anthrax making their first appearance and Metallica making their all conquering return.

Anthrax's Joey Belladonna sang 'Indians' in full Native American headdress and the rest of the band wandered the stage, looking like a gathering of 'surf bums' in their Hawaiian shorts and t-shirts.

Metallica played their first Donington with Jason Newsted now on Bass as the replacement for the sadly departed Cliff Burton. Five tracks were played from 'Master Of Puppets', three tracks from 'Ride The Lightning', two tracks from 'Kill 'Em All' and a few covers. Metallica played mid afternoon, but it would still be another 19 years before they would come back to Donington to play all of 'Master Of Puppets' track by track, including the very rarely played 'Orion' for the anniversary tour of the albums release.

Dio was back after a four year gap, having now scaled the bill to the special guest slot. With a band that now featured the astonishing guitar skills of Craig Goldy (who is still in the band today), the audience was treated to the best of Black Sabbath ('Heaven And Hell' and 'Neon Knights'), Rainbow ('Man On A Silver Mountain' and 'Long Live Rock 'N' Roll') and the best of Dio (including 'Holy Diver', 'Stand Up And Shout', 'Last In Line' and 'Rainbow In The Dark'); an awesome appetizer for the Bon Jovi headline slot.

Bon Jovi at the time in '87 were riding high on the success of the 'Slippery When Wet' album and Donington at the time was probably one of their biggest shows; eight of the ten tracks on the album were played on the day, with a selection from the previous two albums.

For the final encore of 'We're An American Band' by Grand Funk Railroad, Bon Jovi were joined onstage by Paul Stanley (Kiss), Dee Snider (Twisted Sister) and Bruce Dickinson (Iron Maiden); Bruce let the 'cat out of the bag' that he would be back to headline with Iron Maiden the following year and Kiss would make their debut the following year as well.

Jon Bon Jovi was wearing a beard at Donington for this performance and looked very unlike his usual clean cut, boy next door, rock star image.

This year was also the first appearance for the Bailey Brothers, the music channel Rock & Metal poster boys and they recorded a lot of interviews and footage backstage for MTV; they would also return to host the show in 1988.

"It was our first Donington with Jason; we had played the '100 Club' a couple days before as a little 'warm up' gig. I believe we had our first backdrop, 'Crash Course In Brain Surgery', a Pushead take on the Budgie song.

I remember there was a lot of expectation that day; I remember the general reception in the British media was that we were 'luke warm' that afternoon; I'm not sure that I remember us being radically different in our performance of luke warm?

I remember Jason having these baggy camouflage pants, on that may have been the most visual thing onstage, other than the Pushead backdrop.

It was a great week in London where we had played a brilliant gig at the legendary 100 Club a couple of days earlier, where the temperature far exceeded 100 degrees; probably the hottest gig we'd ever played. I remember Steve Harris from Iron Maiden was there watching us and we were like 'oh my god, Steve Harris is watching us', so I think that made us want to play better, but actually made us probably not play as good as we were nervous."
Lars Ulrich (Metallica – Drums)

"I remember that Jon came over and said that we were all going to go up on stage and sing during there show as a finale. Paul Stanley was there and some people from other bands, so I said that I'd think about it, but I didn't do it, it just wasn't me. I certainly hope that Jon doesn't hold that against me for all those years, but it was my decision and I didn't do it.

The Donington festivals were always handled so well, Maurice Jones who did all those was a really good friend, so it was nice be around people that I had known and liked for a long time.
I just remember the show being somewhat like the show that we did in 1983. It's a spectacular audience that are really into everything and they've always been extremely nice to me, as a matter of fact.
I found that both were great days, but the first one was the best, because it was the first; it was a great time and I remember them both very positively.
I'd love to play it again, with either band, Dio or Heaven And Hell."
Ronnie James Dio (Dio – Vocals)

"I remember meeting Gene Simmons and Paul Stanley that day. They were sitting in with Bon Jovi later in their set that night. Both Gene and Paul were very nice to me that day!
I especially remember Ritchie Sambora coming over to me just before we went on and said..."Go out there and kick some ass ...for me"   I thought that was very cool of him to do that!
Then just after that Ronnie came over to my side seconds before we went on and said..."Don't be so nervous...just remember who you are!!"   That was a time in my life where there was a string of firsts....and that was one of them. Playing in front of over 80,000 people! And I knew that during my guitar solo I was going to motion to the crowd to answer me back. I would play a short memorable guitar melody and then motion to the crowd to sing it back to me!
Well needless to say I was very nervous about that, but after a couple of times they all were glad to oblige me and 80,000 voices answered my guitar!   That was a day to remember......I know...I should know the year...but the plaque is in a storage unit in Colorado and I'm currently trying to get it back...it used to remember the date for me as it was a proud thing to display on my studio wall and will again!!"
Craig Goldy (Dio – Guitar)

"Playing Donington 1987 was the biggest show we have ever played crowd wise up until that point in our career.
I remember arriving for soundcheck and watching DIO come out on stage to do his soundcheck; it was my first time seeing Dio perform live and meeting him. We then went on stage after Dio to perform our soundcheck. We all left after soundcheck and then returned to the venue the next morning. It was raining as it always is in England.
The line up if I recall correctly was Cinderella, Wasp, Anthrax, Metallica, Dio and Bon Jovi.
I was able to catch a few songs from everyone that day and enjoyed all the performances that I saw.
That day was my first time meeting Steve Harris from Iron Maiden as well. Steve was nice enough to invite me, Danny Spitz, Frank Bello and Chris Holmes back to his house that night after the show. We spent the evening there eating Indian food, playing pool and just having fun. Our show was great; it was total mayhem from start to finish.
It was a great experience and the fans did not let us down."
Joey Belladonna (Anthrax – Vocals)

"Lets put it this way, There are some guys in this world that like to go out and Rock'N' Roll and kick some ass, there are some other guys that want to stay home and wash dishes and wear aprons and I Ain't one of those"
Blackie Lawless (W.A.S.P. – Vocals/Bass)

"1987 was an amazing year for the Bailey Brothers, to be on the MOR bill with some of the world's major stars like Bon Jovi and Metallica is something we are very proud of. We were the only British act on the American dominated bill. We wanted to bring something different to the MOR in terms of a visual and audio show. Our idea was to have a huge screen that the audience could watch our videos on. We also wanted a camera filming us back stage interviewing the performers and guests thus bringing the whole event to the fans.
Unfortunately, those facilities were not provided as requested but we still managed to entertain the fans with a mix of good music and the Bailey's banter.

MOR 1987 highlighted the great divide between Glam and Metal and you had the 80's hairspray brigade getting bottles of piss thrown at them from the Metal fans. Somebody had to get out their and pull the fans together before trouble erupted and we rose to the challenge. The response through out the day from the fans was tremendous; to see and hear 70.000 fans singing along with you and clapping their hands is just a real adrenalin rush. Everyone always reports on the bands but with out the fans there is no show and we thank all of them for making us so welcome at the Monsters Of Rock. We also thank Maurice Jones and his team for the opportunity.
Rock Not POP!
During the day we encouraged the fans to write in to BBC Radio One and demand more rock on the radio. We called this petition Rock Not Pop and our catch phrase was born. In the weeks that followed the station was inundated with letters which resulted in them playing rock in the day time. It was good whilst it lasted but at least we made our point.
Back stage the highlight for us was being with Paul Stanley and Gene Simmons of Kiss. It would turn out to be one of many close encounters with the legends."
The Bailey Brothers (Mick & Dez Donington Comperes)

"My first time at the festival was in 1987 when I came over with Anthrax. I was working with them at the time and it was not only my first time at Donington but my first time in England.
I recall the guys in Anthrax "bombing" my room the first night, shaving cream in the bed, etc. Made it very difficult to sleep that first night!
I recall the size of the mosh pit that day and that Scott Ian made me shoot the entire performance from the side of the stage. This is when video cameras where the size of a brick! Not fun but still an incredible thing to see."
Eddie Trunk (USA Rock Radio DJ)

"I did a second Donington in 1987, the infamous "all-American" festival. The headliner was Bon Jovi. I was there with Anthrax. Metallica played also. The sound companies

were Rocksound (from Germany) and Malcolm Hill. Hill had a huge (and very good sounding) system flanking the main Rocksound speakers. I remember reading a telling article in Kerrang! the day before the show. The essence of the piece was an extremely perceptive whinge about the Donington show sound. The author had attended many a show there and wondered why, given the virtual mountain of speakers, all the opening acts sounded weak and puny whilst the headliner sounded massive. What if you didn't give a toss about the headliner? Your favorite(s) sounded lame! Shouldn't every band sound good? You paid your hard earned pounds to see and hear all the bands. The author had heard this at all the Donington Park shows and was quite fed-up.

Though I feel the situation in 1981 was certainly not deliberate sabotage on the part of either AC/DC or the Malcolm Hill company, the show in 1986 was quite another story. As usual, we arrived the day before and did a good sound check. The same system engineer was there from Malcolm Hill, we reminisced about the '81 show and I remarked how good the current iteration of the Hill system sounded. The vibe was pleasant, everything sounded fine.

The next day, of course, everything was different. I had high hopes for a fine show, but as we began I noticed that the system sounded much quieter than the day before and the dynamics were limited. Nothing sounded quite right. At one point I became quite disgusted and took a little walk to my left, the centre of the mixing platform, and took a look at the system drive racks. Yes, there it was, a DBX 165 Stereo Limiter, and, by golly, it was kicking back about 12db on every peak. And it was attached to my mix! I turned to the Rocksound system tech (the sound man for the Scorpions, by the way) and asked, "What the hell is this?" I got a reply burned into my brain even these many years later: "You know how it is!" (Imagine a German-tinged accent and a condescending smile.)

Just in case you are thinking, Ahh, the Malcolm Hill people were engineering a payback for '81; not at all. Malcolm's system tech was quite embarrassed and upset. Remember, his system is attached to the Rocksound array. If it sounds like

ass, his system will sound like ass. And ass it was, through every act until Bon Jovi. Then it was all it could be ("You know how it is!").
After Metallica's less than audible set, Peter Mensch (Metallica's manager with Cliff Burnstein) came up to Big Mick (Metallica's super-fine soundman) and me and he was livid. He knew that his band had been badly treated, but alas, there was nothing he could do. So it goes in the wonderful world of big-time sound. Attitudes like this limit audience enjoyment and essentially rob the audience of what is rightfully theirs: a full and effective show. It's also a pussy move. It implies the headliner does not have the confidence to carry the show without kneecapping the competition.
Does this always happen? No, but it happens often enough to be a real problem for touring professionals. It is an unfortunate part of the politics of the music business. These decisions are almost always band decisions implemented by management with the complicity of the sound company. Are there bands that make it a policy of not doing this?"
George Geranios (Sound Engineer)

"1987 had been another good year that I enjoyed immensely, the highlights for me included a surprisingly mature and entertaining headline set from Bon Jovi which included Jon climbing to the top of the stage for one song and the crowd pleasing turn of having Dee Snider, Bruce Dickinson and Paul Stanley join him on stage for a strange but excellent version of 'We're an American Band', I considered it strange because Bruce looked ill at ease and obviously is not American, the only reason I think he was on the stage anyway was to announce that Maiden would be headlining the following year. Another memory I hazily have occurred during Metallica. Part way through the set someone managed to get past security and onto the stage where he managed to find a rope to climb and proceeded to use it as a swing, he managed to keep this up for at least a minute before being collared by the tardy security that had let him slip through their ranks, he received a tremendous applause.

Jovi, Anthrax and Metallica's sets aside, my other favourite memory of the day was the entertainment supplied by my friend Mat who had designed his own Anthrax T Shirt with various felt tip pens in a primary school stylee, this was by far the worst shirt I have ever seen anyone wear at a gig and was ridiculed by virtually everyone that passed us, which of course had us howling with laughter all day long. Mat also learned later in the day that you should not accept drinks in medicine bottles from mad Irish men; I very much doubt he remembers Bon Jovi after a heavy dose of Pocine.

Another vague recollection I have is of Cronos from Venom stamping on my friends hand as he came stomping through the crowd trying to look all rock star cool, oh how we chuckled. Female attendance appeared to be a lot higher this year than during the previous fests, this probably had something to do with Bon Jovi playing but it was good to see that more girls/women were enjoying what had/has largely been a male dominated and attended genre. The numbers did not seem to dissipate during the following years and continues to this day at Download. An amusing anecdote I always remember, referring to the early eighties was of how strange it always seemed, that David Coverdale would always be thrusting his crotch suggestively at the crowd at his gigs when the attendees largely consisted of teen or early 20's males.

WASP were probably the only band that disappointed me in '87, they were ok but I was expecting better. It had not been that long ago when WASP were considered the most dangerous, noisy, parent scaring band on the planet, they were raw, unpredictable and even a little bit scary, they even managed to get their first single 'Animal, Fuck Like a Beast' banned which of course made them even more desirable to fans. This of course was before the likes of Metallica and their other thrash comrades who now made WASP sound wimpy and possibly a little bit silly. Blackie Lawless and the boys did their best and they rattled through their set professionally enough churning out favourites which included 'I wanna Be Somebody' and 'Blind In Texas' but for me the feeling of danger that got me into them had vanished and I was no

longer finding them enjoyable. On the day though and despite the rain during their set, they went down well enough."
Roger Moore (Glinton, Peterborough)

"I had been to concerts before, but never a festival, so I didn't know what to expect.
It was 6.30ish and I am at my local train station waiting for friends to meet up for the trek to Liverpool to catch the coach to the Monsters Of Rock , I had my leather jacket on and my metal patch denim over the top bleached knotted dyed jeans and my Air Wair boots, the real look of metal.
I noticed one of my friends Lee was there before me. He was lying on a bench with his stomach contents lying on the floor next to him; he had been there all night after his girlfriend had thrown him out because he was drunk.
It wasn't long before everyone of us had met up and were waiting to get on the coach to the festival ,
Liverpool was swarming with metal heads a vast see of leathers and chanting of 'Donington Donington Donington' , excitement grew and loads of beer got drunk on the way down, before we got on the driver said no drink allowed on the coach, as soon as I sat down I was handing out swigs out of my bottles of Mad Dog 20/20 and cans of ale, everyone got their drinks onboard, the coach had a video player on it and someone had made a VHS tape of the bands playing that day and we sang along all the way, backsides shown as 'bum salutes' to fellow festival travellers and food fights between the back half of the coach and the front broke out .
We started to slow down and traffic jams started, looking out the window every vehicle had people going to the festival in them. I knew we were nearly there, cars were parked up on both sides of the road and hordes of rockers making the final part on foot.
"Welcome to Castle Donington Monsters Of Rock '87 the signed said, we were there.
Being young at the time I drank as much as I could and staggered off down to the front to stay there and fight for my place to see the rock gods, nowadays it's: watch a band, go the bar, watch a band, go the bar and so on, I could turn

around in the sea of people head banging in unison to the tunes, the Dunlop bridge hovering over the crowd in the background.

We moved back towards the sound stage tower just to get breath before Bon Jovi came on stage. I will never forget we got standing behind two very drunk guys that were finding it hard to stand straight; they had plastic bottles of Scrumpy Jack everywhere around them and were chugging away on them. One of them picked one up and started to pee in one as they had no way of getting out the crowd; putting it back at his feet after he finished, the other guy, his friend, ten minutes later picked it up turned around and started talking to my friend, he then offered my mate a drink he said 'no thanks' with a grin on his face, the guy turned around and started drinking it, the people in the crowd around us just fell apart laughing.

Dee Snider, Bruce Dickinson and Paul Stanley came on stage with Bon Jovi and did a cover of 'Travelling Band' that rounded off a superb day at Donington, and I couldn't wait for the following year."

Paul Townsend (Widnes)

"My friend Tina was a massive Bon Jovi fan totally besotted by Jon.
She hung around the gate to the backstage area, where if you looked
through you could see limos coming in to drop off the bands.
She saw Bon Jovi's car arrive and pushed passed the security guy,
through the gate, ran towards the car and threw herself on top of the
bonnet!
The car came to a quick halt, the back door opened and Dee Snider got
out, he said "Hey, what's going on, god I've got crazy fans!" he looked
very pleased to see Tina on all fours, quite a sight in her leopard
print mini skirt, bra top, boots and blond big hair...

*Then Tina jumped down off the car, ran up to him, pointing in his face
and said indignantly "Who the hell are you? You're not Jon Bonjovi,
what the hell are you doing here?!!"
He looked a bit deflated but not as pissed off as Tina!"*
Naomi Laughton (Rotherham, South Yorkshire)

*"The triumphant return of Bon Jovi. Whether they were your cup or tea or not, at the time they put on a fantastic show (including lasers…….was this the first time lasers had been used at Donington?). Our gang had tripled in number from the previous year, bolstered by several females which seemed to be reflected in the overall attendance. Donington had become sexy.
I remember Jon Bon Jovi performing part of the set from the top of the lighting rig.
As part of the encore, the band was joined on stage by Dee Snider (Twisted Sister), Paul Stanley (KISS) and Bruce Dickinson (Iron Maiden). At the end Bruce saluted the crowd with a "see ya next year", which indicated that Iron Maiden were in line to play the following years Donington.
The fireworks display at the end of the show was as impressive as ever.
Dio put on their usual highly professional, faultless performance, but somehow they just didn't seem to fit in 1987.
Metallica and Anthrax passed me by I'm afraid.
WASP were a little more theatrical and Blackie Lawless' voice came over very powerful.
Bon Jovi stable mates Cinderella had an impressive debut album out at the time and their performance justified their addition to the bill. 'Night Songs' and 'Nobody's Fool' being particularly strong songs.
The weather was 'on and off' wet."*
Paul Hartshorn (Chesterfield)

1988
Iron Maiden, KISS, David Lee Roth, Megadeth, Guns n' Roses, Helloween, The Bailey Brothers,

Probably remembered mostly for being the saddest year in the history of the festival, due to the heartbreaking death of two young music fans.
Due to bad weather the previous few days, parts of the site had transcended into a mud bath; nowhere was it worse than in front of the stage. With everyone jumping up and down, moshing and crowd surges, the quality of the ground underfoot grew worse during the first band Helloween and the build up to Guns N' Roses.

Helloween from Germany went down well, but the most anticipated band of the day were Guns N' Roses making their MOR debut.

When GNR were originally booked they were nowhere near the popularity level that had reached by the time the festival had come around in August. With the release of the 'Appetite For Destruction' album GNR were catapulted to almost instant stardom. Slash was the guitarist that everyone wanted to emulate and Axl was the singer that everyone wanted to be.

The crowd grew as the GNR set loomed closer and as the band started up it could be seen that there was a problem; jostling fans caused massive crowd surges and the slippery ground underfoot meant that sections of the crowd were falling over and then people from behind them were piling on top of them, some people had no chance of getting out. Give the band their due, Axl did stop the concert several times and ask the people further from the stage to move a few steps back, in order to allow the people at the front space to breathe and help people up that had fallen in the crush. At the time the extent of the chaos wasn't known to most of the people in attendance and the security staff were fighting a losing battle, unable to get into the crowd during the bands performance.

All the sad news would be all over the BBC news that night and the following day; a dark cloud had descended over Donington and would be remembered by all in attendance whenever Donington 1988 was mentioned.

Up next were Megadeth, with Mustaine in fine mood for a set in the mid afternoon; this was their debut at Donington and 2010 will be their hat trick of festival appearances.

Next up was David Lee Roth making his return to Donington after 4 years; this time his guitar maestro was Steve Vai in the position that was filled by Eddie Van Halen in Van Halen. Steve Vai was an ex- Frank Zappa guitar prodigy who had played on the album 'Ship Arriving Too Late To Save A Drowning Witch'; Vai would return to Donington as lead guitarist in Whitesnake, in the headliner position, two years later in 1990.

Special guest this year was none other than the 'mighty' Kiss, without make-up, making their first of three appearances to date.

Playing a mixture of classic and recent songs, Kiss could do nothing but entertain the masses. The line-up featured Bruce Kulick and Eric Carr; the die hard fans were still yearning for a 'full make-up Kiss' playing all the classic 'Alive; tracks, 7 years later at Donington they would get their wish.

Headliner Iron Maiden made their first appearance at Donington and what a performance it was. Another British band topping the bill and a band that could fill the slot with ease.

Playing tracks from most of their albums, including crowd pleasers 'Run To The Hills', 'Number Of The Beast', 'The Trooper' and 'Aces High'.

So another festival drew to a triumphant close, only tarnished by the two fan deaths during the GNR set; the names of Alan Dick and Landon Siggers would be forever etched on the Donington history for all the wrong reasons.

Due to the tragic events in 1988 the festival took a sabbatical in 1989, returning two years later, with increased security, precautionary measures and a greatly reduced capacity.

"You can't argue with a crowd this big and we don't intend to argue, we intend to entertain"
Paul Stanley (Kiss – Vocals/Guitar)

"I was amazed at the enormous crowd and the very metal attitude that was at the Festival.
Gene and Paul were excited even though Iron Maiden headlined. We had such a good hit with 'Crazy Nights'; the fans were very into the band. The stage was SO huge, and that was really cool to be on it. Paul loved the ramps which he used, and what a feeling to look out at the crowd and see so

*many people out there, like an ocean of fans! The pressure was on, but we played great and I remember us all being pleased.
I watched some of G n' R and I was impressed with the reaction. Sad of course that some fans died getting crushed to see them. Backstage, there was press, lots of cool people and quite a good hang for everyone. I still meet people in the industry who say they met me backstage at Donington!
We left while Iron Maiden was doing their thing, and I remember leaving the grounds knowing it was an event that will be remembered for many fans for a long time. I still have the tour book and the souvenir mug!"*
Bruce Kulick (Kiss – Lead Guitar)

*"If every one of these guys had bought the album we would be doing great. I came here thinking this would be the worst day of my life after hearing all the horror stories about Donington but it's the best day of my life".
We are not going to be one of these bands that make an album then disappear"*
Axl Rose (Guns N' Roses – Vocals)

*"The good and the bad goes on here. I found out the responsibility of a band being huge right here.
When Guns played here, the first time the band had got really big in the UK and between getting booked on the bill and the time we played the band had blown up, so we were lower down on the bill; everybody surged forward when we played and that was before they had the partitions and two guys drowned in the mud.
So this festival for me also has a really serious aspect to it. This is where I grew up and realised, 'Oh shit. Nobody told me about all this.' This kind of stuff, the responsibility. You start thinking that if the band never got big then those two guys would still be alive; you go through that stuff in your head."*
Duff McKagan (Guns N' Roses – Bass)

"The last time I played here in 1984 Van Halen was peaking, as do all great relationships but the audience were spectacular.
The whole theory of Rock 'N'Roll in England and Europe is different to America."
David Lee Roth (David Lee Roth – Vocals)

"My memory of the gig was that it was massive in terms of size. I'd heard of the Donington event and expected it to be a large crowd but was still blown away by the shear size of the whole thing.
I remember that we played Donington during a period in which Dave was trying to change his image to be "classier" so he had us all wearing suits. At that time Dave wanted to distance himself form the other bands that wore leather and blue jeans or the loud spandex clothes from which he had become associated with just a couple of years earlier. Things were also coming to a head with his relationship with Steve Vai and the "gunslinger" mentality for which he was hired in the first place. I think it was also around that time Vai had gotten a big money offer from David Coverdale to join Whitesnake, which also made things tense out there.
Before the gig Dave and the band discussed the set list, which included songs like 'California Girls', 'Just A Gigolo' and 'Just Like Paradise' that were more in a pop vain. Some of the band thought we should leave out those songs and do a set that featured the harder material rather than the commercial songs because it was of course Donington. Kiss was headlining that day and there were a lot of harder bands like Guns n' Roses and others on the bill.
Well, we did our regular set without change and the crowd responded great and we left with a sense that we had left an impression on the audience regardless of the suits or the set list selection. But there was no question that the Vai era was coming to a close and I was bummed to see that happening.
I also remember being pretty impressed with Paul Stanley's voice. Donington was the first time I'd ever heard Kiss live. They really did rock and the crowd loved them. I've always respected their impact on music and especially their

contribution to the theatrical part of rock and roll. Hats off to them…."
Brett Tuggle (David Lee Roth – Keyboards)

"I have played bigger in my dreams."
Dave Mustaine (Megadeth – Vocals/Guitar)

"Donington 1988 was the first big festival I had played and it had a significant place in my world because I used to listen to the Castle Donington album when I was about 17 years old. That record featured Rainbow (with Graham Bonnet), April Wine, Scorpions and a bunch of other cool up and coming bands of that time. This was when I was at home in Minnesota, before I moved to California and met Dave Mustaine. I remember going 'wow this is friggin' great' because I was getting into all those bands at that time.
I played in '88 on the 'So Far, So Good, So What?' album and Maiden headlined; they were on their 'Seventh Son Of A Seventh Son' album and we played 7 dates with them on that tour, in America just before.
So Castle Donington just sounded awesome, coming from America there was always this affinity and infatuation with Europe and all bands starting out wanted to get to Europe.
So coming over here was huge and to play Castle Donington was the moment that 'you had arrived'.
Donington is an event for everyone and everyone who's anyone is always there, either as a performer or spectator. The day I played there I recall pulling up in the tour bus and there were 107,000 people in attendance. Literally farther than the eye could see.
You can always tell Download because of the barricade split down the middle. So, every time you see a photo you know that it was Download or even AC/DC live at Donington, because you can see that gap and it's a tell tale sign of any 'live' photo.
I remember flying in and meeting the Guns N' Roses guys at the airport. I think that they had been touring America with Aerosmith and they flew the Concorde over, bastards!

So the part of the video footage in the 'Paradise City' music video, where you see the Concorde, that's them, flying to Donington.

So we met at a truck stop and got something to eat with Steven Adler along the way, as our bands were friends in LA. When they played they were kicking ass, they were just great. I remember seeing them open for the Cult when they were this little 'Hollywood bar band' on these big stages. The record was taking off and I remember thinking 'wow' these guys had really spent some time on big stages.

Guns n' Roses played before us and unfortunately 2 people were killed in the audience and I think that after that they stopped having it for a while then reorganised it and eventually it became Download.

David Lee Roth was after us, with Kiss and Iron Maiden to follow. We left when Kiss were playing, so we didn't see Maiden.

The stand out memory in 1988 was that the fans would throw 2 liter bottles of urine at the stage, presumably because they were smashed in so tight in the crowd that they couldn't 'relieve' themselves from their beer consumption any other way than to pee on the ground or in the bottle they just drank from. Having no where to put it they simply threw it at the band!

They were also throwing huge clumps of mud which made for good sport while trying to thrash. In fact, using my bass guitar as a defensive shield against the trash being at the stage was as much fun as the actual show itself On a personal note, that was the kind of the last show for me. I was at the end of a very old life for me; I did a lot of drugs and I was really 'strung out'. To be honest, it was kind of bitter sweet for me because I remember showing up there and thinking I had worked my whole life for this and it was a dream, I was standing on the stage at Donington, sick as a dog, feeling like shit and I remember that after that I went home and started the re-hab circuit."

David Ellefson (Megadeth – Bass)

"I was here for Rainbow in 1980 - I had waited all my life for this moment."
Chuck Behler (Megadeth – Drums)

"I was really excited, to see Guns n' Roses and David Lee Roth, who was brilliant, really brilliant, 'cept this big bloke in front who kept shouting 'DAVE' at Dave Lee Roth and trying to give him a cigar.
GNR were like giants, they were fantastic, they were brilliant."
Tony Wright (Terrorvision – Vocals)

"I went in 1988 as a paying customer with my girlfriend at the time and we'd got the bus down from Glasgow. We were drunk out of our minds.
There were around 107,000 people there that year and it was the year that unfortunately those two young lads lost their lives during Guns n' Roses; obviously the hype regarding G'N'R was huge and the crowd was just out of control. I remember being stuck in the crowd and we were in a situation where you couldn't even get your arms above your head.
We had just started the Almighty and we were about six or seven months into the bands career and I remember standing there thinking 'this is amazing; I want to be on the stage and I want to play there'.
Ricky Warwick (The Almighty – Vocals/Guitar)

"The 1988 MOR was one of the Bailey Brothers most memorable and successful performances in our history. Not only were we back on the MOR bill, we were writers and presenters of MTV's number one rated programme. This time the cameras would follow us back stage as we interviewed every band on the mega bill. They also filmed us on stage in front of over 100,000 thousands fans many chanting our catch phrase 'Rock Not Pop'.
Kiss sent us a bottle of Champagne round to our dressing room which was a real nice touch.
Jonathan King thought he could do what the Bailey's did and just walk out on stage. I don't think anyone in the history of the MOR has had more shit thrown at them. He was covered from

head to toe in mud and piss. He came up to us after the show asking for a copy of the film footage. We didn't oblige.

It was almost non stop for about fourteen hours at the 88 MOR for the Bailey Brothers.

We felt we deserved a drink after the festival and hung out with our manager at the time John Doukas. Ex Thin Lizzy guitarist Brian Robertson joined us and nearly got us kicked out of the hotel .We kept this old guy called Bert serving us until 5 AM in the morning but Robbo still wanted more and had a secret stash of lager bottles hidden behind a plant by the entrance door. We all went up to his room and as he was going to take a drink a slug appeared from the bottle and Brian was screaming at the top of his voice," look a Fookin' wee little beastie". He still drank from the bottle as the hotel manager came to try and remove us. We had put the slug in the bath and told the manager we would report him to the environmental health if he didn't leave us alone and he apologized and left us to it.

When Guns N' Roses were booked to play the MOR they were a band on their way up. It was during their set that two fans died although none of us knew at the time. By the time they hit the stage they were the band everybody wanted to see. In all the years of MOR it had never been this full. Sadly one of the greatest rock and Metal concerts in British history will always be tinged with sadness".

RIP Alan Dick and Landon Siggers"

The Bailey Brothers (Mick & Dez Bailey Donington Comperes)

"But the fans themselves were always the best, always polite and always there just for the music (with the bonus of beer and bottle throwing of course...). Apart from the tragic year the two boys died there was very little trouble, very few arrests, maybe six or seven.   Donington was immensely hard work, we took it seriously but we loved it. It played a major part in my life for more than a decade and I rather enjoyed being queen of the rock chicks for a day. I even received a 'Music Week' Top PR Award for my work on it so *we must have been doing something right!"*   **Judy Totton (Monsters Of Rock PR)**

"Iron Maiden and their soundman Doug Hall, for years they challenged any band to blow them off the stage and would provide all the watts they needed to try. As a matter of fact, the 1988 Donington featured Iron Maiden and Doug assembled a huge sound system. Doug gave everybody everything and our Big Mick attested to this. He was once again in attendance (in what capacity I don't recall). I saw him later at another festival and he gave the sound system his highest accolade: "Raging." The 100,000 plus music fans got their money's worth that day.
I hope this little missive informed and enlightened those of you who are interested in these sorts of sordid details. Alas, my many years as a soundman were full of moments like these. But, like, golf, the one great shot keeps you going. The shows where the band and the sound system came together and built a powerful musical experience were some of the finest moments of my working life."
George Geranios (Sound Engineer)

  "Over the next couple of years I'd started listening to heavier stuff - Faith No More had exploded onto the scene and that really expanded my musical horizons. Guns 'n' Roses were quite the buzz band and their inclusion on the bill prompted me to get a ticket. I was driving and had my own car by now, so no coach ticket was required.
One of my best mates at the time was a chap called Dave Shackleton (known to all as Shack). He's now married to Nikki Chapman (from Pop Idol) and a bigwig at Sony BMG (I haven't seen him in years) but I'd known him when he was stacking shelves at Grandways.
He was a big Rush, Saga & Sabbath fan and his ambition in the Grandways days was to be a music journalist. In 1988 he was freelancing for Kerrang! and about to become managing editor of "Metal Forces" magazine.
Shack didn't drive and needed a ride to Donington. I had an underpowered 1.3L Capri MkIII and I gained my first guest

pass to any event in exchange for a lift. I agreed, and managed to sell my ticket for just below 'face value' to a friend in Halifax.

Queuing up to get in, my fan belt went. Not a huge problem as I was there - I'd think about getting home later! Looking for the car parks, Shack said to go to the guest area. We drove up to the paddock entrance, but we didn't have a car pass! Who'd have known that your guest pass wouldn't get your vehicle in! I pulled over as the ever resourceful Shack went into the site on foot, found Malcolm Dome and borrowed his car pass for my car! Sorted. I drove my overheating car into the guest car park. I had AA Membership, but figured they wouldn't manage to get in so left it for the end of the day.

Walking into the little backstage village, there was the EMI pavilion and smaller marquees owned by the likes of Warners & Kerrang!. Girlschool were sat outside the Kerrang! tent, Vixen & Maiden were lounging around in the EMI one. Everyone had free food & drink so I was rather annoyed with my chauffeur role for the day. Kerrang! were just about to launch their 100th issue (they were bi-weekly at the time) and I had the first piece of their guitar shaped cake. At one point queuing up for the toilet Slash stumbled over me, bottle of Jack in hand.

It was a pleasant walk from there to the arena, along a line of trees behind the stage which seem to be long gone. There were people all around the entrance, offering to buy my pass off me but I ignored them and went on in. My attempts to find somewhere to get a Guns n' Roses shirt were in vain - sold out, so I had to make do with a Dave Lee Roth one. We were late in and had missed the openers Helloween, so had to watch Guns n' Roses from the top of the hill. A good job really, considering the events that it later transpired had happened - the crush during G n'R's set. We weren't really aware that anything had happened at the time, we were so far back. Megadeth were ok, never really been my thing. Dave Lee Roth entertained as expected. Kiss were without makeup, and I found them quite dull and we returned to the backstage area to watch on the big screen in the EMI tent while Shack interviewed Vixen on the next table. Of course when Iron

Maiden came on, everybody was booted out of the guest area to go and watch from the arena. It was the first time I'd seen Maiden, and they put on a great show. The latest album was 'Seventh Son Of A Seventh Son' and they had a huge set and backdrop. I think this was also the only time Kiss ever broke their promise that they would never play support to anyone who had supported them in the past...
Trudging back to the car, I remembered the fan belt. This was, of course, before mobile phones so I drove out of the gates, and there was a phone box near the Park Farm Hotel that I called the AA from. Due to the traffic it was three hours before he reached me. One new fan belt later and we were on our way home - I remember dropping Shack off just as it was getting light."

Phil Hull (Download Forum Administrator)

"1988 was the one and only time of my visiting the 'Monsters of Rock' at Donington, but it was a real eye opener.
It was the first time I'd gone to any festival, so it was a great start. Having arrived by coach early, there was a time of hanging around and waiting in anticipation. When it was time to go in, I was scared and excited all at the same time. All the hoards of people heading towards the stage area waiting for the first band – being Helloween. I was quite new to their music, but I do remember 'Dr Stein' being played and thoroughly enjoyed it. There were a couple of people in front of me throwing oranges at the stage and I was really annoyed, but I was too young and too nervous to say anything.
Guns n' Roses were fantastic. I had been looking forward to seeing them and it was just before they became well known. It was a time I still had enough room to dance to their tracks on the dance floor at the local rock night, but you just knew they were going to be really big. I would say it was the best time to see them live, Axl Rose looked stunning and you were actually able to get close enough to see. They played a really good set that included 'Mr Brownstone' and 'Paradise City' to name just two.
Megadeth were disappointing to me, but only because of all the swearing. I remember the comment of 'thanks for giving

us all your f**king money'. I can remember the music being good though, but only if you could get past all the obscenities in-between.

Dave Lee Roth. What a performer! He put on a fabulous stage show and although I would have classed him as being fairly commercial, you couldn't help but enjoy yourself. He was already a legend at that time, and so it was a real treat to see him live on stage.

Kiss were on next, but this was the one band that didn't appeal so much to me personally, and so I took the opportunity to go and buy a t-shirt. It was a good idea at the time, but the only t-shirts that were left had several different bands listed on the back that didn't actually play! I remember Anthrax being listed at the bottom, and felt really gutted that they weren't actually there.

At that time, Iron Maiden was my favourite band. I worked my way up to the front and got hit on the head with a couple of two litre bottles, but did not want to think about what they contained. I was determined to stand my ground, as I'd seen them live before and had a huge crush on Bruce Dickinson. I also wanted to get a good look at Eddie on stage. If I remember correctly, it was the time of their 'Somewhere On Tour' and I had my 'Somewhere In Time' watch on (which I was very proud of). I then got hit with a small lemonade bottle and had to give up and move back, as this one really hurt. I didn't miss too much though, as they had large screens on each side of the stage that I could watch. I was on a high as they performed an amazing show - again.

The down side was when we heard about the people getting crushed at the front and later found out how serious it had been.

The day was over, but the ordeal continued with trying to find my coach. I found out that the one I should have been on was in amongst all the coaches heading for Glasgow. I didn't know this, as they weren't there when we had arrived and it was now dark, so I didn't have a clue where I was. I did manage to get on another coach heading in the same direction, but I was absolutely exhausted. My friends supposedly kept asking me questions that I had been answering in my sleep, but with

answers that didn't make sense. I then woke up thinking that we'd stopped at a service station, but to find out that we had actually broken down. Looking back now though, it did add to the fond memory of a brilliant day that happened all those years ago.
Thanks for the experience Donington!"
Diane Newman (Plymouth)

"We were there with an army this time.
This year it seemed different; more excitement, much bigger, more build up than the year before and the line up was fantastic. I can honestly say it was my all time favourite line up. Helloween, Guns N' Roses, Megadeth, Dave Lee Roth (with the legend Steve Vai on guitar) Kiss and Iron Maiden. The weather was bad but that didn't put anyone off, I recall one of the video screen collapsing in the wind. The crowd was this huge, massive, energy charged monster that exploded when the first band Helloween came on stage. One second I was on the right hand side of the stage midway from the front and sound stage then a second later I was on the left side of the stage and my feet never touched the floor! I was grabbing on to anyone around me and everyone else seemed to be holding onto me.
Guns N' Roses were due to come on and the crowd was getting more packed. I could feel nothing but pain as I was squashed, but this was the band I wanted to see. Some girl got in a panic and me and a few guys got her over the crowd and carried down to the front. When they came on I have never seen or been in a crowd like that, or since. Another small girl was frantic to get out. There was no way she could escape, people were pushing people out of the way to pick her up off the floor, they got her up and managed to put on some dudes shoulder where she hung on for life, they were band of the day for me.
Iron Maiden later put on the best show they had ever done. Sore wet drained we made our way home.
We never had mobile phones back then, when I got home in the early hours all the lights were on. I opened the door and my girlfriend was up and my family were there, she was upset

I asked 'what is up?' She showed me a video of the news from that day, the news had a caption saying Guns N' Roses, but the footage was of Helloween then it said that two people had died, my heart sank, and she was upset because it could have been me."

Paul Townsend (Widnes)

"When entering the arena on this tragic day it was obvious to me that something was wrong, there appeared to be far more people attending than any previous year and obviously far more than the 80,000 'ish that I thought was the limit. The crowd usually thinned out significantly at the back around the track area where the stalls were located, however, on this day it was even packed around this area. We later learned that there was something in the region of 107,000 there, many of which I believe had got in over the walls etc.

We moved somewhat slower than usual to our preferred location stage left (which always seemed to have more room than the same area stage right) just as Helloween started up, these fun German nutters were riding on the success of their popular 'Keeper of the Seven Keys' opus and went down relatively piss bottle free.

During the end of Helloweens set the scaffolding and video screen on the left collapsed forward and ended up being held just above the crowds heads by the metal fence at the back, if the fence had not been there I think that the scaffolding would have ended up hitting a good few tightly packed punters underneath it.

I was yet to get into Guns N' Roses and so had no intention of trying to move further forward for their set, looking back I am glad that this was the case as who knows what would have happened if were was unfortunate enough to get caught in the crush that occurred during their set. Besides, this was the first time I had taken my girlfriend (later and still Wife) Sue to a festival and there was no way I was going to jeopardise her safety.

From our vantage point, the crowd looked rowdy but it was not until Axl started to talk about people being hurt, I forget his words exactly but at one point just before 'Welcome to The

Jungle' he asked the crowd to step back as there were people unconscious. It became apparent that it was worse down there than it appeared to us, in fact we were oblivious to the severity of what had happened until the end and did not understand the it properly until we got home and turned on the news the next day. It was however apparent that the front was not the place to be and that people were being injured! During the interval after G n' R's set I saw a youngish bloke stumble passed us, covered in blood, with a garden cane sticking out of his neck, strangely he was laughing, I have no idea whether this was real or an elaborate make up job but it looked real enough to me. We also heard from passers by that people had been injured.

Although the atmosphere was somewhat less jovial than previous events we continued to enjoy the strong lineup and of course the contents of our 5 litre beer containers. Next up were Megadeth who were ok but seemed to suffer from a less than great sound, I was not overly impressed especially as the largest woman on the planet was blocking our view decked out in the most shockingly pink rain coat and matching umbrella that I have ever seen. Every time we tried to move this pink elephant seemed to move with us.

After what was surely the bottle fight to end all bottle fights, David Lee Roth was next up, and thankfully the Pink one had moved on to annoy other unfortunates. The master showman soon had us eating out of his hands as he ploughed through Van Halen classics such as 'Hot for Teacher' and 'Jump' along with his solo material, the best being 'Yankee Rose' always memorable because of the conversation he always had with Steve Via's Guitar (guitar responding to Dave's queries). Part way in to the set Dave seemed to be experiencing problems within the crowd and had to stop at least twice until calm was restored, at one point a security guard got on stage and was told to 'Get Off My Fucking Stage'. I was unsure when we first heard whether the deaths had occurred during GNR or DLR as the crowd seemed possibly denser during Dave's set.

During the next interval we decided to have a wonder around the stalls but soon gave up due to the sheer amount of people milling about, it was like wadding through treacle trying to get anywhere and had become a mammoth task just trying to get to the toilets. I felt particularly sorry for the ladies who had to endure massive queues, worse than on any other occasion at any festival I have attended to date.

A new phenomenon seemed to be emerging during this show, it was of course the human pyramid, I had never witnessed this before and it may have started elsewhere but there seemed to be a lot of people trying it out on that day, some where quite impressive and had reached at least five or six high. This of course was deemed mega fun for the bottle throwers who all aimed their missiles at the pyramids until they collapsed under the onslaught, this was a great way to spend the interval time for all concerned: pyramid builders, bottlers and observers, I remained in the latter category as I could not be bothered with either of these activities.

It was soon time for Kiss to hit the boards. The version of Kiss that graced us with its presence on this day was of course the 'Crazy Nights' era incarnation minus the make-up and to a certain extent, the fun. Musically I quite enjoyed them during the 80's and with Eric Carr and Bruce Kullick on board they were certainly way more technically proficient, however, live they were simply not the same beast without the gimmicks, pyros and most importantly the outfits. That said, I enjoyed their set but had that nagging feeling that they were not firing on all cylinders (this was proven correct when I later witnessed the original masked lineup, several times, including their stunning Donington headline of '96).

The year before, during Bon Jovi's set, Bruce Dickinson had announced that Maiden would be headlining the following year, so there was no surprise when this was confirmed in Kerrang! sometime after Christmas. At the time Maiden was still one of my favourite live bands and as it was their first appearance at Donington I was eagerly anticipating their set. Again, I was not disappointed, we were treated to arguably the best stage show of any MOR so far and one of the tightest set lists, Maiden reigned supreme on that day.

I have mixed emotions when thinking back to what was easily the most memorable of the Monsters Of Rock gigs, on one hand, the music was superb and company great as always, on

the other hand, it was hard to come to terms with the fact that two people had arrived at the festival as we did, expecting to have the time of their lives but never returned home. On the plus side, the events of that day have forced changes in festival safety which have been implemented and improved ever since. I now feel incredibly safe standing near the front at Download or elsewhere and thankfully have never witnessed that kind of chaos since.
RIP Allan Dick and Landon Siggers, you shall always be remembered."
Roger Moore (Glinton, Peterborough)

"What I can remember is the night before MOR (1988) me & my friend went to a local rock nightclub, left at 4:00am-ish grabbed a couple of hour's kip, and then headed off to meet up with some other of our mates; jumped in the back of their van and headed off.
It was the first really big rock festival we had been to. We couldn't quite believe that we were able to see so many bands on the same day!
I'd never seen so many rockers in one place. They were everywhere...it was an incredible sight...I still remember the Dunlop tyre... (Now sadly gone) standing out...
It was very muddy as it rained heavily most of the time and at one point we ended up wearing the famous black bin bag coats.
Later (after plenty of Cider) when Guns N' Roses were on, we were stood about a third of the way back, when the crowd surged forward, but my mum (back at home) panicked when she heard on the radio about two people getting crushed and remember it was in the days before mobiles. She had no way of contacting me, worse for her was that all the previous rock gigs I'd
been to, I had always been at the front. So she was very worried to say the least. So when I returned home safe. Her face was a picture.
Having said that, all in all (excluding the 2 unfortunate deaths of course) I can say it was a fantastic experience and has led to me continuing going to festivals and rock gig for over 30

*years!
And long may it continue."*
Deborah Mowforth (debbywebby)

*"1988, still at 6th form and a skinny 17yr old. I just about managed to scrape enough money to go to Donington.
I worked in a pub bottling up and one of the regulars was going with his mate to the festival from Newbury! (Can't remember his name) So myself and a good friend Mike (He introduced me to the 'Appetite For Destruction' album about 2 months before, so I couldn't wait to see them) scrounged a lift in a tiny mini metro to MOR.
Pink & purple swim shorts, a Reading Festival 1987 tour T-Shirt, doc martins, topped off with an old brown leather jacket that I bought from a friend for £10 and I was ready to ROCK.
We eventually made it to Castle Donington, my first of many MOR/DL concerts. I can remember walking over the race track near the famous tyre and looking down (the stage was at the bottom of the hill in a bowl) and the area was pretty full considering no one was on stage yet.
I think we quaffed a few lagers and made our way down for Helloween and positioned ourselves behind one of the speaker/lighting rigs to the left hand side of the stage.
When GnR's hit the stage, wow, by that time we had ventured forward as close as possible, no room to move and then they kicked off with 'It's So Easy', I can remember all of a sudden being about 30 ft from where I was first stood. Jesus it was insane, trying to stay on your feet as the ground was a bog pit! The 1st song went by and by this time I had lost my friend Mike and the other 2 that we had come with! I was now squeezed in about 20-30ft from the front. Next song kicked off and yet again it was just a case of trying to stay on your feet. I remember helping people who had fallen or ended up on the floor, pulling them up and then bouncing along with them in the scrum.
At one point they stopped the set and asked people to move back as the people at the front were getting crushed, so for about 20-30 seconds we could breath a bit, then the next song*

started and back to the mass of bodies running from left to right, trying to stay upright.

At this point 1 guy had fallen over and I picked him up with another chap, he was semi conscious and we held him under his arms and started to make our way back as there was no way he could stand on his own. I remember shouting and yelling at people to 'get the f*** out the way', as myself and this complete stranger struggled to carry the chap out of the masses. As we struggled towards the speaker/lighting rig, which was fenced off, I thought my legs were wet.....and yes the chap I was carrying had thrown up all over my shorts and legs, um lovely.

All I remember then is that we eventually got this chap to the fenced off lighting/speaker area and not so much threw him but tried to place him in the safety of this area. I'm not sure what happened to this chap but I'd like to think that the 2 of us had helped him survive?

From there I ventured back away from the bouncing masses to the relative safety of mid viewing. I look back and think it was one of the scariest times I have ever experienced at a gig and only that I stayed on my feet stopped me from becoming a statistic.

After GnR's, I decided not to go to close to the front to watch the remaining bands. Although for DLR I did get right to the front, but that was it.

I didn't find any of my friends until I went back to the car after Iron Maiden. One hell of an experience and I was so hooked and had one of the most memorable days at a festival. So much so I went to MOR in Bochum Germany the following week, Awesome."

Russell Kennerley (Newbury)

"At long last British Heavy Metal heroes Iron Maiden finally got their shot at headlining Britain's top rock festival.

Their show was based around the 'Seventh Son' album. And with an impressive stage set and song selection they wowed the crowd with an excellent performance worthy of their position at the top of the bill.

However there was an impressive line up beneath them……

Kiss performed a no nonsense, no make up set, that would have set the crowd alight had it not been for a very colourful Dave Lee Roth and co. strutting their stuff with typical American bombast and flair immediately before them. Steve Vai brought out his triple necked, heart shaped guitar at one point.
The Dave Lee Roth T-shirts were probably the best of the day also.
We all know what happened during Guns n' Roses performance, although we didn't at the time. The bands meteoric rise to superstardom had caught the organisers out (they were only second from bottom on the bill, which was probably right when they were originally booked). A sad day for rock music.
Both Megadeth and Helloween were OK, but nothing special. The weather was windy and wet.
Due to repercussions following the deaths of the two fans during Guns n' Roses' set there was a year out in 1989."
Paul Hartshorn (Chesterfield)

"I have numerous experience's from Monsters of Rock, the first year I went was 1988 with my Mum and Dad (I was 14 and lucky for me they loved their rock music, they still do in fact!) and I was hooked. I was such a huge Maiden fan from the age of 7 as my Mum and Dad use to hammer "Number of the Beast"; so to see them in a scale so big was out of this world. I have not missed a MOR or Download since so that's quite a few years!   Memories that stand out for me on this wondrous one day event (apart from the horrible drive home after drinking too much warm beer), were the human pyramids, I remember my first year attempting one, I ended up in A & E the next day with 5 other people dressed in Monsters of Rock T-shirts who I had never met adorning the same type of bruises I had. They were definitely not for the faint hearted and luckily enough they have kind of gone out of fashion! I remember a load of us had piled down in a transit van with no windows and just a mattress for protection in the back, we pulled up near the Hallowed Turf next to 3 other transit vans who's doors opened and what seemed like hundreds of

people rolling out the back, believe me if you ever wanted to know how many people you could fit into the back of a transit van……..it was a hell of a lot!
Also, one thing that had always tickled me is how some people had a total utter need to wear their full tasselled leather jackets with patches and some even with the denim cut off jacket over the top in 90 degree heat!! Then again I guess that still happens but with the addition of New Rock Boots in Download Festival!!"
Jude Wright (Wallasey, Merseyside)

"During the Guns n' Roses set in 1988 and the resulting crush that unfortunately took 2 of our fellow fans, myself and a friend were about 10 metres from the barrier and feeling the pressure from all the people around us, so we decided to get the hell out of there..
As we turned to get away a girl was also trying to get out, but she was heavily pregnant; we advised going over the top of the crowd as the quickest and probably safest way out for her, but she wanted to walk out. So we got the girl between us, with my friend at the front and me at the back. We somehow managed to get all 3 (4 if you include the baby) out of that hell. She thanked us for our help (as if we could say no) and that was the last we saw of her.
I often find myself wondering how the girl got on and hope that her baby was well and who knows might be attending the festival these years, as he/she will be what 22 years old now....I can only hope."
Martin Scott (Ayr)

"What an amazing festival line-up that was, Maiden, Kiss, Guns n' Roses, David Lee Roth, Megadeth etc.
By the time we entered the main arena we were pretty much hammered, early on we were sat near the beer tents at the back.
When Guns n' Roses came on I made my way to the front to get a better view, but Presh stayed further back to carry on his drinking, I made a note of where he was and was gonna join him in about 40 mins, this was mid afternoon and I'd left all my

money, beer and food with him; I wasn't going to be long, as soon as Guns finished I was gonna make my way back to him to carry on drinking.
Problem was though, finding the fucker again. I could've sworn I knew where he was, but I must've walked round that field dozens of times trying to find the twat; nowhere to be seen! What a bastard, never saw him again all day until we got on the bus to go home, I was starving hungry, dehydrated and dying of thirst. He'd had a great time, eaten my grub, drank my beer and spent my money, bastard.
He said he never moved from the spot, I still don't believe him."
Gary 'Fozzy' Forrester (Hull)

1990
Whitesnake,
Aerosmith, Poison, Quireboys, Thunder

After the melancholy feelings of Monsters Of Rock in 1988 came the sense of elation at the festivals return two years later, with a bill that was a 60% British and 40% American. There was reduced festival capacity and more safety precautions in place; so problems like the year before would never happen again.

Making their first of three appearances at Donington (ending with their 'secret band' slot at Download 2009) Thunder opened the proceedings for the day and set the bar very high for other bands to try and achieve. Playing tracks from their debut album 'Backstreet Symphony', Thunder were the quintessential British band, with their feet firmly stuck in the '90's but their roots in the classic rock sounds of the '70's.

Another British band was up next, the Quireboys, hailing from Newcastle with their brand of 'Faces' music for the modern rock fan. Managed at the time by Sharon Osbourne (before she hit mega stardom) the Quireboys were the ultimate party band; singing their way through a set peppered with tracks from their debut album 'A Bit Of What You Fancy'; we were covered in 'Roses And Rings', woken up by '7 o'clock' and invited to a 'Sex Party', 70's party rock with a 90's slant.

Poison were loved enough at the time to play all their hits and have female fans drooling at the front, whilst their boyfriends hung back in the crowd waiting for Aerosmith to play. 'Talk Dirty To Me' was their most popular of the set, proving that their debut album was still the best Poison release to date and the one that the fans longed to hear tracks from.

Eventually, the wait was over and Aerosmith made their all singing, all swaggering, all sexual innuendo oozing Donington debut.

Playing a career spanning set from 1973's 'Dream On' right through to 'Love In An Elevator' from the 1989 album 'Pump'. Aerosmith were the band of the day and the most anticipated by the crowd, having not played in the UK for nearly a year. Aerosmith also pulled a masterstroke by bringing on Jimmy Page of Led Zeppelin for their encores, which was an unexpected treat for all the avid rock fans.

Finally the headliner for 1990 was another British band, back for their 'rock 'n' roll hat-trick'; three appearances at Donington, two in the headline position and what a different beast Whitesnake were now!

The 90's Whitesnake was the 'MTV friendly' totally Americanised version of the classic British rock band. Thanks to the constant MTV airplay of the 'Snake videos for 'Is This Love' and 'Here I Go Again' (a re-recording of the original from the 'Saints & Sinners' album in 1982), Whitesnake were reaching a totally diverse audience. From AOR fans, to metal fans, to soft rock fans and fans of David Coverdale's wife to be (at the time) Tawny Kitaen, who featured heavily in the erotic styled videos, the 'Snake was slithering its way across America and picking up more fans worldwide than ever before. Whitesnake had also re-recorded 'Fool For Your Loving' which again featured as a more 'bluesy' rock standard on the 1980 release 'Ready An' Willing'; the new versions of the classics were dividing the fans.

So, the 1990 performance of Whitesnake had been upstage by the old pro's Aerosmith, who were again on steep curve to renewed success. Whitesnake would return to play as special guests to Def Leppard 19 years

later, but we would only had to wait 4 years for the return of Aerosmith, then boosted to the headline position.

"There are two clips from the 1990 which are THE most requested videos on Whitesnake.com; videos from that Monsters Of Rock."
David Coverdale (Whitesnake – Vocals)

"For me it's a personal triumph, I have always been a lover of British Rock'N'Roll .It was always my dream to be in a British band and to Headline a   major festival in England where people have come from all corners of the   earth."
Rudy Sarzo (Whitesnake – Bass)

"We want to take this time to thank the fans, we had a few technical problems we ironed them out but that shit happens in Rock'N'Roll you know.
For a lot of times shows are consistently tough to do but this wasn't. It was an above average out door show, but hey it takes two to tango and the fans were fantastic."
Brett Michaels (Poison – Vocals)

"Before Donington we were on tour in America and every show on that tour was sold out.
We were never 'glam rock', we were more like 'Steptoe and Son' on speed, it was our gypsy look.
I spent most of the day, before my family turned up, with Jimmy Page, because our tour manager was Richard Cole, who was Led Zeppelin's tour manager. We had been on tour in America and had gone through about four tour managers and I remember that we were in somewhere like Bumfuck, Idaho and I saw this guy and he was pouring a bottle of Jack Daniels down the drain, by a tour bus and then a bottle of vodka and I said 'what the fuck are you doing?' and it was Richard Cole.
When we played it was very weird watching 70,000 people singing along to your songs in the broad daylight; 'Meet the gangs 'cause the boys are here, the boys to entertain you…..' that was our intro tape.

*It's always a good time with the Quireboys and everyone loves a tune that you can whistle.
After Donington they all left and I was left with Thunder; the Thunderbirds were the most embarrassing thing you've seen in your life."*
Spike (The Quireboys – Vocals)

*"When we came to Donington it was a real event, with 5 or 6 bands and 72,000 people.
When you go into Donington as a band, in a bus, you go over the top of the hill and you could see the audience, this huge audience and that's when you get a daunting feeling.
Everyone has probably seen the footage, but when you go up these stairs and you can see from the side of the stage this sea of people, that's when you go 'oh fucking hell'. But luckily enough we were in our early twenties and you have that confidence to go out and do it; I'd probably shit myself now!"*
Guy Griffin (The Quireboys – Guitar)

*"Donington was very different for us, we had started make some money.
We'd recorded an album in LA in '89 and Sharon (Osbourne) was our manager, so by 1990 things had changed quite a lot. We'd toured at the end of '89 and then again March and we'd also done Top Of The Pops.
We had already played with Aerosmith. We had our dressing room all day, which was different to Reading, so we stayed there all day and had our friends over! The stage was a lot bigger and the crowd was around 77,000.
Playing in daylight was quite bizarre and the wind was blowing you around, which was different as we were used to club dates and we played above Thunder.
We wandered around backstage saying hello to Steven Tyler and Whitesnake. Back then Whitesnake were quite friendly, but we've recently done a tour with them and got thrown off it!"*
Nigel Mogg (The Quireboys – Bass)

"The first time we played was quite spectacular and we had a lot riding on it.
We had a few small 'warm up' gigs before Donington and Danny had a throat virus and lost his voice on the tour. It was four days before we were due to play at Donington to 93,500 people and there was a lot of anticipation because the year before it had been cancelled, because of what had happened the year before that and we were opening and it was a really cracking bill.
Danny went to see his Harley Street specialist and he said 'I am going to give you an injection and you mustn't talk for three days', which for Danny is quite difficult.
So he went away and rested and we just sat in corners and worried a lot.
Even the day before we played he wasn't aloud to speak; so we turned up on the day and even he didn't know if anything was going to come out!
We went and sound checked without him. We went out onto this huge stage, in front of this huge field and I was thinking 'I wonder what it's going to look like when it's full of people?'
The sound check went nicely and we were still worried about Danny. He still hadn't spoken a word and he had no idea what was going to come out of his throat.
I remember that the stage manager came in and said ½ an hour and we all went quiet, especially Danny! We couldn't get away with all instrumentals; we're not a 'prog rock' band are we!
We turned up on the stage and the first number we were in was 'She's So Fine' and there's one particular note and if he hits that we'd know everything was OK. He hit this note absolutely spot on with laser like precision and if you watch the video of us on one of our DVD's, you can see the look of relief on all of our faces; you could see us all going 'everything's going to be OK.
It was a magical moment and from that point on we were so happy and it came out in our performance and we had one of the best gigs of our life.
It was a great day, really beautiful and sunny.

I couldn't believe how spectacular it was with the field full of arms waving.

At the time we were signed to Capitol records in America and they were really interested in English rock, or in fact, rock music at all.

The president of Capitol at the time said to us that he cursed the day that he signed Poison, who were one of his biggest selling artists at the time.

We were being courted by Geffen Records who had Whitesnake, Guns 'n' Roses, Aerosmith and Cher and just about every good rock band that you cared to mention.

We had a bit of a 'celebrity fan club' at this point and David Coverdale, very kindly, was talking to David Geffen and John Kalodner about us, 'you've got to hear this band Thunder'. Axl Rose was doing the same, he was a big fan; he stopped us in a car park at the Rainbow Bar and Grill (LA), while he was getting mobbed by people and shouting 'you shouldn't be listening to me; these are the boys you should be listening to!!' So he was telling Geffen to listen to our band and Aerosmith were doing the same!

Subsequently when we supported Aerosmith, we found out that on their tour bus, on the way to Donington, Radio One was broadcasting the concert live and they were listening to it on the radio and Joe and Steven were on the tour bus with John Kalodner. They said to him that this was the band that they were telling him about and he said 'well I'm here now, I guess I can check them out', so the fact that we had a particularly good show that day, got us signed to Geffen America and we got off of Capitol/EMI which had never been done before."

Ben Matthews (Thunder - Guitar)

"That was a crucial point in our career, we had started Thunder in 1989 and had gone out and done a lot of touring the clubs and a few shows with Aerosmith and a few shows with Heart.

We hadn't realised how popular we'd become and on the day all the hands went in the air and we went wow.

It added poignancy as 1989 had been cancelled, when the kids got killed in the crowd, so this had to go well and the promoters were quite nervous and everything was a bit tense. We were the first band on, the weather was beautiful and as a result of that show our first album went gold and we sold out some shows in the states."
Luke Morley (Thunder – Guitar)

"Danny lost his voice the week before, we had been very busy, we didn't stop."
Harry James (Thunder – Drums)

"I had to go and see a doctor after Nottingham and he told me to take a few weeks off (yeah right).
We had to cancel Friday's London Marquee show which I was upset about but I got through today.
We had the audience clapping and singing along it was tremendous."
Danny Bowes (Thunder – Vocals)

"Last time we played here was interesting back in 1985. We haven't been able to get back due to recording schedules and touring. We are coming back here in October for some shows and maybe we will do Donington next year and really kick you in the ass."
Stephen Pearcy (Ratt – Vocals)

"The promoters once again played it safe with the choice of acts for the 10th Anniversary of the Donington MOR 1990 Thunder and Quireboys provided traditional British Rock at its best whilst Poison had a party atmosphere going down.
Back stage all eyes were on Steve Vai who seemed to have cameras following him everywhere he went. The dude looked so cool but he had competition for the lenses with the one and only Rock Star duo Steve Tyler and Joe Perry of Aerosmith. Meeting those guys in the flesh was a pretty amazing experience and they gave Whitesnake a real run for their money.

We interviewed a lot of the bands for our radio show and everyone was just thrilled the MOR was back.

The first decade of the Monsters Of Rock would set precedence for decades to come. The courage of the promoters, the dedication from the fans and the performances of the artiste on the bill will proudly grace the pages of British rock history.

The Bailey Brothers brought the Monsters Of Rock into the homes of millions of fans across Europe via MTV and those shows are still circulated and enjoyed to this day. The Donington Monsters Of Rock was the jewel in the crown and we were all kings of the Castle at least for a while!"

The Bailey Brothers (Mick & Dez Donington Comperes)

"1990 was the year of big hair at Donington. Everywhere you looked there were masses of backcombed hair-sprayed barnets, skin tight jeans and cowboy boots as Donington went glam for its 10th birthday party event. To celebrate this event highlights of the day also went out live on Radio 1 for the first time, which gave many a performer the chance to say a few choice words.

The day was bathed in glorious sunshine (surely another Donington first?!), and the day was completely stolen by the days opening band and relative newcomers Thunder. Danny Bowes and his merry men came on and played a complete blinder and by the time they wound their set up with a drawn out 'Dirty Love' they had everyone singing and dancing along like drunken idiots.

The Quireboys followed and while they couldn't match the euphoria brought to the day by Thunder, they played a solid set and were well received.

Poison hit the stage next and seemed to split the crowd, with those like myself deciding it was more fun to throw bits of melon and any other bits of available rubbish at the band and at others, than put up with their cheesy brand of glam.

Aerosmith got the place jumping again and their set also featured one of the finest collaborations in Donington history when Jimmy Page strolled out onto the stage to join Aerosmith for a blistering performance of 'Train kept a Rollin'.

Once Aerosmith finished it was all downhill from then, with David Coverdale's new version of Whitesnake featuring guitar hero Steve Vai providing a pretty awful performance to finish the day on a downer.

Whitesnake are one of this countries finest exports of blues rock, and with Steve Vai widdling his 'cosmic tapestries' over classic blues rock numbers most were left wondering what the fuck was going on. Time was even given to nearly every band member to bore the crowd with drawn out solo spots and the crowd started to thin out as people decided a more fun way to end the day was to drink themselves to oblivion while devouring some legendry Donington death burgers.

While standing waiting for the appearance of Aerosmith a fellow punter in front of me decided to have a fag. While sparking up his lighter Aerosmith came onto the stage and the crowd surged forward pushing him and his naked lighter flame into the woman stood directly in front of him. Due to the copious amounts of hairspray on this poor woman's hair the naked flame ignited her hair which went up quicker than Gary Glitter outside a primary school.

The woman was still completely oblivious to this fact until everyone behind her started to throw beer over her to douse the flames. This of course inflamed the matter even more as she turned around and started throwing punches completely unaware why she was the target for everyone to throw beer at. Someone soon managed to let her know her hair was on fire as people continued to throw any available liquid over her head until the flames finally went out, leaving her with a badly smelling, black crispy hair do."

Nigel Taylor (Plymouth)

"My first Donington experience was in 1990. First up were Thunder, the sun was beating down and Danny Bowes belted out those songs, what a voice! I still remain a fan to this day. Next up were the Quireboys they whipped up the crowd good and proper, I recall an inflatable Newkie Brown bottle or two bouncing around the crowd; I'm thinking Spike probably appreciated this... Later the mighty Aerosmith and Tyler back in the day, when he could

still back flip across the stage, what a set list topped off by Jimmy Page. Then Whitesnake, Coverdale's vocals and Steve Vai's guitar just completed the day's hard rockin' goodness. I remember getting back home in the wee small hours thinking that it just doesn't get any better than this..." **Matt Allison (Plymouth)**

"I went to Donington Monsters Of Rock festival in 1990. I was eighteen years of age.
Whilst there I was hit, with considerable force, by a passing tennis ball.
It hurt."
Mrs Holly Allison (nee Taylor as I was then, Plymouth)

"1989 was cancelled while the powers that be decided on the future of the festival after the tragedies of '88.
I was quite relieved when they announced that 1990 would go ahead, this was the correct response, learn from the lessons, implement the changes and get on with it. I think that cancelling indefinitely would have had a disastrous effect on all major outdoor music events.
So line-up released (surprisingly only 5 bands this year) it was time to dust of the cordial containers and head off to sunny Derbyshire again. I must admit that Aerosmith aside, I was not overly excited by that years line-up and considered it to be somewhat weaker than the previous two, however, this was Monsters of Rock and I would have probably attended if the Wurzels were headlining, just being there and soaking up the atmosphere was enough for me at that time.
It was noticeable on entering the arena that the crowd was considerably less than '88 and was back to a more manageable size, this was way better and meant that you could actually visit the stalls at the back again without the risk of losing the crowd you were with.
Thunder were today's openers and were well received by most of the early day crowd, our group included. They played all of their radio friendly hits from what was easily their best album ever, the sublime 'Backstreet Symphony' and left us in

jovial spirits, a great party band and possibly the best opening performance of any band at MOR.

I was not a fan of the Quireboys so their set largely passed me by, they seemed to get on ok and got away without being bombarded with too many missiles. I thought that they were a bit of a come down after Thunders sing-a-long set.

Poison were the first of only two American bands on that day, this was weird and in complete contrast to '87 where all of the acts were from the states. Poison were a bit of a marmite band, you either loved them or would prefer to stick your head in a barrel of acid than subject your ears to their poodle haired sounds. I fell into the former category but I also refused to fall into the silly thrash vs. glam nonsense that was prevalent at the time, I liked both.

I remember Poison's set being somewhat unremarkable and suffering from a sound mix that was being carried away by the slightest gust and completely drowned out by the usual low flying 737's. Apart from the usual enthusiastic first ten rows, the crowd seemed to react lethargically to their set and it passed; not threatening to go into the list of legendary Donington performances.

On that day, Aerosmith could have played anything they wanted and I would have been hooked. It was my first chance to see the Toxic Twins who were at that point in time, within my top five favs. I was hooked from the off, Steven Tyler with white and black scarved mic in tow ran about the stage like a man possessed as they went through mostly newer stuff early on but for me it was the trio of 'Sweet Emotion', 'Toys In The Attic' and 'Dream On' that got me really singing along. And then to top it off in style, Jimmy Page joined them for an incredible encore of 'Train Kept A Rollin' and 'Walk This Way'.

Bottle fights occurred as usual, as did peoples liking for recreating Egypt's finest monuments but I do not remember either activity being as prominent as previous years. In fact I fail to remember witnessing any event that was particularly odd or outrageous. Where were the naked sports people, fire starters or Hells Angels tipping over burger vans? Maybe they were all there but I managed to miss them all.

I was not particularly looking forward to Whitesnake, apart from a handful of tracks. I did not care for their recorded material, even more so since they had ditched their better blues style in favour of a more commercial hair band, widdly diddly, and power ballad mad style. What's more, I could not stand David Coverdale, his pompous, big headed, patronising attitude got right on my tits. That said, I did not hate their performance that night and even sang along to the tracks that I could bear. Their sound mix was top notch and the majority of the crowd responded enthusiastically. This set was going out live on BBC1 albeit with several seconds delay to help remove any foul language! Coverdale responded to this accordingly and was deliberately littering the set with as many 'Fucks' as he could muster between and during songs, I believe that a few got through which must have had the good old Beeb fuming.

Although I do not consider 1990 as being one of the better lineups, I remember it as the most relaxing of these fests. The mood was friendly as usual, the weather was pretty warm and the drink flowed well; most importantly we had lots of fun and it was great to have the festival back, it could have been taken away from us for good!"

Roger Moore (Glinton, Peterborough)

"Only five bands this year and the headline slot saw the return of (the now) MTV friendly Whitesnake. Their traditional blues rock had been sidelined for a sleeker USA style heavy metal. Their show was based around the 'Slip of the Tongue' CD and just didn't excite me like the days of old……the only real nod to the past was a perfunctory version of 'Ain't No Love In The Heart Of The City'. David Coverdale's voice had also lost some of its magic.

Disappointing to say the least.

Aerosmith hadn't played these shores for a while, so they were eagerly anticipated. They didn't disappoint, even Jimmy Page joined them onstage for the encore. Band of the day…..easily.

Poison could have done better, but at least they played 'Every Rose Has Its Thorn', which my wife (whose name is Rose) enjoyed.
Not too sure that The Quireboys were right for the show, but they entertained a sizeable portion of the crowd, so who am I to complain.
Thunder were fantastic. From the moment Danny opened his mouth at the start of 'She's So Fine' to the end of 'Dirty Love'. I was near the front and thought they were great…..best opening performance of all the Doningtons.
The whole concert was broadcast live all day on Radio One. The weather was fine.
Also this was one of the first years where alcohol had affected my recollections of the day."
Paul Hartshorn (Chesterfield)

1991
AC/DC,
Metallica, Motley Crue, Queensrÿche, The Black Crowes

This year would be mostly dominated by two major facts,
1) AC/DC were playing again and the appearance would be their 3rd headline slot within the 12 festivals career span so far.
2) Metallica had gradually risen from the mid-afternoon slot, to now being in the 'special guest' position, playing just before the headliner.

First on were The Black Crowes, a slightly random choice for Donington, but as the festival encompassed 'all that was rock', why shouldn't they play?

With 'Shake Your Money Maker' released the previous year, the majority of the crowd were aware of or absolutely loved, the tracks played on the day. Getting an airing from the album were many of the gems that had made the album a multi platinum seller in their native USA, these included 'Twice As Hard', 'Hard To Handle' and 'Jealous Again'.

Next on were Queensrÿche. More suited to the atmospheric conditions of a dark club gig, Queensrÿche lost some of their aura in the open field in the middle of the afternoon, but still put on a great show. Playing tracks from their astounding 1988 concept album 'Operation Mindcrime' and the 1990 release 'Empire', they showed the crowd how 'progressive metal' could be done, polished, note perfect and hard hitting.

Coming back for their 2nd appearance at Donington were Motley Crue, seven years after their opening slot debut and 6 months before Vince Neil would leave the band. The album 'Dr. Feelgood' had been released in 1989 and had been a multi platinum success, but there would be no more Crue albums until 94's 'Motley Crue' which would feature John Corabi (ex of The Scream) on lead vocals; Motley Crue were a band in turmoil.

Playing tracks from most of their previous albums, with the exception of 'Theatre Of Pain', they included a cover of 'Anarchy In The UK' as the final track of the set.

Metallica were on next and it was only 5 days after the release of the 'Black Album', which would see them rise to stadium and festival headliners within the year.

The set featured 'Enter Sandman' and 'Sad But True' from the new album and tracks from their whole back catalogue plus the usual two covers.

At the time Metallica had been on a major support tour with AC/DC so they seemed the obvious choice to be in the 'special guest' spot at Donington and they certainly now were something special.

AC/DC returned for their 3rd top of the bill; we would have to wait another 19 years before they returned to headlining Download 2010, making them the band that has headlined equally the most times at Donington with Iron Maiden.

With a set featuring all the best songs from their career, the show was released as the video (then DVD and now Blu-Ray) 'Live At Donington', featuring cannons, inflatables and the giant 'Hells Bell'.

AC/DC were a band at the top of their game, with continuing success and still churning out platinum albums. The ultimate singalong rock band, with more hits and well known tracks than most headliners AC/DC had created a legacy at Donington.

"We were doing a whole run with AC/DC and it was right when the 'Black Album' was coming out in August of 1991 and we were doing about six or seven weeks with AC/DC and it was just amazing.
We had started fourth from the bottom, then third and then second on the bill.
We were on before AC/DC, we'd had Motley Crue on before us and 'Enter Sandman' had just come out. You could just feel the whole thing was about to go to the next level; there was just a confidence and excitement in the air that was exciting. We played two new songs from the 'Black Album', 'Enter Sandman' and 'Sad But True' and they went down well and we were just young and 'full of spunk' and going for it big time, definitely feeling confident and getting ready to play the 'big league'.
It was just great to be part of the AC/DC thing and get to watch them every night. I'd go and behind Chris Slade and watch them every night; hanging around AC/DC for six weeks was just amazing. Once in a while I would get invited to have a cup of tea with Angus which was so amazing. We would share our rock 'n' roll lives, which was very cool; also having Motley Crue there was very cool, because it meant that there was definitely a debaucherous element there at all times. It was a great late summer."
Lars Ulrich (Metallica – Drums)

"It was pretty much socialising with the other bands; we did some interviews and then got up and played. From the band stand point, they are all pretty much the same; some have better food and better trailers, but usually not.
Well this time it wasn't raining which was a kind of a change. A lot of times there are the paying audience and the ones that are just there to watch; it's better for everyone when the crowd just lets themselves go. We like the people in the audience to bond in a way that's really beyond words; it's one of those things that's indescribable and it goes across all countries, social, political, religious, you name it!
It's very mystical and beyond language and you really feel that at some festivals where the audience is really 'there'. I do feel

that the media is based on a 'sports model', but concerts aren't based on that model and it's hard to score.

So, of all the gigs that we have done in our career, the gigs that really stand out for me the most are the ones where the people are really letting themselves experience it and that's a great feeling.

One thing that I like about Donington is that they tend to have a more eclectic type of bill."

Geoff Tate (Queensrÿche – Vocals)

"In my opinion, 1991 had a very strong, diverse line-up that in theory should have kept everybody happy. We had the new raw sound of Pantera, the bluesy swagger of The Black Crowes, some modern Prog rock from Queensryche, Motley Crue for the glam / sleaze crowd, the ever growing beast called Metallica supplying the Thrash and last but not least, the mighty AC/DC racking up their third (and final) headline slot.

I was happy as the proverbial sand boy when I saw that line-up in Kerrang! and hurriedly collected some tickets from our local ticket shop (which disappeared soon after the emergence of the internet). We had six bands this year again and August could not come around quick enough.

By now we considered ourselves veterans and had the whole thing down to a fine art! We travelled light but still had adequate provisions to last us all day, we were also prepared for all potential August weather conditions. Every year at least one festival virgin would join us and despite continual reminders of what to take, they would always come ill prepared. My girlfriend Sue's friend joined us one year and insisted on wearing high heel shoes, this was a decision that she would later regret as they sank in the mud constantly as she trudged slowly around the toilet blocks.

Pantera were an emerging force to be reckoned with and they hit the stage like an uncaged tiger, their sound was brutal with riffs that could skin cattle at 200yds. I was only just getting into them at this time and only new the odd track from 'Vulgar Display of Power' such as 'Walk', however, this performance was suitably impressive enough to encourage me to buy the two albums they had released so far. It was noticeable again that there were very few bottles heading in Panteras direction, maybe people were just too scared of Phil Anselmo and did not wish to be on the receiving end of some five knuckle retribution .As expected Sue hated every minute of their set. The Black Crowes were about as far removed from Pantera as it could possibly get, their sound was more southern blues but they kicked ass in their own way and were always entertaining to watch. Their 'Shake Your Money Maker' album was riding high in the rock charts and they belted out energetic versions of 'Twice As Hard' and the big hit of the time 'Jealous Again' to an appreciative audience.

Queensryche were at that time (and for at least a decade after) myself and Sue's favourite band. We had witnessed them at Hammersmith Odeon twice and they had put in fantastic performances playing 90% of 'Operation Mindcrime' with the entire crowd singing along to every word. As an indoor live band they were one of the best out there and always gave 200%. Unfortunately it quickly became apparent to us that the energy and atmosphere they created indoors could not be recreated in an outdoor environment, it just did not seem to work and was a sad experience for us. The band did not play badly and Geoff Tate's vocals were as brilliant as ever, there was just something missing which was not helped by the set list which was less than inspiring and the crowd did not really warm to them on that occasion. Thankfully, we have seen them countless times after this and they have been superb every time.

As far as I can remember the weather remained good all day but to be honest the weather was rarely that bad and if there was a downpour it never lasted particularly long. On most occasions I did not need to dig out the trusty bin liners, and if I did it was usually for seating purposes which is the preferred option over sitting on chips and Chinese noodles.

It was Motley Crue's second appearance at the festival but this time around they were for obvious reasons much higher up the bill. The Crue were another band that you either loved or hated, the Thrash Fans in the audience would absolutely despise them but I loved them. I will never fathom out why *some people get into this mentality of dissing particular styles of music which are effectively in the same genre, if you don't like it don't listen to it and let us who want to , do so in peace. Apart from Mick Mars (as usual), the Crue were full of energy and treated us to some choice cuts from 'Dr Feelgood', 'Girls Girls Girls' etc but from my vantage point they were not going down as well as they had in '84, the crowd was receptive but not overly enthusiastic. Vince Neil has never been the greatest vocalist in the world but gets by well enough and is well suited to their style, on this occasion he seemed to be having a problem reaching all of the notes which probably added to the crowds mostly lethargic reception. That said, the crowd got moving a bit more for the set closer, a decent version of 'Anarchy In The UK'.*

In '91 it was becoming apparent that Metallica would soon be the biggest metal band on the planet. The pioneers of thrash were starting to lose many die hard fans after the release of the 'Black Album' but on this sunny August afternoon they were still kings of the hill in many peoples eyes. Their last opus 'And Justice For All' had sold bucket loads but was not held in as high regard as its predecessor 'Master Of Puppets' but still had some killer cuts such as my all time favourite 'One' and a large proportion of the masses in attendance (Glam die hards aside) were well up for this performance. Wearing the traditional black against a black backdrop James and the crew pummelled us into early submission with new and soon to be most famous track 'Enter Sandman' then another favourite of mine 'Creeping Death'. Other highlights included 'Fade to Black', 'Master Of Puppets', 'Seek And Destroy', 'One' and finally a brutal headbangers favourite 'Battery'.

I do not see the need to wax lyrical about AC/DC's performance, proof of how good they were that night is available for all to see in the form of the Video (or DVD in the techy modern world) that they shot of the entire performance. When I watched this video several years later I was glad that it captured the show just how I remember it. I could not fault the show or performances that night, it was the last time that I saw DC and if I do not witness them again at least I can whack in the DVD for a quick refresher of them at their peak.

We travelled down by minibus again that year and of course had to cough up the usual ridiculous fee so that we could wait for hours before we actually got out of the car park. This waiting time was usually spent blasting out the stereo, which of course everybody else was also doing in their vehicles making the din somewhat undecipherable. During this wait at some point everybody would need the use of a WC which of course was not provided in the car park, therefore any old tree or car tyre (or bush in the case of the ladies) would have to succumb to our urinal needs. Car tyres seemed to be the prime choice of one of my regular colleagues, I don't know what it was but he seemed to have a thing for them, this proved dangerous on several occasions as several of the vehicles were occupied at the time, on one occasion an Oak tree sized biker type jumped out of his land rover to remonstrate with our pissing friend but luckily was calmed down before face punching could commence.

In '90 I remember that my brother got out of the van via the back door to relieve himself just as we were able to actually move, therefore we decided that it would be a fun game to drive off and stop about 50 yds away, this of course became the age old fun game of "lets wait for him to catch up then drive off again" we continued this game for at least ten minutes, It is amazing how childish games can keep you occupied in such circumstances, the atmosphere at festivals does have that effect on people though."

Roger Moore (Glinton, Peterborough)

"This was the first time our now depleted gang had not travelled down in our own transport. Instead we caught the train to Derby, then the organised shuttle bus service to the site. At the end of the show we did it all in reverse.

1991 saw the most impressive stage show of them all, with AC/DC having twenty-one cannons lined up across the top of the stage.

This was the best (by far) of the three AC/DC headlining shows at Donington, culminating in a very loud 21-gun salute at the end of 'For Those About to Rock'.

Angus also performing his guitar solo spot on top of a podium in the middle of the crowd during 'Let There Be Rock'
One of the best Donington shows ever.
Supporting 'DC was Metallica, who with the release of their 'Black' album had suddenly leapt into the mainstream of rock. From a personal point of view their new direction suited my musical taste buds at the time. I went on to enjoy all of their 90s material and concerts.
Another big name on the bill in 1991 was Motley Crue, to be honest not exactly my cup of tea, so I don't remember much about their performance.
Queensryche & Black Crowes were also on the bill."
Paul Hartshorn (Chesterfield)

1992
Iron Maiden,
Skid Row, Thunder, Slayer, WASP, The Almighty

Iron Maiden headlined Donington 1992 for their 2nd time; in 2003 they would return again for their 3rd appearance and making it the 4th time in 2007, smashing the record set by AC/DC and Metallica. AC/DC will equal this record with their 4th headline appearance in 2010.

The performance by Iron Maiden was recorded for the video and double cd, called 'Live At Donington'.

Iron Maiden are one of the three bands that are most recognised as 'Donington Icons', the other two being Metallica and AC/DC. Who can forget the battle cry of Bruce Dickinson cutting through the night air as he yells 'SCREAM FOR ME DONINGTON'.

The Almighty, who opened the day, also recorded their set for a future cd release. A hard rocking set from 'north of the border' was just what was needed to blow away the cobwebs and clear the heads, that were already topping up with the first pints of alcohol of the day. Ricky Warwick, the lead singer of the Almighty, would make his solo debut at Download Festival in the tent, playing his 'Americana' based solo music, 11 years later in 2003.

Back for a second appearance, W.A.S.P. played another good selection of tunes from their back catalogue, including their latest album 'The Crimson Idol', but they were not as threatening and exciting as the were the first time that they played, though their career has had great longevity and they are due another appearance.

Slayer were making their very first appearance at the festival in '92 and it was also their first appearance since Dave Lombardo had left; their new drummer, Paul Bostaph, had previously played with Forbidden. Slayer were the last of the 'Big Four' to play Donington. The Big Four were Metallica, Anthrax, Slayer and Megadeth and it referred to the main players in the world of thrash metal. Of the four bands, Slayer were the most aggressive, with the most controversial songs included songs like 'Angel Of Death' and "Raining Blood'. An excellent set, by the masters of 'Satanic thrash'.

Thunder were back for their second appearance in 2 years and had risen up the line-up from openers to 3rd from top. Another solid classic rock set, Thunder always delivered and were again a very popular performer on the day.

Skid Row were special guests on the day and very deserving of the position. Having played as the opening band at the Bon Jovi Milton Keynes show in 1999, their increasing popularity, mostly due to their enigmatic frontman Sebastian Bach. With a set featuring all their most popular songs from '18 And Life' and 'Youth Gone Wild' to newer ones like 'Monkey Business' and the set opener 'Slave To The Grind', Skid Row were the slightly less crazy GNR and their frontman was a much better singer than Axl, these were a band on the way up.

So it was up to the mighty 'Maiden' to finish the day off and they did in grand style; a British band blasting out their many hits to an adoring crowd of denim and leather clad metal heads. They wouldn't return to the hallowed grounds of Donington for another eleven years.

"In 1992 it pissed down with rain, which is always a bit difficult for an audience at a festival, it doesn't get them in the best possible mood.
It was a couple of days before our second album. I think the bill wasn't as good that year as when we did it in '90 it was Whitesnake and Aerosmith and it was a difficult bill for

Thunder to be on with Maiden and Slayer, but god bless our punters, despite it pissing down with rain, it was a good day"
Luke Morley (Thunder – Guitar)

"The second time was good fun as we were further up the bill, which was a lot nicer, but it was pissing down with rain, which is a nightmare.
It's really difficult playing in the rain, as it doesn't come straight down and blows in your face, all over your hands, all over your fret board, all over the stage, all over your leather boots and I remember Sebastian Bach slipped over twice; he came flying out, said 'hello Donington' and fell flat on his ass!
The weather definitely put a bit of a damper on it.
Playing in the driving rain is very difficult; it plays havoc with your hair as well!!
It's a very important festival. It has served us very well indeed and a lot of the press said that we were the best band of the day."
Ben Matthews (Thunder - Guitar)

"August 22nd 1992 was a huge day for me because Donington was the 'Holy Grail' of metal. It was just a huge dream come true for me, having been there in '88. I kept thinking most of the day that I had done it; I had fulfilled one of my dreams to play there.
We opened the show, full of excitement, happy to be there, very nervous and a complete feeling of wanting to do well. The rest of the day goes into a bit of a blur. We came off, started having a few drinks, hanging out and we started doing interviews. But the actual being on stage I remember really vividally and just looking out at a sea of people, it was just amazing! I wasn't able to get my breath for the first two songs, it was just like 'oh my god, this is just mental!!' Then I started to relax and get into it and before you knew it, it was over. But in the lead up to it, I remember staying in a hotel the night before and listening to the radio and hearing our name getting mentioned that we were opening it up and then waking up in the morning and knowing that today we were going to open up

Donington, for a soccer player it must be like going to a cup final, for us it was like going to a cup final!"
Ricky Warwick (The Almighty – Vocals/Guitar)

"We opened up the show in '92. I had never played to an audience that size before and as soon as we got out there adrenaline just took over; it was easily one of the highlights of my gigging career and I have done thousands and thousands of gigs. Donington and supporting Metallica at Milton Keynes Bowl the year after are pretty much the two best gigs I have ever done.
I remember seeing Tom Araya at the side of the stage smiling, which was cool.
We didn't get to see much of the other bands as we were stuck in a portakabin doing interviews for most of the day and by the time we got out it was pretty much done and dusted. But we managed to watch Maiden and also saw a tiny bit of Skid Row and they had the worse weather of the day."
Pete Friesen (The Almighty – Guitar)

"Little did I know that 11 years later I would be playing bass in the opening band?
Our agent John Jackson had our dressing-portakabin loaded with Huggies and talc. Thankfully they weren't needed."
Floyd London (The Almighty – Bass)

"What I do remember was that Tommy Vance was going to introduce us on stage, but when they tried to get us on stage, he decided he wasn't going to. So we had to get our man Bomber to do it, the same guy who introduced us on the live Album; 'Donington can I welcome to the stage, the All Loud, All Wild, the All Fuckin' Mighty'; he did that at the last minute, as he was forced to do it.
All the stuff hat I had thought about before about being calm went out the window and I played 'Crucify' at twice the speed it should have been!
We were the first and usually the first band doesn't get much of a reaction, but the whole crowd was there and we got one of the best reactions, apart from the headliners of course.

*We had just come back from Australia at the time and it was great to get that amount of cheers.
After that, the set was a blur. There were lots of Scotland flags being waved and lots of cheering.
Then we went backstage and I met Steve Harris and Sebastian Bach and it just went downhill from there and there's not much more I can remember."*
Stump 'Stumpy' Monroe (The Almighty – Drums)

*"I have one odd memory from before 3 Colours Red... I was drunkenly stumbling around the festival in '92 when a girl randomly stopped me and asked for a photograph, don't ask me why... but I'm like, "erm, ok then!"
That to me is what the festival is about; the crowd is friendly and always really pissed! I don't know how many times I've walked around the crowd trying not to step on hung-over rock fans asleep clutching a bottle of their own piss! Donington rules, shits all over Glastonbury because it is rock, and we all know that rock has the best fans and the best music."*
<u>**Pete Vuckovic**</u> **(3 Colours Red – Vocals/Bass)**

"I don't think I ever saw anybody's set in all those years; I was always too busy running around backstage. I do remember, though, being in the photo pit for Slayer's sound check one year....let's just say it was a life-changing experience!"
Judy Totton (Monsters Of Rock PR)

"I was a teenager when I first went to Donington in 1992. My friend and I went on a coach trip to Monsters Of Rock, which was headlined by Iron Maiden that year. I remember being SO excited to be in the same field as Skid Row!"
Emma Watson (PR – Bowling For Soup/MC Lars/Zebrahead)

"My best memories of Donington Park go way back to 1992 when the festival was still called 'Monsters Of Rock' and the mighty Iron Maiden were headlining for a second time.

There was such an awesome bill that day with British upstarts The Almighty kicking off the day quickly followed by W.A.S.P., Slayer, Thunder and Skid Row as special guests.
I remember this festival most as this was my first ever gig and I would be seeing my favourite band Iron Maiden and I pretty much liked every band that was appearing that day.
The campsite was an awesome experience, something I didn't expect. We got together with a bunch of guys from 'up north' who had accidentally burnt their tent down and we had this huge tent so we offered them part of it for the weekend. One of the guys from what I remember was a Dave Mustaine look alike and had passed out quite early on in the night.
When I finally dragged myself into the tent for some sleep I found myself quickly awakened by the constant taking off and landing of the planes overhead. The next morning I woke up and the guy was still dead to the world, everyone else was awake so I gave him a shove to see if he wanted a beer. When he woke up I said to him 'how the hell did you sleep through the racket of the planes and the car stereos blasting out throughout the night?'; at this point he tucked his hair behind his ears and proceeded to turn on his hearing aids, I felt like such a tool, I didn't even realise.
The best memories of the gig were Skid Row front man Sebastian Bach's impressive stage dive at the start of the set when he went arse over tit from all the rain, but they played an impressive set and witnessing probably one of Iron Maidens finest shows, which I relive on DVD regularly and the loudness of 72,000 people singing every word in unison."
Neil & Maria Bees (Perth, Australia)

"Iron Maiden returned to show the world they could still cut it. And cut it they did, although I must admit to being very drunk by the time they came on stage.
After the fireworks had finished we made our way through the exits with the rest of the crowd, but for some reason I decided to run up a grass bank, only to lose my balance and fall heavily back down to the bottom. Several minutes later I was in the back of an ambulance on my way to Derby Royal Infirmary with a dislocated thumb.

The pain sobered me up somewhat.
The embarrassing part then was to telephone my eight month pregnant wife at four in the morning to come to collect me. I didn't get much sympathy.
I don't know whether it was my musical tastes changing or the rock world in general (I blame Nirvana and the whole grunge movement) but from 1992 onwards the Donington line ups weren't exciting me as much as they used to. Don't get me wrong, I was still enjoying the whole atmosphere and the day out, but looking back in hindsight is that all it was towards the end….just a good day out.
Skid Row, Slayer, WASP just came and went
Even Thunder just weren't as impressive as they had been two years earlier, maybe I had seen them too many times in a short period of time (five or six times within the last twelve months).
1992 had been memorable, but not necessarily for the right reasons.
Once again their was a hiatus the following year. Maybe this would recharge the festivals and my batteries."
Paul Hartshorn (Chesterfield)

1994
Aerosmith,
Extreme, Sepultura, Pantera, Therapy?, Pride and Glory

2nd Stage:
The Wildhearts,
Terrorvision, Skin, Biohazard, Cry of Love, Headswim

After a break of a year, Monsters Of Rock returned in '94, this year with the addition of a 2nd stage featuring smaller popular rock and metal bands.
The second stage featured British favourites Terrorvision, Skin and The Wildhearts in the headline position. The Wildhearts came back to play Download in 2008, Skin played the mainstage in 2009; Terrorvision have yet to

return to Donington. Headswim, Cry Of Love and Biohazard also played; Biohazard had their set cut short after two songs when they overly encouraged the crowd to come on stage and there was a massive stage invasion.

Pride & Glory were the first band on the mainstage, a band that featured Ozzy's guitarist Zakk Wylde on lead guitar; this band was the band that Zakk formed before Black Label Society where he would see much more success.

Therapy? were on next and this would be their first of four appearances. Gaining chart success since the release of their most popular album 'Troublegum' in February 1994, the set was popular, though they were not a normal type of MOR band. Over the next year there popularity would increase even more with the release of 'Infernal Love' and they would be back to fill the 'special guest slot'.

Next was a 'double whammy' of extreme metal in the shape of Pantera from the US and Sepultura from Brazil; but to follow this with the soft rock of Extreme, playing hits such as 'More Than Words' was a bizarre choice. The metal fans wanted thrashing metal and what they got was the popular radio sounds of Gary Cherone and the boys from Massachusetts, a lot of the fans in front of the mainstage weren't happy.

But most people were happy with the final band, Aerosmith were back now in top slot and four years since they had supported Whitesnake at Donington.

Steven Tyler and Joe Perry were American music icons and were seen as the American rock version of Keith Richards and Mick Jagger from the Rolling Stones, with a similarly large music selection to back them up. Playing such hits as 'Dude Looks Like A Lady', 'Sweet Emotion' and 'Walk This Way', they had the crowd eating out of their hands and who could not love their style of performing, the back flips, the posing, the playing up to the crowd, they were a massive success.

The return of Aerosmith in 2010 will equal the three headline appearances of Metallica and only Iron Maiden

and AC/DC will have headlined more times, with AC/DC's 2010 appearance notching up four top slots and equalling that of Iron Maiden.

"Donington's a weird one. I grew up on punk rock, I was a 'punk kid' and I formed Therapy? with Michael and he was a 'metal kid'.
The people we hung around with, in the small town we're from, 'the outsiders' liked punk and metal, Ramones, Motorhead, AC/DC and Iron Maiden. But whenever I met anyone from our village that'd been to Donington it was always long hair, cut off denims and patches, which wasn't really my scene.
When Therapy? Started out I was only into Thrash metal and the only metal bands I liked were early Iron Maiden, Motorhead and AC/DC, everything else was a bit too pomp and theatrical and not really what I liked.
The first time we got offered Donington, all I remember was the outrage at the time because we had short hair! A few years ago Metal Hammer did a 'piece' on 'Days That Changed Metal' and one of them was Therapy? played Donington in 1984.
We were second on the mainstage and we had short hair and bands like Skid Row were on. People were thinking 'well Kerrang! has championed the band and you're hear in front of the Metal faithful, but if you go down really badly that will be the decider'! Michael he was up for it and I just went onstage and by the end of the set it was absolutely brilliant.
Troublegum was out then and we'd had a few singles in the charts and then after Donington the album just went up the charts and we did Reading the same year and we got a Gold disc out of it. But, I remember Donington was the most daunting one because the NME had extensively covered the band, so Reading was like a safe bet. But just before Donington Kerrang! had latched onto the band, but we did get letters in asking why we had short hair.

But, I remember the gig being very good and after about 4 songs in thinking this is great and the crowd's fantastic."
Andy Cairns (Therapy? – Vocals/Guitar)

"When we played at Donington, I got out of the van, to have a wee (because I was that excited) before we'd even got in and the van drove off!
For some reason I had my rucksack and my bags for the mainstage and I had to walk in with the crowd and blagged my way past security, telling them that I was playing on the second stage.
I remember standing on the hill and Sepultura had just finished and then everyone came over to the second stage. Considering these people had come from watching Sepultura, to come and watch us, with our 'doo wops' and singing about 'Our House' it was fantastic.
They all put their hands in the air and gave us a taste for more.
It was a bastion of rock!!!
If we had a 'fuckin' brilliant album to come back with, we would come back."
Tony Wright (Terrorvision – Vocals)

"Early 94 saw us break thru into the charts and offers to play both Donington and Reading dropped onto our doormat. How cool was that???? Donington was great 'cos we'd always been there as kids and we were sandwiched between Sepultura and Pantera!"
Leigh Marklew (Terrorvision - Bass)

"Terrorvision played literally thousands of festivals, it's hard for me to distinguish one from another, mainly due to the state I have usually been in at these events. The nineties may have been a blur but a couple of memories are surfacing through....
Mid nineties, the hardcore/ thrash/ macho thing was happening, circling us (TV) like Apache Indians around a small gathering of fun loving cowboys. This didn't affect us in the slightest; in fact it made us more stubborn about writing pop songs, not only with infectious hook lines, but with longevity

too, (as we have recently proved).
So when we played on stage at Donington in between Slayer and Pantera it was quite a feat winning over the audience to the point of them all singing "doo wop" and waving their tattooed arms in the air! Think we got away with that one. Another time we hijacked several golf buggies and rampaged the Donington site, picking up punters here and there, turning them over now and then (buggies not punters). Needless to say there was a Wildheart or two involved as well!"
Mark Yates (Terrorvision – Guitar)

"When Skin was asked to play in 1994 it was a dream come true. The adrenaline was so high at the time I don't remember much about it, but we filmed our video to 'Tower of strength' at Donington so when I watch it, you kind of relive it.
When I was thirteen, my sister ran the ZIGZAG club, a venue that held about a thousand people. One particular evening a band called Girl headlined, and at soundcheck there guitarist let me play his Les Paul, and stand on stage and play through his Marshall Stack. That guitarist was Phil Collen, now With Def Leppard, and that day changed my life.
In 2009 Def Leppard are headlining and Skin will be playing on the same stage, same day. Unbelievable."
Myke Gray (Skin – Guitar)

"Donington was an unforgettable experience for me."
Bobby Hambel (Biohazard – Guitar)

"There was no festival in 1993, I cannot for the life of me remember why it was not held as it was originally planned, we were now starting to worry that all was not right in the camp and that our beloved fest would soon come to an end. This festival had for so many years been an exciting regular part of our lives that we assumed that it would be with us forever.
'94 was the first time that the organisers would be experimenting with a second stage, I looked on this idea mostly positively as it could cut out waiting times between bands and allow us to see twice as many. On the minus side, if you wished to see all or most of the bands on the second

stage it would limit time for wondering around the stalls, queuing for beer/ toilets etc.

'94 was also the first time that the fest had been held in any other month than June, I did not particularly like this idea as it meant that the headliner would not be playing the majority of their set in darkness, I do not know why it changed but it sucked in my opinion.

We arrived late this year due to not being too bothered about the first few bands on and also bad traffic on the usual approach roads around the airport, in fact we arrived just in time to see Biohazard being kicked off for allowing the crowd to invade the stage, I believe they managed two songs before the organisers intervened. I cannot say I was too upset with this outcome as I was not and am never likely to be a fan of theirs.

Biohazard were on the new second stage, this was obviously a lot smaller than the main stage and was located at the back of the arena to the left, an ideal location which did not take long to walk too if you were standing at the back or right side of the main stage.

After watching another brutally efficient display from Pantera which was not too dissimilar to their last several years earlier, we headed back to the second stage to catch Skin. My most vivid memory of Skin's set is of the two six and a half foot 'Hair Bear Bunch' look-alikes that kept blocking our view despite us trying to move out of the way, this did not totally ruin the set as the band played a good sing-along set which included good time ditties such as 'Look but Don't Touch', 'Tower of Strength' and their slightly changed cover of EMF's 'Unbelievable'. Skin didn't seem to last too much longer, they produced at least one more album (may have been two but if so I did not hear it) then just seemed to vanish from the scene. Skin reformed to play last years Download and I was surprised by the amount of people who could not remember them, even stranger was that two of them had been standing with us watching them during their '94 performance, memories and fish spring to mind.

Next up were Brazilian Thrash giants Sepultura, none of our group had gotten into this particular take on the genre so the unanimous decision was to take root at the back of the arena and fill our faces. Max and his troupe seemed to go down well and they seemed to be doing what they did well enough but it was just not for me, I could appreciate them musically but have never been a fan of those bands that utilise the Growl/ Grunt/ What the hell is he going on about approach to the vocals.

Not too impressed with the late afternoon lineup of Terrovision and the Wildhearts (who I now love), we decided to make the traditional wonder around the stands. Food stalls have never been a highlight of any festival but I remember them as being worse in the '80's and '90's, the variety was poorer than now but the prices were equally as extortionate. If we could get away with it we never purchased any food from these rip off merchants which was not too bad a ploy with a one day event as long as you took adequate provisions.

The other stalls also had less variety on offer than there is today. Whereas you can now buy anything from a skull on a stick to an inflatable three piece suite, then there was not much more on offer other than the stalls selling Official MOR and Band tour T Shirts and the odd stall selling flags, posters or non souvenir shirts.

Extreme were an odd choice for special guests on the bill that day; they had risen to a fairly lofty level with their 'Pornograffitti' album but had also driven everybody mad with the 'More than Words' acoustic ballad that seemed to be played everywhere you went, the last straw for me was hearing it in a DIY shop one day. So, as the early evening sun shone, Gary, Nuno and the boys tried their best to get a reaction out of a crowd that had largely been listening to harder edged stuff all day. I didn't mind them too much and I thought that they put in a decent energetic performance of some of there harder, funkier tracks like 'Decedance Dance' and 'Get The Funk Out'. That was all ruined of course when they got their stools out for a tortuous version of the dreaded 'More than ....', they lost the crowd completely from then on but gained plenty of plastic receptacles from the 'boo boys'. They were an odd choice for special guests and were always going to be battling against the rabid Sepultura and Pantera fans.

Aerosmith were of course excellent, treating us to the usual greatest hits set with a smattering of tracks from their current long player 'Get a Grip'. It was an exactly what it says on the tin set, Steven danced, twirled and jumped, Joe created his usual cool poses whilst playing faultlessly and the other boys did as they do best, play well but not wonder from their spots very often. I enjoyed it and everybody around us also seemed to also. Aerosmith were at the height of their commercial success and a good choice for headliner, it's a shame they started to lose the plot not long after.

Overall '94 had its high points (Aerosmith and 2 stages) and lows (June date and not the greatest line-up) but it was still a great day out and I would not have missed it for the world."

Roger Moore (Glinton, Peterborough)

"The festival was moved from its usual mid August slot to early June. This didn't improve the weather any….it was bitterly cold.

There were also two stages this year.

On the smaller stage both Cry of Love and Skin both impressed. Skin released their set on a series of CD singles shortly after the show.

Aerosmith returned to headline the main stage. Although not as good as their support slot four years earlier, they still put on a solid show. Due to a lack of late trains home (we were using this option once again…the gang was now down to two stalwarts) we had to miss the last portion of Aerosmiths' show. We could see the fireworks in the distance as we travelled down the Derbyshire country lanes towards the station.

Extreme were OK, but not as good as I had witnessed at the NEC at couple of years earlier.

Other bands such as Pantera and Sepultura were in my opinion amongst the worst bands ever to perform at Donington. The 'new' Donington crowd seemed to think otherwise though and they both went down well.

The future didn't look too good through my eyes."

Paul Hartshorn (Chesterfield)

*"I have been attending Donington since 84 but something different from the usual carnage occurred in 1994.
Myself and some friends had been watching a very enjoyable set from the band Cry Of Love on the second stage and decided to chill out at the rear of the main arena when Kelly (?) the lead singer of COL walked by so we called him over for a chat and to congratulate him on a good set.
Kelly sat down and chewed the fat for a while and then noticed one of our group, a mad man by the name of Eastie, was chugging away on a 5ltr drink container full of a dark sticky liquid. Kelly decided he would ask Eastie for a swig, Eastie duly obliged and told Kelly it would put hairs on his chest. Unbeknown to Kelly the dark sticky liquid was a mix of vodka, southern comfort, whiskey & jack Daniels! Kelly took a good swig, his eyes went as wide as dinner plates his skin turned green and foolishly he tried to stand and walk off nonchalantly........ hence the never forgotten sight of an American rock singer staggering sideways down the hill making excuses that he had to meet someone back stage! Hilarious and one of many fond memories of the Monsters of rock."*

Simon Rucastle (Carnforth)

1995
Metallica,
Therapy?, Skid Row, Slayer, Slash's Snakepit, White Zombie, Machine Head, Warrior Soul, Corrosion of Conformity

This year the second stage had disappeared and the festival had another name; instead of MOR it was re-named by the headliners Metallica as 'Escape From The Studio' as they were taking a break from the studio, whilst recording 'Load'.

First on was some 'old school thrash' from Corrosion Of Conformity, favourites of Metallica and then followed by the whacked out 'Acid Punk' rock of Warrior Soul.

Machine Head made their first of many appearances at the Donington site and left quite an impression on the people who caught all of their set. This was a band that had 'staying power' and are now headlining arena shows in their own right across the UK, 15 years later.

The eerie 'horror metal' of White Zombie would have always been a popular choice on the day; the return of Rob Zombie is still eagerly awaited and the Download festival forums are always full of people requesting that

Rob plays every year. White Zombie made the most of their short trip to the UK and played Donington on the Saturday, following it up with an appearance at the Reading Festival on the Sunday.

The return to Donington by Slash was a popular choice to watch in the mid afternoon slot and was a lot less eventful than the Guns N' Roses appearance in 1988 when the crowd disaster had struck. Slash's Snake Pit was a bluesier band and really just a vehicle for the guitar skills of Mr Hudson himself. Slash would return again in 2005 & 2007 with Velvet Revolver, a more popular band and a proper group, including Scott Weiland of Stone Temple Pilots on vocal duties.

Slayer made their 2nd appearance in the same spot on the bill as they had occupied 3 years before. Slayer did exactly what it said on the tin, thrash, thrash, quality thrash.

Skid Row were back again this time one position below the guest slot , but still an incredibly popular choice, with an extremely vigorous and energetic performance. Sebastian Bach was still with the band and when they lost him the main focus of the band was gone, though the amazing songs were still there as a testament to their once greatness.

Therapy? had now risen to the 'special guest' slot and even had a cello player, something that wouldn't be seen at Donington until the debut of Apocalyptica in 2003.

Metallica were back to headline the festival for the first time and they were now a band that was unstoppable and musical world domination seemed to be the name of the game.

Playing some of the most precise thrash that had ever graced the stage at the festival, Metallica were such a popular choice most of the people in attendance.

Metallica would be back to headline for the 2nd time in 2004, followed by their 3rd slot in 2006.

So, another Monsters Of Rock had finished, but we didn't know that the following year would be the festivals Swansong; the end of an era, the end of the line, final orders etc. Monsters Of Rock was coming to an end and a much needed different brand of festival would be needed to fill the gap, this would happen with the beginning of Download in 2003, 8 years later.

"Metallica headlines Donington 1995!!!
We were in the middle of the recording of 'Load' and took a break from the studio to come over and play Donington. I think we played a warm up show underneath the Astoria, in the Astoria 2; it was the first time that we played a couple of the songs that ended up being 'Devil Dance' and '2 x 4' that ended up on 'Load' and 'Re-Load'.
It was great to get out of the studio and it was obviously great to headline Donington. It was a very relaxing day; I remember that whenever we played Donington, we were always wound up and nervous and kinda all over the place, but I remember that there was a really calm atmosphere backstage. I remember that we were just hanging out talking to Sebastian Bach and Kerry King and it was just a really effortless day. Everyone was in a good mood and there were no dramas. We opened up with 'Breadfan' and we played two new songs and we got do a full 2 ½ hour set; it was an incredible day. Afterwards we went for a 'piss up' down in Birmingham at Edwards Number Eight club. I remember that all the Metallica guys, the Skid Row and Slayer guys 'caravanned' down to Birmingham; we were off the freeway, or the motorway as you call it and we had all been drinking beers and everybody had to piss. We literally stopped somewhere outside of Birmingham, it could have been Wolverhampton or somewhere and the guys from Slayer, Skid Row and Metallica got out and all just started 'peeing' on some guys lawn. We were standing there at 2 o'clock in the morning on the way to the 'After Donington Piss Up Party' and we were all pissing on some guy's lawn in a suburb of Birmingham, it was quite funny."
Lars Ulrich (Metallica – Drums)

"Metallica were playing Donington as a 'comeback gig' and they've got a more hardcore fan base that like Metallica and nothing else, so it was a lot more difficult for us.
We had a cellist onstage with us at this point, as we'd brought out 'Infernal Love' it had gone Gold and sold a lot of records and we were second from top.
I remember the first half of the set was a lot more difficult because it was Metallica and they weren't really 'indie friendly' and we were in that cult kind of thing, straddling both camps.
It came to opening for Metallica and we'd sold all these records around the world and we opened with the cellist onstage and the Joy Division cover of "Isolation". I remember being conscious for the first few songs that this could go either way.
There was a hardcore of Metallica fans down the front giving us really bad looks. We kind of managed to pull it off towards the end, but it was a lot more nerve-racking than '94. People who were fourteen or fifteen absolutely loved it.
I think a lot of the 'old guard' had been put out of joint by the like of 'Troublegum' and Faith No More, Helmet and Grunge and the fact that we had short hair.
I do remember that it got a lot more corporate for us and we had a big promotional tent backstage and we were whisked 'from pillar to post' doing lots more interviews, but at the end of the day the gig was still fantastic."
Andy Cairns (Therapy? – Vocals/Guitar)

"WAKE UP!!!! You've got five minutes to get on stage!" was the first thing I heard that day.
We had fallen asleep in the tour bus late the night before, and no one had bothered to wake up me or Rob that morning at Donington. Although we were in the middle of the line up that afternoon, it was afternoon, and time to perform. We threw on some clothes, and were immediately whisked on stage – no coffee, no warm-up, and only the biggest, most important show ever! Talk about an adrenaline o.d. – waking up to so many thousands of people – it was amazing!
We had the unusual title of being the first band ever to play Donington and Reading back to back, which many bands

would covet but made us extremely nervous. What if the metalheads thought we were too alternative, and vice versa at Reading? We had heard nightmarish stories about how the British fans might react – bottles of piss hurled at you, sharpened coins, you name it. It was nerve wracking, walking out on to that stage. Especially jolted awake just seconds earlier.

Of course the crowd was fantastic, and it definitely is in the top 3 White Zombie shows ever. Someone recently showed me footage of us that day, and it looks as crazy as I remember it. Besides the pleasant shock of 80,000 fans going nuts, my next strongest impression was the sharp pain in my ribs: the stage seemed as big as a football field, and we were doing our normal stage thing of running back and forth like nuts. I was completely winded by the middle of the first song, but had way too much adrenaline to slow down.

Afterwards I found out I had personally garnered another title that day: "2nd Female to Grace the Stage since Doro". I'm sure there have been many more since me, but it was a newsworthy at the time, and I suppose I was the only female musician there that day. That seems weird now, but at the time it was normal.

After our performance we met Kirk from Metallica, and he invited us to stop by his private tent for Martinis later, which was very cool of him. Next thing you know Skid Row are on stage, and Bas is kicking ass! He owned that day; I have never seen someone so "on" and working a crowd like that. The last thing I remember was watching Metallica from the wings, finally evening, outdoors, lights, action, amazing. A perfect day, if only there had been coffee and breakfast!"

Sean Yseult (White Zombie – Bass)

"The Donington experience was a fantastic dream to me, brought forth by nature spirits, it seems.

We flew in the night before from Los Angeles. I was very excited about the event because I have always been intrigued about the "Earth energy secrets" for which Donington is well known. Plus, I dig the shit out of castles (who doesn't?). Ideally, I would have liked to share a snifter of brandy next to a lit fireplace with Diane Cilento and Christopher Lee, singing dirty limericks in the gatehouse, but hey, I'm like Wickerman damaged (I fucking love that movie). As it happened, we flew in and were on early. The time window was so short that we literally had to leave for home almost immediately after the show.

I do remember Slash and I hanging out with Ben Shepherd of Soundgarden sometime before driving to the event. We had a smoke out in the front of the hotel, loitered a bit (like proper rockers should), and then drove to the stage.

I looked out amongst the thousands before our set and thought, "Fuck, yes! This will be a real memory, not some blank weekend warrior recollection!"

We got on with the gig, and I remember that indescribable feeling of energy. It was electrifying and tremendous to play for so many and in such a setting.

We ended our set, said good evening and here comes Metallica!

We then were taken offstage to a V.I.P area somewhere further away (but not behind the stage, so we could still see the show).

I remember a few last things.

I have never heard the real sound of a mechanized armor unit on the move in person before, but from the moment Metallica got on, that's what it sounded like! I dug the hell out of it. It could have caused pensioners and small children to poo themselves! It was that loud right down to the twig and berries chakras.

We spent the last while before leaving for the airport chatting in the tent with people, enjoying the English countryside, laughing, a few drinks, kiss kiss. Bye.

After the lag wore off in L.A., it was back to 'Eric Dover, did you pay the electric bill?' and 'Can you run to the bank?' Back to the normal daily affairs. <sigh> For a few weeks afterwards, though, I was still tripping about how whirlwind cool and mythical it was. I would be in a supermarket and look at all the food and think,

"I can BUY ANY of this fucking food I want! I played at Donington, bitches!"

Eric Dover (Slash's Snakepit – Vocals)

"As a kid growing up and listening to rock and metal music, I went to my first Donington in '95; Metallica were headlining with Skid Row, Therapy?, Corrosion Of Conformity and Machine Head and having seen a massive festival like that as a kid, I never thought that I would end up playing it. If someone had come up and told that 13 year old rocker kid that I would have been playing in the same position that Corrosion Of Conformity played, I wouldn't have believed it."
Dave Warsop (Beat Union – Vocals/Guitar)

"I remember this Monsters as it was my first and the one I developed chicken pox at. I got sicker and sicker throughout the day and the noise of the bands did nothing to improve the throbbing pain in my head!!!"
Mike Horton (Plymouth)

"We had not heard about Metallica headlining the 'Escape From The Studio' show in 2005 until late and by then we had made other plans.
To be honest, I do not think that it was organised or announced until fairly late on, which was a shame as it had a pretty damn good line-up."
Roger Moore (Glinton, Peterborough)

"Metallica's fourth appearance saw them headline for the first time and they kicked a bit of life into the old festival with a mixture of old and new numbers (even a couple of brand new songs).
It's a pity I can't say the same about the rest of the day.
As in 1994 bands such as White Zombie and Machine Head were awful to these ears.
Special guest slot was occupied by Therapy?. Not what I would call a Donington band (or not the kind I wanted), but they performed satisfactorily and were OK.
I also enjoyed Slash's Snakepit for their short early in the day slot.

*I was the last of the old gang to attend this year. I got a lift with some younger Donington newcomers.
I could sense the old beast was beginning to breathe its last."*
Paul Hartshorn (Chesterfield)

*"Back in 95 the weather was scorching, (so I remember) anyway, me and a mate had just finished watching Slash's Snake Pit. I was absolutely starving so decided to go grab a bite to eat.   We went to the nearest available burger stall. What with Donny's reputation for their 'dethburgers' I ordered 2 hot dogs. Carrying one in each hand. While walking back to where we were sat beforehand walking down a grass verge I felt my legs slip from under me. And landed in the only stretch of mud for miles.
Looked up and there was a single tap water point where the remainder of water had been draining all day and made a mini mud slide. It was about no longer than 7 foot long and a foot wide and I had managed to slip on it. Claire (my mate) laughed hard. To which I received a large cheer and a round of applause from the hundreds of people sat watching me. I took a bow and disappeared rather quickly. My legs / shorts were caked in mud and my mate couldn't stop laughing. In my defence I didn't drop either of my hotdogs though."*
Mike Fairhurst (Urmston, Manchester)

1996

Kiss, Ozzy Osbourne, Sepultura, Biohazard, Dog Eat Dog, Paradise Lost, Fear Factory

2nd Stage

Korn,

Type O Negative, Everclear, 3 Colours Red, Honeycrack, Cecil

This year saw the return of the second stage and also the return of Kiss as joint headliners with Ozzy Osbourne, who was also making his 3rd visit.
The line-up for the day was very diverse, especially across the acts on the mainstage. Opening with the 'industrial metal' of Fear Factory and having Dog Eat Dog's 'nu metal rap crossover' hybrid playing later that afternoon, no one could complain about the lack of variety on offer.

Early afternoon saw the British 'gothic metal' band Paradise Lost draw a considerable crowd and include in their set tracks from their album 'Draconian Times' which had been released 2 months earlier.

After Dog Eat Dog, Biohazard returned to Donington after their truncated set on the second stage in 1995.

The show for Sepultura was a very strange and sad one. Max Cavalera's step son had been killed in an accident and so rather than cancel the show and let down any of their growing legion of fans, Andreas Kisser stepped up to the mark and sang all the songs for the set instead. Max stayed at home, to be near his family.

Over on the second stage there were performances from Cecil (whatever happened to them?), Honeycrack and 3 Colours Red, who have both since split up; the members of Honeycrack have gone on to other careers, Hugo Degenhardt the is now playing the part of Ringo Starr in the Bootleg Beatles, CJ is in the Wildhearts and Willie Dowling is writing music for TV shows and films.

Elsewhere on the 2nd stage, Everclear, the multi million selling 'alt rock' band from Portland, Oregon, USA, put on a fantastic show and were a big success on the day.

Also gaining many fans were Type O Negative, putting in a rare appearance on the day; playing a whole set that only consisted of three songs over a period of 30 minutes, but what a great 30 minutes they were.

Finally the 2nd stage came to a close with Korn, who at the time were a very much 'underground' act and won over the crowd; who couldn't love a band with a dreadlocked bagpipe player?

On the mainstage Ozzy preceded his set with a montage of amusing video clips, with him superimposed in famous historical clips and music videos.

Always a popular choice and making his third appearance at the festival, Ozzy played all the classics 'Iron Man', 'Paranoid' and an encore of 'Crazy Train' and 'Bark At The Moon'; he would return to headline the Ozzfest day at Download 2005, 9 years later.

Finally, Kiss were back, this time with full make up, the original line-up and a set that featured all the classic Kiss songs. Playing a twenty songs set, with music only from their 'make up days', Kiss proved why they were a band at the top of the rockpile and put on one of the most amazing shows ever seen at the festival. Starting with 'Deuce' and ending with 'Rock And Role All Nite', the crowd was entertained by the worlds number one showband; it would be another 12 years before Kiss would return and by then Peter Criss and Ace Frehley would both have been replaced in the band.
So that was it, the final Monsters Of Rock at Donington. Going out on a high, with a double headline slot was a great way to end to an iconic festival, though it would return in a slightly different guise at the Milton Keynes Bowl in 2006.

"I remember being on stage and I thought I was seeing amazing kind of special effect, twirling through the air, but it was water bottles filled with piss."
Paul Stanley (Kiss – Vocals / Guitar)

"Donington was a major part of breaking our career here in Europe.
I remember that at our first show in '96, there was a big lead up to it with 'Korn's coming, Korn's coming', thanks to Rob Flynn from Machine Head who was talking us up a lot in the press, in Kerrang! and a lot of other magazines. He was saying 'you've gotta hear this band called Korn, you've gotta check 'em out', so there was this buzz going round about us. That was really our 'coming out'. We had come over before with Primus and nobody really knew who we were, but Donington was the show that really blew the doors wide open for us; there was no turning back after that show.
It was a magic show, a funny show that I will never forget."
Jonathan Davis (Korn - Vocals)

"At this time in our career, Dog Eat Dog was used to playing large festivals, but sharing the stage with two of our all time favorite bands, KISS and OZZY, was a dream come true! It was like a big party with our friends Biohazard, Fear Factory, and Sepultura also on the bill. Add in the beautiful weather and this was a day we'll never forget. I got to shake Gene Simmons and Paul Stanley's hands as they walked thru the backstage. John got to meet Ozzy. Everyone was happy. This was one of the most important shows in DED's history and we will always remember it fondly."
Dave Neabore (Dog Eat Dog - Bass)

"First of all I was so stoked to play with Ozzy and Kiss, being a kid of the 70s and 80s; Kiss were there and I had an all access pass. All I knew about our stage was this band from Cali called Korn was gonna play after us.
The year had been a whirlwind of radio/summer festivals. We had no pull in Europe but things were going well for us in the States.
When asked to do the show I jumped at the chance while the rest of the band resisted. I was a HUGE KISS fan and knew that Ace was gonna be on the grounds.
So we set up, got everything in place and I remember seeing people drink alcohol or something out of what looked like plastic pouches. Ok... your gonna be there all day bring your own drink, I thought. Our crew began to set everything up.
Korn was to go after us and they were very stoked to play, Munky and I hung out for a while, super cool guy!!!
I think the crowd was ready for Korn but we were next. So while our crew was setting up a few, maybe 3-4 people threw their bags on stage hitting our trusty road crew. They wandered off stage asking, "Why would they throw beer at us?" Well... after they finish drink the beer/alcohol from the bags... it becomes somewhere to piss. Our road crew became targets for their piss bags. Not sure why?
I also hear that Ozzy was not singing that day and there was a guy under the stage singing for him.
I was back stage "MAIN STAGE" and saw two young women holding ACE up cuz he was sooooo fuckedup. GENE and

PAUL came out and were the usual freaks, Gene looking for girls and Paul looking for guys."
Craig Montoya (Everclear – Bass)

"We played the last ever Donington Monsters of Rock Festival, the headliners were Kiss.
It was an amazing event to be part of as the Monsters of Rock Festival was something everyone dreamt of doing in those days.
Our label at the time was Music For Nations. They had a tent set up for us backstage in which everything was black; food, drink, everything, pure Spinal Tap and the black sandwiches weren't very popular.
It was also an honour to be playing the main stage.
The show was awesome. A sea of people and even some banners just for little, old us."
Gregor Mackintosh (Paradise Lost - Guitar)

"Donington meant everything to me, I remember watching AC/DC and Van Halen being interviewed by Andy Kershaw for the Whistle test in 1984, also, my old man would drive us up from Devon as a kid some years, one of my earliest memories...
So to get the chance to play there was almost other worldly, 3 Colours Red, to my knowledge were either the first, or one of the first bands to play the event as an unsigned act, I think it was '96 so it was a bit nerve wracking, the crowd were well up for it which was great because we were brand new. I remember looking at the massive tyre and being at a loss as to what to say for once, so I tried the line - 'knowing us 3 Colours Red, knowing you Donington', the whole crowd shouted 'A-HAAAAAAAAAAAA'... Awesome."
Pete Vuckovic (3 Colours Red – Vocals/Bass)

"My main memory of Donington is of seeing Kiss' helicopter fly in and land backstage, and later on watching them tottering towards the stage on their
platform shoes in full rig, thinking "Wow. That's Kiss".

Our time onstage was just a blur of adrenalin. And volume, of course."
Hugo Degenhardt (Honeycrack – Drums/Vocals)

"I couldn't go that year; but I remember when I was a kid taping the rock show on Radio One and Max from Sepultura's step son had just been killed and I remember Andreas doing all the singing for them and it was amazing."
Tom Lacey (The Ghost Of A Thousand – Vocals)

"My first experience of Donington was a near-death one aged 16 at Monsters Of Rock 1996.
My mate Simon and I crawled a quarter mile through a trench that ran under the security fencing and found ourselves in the VIP area - Valhalla to a young metal kid!
After drinking more free booze than we could handle, and making acquaintance with members of Cradle Of Filth and Anathema, we all decided to go back to the main arena to watch Kiss, but got caught in a dust storm as their helicopter landed.
We just lay on the floor until the explosions (they had a LOT of pyro) stopped, and got up shaking, with sand, mud and shit in our hair. Then we watched Kiss jump out of said helicopter. That event pretty much solidified my entire future, and I've been lost in rock ever since."
Adam Sagir (The Noise Cartel)

"The next trip was 1996 - The Ozzy/Kiss double header. This time it was a minibus full of drunken idiots and a lunatic for a driver. I was married by this time and we all got picked up in the early hours. A crate of beer in the back and a few "herbal" cigarettes going round meant we were in fine spirits when we arrived. The sun was shining, a first for my Donington trips I believe, and we got to the gate. "Can't bring bottles in" said the guard, offering us a plastic bag with a tap on it "but you can have a couple of these for a quid each."
Decanting our various bottles and cans into these, which looked suspiciously like a bag of piss, we made our way in. To be honest, the drink we'd had on the way down means that it

wasn't the most active or memorable of MOR's. My "Donington moment" seemed odd with a second stage at the top of the hill. We found a spot about halfway back, basking in the sun and just drinking in the atmosphere.
Shops made a welcome addition to the burger vans, and I ended up buying my wife a pair of leather trousers. Burger vans were being edged out by Noodle bars - what variety. Biohazard were ok, Sepultura were impressive if incomplete - Max was absent due to the death of his stepson - and I remember lying down half asleep while Ozzy was on. Everyone in the group got bored watching Kiss - who were doing a much bigger show than in '88 - and we left before the crush at the end of their set and watched the fireworks from the van. I don't think we even bothered to check out the second stage at all. I mean, who the hell were Korn?
And that was Monsters Of Rock. Time went by, I got divorced. After a fallow period with music, I started listening to new music again.
Phil Hull (Download Forum Administrator)

"Kiss had reunited for their 'Alive' world tour, and were in full makeup; what an iconic performance.
Ozzy's performance, despite the fact that he looked like he could have done with some sort of assistance walking, was also amazing."
Mike Horton (Plymouth)

"August 17th 1996 could not come round quick enough for us, the main reason was a one word reason - KISS. Yes, we had seen KISS four times previously but this was different, this was the original line-up reformed with full makeup and 'Alive' era stage show to boot. This was great news and only got better when it was announced that Ozzy would be co-headlining (although his set was really only a 'special guest' spot). From then on I was not bothered who else got booked, these two were enough for me, in fact when the rest of the bill was announced I could not be bothered with any of them, Fear Factory aside.

In reflection, I think that for us the last few years Monsters Of Rock bills were far inferior to the mega line-ups of '84 and '88, they had more bands with the two stages but we found the under card to be somewhat lightweight. I do not blame the organisers for this, I think that it was as a result of Grunge which had destroyed the Glam scene and was steadily destroying everything else 'Metal' in its wake. To be honest, if the Headliners had not been great, we may have missed '94 and '96, this would have been bad looking back at it now, as we had no idea that they would be the last two under the MOR banner (although I am still unsure whether '96 was called MOR as the ticket just says Donington '96).

We arrived late again that year, about halfway through Dog Eat Dog's set, I was only disappointed that we did not miss their entire set as their Metal/ Rap crossover was definitely not my cup of tea. In recent years I have come to appreciate some of the bands who fuse Metal and Rap (Linkin Park, Bodycount and Stuck Mojo to name but three) but in those days I considered it sacrilege, shit! I was still smarting over the whole Aerosmith - Run DMC thing.

After a quick mosey round the stalls and obligatory wait around while the ladies joined the ridiculously long toilet queue, we headed over to the second stage to catch Type-O-Negative.

This year they had moved the second stage around so that it had the back of the stage facing the main stage; I am not sure why they did that? Maybe they found that this afforded better views or less sound leakage in the wind? I have to say, I was impressed with Type-O-Negative, their doomy, gothicky music appealed to me in a kind of Sabbath meets Sisters of Mercy way and their giant vocalist Pete Steel had the right type of deep voice that complemented their sound. I cannot remember what they played apart from 'My Girlfriends Girlfriend' but they hit the spot enough to ensure that I would buy their next three albums.

My opinion of Biohazard had not changed since their last visit in '94, so the chances of me giving them any time was nil. Unfortunately, with no other band playing on another stage at the same time, to drown them out it was impossible to escape

from having to hear them. I promised my ears that they would get a treat later for having to suffer this annoying din.
I had heard some rumours about this band Korn and some bloke who plays bagpipes but had not actually heard them. Due to some kind of vote within Kerrang!, Korn were chosen to headline the second stage, this was odd to say the least for an up and coming act, however, on the day there was a huge crowd trying to watch them; we went over but could not see anything, instead we resigned to sitting as close as we could to listen. What I heard was slightly different and definitely something new; in fact I could not decide whether or not I liked it? However, I thought that the fact that I definitely did not hate it was a plus sign, about five years later I brought their back catalogue and liked at least 50% of the material!
There was one thing for certain, the huge crowd that were trying to squeeze in front of this relatively small stage were loving it, and the band responded in kind with the most energetic performance I ever saw them play. I think that this performance broke Korn in the UK and from that day on they appear to have almost secured a residency at the venue as not many Download festivals go by without them on the bill or a Korn solo project.
We were only half watching/ listening when Sepultura came on however, this time it was minus frontman Max Cavalera? We were advised that his absence was due to a personal matter that had forced him to return to Brazil, we later discovered that this was due to the tragic death of his stepson in a car accident. I was still not a fan of Sepultura but I admired the fact that despite what must have been an event that affected them all, they soldiered on with Andreas Kisser taking on the vocal duties.
'96 was another Donington day when the weather was good, from what I remember all day. And who better to watch on a hot summer's day than Ozzy! The Oz man has always had a penchant for slinging buckets of water at the crowd, this is usually welcomed by those hot, sweaty individuals at the front but those of us further back usually remain dry. Ozzy being a creative individual had remedied age old problem of soaking us stood further afield on this day by purchasing a water

cannon, what a genius, he regularly doused us down and I am sure kept several people from flaking out. I have always been glad that Ozzy has his obsession with this particular element and not any of the other two!

Before Ozzy came on we got a five or so minute video of various famous film scenes with Ozzy appearing in them, including him knocking on the window of Apollo 13 trying to get in, this was a great way to start the set and got everyone in high spirits. Ozzy bounced on to the stage shortly after the vid and treat us to his usual greatest hits style set with a couple of new tracks (I remember 'Perry Mason' I think but none of the others). He was as enthusiastic as ever and kept telling us over and over that he loved us (as usual); his singing was not as good as I have heard on other occasions but this was easy to forgive when the set is good and the band having such a good time. I have seen Ozzy many times as a solo artist and with Sabbath and he has never given anything less than 100%, he is a man possessed on stage with boundless energy and a joy to watch.

During the interval it was time to get on with the usual chores i.e. replenish the beer supply and drain the all ready consumed beverages, I considered this to be absolutely essential on this occasion as I did not want to miss a single minute of today's headliners set. Due to the queues myself and a not to be named acquaintance decided that we could not risk waiting any longer so we decided to use a security fence as a plan B. As we reached the fence there was no sign of any unwanted security so we went about our business watering the said fence and chatting. Before we had finished a whirring noise started and a KISS helicopter appeared (from behind the stage I think) this was of course a signal to get back to our group, I quickly zipped up, but my slower friend was still in mid flow when from out of the darkness leapt a gigantic Rottweiler and hit the fence at with such impact that it knocked my friend over. I picked him up and we headed back into the crowd, however, he was obviously a bit stunned? When I questioned "what the fucks' up with you" he informed me that the friendly canine had missed biting off his old man

by centimetres, he swore he felt the mutts nose on his lucky love gun, a lesson had been learned.
We luckily found our group where we had left them just in time for KISS to hit the stage. For most of the next 90 minutes we were treated to the best visual display I had ever seen, this was light years away from their '80's incarnation, just simply stunning.
We got the whole package, Gene breathing fire and spewing fake blood from his platform that he fly's to at the top of the stage, we had Ace firing Rockets from his guitar, we got elevating drum kits, platforms than swing out over the crowd and more pyros than you can shake a stick at. The set list did not disappoint either, it was all old stuff such as 'Deuce', 'Hotter Than Hell', 'Detroit Rock City', 'Beth', ' I Was Made For Lovin You' and of course finished off with 'Rock n Roll All Nite'. They came, they saw, and on that night (for me anyway) they ruled."
Roger Moore (Glinton, Peterborough)

"My memory of Donington at its best - dodging the dodgy content bottles that always got thrown!
Seriously, I really miss Monsters of Rock! They had the best acts and the best newcomers for you to see first hand.
My best bands have got to be Skin, White Zombie, Metallica and Pride & Glory - they were all fantastic live!"
Gill Talbot (Gravesend, now Carlisle)

"Apart from the co-headliners in 1996, KISS and OZZY, once again there wasn't too much on offer for me during the day. But I rallied myself to go (it was now mainly because I had been to all the previous ones and didn't want to miss it…I was clinging on to my youth….I was now 33 years old).
I travelled down with a new group of festival goers (which included John Slater guitarist-to-be with Blaze Bayley's band after his departure from Iron Maiden. John lived in the same village as me).
The beer flowed quite freely and I must admit I really enjoyed my last Donington.

I went down the front for both Ozzy and KISS and had a great time, the downside being that I lost my camera in the melee at the front shortly after the start of the KISS set.

If Donington was going to go out with a bang rather than a whimper then I suppose KISS in full reunion make-up were the right band to do it. Their stage show is legendary and spectacular 'Rock 'n' Roll All Nite'.

So there you have it, my brief memories of THE MONSTERS OF ROCK festival at Castle Donington 1980 to 1996.

I wonder how many other people attended all fifteen shows…..maybe someone could arrange a reunion…..who knows."

Paul Hartshorn (Chesterfield)

"I remember the first year Monsters of Rock had two stages, one of my mates scooted off to watch one of the bands on the 2nd stage and came running back to grab us; all he said was "Shit man you won't believe it ya gotta see this band, the lead singer is playing the f#*king bagpipes!?!" Hence to say this was our introduction to Korn!

I could name so many amazing bands I have seen over the years, I feel so privileged to have been a part of Donington so many times, with so many friends. The atmosphere never fails to make the hairs on the back of my neck stand up, and on those barmy hot days when you're sitting in a field with like minded people, a cold beer in your hand watching and listening to music you love, you will never experience a feeling like it." **Jude Wright (Wallasey, Merseyside)**

2001
A Day At The Races
Stereophonics,
Ash, The Black Crowes, The Crocketts, Proud Mary

In a total contrast to any of the Monsters Of Rock events, the 2001 'A Day At The Races featured a host of indie/pop bands and one band that had played at a previous MOR in 1991. Monsters Of Rock was put on a backburner and the ghosts of metal past were banished forever into the very soul of Donington Park; or were they?

First on were the Crocketts who have since evolved into the 'Top Of The Pops' appearing stars the Crimea. Minor hit makers and indie crowd pleasers, the Crocketts played tracks from their debut album 'We May Be Skinny And Wirey' and their 2000 album 'The Great Brain Robbery'. Popular on the day, but still relatively unknown, the Crocketts split up the following year.

Next up were Proud Mary from Oldham. Favourites of Noel Gallagher of Oasis, they were the first band that Noel signed up to his Sour Mash record label, due to their 'classic' rock 'n' roll sound. They played a set that mostly consisted of tracks from their debut album 'Same Old Blues', including the popular single 'Very Best Friend'. Finally, a band from the MOR days was back to grace the stage with their Southern Blues-Rock style, The Black Crowes. Having played in 1991, the Black Crowes were back for another bite of the Donington cherry, slightly higher up the bill by two places and standing out from the other bands playing. What the audience made of the band from Atlanta, Georgia on the day was any ones guess as they certainly weren't anything like Stereophonics or Ash, who were on next as 'special guests'.

Ash from Downpatrick Co. Down in Northern Ireland were making their Donington debut this day, but would return as 2nd on the bill to HIM, on the 2nd stage at Download Festival in 2008. Playing a massive amount of singles including 'Girl From Mars' and tracks from their latest album 'Free All Angels' including the remarkable 'Burn Baby Burn, Ash were an excellent choice for the special guest spot on the day.

Stereophonics show at Donington was part of a two gig series, the other at the Millennium Stadium; the original choice for the other gig had been at Chepstow Racecourse, hence 'A Day At The Races', but due to the 'foot & mouth' crisis it had to be moved.

Playing tracks from their recently released 'Just Enough Education To Perform', Stereophonics trawled through the stand out album tracks and yet to be released singles; 'Mr Writer' and 'Have A Nice Day' had already been chart hits from the album, but 'Handbags And Gladrags' was yet to be released.

Hit after hit were played and the event was a great day out, but it wasn't Monsters Of Rock; but at the time we didn't realise that metal was on its way to Donington once again this time in the shape of Ozzfest, the Ozzy Osbourne organised one day event, which would arrive at Donington Park in May the following year.

"It was just massive, we were checking out the crowd. We'd played at Reading a lot of times and Glastonbury, but this was equally as big, with a sheer amount of people."
Mark Hamilton (Ash – Bass)

*"I remember thinking that the Monsters of Rock Festival was the 'ultimate festival' as we grew up as kids and I remember listening to Tommy Vance.
So, when we got to play here it was a big deal; the stage was very cool, like a natural amphitheatre.
I really like playing out doors, especially in the UK, where people know us."*
Tim Wheeler (Ash – Vocals Guitar)

"I like it when we played with the Stereophonics because it was like a natural amphitheatre with all of the crowd looking down."
Rick McMurray (Ash – Drums)

2002 Ozzfest
Ozzy Osbourne

The well needed return of 'the metal' to Donington was a moment to rejoice, although the weather on the day wasn't.
The one day Ozzfest event was sadly marred by the torrential rain which occurred on and off throughout the day, drenching the crowd, but not dampening their spirits; the crowd were definitely up for another great day of rock.
The initial Ozzfest at Donington (it would return on the Saturday of Download 2005) was headlined by the 'Ozzmeister' himself, Mr Ozzy Osbourne and a fantastic supporting bill.
The second stage was positioned in the exhibition centre and so was packed all day long due to the rain outside. The stage was headlined by the British band Hundred Reasons with a fledgling Skindred and Otep also playing earlier in the day, but there were so many that played which have since disappeared, where are Cyclefly? Where are Pulse Ultra? Where are Flaw?
For every success story there are always a host of other rock 'n' roll casualties who get lost along the way and the second stage at Ozzfest seemed to have an abundance of them.
The main stage was however a totally different story with a line-up that featured three future Download headliners; System Of A Down who headlined in 2005, Tool who filled the top spot in 2006 and Lostprophets who closed the festival on the Sunday six years later in 2008. Slayer, another staple of the Download festival played on the day and have been one of the few acts that have played

Monsters Of Rock, Ozzfest and Download all at Donington in the last 30 years.
Ozzy closed the festival with a show stopping performance and would return again for 'Ozzfest day' at Download 2005, but this time he would play his only performance at Donington with the mighty legends that are Black Sabbath.

"It was raining and cold, they had the semi-circle at the front and it was half empty. The only people, who could get in there, got there early and they'd gone off drinking and Slayer were on after us, so everyone was ready for Slayer.
But, I love Slayer, but their fans are probably not the biggest fans of us.
You needed special tickets to get in the semi circle and it looked empty, beyond the semi circle it was rammed but nobody could get anywhere near the stage."
Ian Watkins (Lostprophets - Vocals)

"We played Ozzfest at Donington, just before it turned into Download and it was horrible, one of the worst shows that I've ever played, disgusting.
For me whilst I was growing up the Monsters of Rock was huge. I remember Metallica headlining it and all these great bands and it was like WOW 'we're going to play Donington!' It's like every metal kids dream to play Donington and it was shit, it was like the most disappointed I've ever been. Because I was so worked up for it, we were finally going to play Donington!!"
Mike Lewis (Lostprophets – Guitar)

"We were afraid that we were going to be trying to get everyone to sing-along and that they would hate us, so we were all pretty nervous before the set.
Then there was a massive rainstorm so the tent got absolutely mobbed; there were about 13,000 in there and they stopped letting people in, because they couldn't physically fit anymore in!

It was packed and we were very nervous, but as soon as we went on it was brilliant. I actually have a BBC CD recording of that show and I listen to it when I'm depressed about anything, because it's fantastic and you can hear the crowd, louder than the band, singing along to all the songs.
They had an after party that night, in a big tent, which was an absolute disaster, because of all the mud."
Larry Hibbitt (Hundred Reasons – Guitar)

"I remember playing Donington the once and we were sandwhiched between Mushroomhead and another band of that ilk.
I suppose it was when 'Nu Metal' was at the forefront and we didn't really see ourselves as a 'Nu Metal' band. I remember coming out and playing softest, most melodic, quiet tune to the horror of about 15000 kids who obviously didn't know who we were. After about half a minute of bottles coming over, I think everyone calmed down and realised we were trying something different. I seem to remember after that the gig went really well and for years afterwards people were coming up to us and saying they saw us there.
Probably the first time I ever went there was to play it and I always remember the Guns 'N' Roses video, that was my image of Donington."
Joe Birch (Hell is For Heroes – Drums)

"I remember we were supposed to be playing Donington a couple years ago and it clashed with another European festival that we were going to do, so we had to pull out. So, they had to find a worthy replacement for 2pm on the second stage and it ended up being Metallica. They took our slot and left people somewhat dissapointed, I bet, that we weren't around"
Will McGonagle (Hell Is For Heroes – Guitar)

"As a kid being a huge metal fan it was a quite a big deal to play Donington as I'd followed it for years. All I really remember about the gig was ducking bottles, that was it…..
'DUCK'"

Tom O'Donoghue (Hell Is For Heroes – Guitar)

"My memory of Donington was when Ozzy had to pull out at the last minute 'cos he wasn't feeling too good, but it was probably because ot was cold and raining and he didn't feel like getting out of bed.
It was an anti climactic end to the festival where the headliner had pulled out, it was miserable weather and everyone was feeling down. Tool took to the stage as the replacement headliner and I managed to blag myself to the side of the stage and it made up for everything as it was an amazing gig that I will never forget"

Justin Schlosberg (Hell Is For Heroes – Vocals)

"Our Donington started the day before with sound check. Since we were first
on the main stage, we got to sound check after Ozzys guys. BLS were there
too. It was great to get an idea of the stage and sort our sound out the
day before.
We were the first band on the main stage that day and there were 43,000
people through the gate when we came one...it was a big crowd! In his usual
quest to push the boundaries of decency, A. Product came on dressed up as
the Queen Mother...she had recently died...with the hat and everything...the
crowd loved it...then we all followed him on and started our set.
Life is all a valuable learning experience and that day we learnt not to
play a pop set at a metal festival! Our insidiously catchy, hook laden
PopMetal Rock certainly got a reaction, and a number of bottles hurled in
our direction. This incited A. to demand that they throw more but to fill

them with urine too. Fortunately it was still so early in the day that
there was not much urine on hand.
I thought my guitar was wireless, but a problem with it just before we went
on meant I was on a lead. My tech swears he told be I was on a lead, but I
didn't hear it. I was looking at the crowd thinking come on...lets 'ave it!
So at one point in the show when I went to run across the stage to go and
pull an Angus type shape in front of the huge PA stacks, just as I'm really
picking up speed the lead runs out and I get whip lashed back, only by the
grace of god not falling on my arse. 300 or so of the people stood in front
of me let out a massive cheer and raised their arms...I always check now if
I am on a lead or not...that will never happen again...but my one and only
time was at Donington in front of 43,000 people...I shall always remember
Donington fondly for that!
The bottles kept coming and A. kept demanding more and complaining about the lack of urine. One of the bottles was filled with brown shit that looked like soil so A.Product poured it into his mouth (he said after that it was pleasantly actually crumbled up chocolate muffin).
In the accapella section of Arms around the World (our Bohemian Rhapsody) a chant of FUCK OFF started...it was cool though. We aim to make people react and that day the people of Donington did...not necessarily in the way we would have chosen, but oftentimes a hostile crowd will make you dig in that
bit further...after a point you have nothing to lose so you give it all...
so making it a better performance. I have spoken to many people in the

ensuing years who were there and loved it....as I did...it was one of those
you had to be there times in the AntiProduct story!
We were lucky with the weather, it was dry and even a little bit of
sunshine. It got progressively worse throughout the day with torrential
downpours while Cradle of Filth were on stage. The Lost Prophets,
Millencolin and Cradle of Filth all got more bottles thrown at them than we
did and there was plenty of urine flowing by then too.
I got to see a bit of System of a Down (one of the best bands in the world
today) before we had to leave for the next Ozzfest show in Ireland, they
were awesome. There was problems with high winds and lighting rigs though
and everyone was cleared off the side of the stage as we were leaving.
All in all an awesome day!"
Clare Pproduct (AntiProduct – Guitar)

"To say I was chuffed when they announced Ozzfest 2002 would be an understatement, having attended the previous event at Milton Keynes Bowl I was sure that it would be well worth attending, and what's more, this time it was going to be held at Donington – perfect.
This had all the makings of being one of the best fests ever held at Donington, fantastic line-up held in the spiritual home of Hard Rock, unfortunately this was nearly all undone by possibly the worst organisation ever witnessed at this venue. Early after entering the arena it was evident that whoever thought up the layout did not have their brain fully engaged, the main stage area was as it had always been, however, the second stage had been placed in the conference centre which was not an ideal location and suffered from poor access and egress. Throughout the day we attempted to get into this area several times but the queues were ridiculous and we only

managed to get in once as Mushroomhead were finishing their set, we started to queue twenty minutes before they came on. What made it worse was that they had placed the rear exit to the main stage in the same location as people were trying to get into second stage, and even worse had placed the toilets beyond the point that these two queues met which meant that there were three lots of people trying to move about and all meeting at the same place creating a huge bottle neck. On one occasion when I was trying to get back to main stage I was caught up in this bottle neck and it became so tightly packed that the weight pushed the surrounding barriers down, this was a relief as someone may have been hurt if these fences had not given way. Security was in plentiful supply in this area but all stood around seemingly clueless as to how to handle the situation.   As it was virtually impossible to get anywhere without encountering a mass of bodies trying to move in the opposite direction we quickly decided to remain in the main stage area for the rest of the day, this was a shame as there were several bands playing second stage that we really wanted to see.

It also became apparent that the weather would not be as kind to us as it had been on some of the previous MOR's but luckily the showers did not last too long each time until, that is, near the end when it rained constantly. May is not the ideal month to hold an outdoor event.

The line-up was probably the most diverse in the venues history of holding events in this genre, we had Punk, Thrash, Nu-Metal, Black Metal, Pop Metal, Prog Metal, Reggae Metal, in fact, something for everyone plus we had good old dependable Ozzy to finish off the proceedings.

We joined the queue for the now fashionable beer tokens just as Black Label Society came on, Zack and his crew were suitably impressive and churned out their biker metal, Sabbath enthused tunes to an appreciative busy early day crowd. I did not know any of BLS's songs at that point but enjoyed what I heard and saw from my vantage point in the painfully slow queue.

After procuring a pocketful of tokens so as to avoid enduring the queue for the rest of the day, beers in hand we made our way to our old haunt, main stage left to check out Japanese nut jobs, Mad Capsule Markets. Not long into their set we established that this lot were not our cup of tea; however, since it would prove fruitless trying to move elsewhere we stayed put and tolerated whatever they were shrieking about in their native tongue? Whatever it was we were glad when they stopped.

Drowning pool were a welcome relief after the shriek fest of Mad Capsule Markets, I had recently picked up a copy of the 'Pools' debut album, so for the first time in the day could sing/mumble along with the set especially the very familiar (as in sticks in your head for days) 'Bodies'. I do not think the other three with me knew any of Drowning Pools ditties but they seemed to enjoy them regardless, but then again, they would have probably been happy with a skiffle set by the Chuckle Brothers after MCM's. Millencolin were obviously not as popular or as well known with the crowd when they came on, the crowd thinned along with the atmosphere which was a shame as I thought that they played a nice tight set with plenty of energy. I was back in unknown material territory again and apart from something that had been played constantly on Kerrang! TV, this did not detract from my enjoyment of their set and I vowed to myself to pick up something from them on my next venture into Virgin Megastore.

Most drinks containers had now been banned at festivals, you could usually get bottles of water in but that was it, this of course meant the death of the legendary Donington bottle fights where you would witness a mass of containers in the air that threatened to block out the sun. Bottle/anything else throwable fights continued as they did on this very day but they now looked wimpy in comparison as empty waxed paper cups just do not have the same effect as 2 or even 5 litre bottles. It was rain coat time again during Cradle Of Filth's set, a set that was partially enjoyable and partially shite. Musically COF are a tight, talented set of musicians who unfortunately are fronted by Dani Filth who can not sing for toffee and seems to consider himself a bit of a stand up comedian. The sound they generated was impressively doomy but it is impossible to take them seriously when the front man comes across as about as threatening as an Ewok. Thankfully they did not try to play it too straight with Filth making wise cracks at their expense between each satanically titled track. The bizarre inclusion of people in odd costumes wondering the stage added to visual entertainment but I remained a non-fan after the band exited stage left. We missed Lostprophets set due to the unwise decision to give it another go at the second stage; this again proved a fruitless and frustrating expedition which required some liquid refreshment to get over.

Despite the now frequent downpours, Slayer were never going to disappoint us, it had been at least six years since we last encountered them live so we were expecting to enjoy this. If nothing else, Slayer are consistent, they play their ferociously paced music and there is rarely any talking between songs. On this occasion, not unlike any other time I have witnessed them, they played a couple of tracks from whatever new album they had just released and the rest of the set was made up mostly of classics from 'Reign in Blood', 'Hell Awaits' and 'South of Heaven'. My favourites on this occasion were 'Angel of Death' and 'Raining Blood', hey! What am I saying? These are always my favourites. They came they played, they did not talk to us as usual; but they left the majority of the crowd happy.

I had recently got heavily into 'Toxicity' so was awaiting System Of a Down with eager anticipation but not quite sure what to expect, the other three with me had only heard 'Chop Suey' so were grilling me on what their stuff was like, I could not really give a definite answer so just stuck to weird. Weird was correct but entertaining and brilliant sprang to mind half way through their set. They seemed to play most of 'Toxicity' along with some debut album tracks that I only semi knew but it was all immensely enjoyable. It was obvious that guitarist Daron Malakian was mad as a hat stand as he talked absolute cobblers between songs and calmed the crowd with a rendition of some strange song about raining whilst a technical fault (that cut the set short) was being sorted out. I was quite surprised as I did not recall Serj Tankian actually speaking to the crowd which is odd for a vocalist.

As the early evening drew in the rain continued to annoy us with shower and at one point hail which did not particularly amuse. Of course with rain comes mud and there were plenty of inebriated folks wondering about absolutely covered in it; I suspect that some people deliberately covered themselves in it, maybe to provide some warmth as it was getting colder and colder as night came.

I had enjoyed most of Tool's set at the previous Ozzfest but about half way through I started to get bored as they are a peculiar band to try to watch especially as Maynard had just stood in one spot standing sideways on at the back of the stage. This year I think that they managed to keep my attention for about 10 minutes longer but it was the same type of show as before, Maynard complete with black stripe on face stood still and the video screens showed weird animated images (the same as the music videos to tracks such as 'Schism'). Musically they were as tight as a gnats chuff and I particularly enjoyed the earlier tracks such as 'Stinkfist' and overall I would say that they went down well generally but it is hard to remember because you find that you become drawn in by the weirdness on the video screens and do not notice anything else.

Ozzy came on after another bunch of piss take clips that he had made played on the video screens, I do not remember for sure, but I think that some of them were the same as had been played in '96. Practically as soon as Ozzy hit the stage the rain decided to up the ante and my weather proof rain coat was now deciding that it was not entirely weather proof.

Ozzy was as animated as ever and was running and jumping around the stage as frantically as ever sporting very fetching black Benny hat. I do not remember the set list exactly but it included all of the usual suspects and was enjoyable. Unfortunately when you are getting soaked even the best of shows can become a chore to watch and this was starting to be the case here, I was not too upset when the set came to an end so that we could go and find some shelter for a few minutes before trying to find the taxi we had booked.

In 2002 we decided to take the cosy option and book a B&B, unfortunately the nearest one that we could get at short notice was in Hathern which is approximately 6 miles from Donington Park, not too bad we thought we shall get a taxi back. We took a taxi from the digs to Dony and booked the same driver for the return leg agreeing with him the pick up location and time. After the show we made our way in the rain to the agreed pick up point to find that there was no cab waiting, no problem I thought, I shall ring the firm which I did and was told that he was nearly there. 20 mins passed along with more heavy rain and still no show so I rang again to be told the same thing? By this time we were trying to flag down other cabs to no avail. I believe I rang this firm about 12 times and was bullshitted to on every occasion, at one point I was informed that the driver had been held up because there was an accident at the DHL roundabout, I quickly explained to the chap on the end of the phone that this was not exactly the case as I was standing on the DHL roundabout.

Enough was enough, we were cold and ###### off, it was now nearly 2 hours after Ozzy had finished and we needed to get back to the B&B to recuperate. By this time one of our party had decided that he was going to warm himself up by way of a full work out which included jogging up and down the street and middle of the road push ups and sit ups, I could tell that he had lost it.

After a lengthy stroll to East Midlands airport for some well earned shelter we managed to secure another cab which was a relief, and as a special treat many bewildered holiday makers were subjected to my crazed colleague minus most clothes continuing his exercise regime in the check in area. We vowed never to stay outside of walking distance ever again.

Ozzfest was the final one day festival to be held at Donington and arguably one of the worst festivals in terms of the general organisation. Despite that, we still had a great time and although we had plenty to moan about it leaves you with plenty of memories."

Roger Moore (Glinton, Peterborough)

"Ozzfest 2002 was my first music festival. I went with one of my friends from school and around halfway through the day my friend insisted on seeing a band I'd never heard of and I wanted to see Drowning Pool.
We split up to see the bands we both wanted and agreed to meet up later, as Drowning Pool were my favourite band at the time. They played up to my expectations and the chaos during 'Bodies' was insane when I was 14.
Even though that day I saw System Of A Down, Slayer and Ozzy they were the band of the day for me.
What makes it even more special was that it was Dave Williams's last UK show before he passed away."
Adam Curson (Hinckley)

2003
Iron Maiden, Audioslave

Rising like a metal phoenix from the ashes of the destroyed Monsters Of Rock festivals, Download was a shot in the arm for events at Donington and the start of the successful Download brand. Initially devised as a two day festival, with the option to grow into a three day festival if proving popular, the first year was a great success and so the seeds for developing into a fully fledged festival were starting to be sown, over the two stages.

Headlined by Iron Maiden, making their third headline appearance at Donington on the Saturday and Limp Bizkit on Sunday, all was set for a fantastic start to the new event. However, close to the time of the festival Limp Bizkit, who were huge at the time, dropped out and their slot was filled by Audioslave who were originally the 'special guests'. Metallica had wanted to take the top spot in the absence of Limp Bizkit, but already had a commitment to headline the Reading & Leeds festivals so were not allowed to headline another festival due to the clause in their contract with the Mean Fiddler organisation; Metallica couldn't be stopped though from playing a mid-afternoon 'secret slot' in the tent. Possibly one of the worst kept secrets in the festivals history, the tent was packed with fans and other bands all ready to catch a small, intimate show with the 'Mighty Metallica'

and that's just what they got. From the taped out Metallica logos on all the gear, to the rumours flying around the site, anticipation was high for one of those rare and special festival moments; an 'I was there moment' and every year Download is full of those moments. From seeing small bands developing on a small stage to classic headline
slots by major artists, Download had arrived and it was going to be here to stay.

The mainstage featured a supporting bill which looked like the 'shape of things to come', The Darkness, Evanescence, Funeral For A Friend and Stone Sour all would go on to greater things and greater festival billings, both at Download and elsewhere. The mainstage also featured some Download stalwarts in Marilyn Manson and Deftones.

The second stage was headlined by A on the Saturday, who would come back to the mainstage on 'Ozzfest Day' in 2005 and by NoFx on the Sunday who have never returned; the Sunday bill was filled with punk bands from the 'Deconstruction Tour' but none of them have returned since.

So the festival had laid its roots and would definitely return again, the rock was back at Donington and it was there to stay.

"We were going around Europe doing some promotion for 'St. Anger' and doing some TV shows, Maiden were headlining that year and our booking agent John Jackson had the idea that we should go into Donington 'under the radar' and play in one of the smaller tents in the afternoon; have some fun and do it 'guerrilla style', which we did and it was great idea.
We were on in the middle of the afternoon; we just rolled in and all our crew had been instructed to cover up the Metallica logos on all our equipment.
We went onstage and opened up with 'Blackened' and we played just less than an hour. We played hard and it was fun; the great thing about it was that we were off by about four so I got to do something that we don't get to do very often and that

was to start 'cracking some beers' and hanging out with all the other bands; when you're headlining and you get off stage everybody else had left. So, we had few drinks with some of the road crew and the other bands and a chance to hang out, watch some bands and have some fun.

It was the worst kept secret in England, but it was a lot of fun and it's just great that we still get to do those things and play 'guerrilla style'."

Lars Ulrich (Metallica – Drums)

"It was huge; it was my first festival and we were on the mainstage. It was a very bizarre experience being up there and seeing that many people rocking out and throwing themselves around; it was maybe too much for my little brain to handle!

It all went by in a bit of a blur and I remember losing my favourite Black Flag t-shirt, so I was gutted and very depressed, so I actually went and got really, really drunk. I remember wandering around looking at bands, as you do and going from stage to stage. According to a source, a friend of mine saw me in the back of a transit van (and I'm not sure of how much of this I believe) with a bunch of girls and I was passed out apparently.

For a first festival it was pretty cool. You hear all about Donington and Download and it has such a history and to be a part of that, playing with all these fantastic bands and having such an amazing crowd, it was a great experience. I feel that audiences of aggressive and alternative music are really into it and everyone is so respectful. At the festival you get the feeling that more people are just there to hang out with their friends and get wasted; you get a definite sense of community when you play Download."

Matt Davies (Funeral For A Friend – Vocals)

"Our experiences of playing at Download have always been really good ones. The first time that we played, it was still Donington Monsters Of Rock, in my head and it still is really.

It was not only great to play Download, but the fact that it was Donington and that I had grown up watching those great bands at Donington, it was a really good experience.
It was a little unfortunate for the first two songs that the sound guy had forgot to turn the lead vocals on, or had some difficulty in doing so. Rod Smallwood, who's Iron Maiden's manager and co-manager of Funeral For A Friend, was standing at the desk at the time and I'd just like to say that the services of that sound man were dispensed with, from that very moment. He got his P45; so if Rod is standing at the sound desk, don't fuck it up!
It was Rod who discovered us and hooked us up with Sanctuary Management."
Ryan Richards (Funeral For A Friend – Drums)

"We played Download in 2003; I know this because I have a plaque on my wall at home. They gave us these plaques, in a frame, which was a poster and it said 'Less Than Jake Donington Download Festival 2003' and it's hanging at home, on my wall in my office and I always look at it and think 'wow, that was a really crazy gig'.
It was the first Download Festival and going into it we didn't realise that it was the same place that the original Monsters Of Rock Festival had been. As a kid growing up it was one of the places that you wanted to play and looking at the other bands playing that day, we were 'tripping out' that we were playing the mainstage.
I remember the show being really good, but the thing that stuck out the most to me was going to watch Metallica play on the 2nd stage. I remember going up to the stage and seeing all these road cases that had Metallica 'duct taped' out, so that people didn't know they were there; but everyone knew they were there. I remember I had never seen Metallica live before and to see them in that intimate setting for a band like that, it was pretty intense.
Looking back on it, I would love to do it again; maybe we will get back there at some point to do it. But all the memories that I have of that festival, as blurry as they are were good. I think

that maybe to keep the 'vibe' they should call it the 'Monsters Of Download Festival'."
Peter "JR" Wasilewski (Less Than Jake – Saxophone)

"I remember that we were all excited, Chris was especially excited as he is a huge 'metalhead'.
There were two things that stuck out in my mind one being that it was the first time that I had heard of the Darkness and we had a chance to see them that day and I was blown away; truly blown away. I was staring at their bass player, who they had then, a tall guy with a Japanese flag tied round his head, I was thinking 'what the fuck is this'. But then seeing the response that they got from the people blew me away, because people were 'feeling it'. They put on a great show and I remember leaving it thinking that they were such a great band. A few weeks later we got back to the United States and started to hear rumblings about this band and they were a bit 'kitschy', a bit Queen inspired and a rock band from the UK; I laughed because Americans didn't know what they were getting, until they got it. My introduction to the Darkness.
The other thing I remember was that Disturbed played also on that day and their backing tapes stopped working after one song. So here they are in front of a massive crowd and literally the sad but true fact was that their set consisted of that one first song and then two acoustic songs after the fact. For me I looked at that and thought:
1) *I'm glad that we don't run tapes*
2) *That if I was playing in front of that many people I would have a back-up of a back-up of a back-up to do that.*

Those were the two main things that I remember the Darkness and the debacle of Disturbed and also Metallica obviously. Just the feel of it, from being a 13 year old knowing about Monsters Of Rock on MTV news and Headbangers Ball, to being there, it's just cool."
Vinnie Fiorello (Less Than Jake – Drums)

"We were chucked onto the mainstage; at the time we were like 'show us a mainstage and we'll give you a show'. Download was probably one of the scarier ones, not that we were worried, but whether it would go pear shaped and if we would be accepted.
Strangely we always found that we went down well in the Darkness; we went down well with Metallica, the only band we didn't go down well with were Disturbed, but that was because they were a bunch of assholes."
Dan Hawkins (The Darkness – Guitar)

"That was the last tour we ever did, it was on the Iron Maiden tour.
Playing Donington was something I think we all grew up wanting to do, because of the 'Monsters of Rock'. We'd watched all the 'Headbangers Ball' stuff and for years all these bands we'd grown up on and it was like one day I'd just love to be there and then to actually play it, it's a whole other thing!! Walking up that stairway to the mainstage, it's a big stairway; it just keeps going, keeps going, keeps going! At the side of the stage you get butterfly's going! The crazy thing is it's over before it even starts, because it's a show. You walk out, do it and walk off again. What do you do now, you've just played Donington!
You almost wish something really crazy would've happened, just so that it would live on. Because other than just playing your gig, it's a show. Unless, somebody dies or loses a limb, which I hope is what happens next time, wishful thinking!!
We actually had a guy on stage telling us to hurry up. It happens so fast, it's just another gig, but that one's a special gig".
Wednesday 13 (Murderdolls - Vocals)

"It was cool; we had a good day and a good crowd. I would love to play there again, but I haven't been there since we played.
We were so busy on tour at the time that we didn't get to see many bands as we had to leave.
It was near the end of Reef's run."

Jack Bessant (Reef – Bass)

"When I played here with Mudvayne it was down pouring; it just looked like a heaving pile of mud out there with all those kids. We played in the afternoon on the mainstage and everyone was into it, we were well received, it was a good time to play."
Greg Tribbett (Mudvayne– Guitar)

*"My first Donington experience was way back in '88 at the 'Monsters of Rock' festival, watching the likes of Iron Maiden, Guns 'n' Roses, David Lee Roth and Kiss. Not bad for a first effort. I couldn't believe the size of the festival, even though back then, when there was only one massive stage, and between acts you pretty much had to stand around in the rain, waiting for the next band whilst avoiding plastic containers filled with warm, yellow liquid!!?? It was unforgettable... it was amazing.
I was hooked.
 One day..... I was gonna be up there playing. One day. One day' as it turns out whilst typing this, has been 'three days'. I've been fortunate (lucky!!) enough to play at the Donington Rock / Download festival on three separate occasions. Twice in my first band 'A' and once with Malpractice.
The first time I played it with 'A', we were headlining the second stage, while at the same time Iron Maiden were playing their only UK date of the year on the main stage. We couldn't believe it. On one hand we were chuffed to bits to be playing the gig, but going head to head with Maiden is always going to be a struggle. Especially when you're a massive fan of 'em and you really want to watch them rock! Ah well, no one said it would be easy. And we had a great gig."*
Mark Chapman (A – Guitar)

*"The one that I'm recalling is the one where Marilyn Manson was playing, it was my birthday and our old drummer Carlos quit that day.
It was a great day actually, but I don't remember that much*

about it. I remember we got there early and it was my birthday. I only remember things if they revolve around me!!!
I remember being backstage and the dancers from Marilyn Manson were back there. They walked by and half of there faces were normal and they were gorgeous, gorgeous, gorgeous, beautiful girls in makeshift Nazi uniforms, which was a little weird, but they were still very attractive and then they'd turn around and the other side of their face was grotesque and mangled and I got an even bigger 'boner'. I was turned on by that, I don't know why?
I remember we were a lot heavier...... we all weighed a little more!
It was before we got into transcendental meditation. That was a whole three or four weeks before we got into transcendental meditation. We'd heard all about the multiple orgasm things without the actual ejaculation and that appealed to us on a level that we probably shouldn't really talk about.
I remember it was outside, but we were under something like a tent and we played some songs on our instruments, as a band."
Scott Klopfenstein (Reel Big Fish - Trumpet / Vocals / Guitar)

"I remember we only played it once, I guess they didn't like us?
We may seem happy and wacky, but we are the biggest bunch of assholes that you could ever meet.
I remember there were all metal bands and us, so we didn't really fit in, but we kicked ass!
In fact we are the Iron Maiden of Ska!"
Aaron Barrett (Reel Big Fish - Vocals / Guitar)

"I remember being a little apprehensive about playing the Donington show because it's a legendary Heavy Metal/Hard Rock kinda show and we were going to be these goofballs hanging out! Also, we were going out at the same time as Iron Maiden, so that was pretty daunting and we were afraid that on one would be in the tent we were playing, so we get on stage and the tent was full and everyone was rocking out!

We thought everyone's gonna leave in a minute and go and see Iron Maiden, but they stayed for the whole set and then when we were done they all ran off to see Iron Maiden, it was pretty flattering."
Dan Regan (Reel Big Fish - Trombone)

*"I have some good things about Donington 2004.
That was the day I got to play 3 songs with Metallica in their backstage rehearsal room when Lars couldn't make it."*
Sal Abruscato (Life Of Agony – Drums)

"We did Download in 2003 I had real trouble getting in; I actually had to use the line "I'm playing here this afternoon" to the security! But the gig was fucking great, at the end of the last song you can hear the entire crowd chanting '3-C-R, 3-C-R, 3-C-R' which went on for ages from the Radio 1 recording, real tingle up the spine moments."
Pete Vuckovic (3 Colours Red – Vocals/Bass)

*"The first time we played, we were the first band to play the second stage, on the first day of the festival.
We almost didn't make it because we were playing in Holland the night before and we showed up literally 30 minutes before we were due to go onstage.
I remember being SO excited as it was our first festival ever and I had a look in the tent and there were about five people in there. I thought we'd rushed all this way for nothing and that it was going to be stupid. But, when we walked out on stage, it was an over packed tent and they had to stop letting kids in, our fans there were rabid!
It was definitely one of our best memories."*
Mark Hunter (Chimaira – Vocals)

"I didn't see any of the mainstage bands and I don't know why? I would have loved to have seen Amy Lee and Evanescence and all my gay friends in Less Than Jake. All I can remember was being unable to get on the stage to watch Metallica, some of the rest of the band did, but I didn't."
Michael (Bouncing Souls - Drums)

"I remember watching Metallica. There were rumors going around all morning that they were going to play on the side stage that we were on.
Right before we played it started pouring with rain and everyone ran into our tent which was awesome and great timing."
Pete (Bouncing Souls - Guitar)

"Damn bloody ferry boats! We came into England's Port of Dover around 6:30am after battling the choppy ass English Channel. It's not very easy to sleep when the Ship is at a 10 to 35 degree angle, but I think I got a couple hours.
Upon arrival we all had to get out of our bunks and go through British Immigration. Inside we found the Boy Sets Fire team going through the same ordeal. We all took our turns, showed our passports, and went back out to the bus to get more sleep. When I got up again we were just getting to Donington Speedway. Today the Deconstruction tour is a part of the Download festivals featuring Audioslave, Zwan, Deftones, and about every bad nu-metal band you can mention. The real news is that Metallica is rumored to be playing a surprise show, on our stage!! Thrice's manager Nick said he heard it's true, but I can't quite believe it. Well all doubts were squashed when Chris and I went over to our stage and beheld Metallica's massive backline. Ok, this is really crazy!! Sure, they haven't done anything good in over 10 years, but Metallica used to be my life. Between 1987 and 1991 they shaped my entire musical being. My first concert, first songs on guitar, first bongload....all Metallica. So yea, I'm about to freak!!
Their set to go on at 3:30 giving Chris and I only about a half hour to get back to the bus and get high and tell the others. We did that shit and rushed back to the stage, only to find out that no one could stand backstage to watch the show. I found Rugglie, NoFxs tech and we pushed as close to the front of the stage as we could. At this point no one in the crowd knew who was next, so we got right to the front. We told some kids around us who were sceptical, but within minutes their 18 full

stacks were brought onstage and a wave of metal madness began to overtake the room!

They opened with 'Blackened' into 'No Remorse', into 'Harvester of Sorrow'. Shit got so crazy around me that I went back to the soundboard to get some photos. More classics included 'Sanitarium', 'Creeping Death', and 'Master of Puppets'!! Seriously, I couldn't write a better set list!!

They finished up and I went backstage to find everyone, and maybe meet some of the old bastards. Backstage was pretty much a zoo. Our room was right next to the Murderdolls, which afforded me the privilege of seeing them in their skimpy ass neo-glam stage clothes. Or maybe they always wear that shit. I downed a few beers and went over to watch Thrice rock their set.

The crowd today is unusually calm and unresponsive, or maybe that's the norm for these shows. I had heard this about London, but we've never had this problem with our club shows. Thrice killed it as usual and we were up next. It was strange enough playing on the same stage as Metallica after them, but it was also about the dullest crowd we've ever played to. What a shame, I had such high hopes for today.

We finished out set and I went back to our room to get drunk. By now it was dumping rain so I had to sprint from tent to tent. I met up with Josh from BSF and he helped us finish our bottle of Vodka and scatter some uneaten food around the room. Our room was divided by a heavy cloth that was draped across the middle. At one point Rob started to pull down the cloth, only to have the crazy bozo hawk 'Firestart'n' singer of Prodigy stick his head through. I gotta say that's the last fool I expected to see!

Once the rain had stopped we exited our room and walked right into Lars Ulrich and Rob Truijo who were getting into their van. We said hi since this is probably our only chance to meet these guys. Lars was totally nice, and he hit it off with Chris since they are both huge King Diamond fans. They talked about Merciful Fate and Chris told Lars how he liked the new song he heard them play on MTV icon. He hummed out the guitar melody causing Lars to proclaim" you do that better than Ozzy!!" Ha-ha, pretty cool. We had the guys sign some

stuff and we took a few photos before they were shuttled away to their mega rock super life. Wow, that was crazy!!
We then hit the main stage to watch the day's headliner, Audioslave. Not quite as energetic as Rage was, but an amazing band none the less. Soon I was on the way back to the busses to find the after party in full swing. First we ran into the singer of Mudvayne who told us how much he hates touring. I found Josh and we went over to the Bouncing Souls bus where Fat Mike was in effect. Besides being a great guy, Mike always has the best booze and is very generous. You just can't beat getting wasted with the boss!!
After a bit the party moved outside and I stumbled back to our bus. Downstairs Cappy was giving a girl a backrub and Jordan was making a sandwich. Thrice's TM Nick was outside talking with some girls so I jumped in the conversation. Ahhh... there's something so comforting about a girl with a British accent. This one was really cute so I gave her a big kiss as they started to leave. Gotta keep up international relations right?
The sun was starting to rise and it hit us...we're at a freaking racetrack!! Making the most of the situation we borrowed Cappy's girl's car to take out on a lap. So at 5:30 am Jordan, Nick, Angel, Cappy and myself took this girls early 80s Volvo through the Ferrari garage and right onto the Speedway!! We did a quick lap and snuck back out without anyone noticing!!! Hahahahahhaha, its official it was my craziest rock filled day ever!!!"
Jake Kiley (Strung Out - Guitar)

"We were on the Deconstruction Tour at the time and they combined most of the bands to play at Download. On our stage was NoFX, Boysetsfire, TSOL; but we also had 'special guests' who were Metallica, who played on our stage!
It was insane! Metallica actually played before us, so we got to see them perform eight songs and it we were standing next to their guitars and it was unreal man; but the whole day in general was just really fun.

We got there at nine in the morning, it was just a whirlwind of craziness, there were so many bands playing and all our friends from that tour and we were all just hanging out.
We watched other bands and hung out with other bands; it was a treat just so much fun, it was a blurry day!!
We watched Chris Cornell with Audioslave and Billy Corgan with Zwan and Jordan our drummer had a great time talking to James Hetfield. Awesome, good times!"
Chris Aiken (Strung Out – Bass)

"Well, it was like any other day of a gig for us, grabbed a transit van from a local van rental company and loaded in the gear. You'd never have thought we were playing Donington, a toilet like venue called the Donington Arms more would have been more apt. I mean, how many bands on that day's main stage rolled in all crammed in a Ford Transit?
It summed Stampin' Ground up really, from our humble days of playing back rooms of pubs, to touring with Anthrax and Arch Enemy and headlining our own shows, nothing really changed. I can honestly say the fame and the money never really got the better of us...we were always the underdog of the UK's metal scene.
So, the show. I don't think any of us really let it sink in before we played. We set up and played just like always, just that 30,000+ metal fans we're waiting for us. Myself and the guys actually laughed at each other as our intro tape rolled, Adam our singer even said, how the hell did we get here? It was more disbelief than pre gig nerves. Were we honoured to be able to play that day? HELL YEAH, but we deserved it; it's along road to get there."
Scott Atkins (Stampin' Ground – Guitar)

"The day Metallica opened for us."
Jack Grisham (T.S.O.L. – Vocals)

"We opened up the main stage and played to about 20,000 people. It was pretty early and extremely hot and I was pretty hung-over, since we'd been partying and camping at the festival the night before. It was a good show for us too.

My main memory though was the fact that Metallica were doing a secret show the same afternoon in the tent. The buzz had started to go round by the time we were on stage and it was a bit of: is it true? Is it really Metallica? Within the crowd. And then towards the end of our set Frank announced to the crowd, all excited, that yes it was indeed true...Megadeth were playing in the tent! There was a sort of muted grumble of disappointment from the crowd. I fucking pissed myself laughing!
I checked out the Metallica gig later though, pretty cool to see them open with Blackened!"
Gareth Smith (Raging Speedhorn – Guitar)

"It was a big backstage area, loads of band mincing around and we just went into stupid drunk mode and it was a drinking contest.
Download backstage gay! They had masseurs it's hardly rock 'n' roll!!"
Alex Copeland (Spunge – Vocals)

"As we turned up we actually found the controls for the lights, by the bridge. All the other bands were asleep in the buses and we doing the green for go and had people running under the bridge as we did the stop and start lights on it.
We took the sunroof off the coach and turned the music up and we were dancing on top of the coach."
Damon 'Des' Robins (Spunge – Guitar)

They also had a tent, showing off all the amps and stuff for the weekend, we actually took over the tent for the whole weekend. We were actually told to turn it down by both Iron Maiden and Metallica's people, how cool is that? Someone came along from their entourage on both days, we'd played 4 ½ gigs before we'd even taken to the stage.
Chris 'Jarvis' Murphy (Spunge – Bass)

"The best part of Download was not the gig or the music, but the fact we parked up in the racing pits and a bloke came and

got us in a transit and we blagged him to take us around the track in his transit. It was an absolute fuckin' bargain.

I went to go to the loo in the portakabin bollocks you get backstage and I was in there and the biggest scariest black bloke in the world came in and said "Could you please leave the toilets" and said that I was half way through, it was because matey boy from Metallica wants to come in!!! How gay is that?

Although you got passes and could only go into your own bit, we were in the working class tent, I walked straight down to the posh end, whilst Iron Maiden were playing and I must admit they were really shit. I walked straight past all the security and was actually stood behind all the barriers with the photographers, but they wouldn't let me out, what kind of security is that? But what I do remember was that he had on the 'biggest whitest gayest' Hi Techs ever."

Wol Gurney (Spunge - Guitar)

"We were sponsored by Scuzz (on the Scuzz stage) and the hospitality backstage was fantastic, there was free food and free beer. Then they were like you're giving out free beer to everyone and free food and you're scaring everyone.

Jem King (Spunge – Drums)

"We play after the special guests of the festival who are not listed on the
bill. We don¹t know who it is and we couldn¹t care less but we wonder why
there are about 7563 Marshall stacks placed on stage and all of them got the
name METALLICA written on em..... Nevermind...

After this band called Metallica finished their set promoting their new album called ST. Anger or whatever, their roadies start to empty the stage and take away the 7563 Marshall stacks and another 35 bass drums, 17 cymbals, 35 toms and 53 bass cabinets.

We set up four amps of ours and a drum kit and start one of the heaviest and most emotional concerts of our entire life in front of 26 people who surrendered the Metallica show.

Finally we end up doing our encore in front of 2000 people who made their way back from the hospital just in time to hear us play LET ME IN and some more of our favourite tunes. Thank you Donington, Thank you Metallica...
Heavy metal is the law!"
Beatsteaks

"When we played Download we'd only just hit the UK charts a few months prior, with 'I Wish I Was A Girl' charting at number 25. The singer and I were only 18 at the time, so to be playing Download festival was incredible. We played the 'Scuzz' Stage, playing after Chimaira (who opened the stage that day), and Arch Enemy.
I was a big fan of both bands at the time, and that was the first intimidating experience – going on after two 'Real' bands! I remember we all felt so nervous we could have been sick, and the wait at the side of the stage was absolutely horrible.
We went onstage, got bottles of piss thrown at us by the dregs left behind from Arch Enemy, and launched into our first song. The crowd were a bit unsure on dancing at this point, but we had a lot of fans in the audience and all it took was for our singer, Rodney, to ask them to go mad, and they did.
Personally speaking, onstage at Download 2003 was the best moment in my life. Nothing has come close to the feeling of being watching by thousands of people, and hearing those numbers of people singing along to your songs is unreal.
I made sure I caught the bands we toured with prior to the festival, so I hung out with and watched 'A' and Instruction. One of the weirdest things was finishing playing and having Taproot wander up to us and saying 'hey, they really liked you guys! You're playing with us in a few days so we thought we'd check you out!' It was unreal.
I got to meet our label mates in Deftones and Zwan (Billy Corgan being a personal hero of mine, though he was without a doubt the nastiest musician I've ever had the misfortune of meeting), and got autographs of Chris Cornell, Tom Morello, Lars Ulrich, Casy Chaos, David Draiman and a few others for my girlfriend who only came for the day we played.

We discovered on our arrival of the second day that AAA passes were only given to people playing on the day they were playing, so I used my imagination and rubbed off the marker pen that had the date of the AAA on it, and quickly scribbled in the second day's date in my best 'other person' handwriting, and it worked.

Being interviewed by Scuzz TV during the build-up and excitement of the 'mystery' band was cool. Rodney said to me 'oh my god!' excitedly, as the amps were brought onto the stage, 'look, it was a 'M' on them!' I said 'whoa, it can't be?' and he said 'yeah! It's Mudvayne!' We found out a few minutes before they went onstage it was Metallica playing, and we all had to vacate the area, swiftly. They arrived by helicopter and then got a golf cart to drive them to the Scuzz stage where they played.

All in all, it was absolutely amazing. Any young band wanting to play Download on a stage bigger than the smallest one - just write a song that will hit the charts and you'll get to play a metal festival with your heroes! It's worth it."

Tom Steenvoorden (Violent Delight – Guitar)

"The way that we booked 'Monsters' it didn't actually have the capability to move on; we were still booking big headliners and we hadn't grown it out into a festival, it was still a one day concert. It had got to the point where many of those big headliners could instead go out and play their own stadium shows, so Monsters really ran its course, primarily because we didn't develop it. If we had, I think we would still have been at Donington running a thing called Monsters of Rock still. However, we didn't and in 1996 the last Monsters was held with Kiss; then in 2001 we had Stereophonics with 'A Day At The Races' and then in 2002 we did Ozzfest. We did Ozzfest and what became clear to me was that it wasn't going to be the success that Monsters of Rock was, a) I wasn't sure how many years Ozzy would still be on the road and b) Ozzfests focus was America and it wasn't always going to be able to come to Donington. So we decided that we needed to create a 'modern day ' Monsters of Rock, but that we would use the

Monsters Of Rock still as a heritage brand, hence the Monsters of Rock at Milton Keynes and a few MOR tours. So, we decided that Monsters & Ozzfest weren't the way forward and we sat down to create what we thought a modern day UK rock festival should be. Donington was the obvious place to do it, the spiritual home of rock. We agonised for days, weeks and months on what to call it and eventually I think that it was my assistant who came up with the name 'Download' and the Download Festival was born."
Stuart Galbraith (ex – Donington Organiser)

"I got quite interested in new music again. I decided that I'd go see Audioslave next time they were in the UK."
And that was when I heard of Download. Audioslave got announced - I didn't fancy going and camping, Donington was close enough to get there and back. I bought some tickets and took my best friends 14 year old son to his first ever festival (having taken him to his first ever gig - Rammstein - a month earlier).
Though the gap between '96 & '03 was less than that between '88 & '96, Donington had achieved its "spiritual home of rock" status by now.
Walking through the day ticket gate, I had my strongest ever "Donington" moment standing at the top of the hill as Raging Speedhorn did their thing.
My '96 experience had prepared me for differences in layout and we had a quick explore over the site. A trip to the second stage was brief, but there wasn't anything on that I fancied as it was a punk themed stage that day... though I didn't notice an out of place Apocalyptica on the lineup.
I'd heard rumours - some about Metallica, some about Megadeth, some about Iron Maiden - playing a secret set. I paid the rumours no notice and went to pick out a nice spot in front of the main stage.
The Darkness seemed silly. Disturbed had a microphone malfunction. Stone Sour, Mudvayne and Evanescence were entertaining until someone nearby said "I've just seen Metallica". Sick as a dog.

I got over it though. I was interested to see Flint - being a Prodigy and Pitchshifter fan - even if it was strange to see such a short-lived solo project so high up on the bill.

Zwan were next, and the heavens opened. I mean REALLY opened - scattering the crowd, who pulled up the matting walkways to shelter underneath. These weren't much help, so we got up to the exhibition centre, which was being used as a chill out zone, and dried off. I was all for going home if it didn't clear up - but it did, just in time for the end of Zwan.

So I got to see Audioslave - a short set for a "headliner", but then Limp Bizkit had pulled out only a week or so before, and not replaced (other than the Metallica thing). An enjoyable return, but I wasn't going to miss out on anything like that again. So in January, when Linkin Park & Metallica were announced for the following year, I signed up for the message boards.

As it turns out, that was quite a momentous decision.

The message boards have stretched the festival experience out to five months (or even year round for a number of people) and made Donington the social event where - in addition to a great rock festival - you catch up with all your mates in one go whom you only see sporadically throughout the year. For the Download Message board regular, it's the biggest party of the year and makes the festival the biggest event in your lives. It certainly has for me.

Somehow I managed to run up a high post count in that first year, and that somehow propelled me onto the moderation team. Nothing more than a handful of volunteers who could lock and delete rogue threads. There was no real interaction between Live Nation (still part of Clear Channel at the time) and the mod team, any communication that there was, was between Steve Jenner of Virtual Festivals who was looking after the boards at the time.

By the time of the festival there was a core bunch of people who had met on the boards and it was great to meet people from the forums, share a beer with them. It was no longer the solo event it had been, when the only people you knew were the people you arrived with."

Phil Hull (Download Forum Administrator)

"Donington was my first festival experience, at the very first Download in 2003.
At the time, my favourite band, as an 18 year old teeny bopper, was Limp Bizkit, who were down to headline. They had sold it to me, but so many of my favourite acts were playing: Iron Maiden, Raging Speedhorn and Soilwork to name but a few. Despite Bizkit cancelling, I knew on the train down from Glasgow this was going to be one hell of a weekend- I had finished Uni that morning, jumped straight down on the train with one of my mates and arrived at the now "hallowed turf" of Donington to witness something special. The weekend that came and went blew away all expectations, and I have returned to the festival in 2004, 2005, 2006, 2007 and in 2009, along with a trip to Germany's Rock am Ring festival in 2005 and 2008.
Each year as the headliners get announced, and the anticipation grows in my group of friends who come down annually (this has grown from one in 2003 to over 20 who I meet from all over the UK, some of whom its the only time I get to see them) and we start to buy our tickets, food, camping gear and most importantly, our booze.
The routine is always the same, some come down Tuesday and sleep in the car park (myself included, twice) some arrive on the flight down from Glasgow Wednesday morning (and fly over the arena, and say it's then that the hair stands up on your neck) right up until the festival starts on Friday, the mobile rings, you find their tent and you're sharing a beer with friends new and old, chatting to strangers like you've grown up beside them, and nodding along to the cd player 20 yards away, or yelling out whatever that years campsite chant is.
To me, the campsite experience is almost as big as the actual music itself. My Wednesday and Thursday nights I especially love exploring, sharing out beer and playing "the chair game" which I will now explain, as I did to Corey Taylor who wished he could come play it with us...
It involves a marker pen and a camping chair, and finding some of Downloads more attractive females, and asking if

they would like to sign our Ladies Chair, in exchange for signing T or A. It's proved a fun, popular game these past 2 years and in fact the only guy to sign our chair was Corey himself. We did not get to sign his boobs, or his ass.

Musically, I have seen some of my favourite bands, I've seen some great bands, some not so great bands, and had some special moments, so many in fact its hard to define a favourite. Metallica in a tent is up there. Metallica minus Lars is up there. Prodigy and Korn "on the edges of" the tent are up there. I've discovered some bands I never knew of and become fans of them at Download....Bullet for my Valentine, Sylosis and Enter Shikari for example.

When I look back from the moshpit at just how many people are here for a genre that is considered an outsider, I feel pride at what we as a community achieve each year by attending and being part of an event on this scale.

To sum up what Donington has become for me, it's a place of escapism, of relaxation and of friendship; it defines the 'Spirit of Metal' to me.

In the past, I have came down to the East Midlands out of "festival time" for a couple of gigs, and I have made the trip on the journey to the airport to where the festival is, to have lunch and a beer in one of the local pubs, to visit the festival site, and see it during "down time" and even then, you feel that this is indeed a special place.

A cold December morning and a mild October afternoon I've spent in the village, a quiet place that becomes home to 80,000 like minded, friendly people for just one short week a year.

To me, Download is my home away from home, and long may it continue to be the 'Ground Zero of Metal' worldwide."

Kevin Kerr (Glasgow)

"I can remember driving down the M1 being really excited about going to this new rock festival at Donington Park when on the way a friend of mine called and said there's rumour on the internet that "Metallica" would be playing a secret set on the second stage on Sunday afternoon.

At first me and my mate Nathan were like "no way that's a load of bullshite", but as the weekend carried on we kept hearing the same rumour and eventually we decided to miss a load of great bands early Sunday to get to the front barrier of the second stage in anticipation...
Then I can remember it like it was yesterday, it was mid afternoon and "Eighties Matchbox B-Line Disaster" had just finished their set, their roadies were removing the gear and one accidentally caught the backdrop curtain which in turn exposed the corner of a wall of guitar amps with the Metallica "M" logo on them.
I couldn't believe it the rumours were true and I was smack bang in the middle, at the front holding on to the barrier...
Soon after the intro to "Blackened" kicked in and I witnessed the greatest gig of my life.
At the end of the set I managed to get one of James Hetfields guitar picks which proudly hangs on my wall with a picture I had taken during the show.
Its was my first time seeing them live and no matter how many times I've seen them since the "Download Festival 2003" gig will always be the very best. Thank you DONINGTON!!!
Ash Winter (Shirebrook)

"Back in 2003 I remember setting on a bus reading Kerrang! and noticed a festival, "Download Festival", noticed the date, it was that day, well the camp site was opening
Realising I had some cash saved for something or another, I decided sod it and when I got off the bus I ran to Rock City(Nottingham) as it was listed as an outlet. Bought my ticket there, as a trial as it was my 1st ever festival I didn't get camping as it was too close to the date so they weren't selling them at Rock City and I had the best weekend of my life.
At the end of it I made promise to myself "I will come to this festival every year until it dies or I die which ever came 1st".
As in my promise I have been every year without fail. The minute the dates get announced every year I book the time off work. Now I camp which can only be described as fucking mayhem you see the funniest/random/scariest things you will only ever see at Donington I love the festival so

much I don't even go for the bands anymore; I go for the atmosphere and the people, the bands are just a bonus! Over the years I've made so many long term friends at Download/Downloads online message board; if it wasn't for this amazing festival I wouldn't know 70% of my close friends.
Over the years the festival has improved and it never fails to impress me and I will continue my loyal ness and be attending every year.
One last thing; thank you for taking over my life 7 years ago Download you give something to look forward to every year!!!"
Adam Walker (Nottingham)

2004
Linkin Park, Metallica

Returning again in 2004, as a two day festival, with another stellar line-up and two solid headliners in the shape of Linkin Park and Metallica, Download was already now synonymous with Donington.

Metallica were making their 2nd headline appearance at Donington Park, they would be back again in 2006 for a hat-trick and Linkin Park would be back in 2007 for their 2nd headline slot.

The most controversial occurrence of the festival was the non appearance of Metallica's drummer Lars Ulrich who had suffered a panic attack on the plane on the way to Donington and had been hospitalised in a Berlin hospital; the drum stool duties were covered by Slayer's Dave Lombardo, Slipknot's Joey Jordison and Metallica's drum tech, who all saved the headline performance from the brink of disaster.

Elsewhere on the mainstage Sum 41 and Korn (returning to Donington after 8 years) filled the special guest slots and Slayer and Machine Head also made their return to the hallowed grounds of Donington Park. Sadly Damageplan made their only Download appearance, with their career cut short on December 8th of the same year by the murder of their guitarist (ex-Pantera guitarist) Dimebag Darryl Abbott.

The second stage featured headline turns from Pennywise and HIM; HIM would return in 2005 on the mainstage and
returning again to headline the second stage in 2008. The ever entertaining Bowling For Soup made their first Donington appearance on the same stage playing as 'special guests' on the Sunday.

This year saw the addition of a third stage which featured a majority of bands who have never come back to Donington or have split up since; this stage did however feature performances from the 'new' Bullet For My Valentine and The Black Dahlia Murder.

This year also saw a 'mini Download' in Scotland on Glasgow Green, which featured a selection of 8 bands from the Download line-up plus the addition of Lostprophets; the festival was still headlined by Metallica and Linkin Park.

So Download was now establishing itself as a major player in the festival market and would return the following year bigger and better than ever.

"M.I.A.

Things got a little 'nutty' on that airplane, so I ended up spending our headlining Download appearance in a hospital bed in Hamburg, Germany. I believe that everybody else stepped up and Lombardo, my drum tech and Joey Jordison all saved the day.

It was so weird just lying in this hospital bed with wires and stuff like that, hooked up to a machine. I spoke to James and said 'listen I'm fine, there's nothing wrong, I had a bit of a panic attack; I'm going to get out of this hospital and come over and I will make it' and he said 'you fucking stay there, get some rest and chill out'.

It was the only show I have missed. I was just so bizarre laying in a hospital bed in Germany and it was on the ground floor. I was actually thinking, at one point when I was lying there, of just jumping out of the window and taking off and

hitchhiking down the airport and stealing a plane; Donington or bust!
I have never seen any of the footage or heard any of it because the whole thing obviously left a very surreal taste in my mouth; apart from the fact that it's something I try and compartmentalise as much as possible, I heard that Dave and Joey saved the day and that it all worked out fine. So that day was a big reason to come back in '06."
Lars Ulrich (Metallica – Drums)

"The year we in Sum41 got to play Download was a very special show.
We were just fresh off a week of dodging bullets in Africa and someone told us we had to go play Donington.
I can still remember the camaraderie we had in our eyes before we went on
stage. One of those moments that you have everyday on tour, but this one stuck out in particular, due to our mental states at the time. Looking back it was hilarious as we were all shell shocked little guys going to play a loudass outdoor music festival.
If you've ever been shot at, playing music is one of the best releases especially in front of a crowd like that.
The whole day was filled with good memories as Iggy was there and stopped in to say hello. I believe "Party Boy" from the "Jackass" series punched a member of Electric six through a window. We also had our room raided by the "Suicide Girls Burlesque Tour." Oddly enough all of them were skinny so we offered food and beer to fatten them up. It didn't work as they stayed skinny and talked more 'schupidness raas'.
I love playing festivals as they are always like a one day, 'day camp' filled with some of your friends and favorite musicians. I got to say hello to a very influential set of people on my playing as well. But I missed Arch Enemy's set due to our set starting five minutes after theirs had.
All in all it was a huge mental victory to get back onstage after a very
enlightening trip to Africa. I'd like to thank all in attendance on

our behalf for making some shell shocked Canadians feel welcome."
Dave "Brownsound" Baksh (Sum 41 – Guitar)

"I played with Damageplan, it was awesome and there was a lot of love."
Bob Zilla (Damageplan – Bass)

"The Download Festival to me is a pretty big deal, because I always knew about Donington and Monsters of Rock, growing up as a metal fan and a metal kid.
The first time that we were booked to play the Download Festival I didn't realise that it was the same thing and that it was at Donington.
So our first experience of playing there was pretty amazing because I got to meet Tracii Guns and Nikki Sixx and all these guys that I had grown up listening to.
We played the side and weren't really sure how it was going to go as we aren't a metal band, so we were a little concerned as to how people were going to respond.
It was really good, but we were a little too drunk to play at our first experience of Download, actually a lot drunk.
We were pretty awful; Eric threw up on stage."
Jaret Reddick (Bowling For Soup – Vocals/Guitar)

"The first time that we got to play Download, it was going to be the 'big deal' for us, as we were going to be playing with bands that we all loved, like Slayer.
I'm a 'metal head', so I was freaking out at the metal line up. It was Castle Donington, the Monsters Of Rock; it was one of the biggest rock festivals in the world and I had been reading about this thing in magazines since I was a kid, so it was a big deal.
I got way too loaded, all of us did and our show was 'so terrible', we played like shit, complete shit!
But, the beauty of it was that we were funny and we do have personality and that's our saving grace. Apparently a band like us, in a metal festival, is comic relief, we're the entertainers.

I tried to get someone from Kerrang! to get photos of me being punched in the face by someone from Slayer. I was really drunk and they are my favourite band and I just thought that it would be cool to get one of them to punch me in the face."
Chris Burney (Bowling For Soup – Guitar)

"The first time played At Download, we were the next top last band on the second stage, and HIM played after us, so we were in-between Slayer and HIM.
Kerry King during his set uttered the words,
"I can't believe that we're opening for Bowling For Soup!"
It was great for us .He was taking the piss out of us, but we loved it, Kerry King said our name!
We showed up at about 10am and everyone started drinking, we weren't on until 8pm!!!
We arrived on stage too drunk to play and it was awful, we walked onto the stage with our heads hanging, and in a miserable state. We all knew we had just blew a great opportunity. We got back to the States and the emails and reviews of the shows started coming in and everyone said 'we had such a great time', when you guys played 'it was wonderful, it was so awesome' and our review in Kerrang! gave us three K's.
It was like 'did you guys see the same show that we played?' Because, we played absolutely awful!!! Even our manager at the side of the stage saw us come off and he had the 'I know how you feel face' as we all walked off with our tales between our legs. Then the response to it was absolutely amazing!!! Chris' big deal the whole day, was that he wanted Kerry King to punch him in the face, 'I want him to punch me in the face'. We met them after everyone had done playing and we were speaking to them and Chris was upset because he couldn't get anyone else from Slayer to punch him in the face!
Erik Chandler (Bowling For Soup – Bass)

"We had gotten into town a day early and done a warm up show. We stayed up drinking after until seven in the morning, we're idiots!
We got to Download and we had press starting at 8:30am, so

we were all still hung-over and smashed at the same time. We rolled out of bed, brushed our teeth and someone handed us a beer and we started drinking again. When we got there we did think 'what the hell are we doing in this mix'? It was like a peanut butter, jelly and prawn sandwich something doesn't fit. The bad news was we didn't play until 9pm, so we just continued drinking all day!

I don't think any of us remember being on stage, but there were photos of us on stage, so I'm sure that we were. But, when we got offstage we were blown away by this HUGE festival that we'd just played, but all kinda pissed off 'cause we knew that we'd sucked and probably had one of the worst shows we'd ever played.

We were really worried about how it went over, but we ended up getting really good press from it! The way they spun it was it's this heavy festival and everyone is pissed off and here come these 'drunk ass fat dudes from Texas' who'd rather tell jokes than play songs and they all got some comedic relief from it!

Our sound guy said that he didn't do anything with the sound after the first song because he couldn't make us sound any better, we just sucked.

We went and watched Slipknot from the pit and all the kids who were coming through were asking for our autographs, so we had to get out of there, because the security said we were going to cause a riot.

That night we were playing a dice game on the bus and Dimebag Darrell came by and played and then later we were in the parking lot playing folk songs with HIM.

Jared fell down and hurt his head, his wife wasn't too pleased about that!"

Gary Wiseman (Bowling For Soup - Drums)

"I remember mostly just getting there and us being the first on; seeing people funnel in from the gate. A friend of mine brought a digital camera with a time-lapse function and every 3 seconds it would take a shot of this funnel of people coming in, running. We were setting up and we went away for a bit, then we came back and there were about 30,000 people!

It's always a little weird playing early in the day, but the experience is overwhelming to say the least. Obviously what we were doing was just going by so fast and evaporating, bands like Air sound great outside, bands like us sound like trash; so it ends up being like 'high energy' but 'low accuracy'. I remember watching Opeth after us and it was the same kind of thing 'what is this band doing playing in the day?' It just seems so weird.
We hung out that day and I got a haircut. Bed Head had a booth and my hair was a mess and they were offering anyone free haircuts, so I said ok and sat there and got a haircut. I remember hanging out and having a joint with the Opeth dudes.
I also remember taking a disgusting shower backstage. There was also a big press area and I remember spending a lot of time there doing interviews."
Liam Wilson (The Dillinger Escape Plan – Bass)

"I have some good things about Donington 2004. That was the day I got to play 3 songs with Metallica in their backstage rehearsal room when Lars couldn't make it."
Sal Abruscato (Life Of Agony – Drums)

"Donington Park rocks! The first time we were on the Barfly stage and we were an unsigned act; that was the scariest time."
Michael 'Moose' Thomas (Bullet For My Valentine – Drums)

"Every time I have played Donington with the boys, it's been amazing. We've had a really good time and played with some really big bands there. It's a gig that we always used to go to when we were younger and now it's really cool to be able to pay that show.
The first year was the most exciting because we were getting to play 'DONINGTON'!!"
Jason "Jay" James (Bullet For My Valentine – Bass)

"We came over as a very young band. It was the first year that we started touring in 2004 and we were still 'cutting our teeth'; but Download was (and still is) the biggest and grandest scale gig that we have ever done.
We played on the small stage and we came with great expectations as this is THE most famous rock festival."
Trevor Strnad (The Black Dahlia Murder – Vocals)

"Our very first Experience at Download was in 2004, I believe the headliners were Metallica on our day of the weekend.
I had my wife and best friend to share in the event with us as well. Growing up I knew of Donington and the legendary concerts that had preceded my first visit. It was everything I had thought it would be and more, from hanging out in the backstage village with all the bands to watching Slayer destroy the Snickers Stage.
I Have never been more anxious or nervous to play a show, the crowd was immense and the overall attitude of everyone there attending, playing, and working is just a really positive environment.
I think the highlight that year besides just playing and being a part of the line up was probably watching one of my all time favorite bands, Machine Head. Having toured with them a couple months earlier I could tell by the look on there faces that it was one of there greatest moments on stage. They absolutely owned it that day.
Metallica was also without Lars due to an illness I believe, so backstage you could hear a select group of drummers auditioning for certain songs to play with them in there set.
Overall the first Download experience is something I will never forget."
Brock Lindow (36 Crazyfists – Vocals)

"In 2004 it was totally different to 1992, as I hadn't really kept an eye on it at the end of the 90's or into the early 00's, because I was doing the solo stuff and I was spending a lot of time in America.
To get on the bill, I really didn't know what to expect and I didn't even know what it was like and how the whole thing

was. I remember that I was on really, really early and I was really worried that there would be nobody in the tent to see the show, because it wasn't The Almighty but Ricky Warwick. But it was packed and it was great. I think I went on around 12:30pm and did my stuff, which is not metal, my stuff is like Americana country music and I was standing there playing it thinking 'how is this going to go over?'
I had a full band with me, which is great, but I went down really, really well. Everyone was pleased that I didn't play one Almighty song, which in hindsight is a silly thing and maybe I should have thrown one in, but I got a fantastic reaction.
So, both my performances at Donington were totally different things, but both good and satisfying in their own ways; but obviously the first time round with The Almighty was huge and it was our little band that we had started and we were there, playing Donington and it was so unbelieveable as we had dreamed about it as kids."
Ricky Warwick (Ricky Warwick – Vocals/Guitar)

"Well I can remember quite a few from Download....Probably the most major is when our bus broke down for Download of 2004 and we had to miss our slot for mainstage...but Jason Gong of the band Drowning Pool invited us up during their set and we all played the song "Halo" together....and not to mention all the drunken madness we had that time with Dimebag Darrel, Kronos, the Arch Enemy guys, and Slipknot....."
Tim King (Soil – Bass)

"I previously worked for my friends band Akercocke in '04 and that was a really big event for me. The last five years I had been blagging my way in with other bands, 'teching' or driving."
Luca Grandi (Ted Maul – Guitar)

"The first time that I went to Donington was in 2004 when I played with Akercocke. It went really well and I had never played anything nearly as big and it was large tent and it was full as far back as I could see.

The first quarter of an hour before the show, when you are backstage with the equipment just looking at the crowd, because normally I'm used to playing quite small venues, so that was quite nerve wracking.
Then there was one particular bit of a song where I was quite shaky on, but when that was out of the way I really enjoyed myself and it was fantastic."
Casino Brown (Akercocke - Keyboards)

"We actually filmed most of Silvertide' s EPK DVD at Donington/Download Festival which was awesome because I was so drunk that I didn't remember having a good time until I watched the footage.
What I found to be very hip about the Donington/Download Festival were the backstage arrangements. All of the dressing rooms were in small groups facing a common area which was great because I got to hang out with Nikki Sixx and many other musicians for hours before and after Silvertide played. The concert setting itself feels more like a community of people getting together to have an incredible time regardless of who their favorite band is and the crowd at Donington is the best group of people I've ever hung out and got drunk with. To this day I still keep in contact with friends that I met in the audience, and backstage. I can't say enough about how much of a great time that I had at Download and my only regret is that I haven't invented a way to teleport that crowd to my side of the pond."
Walt Lafty (Silvertide – Vocals)

"Well it was the summer of 2004 - I think! - And a few planes, trains, and SPLITTER VANS later, Silvertide arrived in Donington.
It was hot, there were beautiful girls for miles, and enough rockers crammed into a small outdoor backstage area to raise suspicion... yep it was the Download festival!
I remember that time specifically because we were filming our EPK, and had cameras on us at all times - lucky for them - there was plenty to shoot :) We shared a dressing room with The Brides of Destruction, which was great and really

important, actually. Not knowing it then, I guess we planted some pretty good seeds with Nikki, because a year later we were opening for the reunited Motley Crue.
I know we played under some sort of tent packed with wild and sweaty Rock N' Roll fans - who gave us more love than we ever could have hoped for. It was magic. Filled with topless chicks and fist pounding dudes, that place was fucking lit up. It sounded great, felt electric, and reeked of beer... the way any good rock show should!!!"
Nick Perri (Silvertide – Guitar)

"Donington has been a very good festival to us. Our first time at Download was really cool, we opened up the mainstage on the famous year that Metallica kind of played, but didn't!
So we were in the backstage area with Metallica and all these other big bands.
We had a 'mega mega' response, we had a huge turn out of 30-40,000 at 11 o'clock in the morning and it was great because that same week we hit the Top 40 with our single 'The River' and our new album came out, it was a culmination of that whole era of Breed 77.
There is a huge sense of occasion with Donington always; it is not so much of a festival but an event. It's steeped in history we always think of Monsters Of Rock and I never call it Download, it's Donington! You feel that you are walking in the footsteps of so many famous acts before you. When you do it you have to rise to the occasion and you've got to give more than you usually do.
We managed to get extremely drunk, by 7pm we had been drinking for 7 hours straight and according to police reports everything was kosher and above board."
Paul Isola (Breed 77 – Vocals)

"I played at Donington Festival in 2004 on the Snickers stage with my old
band, Million Dead. My highlight of the day was being able to walk
onstage and announce "It's not Download, it's Donington, and

*it's not Snickers, it's Marathon!"
I remember being a kid and staying up late to listen to Iron Maiden at Donington in 1993 (? I think), so it was an honour to play there.
We met Iggy Pop backstage, flanked by a phalanx of bouncers, apparently because of his ongoing beef with the Hells Angels.
True metal paradise!"*
Frank Turner (Million Dead – Vocals)

*"Being in a band with two ex-metal heads and one Iron Maiden fan, playing Download festival was a pretty big deal to the rest of my band. Playing in front of more than fifty people was a good show for me, so the prospect of playing in front of a few thousand was fairly daunting.
The standard joke of the day was this was Donington, not Download, and one of the stages was the Marathon bowl, not the Snickers bowl. Clearly, we were a hilarious band.
This was my first experience of playing a large festival and the concept of rotating drum risers... "you mean, I get to set up my kit as I want it and you roll it out on stage and it's ready for me to play?.....oh yes...."
For a band that was used to playing punk shows and the hasty change over, this was pure luxury. The idea, too, that Jerome, the man who deals with my Sabian endorsement, was around and I was able to borrow a ride cymbal off him to temporarily replace my broken one (I believe I used Arch Enemy's ride) was just awesome... it was these little things that made the day special and would allow you to imagine, just for a short while, that your band was bigger
than it actually was.
I remember the backstage area being fantastic (and far superior, as I would find out, to any other festivals), with arcade games I could not be bothered to play, a hair dresser for the rock stars and a masseuse (whom I believe Frank, my singer, utilised). There was also the dichotomy of fridges filled with free Carling. It was lots of free beer, but the worst beer ever made by man. Ever. (As a side not, anyone who actually*

orders Carling at a bar out of preference deserves to have their tongue cut out).
The show went very well, the tent was almost packed (we were playing on the second stage at around 3.pm), although I recall checking out reviews on the Radio 1 website where one festival goer had described the tent as empty and us as rubbish, and as I read more and more of his "review" I realised he had mistaken us and the previous band (who's time slot we had swapped with) and was calling us shit because of their performance and them great for ours. It even talked about their female bassist. We had the girl, they were all guys. Nice to know that any one reading that about us would possibly dismiss us
from then on because they'd heard we were shit...great.
The rest of the day was spent drinking with Yourcodenameis: Milo: Milo, praising their tour manager, Stan, for his fantastic handlebar moustache, and laughing at the guys who filmed our video blagging their way past security because they'd "just go in for five minutes to say goodbye to Million Dead and be straight back out" then raped the buffet and walked back out past the distinctly unimpressed security guard with the biggest sandwiches I'd ever seen.
I completely failed to go watch any other bands because, ironically, I hate festivals...great to play but the worst way of watching a band ever. Instead I'm afraid I was very very drunk, and only remember the journey home taking twice as long because our driver was incredibly stoned and was driving at half the speed he usually does.
Safety first."
Ben Dawson (Million Dead – Drums)

"I remember seeing Cradle Of Filth playing in the day, when I didn't think Goths came out, wearing PVC and sweating profusely."
Sean Smith (The Blackout – Vocals)

"We played Download in 2004. Our first album was just out and we were gorging ourselves off the excitement and

anticipation that comes with doing your first festival circuit ever.

We were due to play the Snickers stage on day 2 of the festival and decided to get there a day early to soak up the atmosphere and hopefully, some of Downloads renowned (and rumoured free) hospitality and so that's what we did. We all knew opening a stage on day 2 is a bit of a risky business regardless of what state you might be in. Will the crowd turn out? Will all the gear be working having been thrown about a Splitter van for the last month? Will Paul actually be sick like he claims he will? And will my arse hold out without lapsing into a whiskey induced prolapse before the end of the gig? These were just a few of the things flashing around my mind.

Well they did, it was, Paul didn't and I nearly and it was a great sound and a great show which ended with Paul destroying his flying V. There's a picture somewhere on the net with some lucky guy holding the remains.

It was also incredibly hot that year. Adrian, our tech, sported a skin head which was so burnt by the time Soul Fly had come on the top of his head was actually supplying 30% of the over all heat being radiated from the crowd and putting aeroplanes off course. He didn't mind though as he dowsed the pain with a bottle of Buckfast. Devon's finest.

This was also the year that Metallica played and Lars didn't make it. There were all sorts of rumours floating about as to what had happened to him. He was ill. Customs had got him. Adrian's head heat had forced his plane to land at Glasgow Airport. What ever the reason, we didn't take notice cause we got to sit backstage and watch the stream of other bands drummers marching in and out of the Metallica trailer. It was awesome. In fact I'm surprised there wasn't a massive battle of stick wielding maniacs all vying to play 'Enter Sandman'. Good on them I say. Christ! Its bad enough dealing with one of the fuckers!"

Ian Fairclough (Terra Diablo – Vocals)

"I went to Download with a few of my mates in 2004 and Metallica were playing, but Ulrich was sick or coked up or whatever, so he wasn't there. So they had Joey from Slipknot played a couple tracks and the guy from Slayer, Dave Lombardo, played a couple tracks and that was really cool."

Logan (Sons Of Albion – Vocals)

"For three exhilarating and ground-breaking years between 2004 and 2006, my team and I were contracted to help create and raise a real monster – the online profile and community of Download Festival, the biggest and baddest that had ever rocked the Earth. It was an adventure of epic proportions, packed with stories to tell our grandchildren and lessons we will take to our graves. The rest is history. This is our story...

Whilst most festival promoters would be satisfied with simply having the best rock festival in the UK, Stuart Galbraith and his team wanted their new creation - Download - to go one step beyond that and break new boundaries in digital innovation, a tall order and one that we at Virtual Festivals naturally found tremendously alluring.

By 2003, 99% of festival and concert tickets were being sold online, yet the old-school-dominated live industry was still painfully backward in embracing the digital age. At last here was a major new event we could really work with. We first hit it off with the organisers during the debut event, as they witnessed us beavering away, uploading our online coverage from a little backstage portakabin into the small hours, while our peers were propping up the VIP bar. It was a testament to how seriously they took their online aspirations when they invited us, along with just one other publication (a national newspaper) in to photograph the most anticipated event of that first festival - Metallica's 'secret' appearance in the Snickers Tent.

Then, six months later, the call came in from Clear Channel (now Live Nation) asking for our help in an official capacity to create a powerful online profile and community around the festival. With market-leading case studies under our belts for both Virtual Festivals and, more recently, Glastonbury Festival, this was something we knew we could deliver and we jumped at the opportunity. It was our most exciting challenge yet, as well as our toughest, as Download did already have an online community, albeit one that was very negatively skewed *against the event (and its organisers) doing more harm than good, initially.*

This was common with official festival forums (which is why few events dared have them back then); we're talking long before social networking was a mainstream way of life and these things do need a lot of time and energy invested, especially at the start, in order to bear fruit. I told Clear Channel to give us two weeks to sort it out.

The first step in building rapport digitally (just like in real life) is always to develop a close dialogue with your subjects, in their own language. As with all major festivals, there was a huge culture-shaped fence dividing the organisers (professional company executives required primarily to make the event safe, efficient and profitable) and their customers (who had very different things on their minds). As I've come to see, one of the most thankless things about being a festival organiser is that, the better you do your job, the less it is noticed - the fans will only pick up on your failings.

So it would be no good the organisers trying to make friends online with the fans, any more than it would be for your mum to start messaging your mates on Facebook today. What we needed was a third party who could understand and interface between both sides of the fence. Virtual Festivals was an inspired choice for the 'brain' of this character (If I say so myself) but as John Probyn himself recently stated, we did look like web geeks back then.

We needed a Monster Of Rock, and it turned out that he already existed as a piece of conceptual artwork within the festival's assets. As soon as I saw him, I knew it was time to let the Download Dog out of his kennel.

With his razor-sharp fangs, spike-studded collar, feral glare and pink coat, this guy immediately struck me as the perfect embodiment of rock - wild, aggressive, outspoken, a bit disturbing, funny and camp. Logging-on to the message boards as this character had a similar effect on to putting on The Mask in the Jim Carrie film. The Dog's larger-than-life personality exploded from the keyboard, dousing the forums with an infectious enthusiasm loaded with irreverent attitude (bite), charisma and humour. Anyone who tried to spread negative feeling on the boards got a taste of the Dog's fangs, and boy were they sharp! The fans loved it and in no time, the community was buzzing and the Dog started picking up a loyal, adoring following of his own. Believe me; you wanted to be on this fella's team.

It wasn't just about the banter though - far from it - The Dog had a very important educational role to play too. He took great time to respond to questions and constructive criticism. Vast swathes of Download's audience were won over, for instance, when it was explained to them that the organisers were not withholding artist announcements just to be annoying - there were sensitive contractual issues over which they had no control - and that artist billing orders were most often governed by the evil booking agents, not the promoters. At the end of the day, Download's marauding fans were not a bad bunch. All they'd wanted was for their views to be officially acknowledged. By doing so, replying wherever possible and making them feel like they had some input into the event, these rock kids were putty in the Dog's paws.

We had so much fun with that guy, it was addictive - something we'd look forward to doing each day. As well as responding to posts, the Dog took a proactive role in using his new, fast growing, fanbase to generate newsworthy content. We ran polls and solved some of life's biggest questions such as "What's the greatest guitar solo ever?", "What would the most awesome supergroup of all time consist of?" and, er, "Which celebrity would you most likely to share your tent with?" We even uncovered the cover version that Download fans most wanted Metallica to perform. Then we contacted their management and the band actually played it during their set at Download. Co-incidence or not, The Dog was never more respected. If you're curious, the answers to all these riddles can all still be found in the Download forum archives now.

Aside from fun on the forums we also found the time to populate the content on the official website, establishing a far more compelling, engaging and edgy tone than the characterless 'press release' style of the festival's rivals. We created a page for every act on the line-up, uncovering bizarre and interesting facts about them and involved the artists in the process. I remember sitting on the top deck of the 93 bus once, surrounded by teenagers in Slipknot t-shirts, beaming inside as, unbeknownst to them, I chatted on my mobile to percussionist Chris Fehn (nose) from the band about their upcoming Download appearance.

Another weapon in our armoury was the 'Skinker' desktop alerts application that users could download from the website. Whenever we had something to announce, whether it was a line-up confirmation, a new poll on the forums or just our weekly Friday afternoon joke, the Download Dog would suddenly bound onto the user's desktop, growling as the content pinged-up in a little box! It was cutting edge stuff and Download won several prestigious technology awards for our application of the gizmo. Sadly, Skinkers did not make the final cut in digital's fast moving edit suite, but for a time, you were no-one if you didn't have one and Download remains the first and only music festival that did.

As well as an exciting and fun project, the experience of working for Download was hugely insightful to us. VF was a bedroom-grown operation and I certainly had no formal management or leadership training. So we all, especially me, learned a great deal from our privileged glimpse inside the mechanics of such a big festival. Every fortnight, there would be a Production Meeting at Clear Channel HQ, with all the people responsible for different parts of the event (such as site production, talent booking, PR, marketing, sponsorship, ticketing and my department - online) sitting around a vast boardroom table, reporting in to Stuart Galbraith, who would chair. These could go on for hours at a time, but I always found them absolutely fascinating, both to see how a major festival was put together, and a large organisation managed. It always impressed me how hands-on Stuart was in every minute detail of the operation as he went around the table firing questions from his hand-written notes. Now and again he'd shoot one over to me, and some of the others would roll their eyes, but he always listened intently to every word I said, reinforcing how much he understood and valued the potential of online, which was rare in this industry back then.

If the planning stages were eye-opening, the event itself was off the scale. I had forged a career out of blagging my way backstage over the years, but at last I was given an official All Areas pass. I could legitimately go anywhere, even on the stage. Milk it for England? Would have been a crime not to.

Our main job on-site in that year (2004) was to produce the official coverage of the event, for Download's website. Although I had hundreds of talented, proven writers to call on from VF's barracks, I thought it would nice to involve some kids from Download's forums, real fans for whom the opportunity would really mean something special. Over the preceding months, we had invited creative fans from the message boards ('boardies') to write various editorial preview features and festival survival guides. The best writers were selected for my official festival reviews team (and given backstage passes), and their submissions published in the festival's printed programme. This level of official fan involvement had never been done before and it went a long way in fortifying Download's community. So my little squad would appear intermittently in our backstage portakabin throughout the day, handing over their scrawls on scraps of paper which I would type up and instantly upload to the website giving a running fans' eye commentary of the festival as it unfolded - another first. I know that at least one of these kids has since made a great career as a music journalist; see - the Download Dog made dreams come true.

As the crowds flocked back to their tents for the final time at the end of the 2004 event, Download was well and truly on the map as a major festival, and its online profile was already streets ahead of anything else in the market and picking up awards. Despite an incident where the organisers caught one of VF's photographers partaking in some off-limits 'rock n' roll' in our portakabin (oops), we were praised for our good work and retained to do it all over again the following year. In the big post-event debrief meeting back at Clear Channel towers, the value of the festival's online following was asserted in no uncertain terms when I produced a report I had compiled from comprehensive feedback posted by festival-goers on the boards. Stuart then referenced this document as the basis for the majority of the discussion, ensuring that the fans' wishes were at the forefront of the improvements made the following year. This process would, in later years, expand into an informal physical meeting between the senior promoters and groups of boardies to discuss face-to-face.

It was a monstrous lesson in pulling triumph from the jaws of disaster. The festival's organisers faced a worst case scenario when it transpired that the headliner's drummer, Lars Ulrich, was not 'well' enough to perform. It was too short notice to draft in a replacement act and how do you tell 75,000 rampant rock kids that the band they paid £100 to come and see wouldn't be playing? The backstage compound was a place of panic that day, to say the least.

Metallica then stepped up and proved why they're the biggest hard rock band in the world and, rather than pulling the show and wasting the fans' money, they delivered the most unique, thrilling and historic gig of their career to date. It involved drafting in a revolving cast of guest drummers from other bands on the day's bill, like Slipknot and Slayer.

From my vantage point, illegally stowed between some flight cases on the stage (long story), seeing the awe-struck faces of the crowd in front of me, the band at the side of me clearly enjoying this exciting break from their usual tight routine and the utter sense of relief on the faces of the organisers behind me (who had feared a riot) is indelibly etched on my memory as one of the most amazing experiences of my life.

The most poignant moment of all for me was at the end of the gig, seeing Slipknot's Joey Jordison (who had proven the best and most frequently used replacement of the night) run down the stairs at the back of the stage into the waiting arms of his un-masked bandmates who all hugged him, beaming with pride, Corey Taylor proclaiming: "You just made rock history dude!". I think I had a little tear!"

Steve Jenner (Founder of Virtual Festivals.com & UK Festival Awards)

"This was the year that "VIP camping" (later to be named R.I.P. - Rest In Peace) was launched, and I decided to go this route. Arriving at site, checking in and being handed a goodie bag with t-shirt, program and a few other bits & pieces was a nice way to get setup. Tent up, we managed to meet up with a couple of people we'd met from the boards. Download was still a two day festival at this point (though this was the first time a third stage had been introduced) so as it was the Friday it was a case of settle in, have a few beers and get ready for the music.

The VIP route in was through the paddocks (exciting to see all the tour busses parked up here), through a tunnel and then out into the arena from behind the second stage.

Memorable bands - Iggy Pop and the stage invasion. The sight of 200 of the crowd vaulting over the barriers and then dancing & head banging on the stage. One guy even 'airguitared' his way in front of the speakers/screens, no doubt a lifelong ambition realised.

On the Sunday it was the 60th Anniversary of D-Day and Breed 77 were the only British band on the bill (Their home, Gibraltar being a British Colony). Knowing Breed 77, we'd mentioned this to them a couple of weeks earlier and they acknowledged the date by using a Winston Churchill speech as their intro. This had the impact on me and my girlfriend Carrie of being the first time someone we knew playing the stage, and one of our suggestions making a dent on the events of the festival.

Slayer missed their slot (apparently the band were there but their crew and equipment had got lost!), having to play later on the second stage and bumping Damageplan to the mainstage. Not many people knew who Damageplan were, but when vocalist Pat Lachmann drawled "We've seen the backpacks, the Pantera shirts out there. We're gonna put this one to bed right here..." Dimebags guitar shrilled out the riff to 'Walk' and an arena full of sunbathers woke up and rushed the front. Six months later it became a very poignant performance...

The main thing I remember is being hypnotised by Slipknot (the first time I had seen them) and having such a good time that after Korn had played I only realised that Metallica were late on about 30 minutes after they were due on.

About this time people started worrying - Metallica weren't

known to be late starters - and James shuffled on stage about 30 minutes later to inform us that Metallica would be a 3 piece that evening. Some were gutted to not be seeing a full Metallica show, but I enjoyed the piece of rock history we were given. It was quite something to see Joey Jordison in full Slipknot gear give Lars a run for his money."
Phil Hull (Download Forum Administrator)

2005 Feeder, Black Sabbath, System of a Down

Now expanded to a 3 day festival and featuring 'Ozzfest day' as part of the line-up on the Saturday, Download was steadily growing year by year.

The Download Fan Forum was now very much an integral part of the festival set up and organisers Live Nation were very happy to listen to the moans and groans of the online community and take notice of their concerns; line-up suggestions and recommendations were also listened to by the organisers.

Friday on the mainstage was unlike any other Download day before and since and featured several indie bands including JJ72, The Others, Garbage and headliners Feeder. Friday night on the 2nd stage saw a very busy headline set by Billy Idol, with a lot of the mainstage crowd packing out the tent. Other bands on the 2nd stage included My Chemical Romance, The Used and a pre-Eurovision win Lordi from Finland, who would return two years later.

Saturday was 'Ozzfest Day', headlined by Black Sabbath with amazing supporting bill, including the re-formed classic line-up of Anthrax with Joey Belladonna back on vocal duties, a return by Bowling For Soup & HIM, Velvet Revolver in the 'special guest' slot and the Donington debut at 11am by a little known band, at the time, Trivium. The second stage saw the Swedish sensations In Flames closing the day with a supporting cast of up and coming metal bands Chimaira, Lamb Of God, Unearth and Bullet For My Valentine.

The third day featured a record breaking attempt at performing a set whilst suspended from the ceiling of the stage with hooks through his back by Matt Zane of Society 1, which was one of the most photographed sets of the day.

System Of A Down closed the festival with an amazing and so far only UK festival headline appearance. Third on the bill was Slipknot who would be back for their first headline appearance in 2009.

Motorhead were the headliners on the second stage and Lemmy also came on for one song with MC5 who played just before them.

Therapy? headlined the third stage, making their return to Donington and their first appearance at Download.

Another successful year and the last time that the 'indie day' took place, but it was the third year and the festival was developing all the time and getting better each year.

"Seattle is a long, long way away from here and you knew about Donington. We had Mattel Hot Wheels [model cars] and one of the tracks was Donington and with the rock festival also it became this exotic thing.   Around the world this is considered the Mother Of All Festivals. If you're included on Download, it's the one. There's great festivals –

Rock In Rio, Rock Am Ring – but this is the one. If you're a hard rock band this is where you wanna be."
Duff McKagan (Velvet Revolver – Bass)

"I watched Mastodon, they were great and System Of A Down, Slayer and Slipknot.
UK festivals are great, just as long as they are not pissing down with rain; it seems to be that in the summertime, the weather in England is worse than Scandinavia. We walk around in London and it's a great day and then we head out for the festival a day later and here comes the rain!
It is still a great festival, with a lot of good bands always."
Mikkey Dee (Motörhead – Drums)

"To return nearly 20 years later was great.
It was at the same location, but they changed the name to Download from Monsters of Rock.
It was one of our first shows back together in England and the vibe was great. It was like we were never apart for the 13+ years and the crowd's reception was awesome as always.
The fans are great and have always supported us and I am grateful for that because with out them I would not be able to do what I love to do.
Black Sabbath, Velvet Revolver, Alter Bridge, Lamb Of God and HIM are all the bands I can remember that performed that day."
Joey Belladonna (Anthrax – Vocals)

"We played in 2005 which was the year of the Anthrax reunion and of course I had to see that, being a huge Anthrax fan. I had always wanted to come to the festival when I was much younger when Guns 'N' Roses, Iron Maiden and Helloween played, but I was much too young."
Peter Iwers (In Flames – Bass)

"It's a very special thing really, a legendary place for Metal! It's a really good atmosphere and everyone's up for a good time. It's such a huge site and an honour to play there."
Matthew Tuck (Bullet For My Valentine – Vocals/Guitar)

"We played the Snickers stage and last year we watched a lot of bands and it was like we'd love to play that stage. And free beer!"
Michael 'Moose' Thomas (Bullet For My Valentine – Drums)

"We had one of the biggest circle pits I have seen in my life, with the crowd going 'ape shit', just loving the music and going crazy.
I can remember being backstage before we went on and Sharon Osbourne had heard about us and came over, looked me in the eye and said 'good luck with the show'. It was like 'WOW' some people do know about us."
Jason 'Jay' James (Bullet For My Valentine – Bass)

"Donington was cool for me because it was the biggest show we'd done. Going backstage it was fucking awesome, seeing people walking around, Slipknot, Slayer and fridges stocked full of beer!"
Michael 'Padge' Padget (Bullet For My Valentine – Guitar/Vocals)

"Originally when we were scheduled, we were booked for the 3rd stage and then we did so well on our UK tour and had such a big reaction, that they asked us if we would like to open the mainstage on the Saturday, so we said why not!
We went and did it and there were a lot more people that we were expecting. We went on at about 11 o'clock and there was a massive amount of people, as far as you could see from the stage and it was just unbelievable. We went out and did the best that we could for that early in the morning; it was pretty chilly out and it's a lot more difficult to play when it's cold.
We were standing on stage a half an hour before we were supposed to play and there was no one there and then 5 minutes before we played you could see this mob of people coming over the hill, stampeding towards the stage, full out

running; then in 5 minutes it had filled up. By the time we played there were people from the stage to over the hill.
The crowd went nuts and it was the biggest show that we'd ever played. It was the last show that we had done on the tour and we couldn't have asked for a better ending, to such a great tour and first time over in Europe. Everything so was much bigger than we'd expected it to be and the reactions we got were way bigger and more ecstatic than we thought.
We arrived at Download on the Friday afternoon and got to hang out for the rest of the day, played Saturday morning and then hung out for the rest of the festival. We got to sleep in our tour bus.
Download is more fun that any of the other European festivals, because it's pretty much a 'metal festival'. We were stoked to play as we had heard in the States, all about Iron Maiden and Metallica playing it.
It was one of our most memorable shows and we played the festival and it was more than we had played on the previous tour. People still come up to us now and say that they saw us at Download and how much they enjoyed it. The show was a big 'door opener' for us, for playing in front of a lot of people in one shot.
It's a good festival, lots of cool things to look at, lots of fun things to do and they get great bands to play."
Corey Beaulieu (Trivium – Guitar)

"Getting there the night before it had a real carnival atmosphere and all the bands and crews and fans were gathering and there was a real freak show on the grounds. Lots of weird dance parties and people doing all kinds of shenanigans.
It happened to be a really good show and it was definitely at the point (and I think still) the biggest crowd we'd ever played to the in the UK.
Shortly before we'd played I noticed a big flagpole going up with a confederate flag on waving back and forth, way back there in the crowd, just before we took the stage. That was a warm welcome out there, but someone out there knew where we were from and that was like a warm welcome and a good

omen."
Mark Morton (Lamb Of God - Guitar)

*"It was an amazing experience for all of us. Just to be invited to the festival in the first place and then the slot that we had and the response that we had from the crowd, it was really cool. The kids just totally went off!
Looking back and near the very back of the crowd there was someone holding a confederate flag which was really funny. But the festivals in general are great to come together with all the dudes you've been on the road with before; it's just a great time and a great show.
I watched Meshuggah, of course and they were awesome."*
Willie Adler (Lamb Of God - Guitar)

*"I woke up really early on the day that we played Download. Driving out to the festival grounds cranking Led Zeppelins 'Houses Of The Holy', we were already in a good mood.
I then got off my bus with a beer in my hand and these three, really hot, Suicide Girls came walking by and they hand me these little stickers with a little heart on and said Suicide Girls on it. I said 'can I have a couple of these?' and they said 'you can have all of us if you want!' I was like YEAH ALRIGHT, THIS IS GOING TO BE A GOOD DAY!"*
Randy Blythe (Lamb Of God – Vocals)

"We played the smaller side stage and had an amazing show, it was unbelievable; at the time it was the biggest show that we had played. The reaction that we got was truly flattering and we didn't know that many people shared our enthusiasm about our music and so we were really excited about that show and it always stuck out in my mind."
Chris Adler (Lamb Of God – Drums)

"The second time we played was in the tent, which I preferred really, because within the environment of the tent you can take your stage show to the limits of the tent, so it's a lot more confined and made it a lot more comfortable for me really, as

a performer. There is something really special when you are onstage and the tent is rammed full of people."
Matt Davies (Funeral For A Friend – Vocals)

"The first time that we played at Download Festival was in the tent and it was a rainy day and very cold. It was a great experience and the first time that we had played a festival in the UK.
I remember seeing Motorhead in the tent; it was the first time that I had seen Motorhead and they were really loud.
I was also impressed because there was skateboarding going on, which was really good as it was the first time that I had seen something at a festival that was not related to the music."
Andrea Ferro (Lacuna Coil –Vocals)

"Download in '05 was probably our first really big show and we all very excited to get over. We were on the smallest stage and Crucified Barbara and were on before us; Micky had to lend them some bass gear, I think he was trying to get in there, bit he got knocked back.
It was a great gig to play, a dream come true to play at Donington. I remember listening to Monsters Of Rock as a kid in 1990 with Whitesnake, so it was good to finally make it there.
We had a great time hanging out and watching bands too; I remember Black Sabbath were on and Cormac had a few beers and needed lavatory and jumped over the middle fence where the sound desk was and proceeded to piss there, while Black Sabbath were playing 'Sweet Leaf' and somehow managed not to get thrown out of the whole festival, I don't know how. Ozzy didn't seem to mind too much.
We watched System Of A Down from up on the hill, it was a great weekend."
Paul Mahon (The Answer – Guitar)

"Download to me is everything. When we were kids growing up listening to rock music, you always heard about Donington. When we found out that we were coming to play at Download, our manager told us, it was incredible, it was like we'd made it, we were actually getting some respect for once.

All the legends that have played there over the years it's incredible, every year the line-up is great and there's someone that you want to see.

The first year that we played Therapy? were on, friends from back home. They were a band that we looked up to and our friendship began to grow and now we've been friends with them for many years now.

I also will never forget watching Helmet. They headlined the small tent on the Saturday night and then the next day they played in the morning in the bigger tent; it was like going to mass on a Sunday morning with hardcore; 15,000 heads all bobbing in time.

When we walked out on stage, there were all these black t-shirts looking back at us, it was amazing; it was where we should have been all the time."

James Heatley (The Answer – Drums)

"It takes a special festival or show to really stand out from the thousands of shows a band plays. It usually takes a certain occurrence at that particular show, the reaction of the people in attendance or sometimes the venue where that show happens can make it stand out. With Download there is a certain combination of all those elements that make it stand out as one of the best show memories we have ever had.

From the historic value of the yearly event, to the amazing line ups year after year, to the different stages bands can play, to the backstage village the bands can hang out in and have the party of their lives post show and finally to the amazing energy and vibe the crowd continuously puts out throughout the entire festival is something that rarely happens anywhere in the world.

From our first experience on the fest in 2005 we were hooked. Of course the honor of being invited to play the gig is mind blowing, but then to actually be there and play a mid afternoon set on the Snickers Stage to 10,000+ metalheads destroying the pit, crowd surfing, singing along and throwing their fists

and horns up in the air gave us such a sense of pride that it is tough to explain with words. The adrenaline that one show instilled in our veins on that particular day is something I will never forget.
After the show I got to roam the grounds of the festival with some friends and see In Flames crush the Snickers stage, see the Anthrax reunion (one of my favorite bands of all time) from the crowd as well as the mighty Black Sabbath grace the stage.
Enjoying our set and then other legendary metal bands sets was then capped off with a party with a bunch of our friends in the metal village after the show was over for the night. The amount of debauchery that ensued that evening was epic and all I remember is our tour mates in Lamb of God and Every Time I Die stumbling back to our bus more than an hour late for bus call. Yeah the tour managers and bus drivers were not pleased, but we had a damn good time on that day."
Trevor Phipps (Unearth – Vocals)

"Download was really good, it was really great.
I remember watching Dave Mustaine and thinking that this was really absurd that we were going on after.
The thing that was really cool was everyone was switching stages, so when we actually went on, the field was really sparse and empty. Then everyone started moving over and by the third or fourth song we had a full audience, it filled up. The festivals to me a so large and it's hard for me to have a good time."
Murph (Dinosaur Jr – Drums)

"I thought the field was empty the whole time!!!"
Lou Barlow (Dinosaur Jr – Vocals / Guitar)

"We played the Snickers stage and it was fantastic.
Going to the festival now, most people have short hair and we've got a history of 14 years and we were thinking will the young kids like this, but they did!
What I feel about the metal fans that I do admire is that those fans are the most up for it fans in the world. With a lot of indie

fans if you make a bad record they could all drop you and it may take years to get those fans back, whereas with the metal fans they will tell you that you've made a bad record and that it stinks but they won't leave you.

We have still got quite a hardcore fan base worldwide, because people say 'you've made some naff records that we didn't like, but we'll still come and see you play and buy your new record and see what it's like'."

Andy Cairns (Therapy? – Vocals/Guitar)

"Our second experience of Download was totally different; we played the mainstage in the middle of the afternoon and had an amazing show.

We had a blow up sheep thrown onstage and a banana and we did things to the sheep with the banana!"

Jaret Reddick (Bowling For Soup – Vocals/Guitar)

"This year they asked us back and we got to play the mainstage. Everyone was keeping a close watch on everyone else, 'You're not drinking too much are you?' We didn't show up early in the morning, we had our night out the night before and then got up late in the morning.

It was absolutely amazing, the largest crowd that we've ever played for was that show. It was a very humbling experience to see that many people out in front of you that are enjoying what you're doing.

You'd expect with that many people; you're going to have a certain number of people who like it and a certain number of people who don't give a fuck! But as far as you could see people were on their feet, pumping their fists in the air, it was an amazing thing to see.

It was a marker in time. Walking on stage and everyone stands up and cheers and it was the most people in front of me ever.

There was a cloud of dirt, a thin layer of brownish air about six feet above everybody and it was like their breathing that all shit in!!! Everyone would need to blow their nose when they got home!!!!!"

Erik Chandler (Bowling For Soup – Bass)

"We were on the mainstage after A, so we got to see them again which was awesome and two bands before Anthrax, which was pretty amazing as we got to sit on the stage and watch Anthrax! It was the Ozzfest day.
Erik took a blow up sheep onstage and stuck a banana up its ass!
There was a lot of drinking and not remembering shit!
Gary Wiseman (Bowling For Soup - Drums)

"The next year we got picked to play on Ozzfest day, on the mainstage and we actually made it on the Ozzfest DVD and it was so cool to see that.
To this day when people or family come over, that's the first thing I show them, our Ozzfest performance from Download on the Ozzfest DVD.
I also met Max Cavelera and he was so nice to me and when I walked up to him, some crazy girl was playing with his hair, so he was looking for someone to get him out of that situation and so I stumbled along at the right time.
Dave Mustaine was a really nice to me and I also got to meet Billy Idol"
It was so much fun and so many people and the good thing about that year was that we actually played good!
We actually rocked it!
We did the 'sheep bit' and carried it over to 2007."
Chris Burney (Bowling For Soup – Guitar)

"Download, that was last year? Holy Jesus."
Dave King (Flogging Molly - Vocals/Guitar)

"We all watched Black Sabbath and we started our set with Paranoid."
Bridgette Regan (Flogging Molly - Fiddle/Penny Whistle)

"The Saturday was the metal day and we played the mainstage before Megadeth on the Friday, but when you play Donington you don't care when you play. I don't want to be associated with just the whole metal scene. I'm a metal fan,

but what I do it's metal, it's punk, it's rock, it's a lot of things. We played early at 2 o'clock, which may as well have been 10 o'clock and we carried on drinking and drinking and doing interviews.
Right before we left I saw Steve Stevens and walked up to him and said 'Hey man my name is Wednesday' and he said 'yeah you're in Murderdolls, you did White Wedding, I know who you are' and I was like 'that's cool', I was kind of shocked by it. We had a very hectic press schedule, so we just kept drinking!!
Wednesday 13 (Wednesday 13 - Vocals / Guitar)

"We came back in 2005 and played a lot later in the day, second to last on the second stage and they couldn't stop chanting out name. It was almost like we weren't allowed to play; they just wanted to chant our name!
It was just so overwhelming."
Mark Hunter (Chimaira – Vocals)

"The second time with 'A' we played on the main stage; it was great (especially when a bottle smashed into my guitar at the beginning of the first song!). Apart from that minor glitch we had a great time.... I even managed to blag a Total Guitar front cover pic with Slash, Scott Ian and Mark Tremonti... Three players who have made more than a little impact on me and a few million other guitarists around the world. I couldn't believe it."
Mark Chapman (A – Guitar)

"Playing Download Festival should be a big deal to any band so when we were first asked to play in 2005 it was a huge honor."
Olly Mitchell (Johnny Truant – Vocals)

"Considering the history of Donington and the place it holds in our hearts thanks to the Monsters of Rock festivals, playing the Download festival in 2005 still holds up as being one of the greatest shows Panic Cell have ever had the privilege to play.

The whole vibe, atmosphere, weather and especially the crowd participation were amazing, we couldn't have asked for a better show. Considering that back in June 2005 Panic Cell were pretty much an unknown act, we were astonished that by the time we went on the tent was packed out and over spilling, we could see people outside the tent watching as they could get in... it was that full!! Smiles a million miles wide and plenty of beers were had that day we promise you.
An awesome, mind blowing weekend was had by all, we met a lot of cool people and made a lot of new friends over the time we spent there."
Bobby Town (Panic Cell – Bass)

"The second time we played was maybe a little more special to me though. To this day it has to go down as one of the all time Speedhorn shows! We played second from top in the tent, with our mates Napalm Death.
It was the last show of our first UK tour with Bloody Kev, and he was pretty nervous.
There were so many people in the tent!! I met loads of people afterwards who said that they couldn't get anywhere near the inside of the tent, such was the crowd there!
We were about 2 songs into the set and the crowd was really kicking off! I have an everlasting image of all these extra security guards ascending to the front of the stage to cope with it. It was just unbelievable. It was one of those shows that take your breath away and make you think..."Holy shit!"
When you play 200 shows a year, it takes something special to take you to that extra level, where you're just floating on adrenalin; that was one of those shows..."
Gareth Smith (Raging Speedhorn – Guitar)

"The first thing that struck me was that it as so big, enormous and we were pretty nervous when we entered the stage. We played early in the day at about 1 o'clock and we didn't know if there were going to be any people at all.
We had heard so many stories about the crowds throwing bottles of pee, so we were like 'how's this going to be??'

But, when we entered the stage it was packed and it was really good and we had an awesome gig.
We saw some friends from Sweden from In Flames and Messhuggah and hung out backstage and we saw the Osbourne Family, which was really strange.
It was just fantastic and we hope to be back."
Mia Coldheart (Crucified Barbara - Vocals/Guitar)

"It was really big, like REALLY big! We had to a van to get from the backstage area to the stage.
I remember I had my camera with me and we took photos of people like the singer from Slipknot and they closed the backstage area because Ozzy was coming in there, so we had to wait. I watched some songs of Velvet Revolver. I also remember that they had a massage chair in the backstage area and I thought this was really good, but nobody was using it, I sat there but no masseuse came up; and you could get your hair done."
Nicki Wicked (Crucified Barbara - Drums)

"I remember that it was so big and at night I wanted some cigarettes and I walked with Jesper (Strömblad) from In Flames. We walked for 1 hour to get cigarettes and it was like 'my god, where are we?' We were just walking, walking, walking, walking and finally we got to somewhere to get cigarettes, it was just huge.
I remember some stupid photographers in the press area asking us if we were a band or just groupies? I had never heard such a stupid comment as that before and I thought he needs to get spanked!!"
Klara Force (Crucified Barbara – Guitar)

"I had no idea that Download festival would become a regular part of my job and I'd be able to watch amazing bands, like the original Anthrax line-up, from the side of the stage."
Emma Watson (PR – Bowling For Soup/MC Lars/Zebrahead)

*"We started off on year one and year two as a 2 day festival and then in year three we changed it to a 3 day festival and I think that it was the best decision that we ever made.
To be honest the line-up on the Friday, which was quite 'Indie', was the best that we could do. The interesting thing about Download is that Monsters of Rock ran its course, but was very niche, but with Download I'd like to see it here in 10 years time and if we are going to achieve that it has to maintain its core and its roots as a rock festival, but it's got to have a really broad base. If we keep coming back and doing the same core rock bands, then we are going to run out, I'd like to see bands like Foo Fighters and Muse play here as well; even bands like Linkin Park take us a little bit broader and I think that the broader we make it the longer it will last."*
Stuart Galbraith (ex – Donington Organiser)

"2005 was a massive year for Download which saw it expand to include a third day, boast its biggest line-up to date and achieve sell-out status - no mean feat in just its third year of existence. The online operation scaled-up to match. By this stage, the message boards had become so active that full-time dedicated coverage was required to administer and manage them. I needed some helpers and they came to me in the form of two amazing people called Phil and Carrie. This larger than life couple had, off their own back, already put a lot of time into helping me out with the boards and they seemed to be on there permanently. With Clear Channel's blessing I appointed them the official 'mods' and they're still there running the show today, for the love of it - very special people. As Download's online activities increased, our role began to have a more tangible effect on the shape of the festival. There was a lot of talk about 5-a-side football games being organised in the campsites by fans, on the forums so, at the next production meeting, I proposed that we put in a proper pitch to house this activity. My suggestion was met by a roar of laughter that almost blew me out the room. "Metallers can't play football!" someone snorted. Next time, I arrived with a petition of several hundred fans who claimed otherwise. I was given a space in the market area, £200 to buy some goals and

branded footballs, and told I'd better make this work. As soon as the Dog relayed this info back to the 'boardies', as yet another case in which they had been allowed creative input into the event, they made sure it not only worked but was such a popular attraction that 5-a-side pitches started popping up at festivals all over the country after that, from Reading to T in the Park. Less ubiquitous now is the other attraction we installed that year - giant games of Twister! All weekend-long, this favourite with the girls generated a writhing tangle of limbs as black-clad young rock chicks fought to out-flex each other. It also proved a big hit with the artists backstage, becoming both a magnet to attract curious/bored rock stars to our interview area and a prop to generate unusual content.

To this day, Download 2005 remains the biggest festival coverage operation ever undertaken by Virtual Festivals. Our team that year consisted of 35 people - photographers, writers, interviewers, runners, film-makers, managers and we even had a crew of VJ's mixing up the screens on the Third Stage.

We reviewed all 140 artist performances separately and uploaded these to the official website, with photos, within an hour of the artist leaving the stage. Nothing like it had ever been attempted before, and has not been since. We interviewed more than 60 acts on video, with many of these edited and uploaded on-site. Physically, it was the most exhausting thing I have ever done, and we were carried through on the sheer adrenaline and excitement of the situation. Most nights we didn't turn in until 3am, then the beers would flow as we'd be so wired, and we'd be back in the portakabin at 9am to do it all again.

Being based backstage, we got to spend a lot of time hanging out and bonding with artists, many of whom were intrigued by our operation. Some were very distracting; especially the pair of acts who had a full-on brawl, trashing their dressing room next door to us and had to be escorted off the premises! Then there was the American supergroup who used our laptops as suitable surfaces for laying some train tracks. Others were charitable such as Velvet Revolver (and former GNR) superstars Slash and Duff McKagan who hand-delivered us their entire rider of pizzas one night and Black Sabbath's Tony Iommi who popped his head around our door after their headline performance and kindly invited us to help ourselves to their rider too. Hoping for enough unopened booze to last us the night, we realised we'd now seen it all upon discovering just a load of (quite expensive looking) exercise equipment - bikes, steppers, a treadmill - left abandoned in their quarters! 2005 also marked the year in which the Download Dog made his first 'live' appearance at the festival. I can reveal now that it was actually a man (a Clear Channel employee) wearing a custom-made suit, but we had the job of taking our loveable mascot out for a walk in the arena to greet his minions. He had his own security guard, but one was not enough, as word spread around the site like wildfire and kids turned their backs on the bands performing to swarm around their idol in the hope of a hug, photo or autograph. Never mind John Lennon, the Download Dog was bigger than Jesus at that festival.

As the big screens flashed up with a message of thanks to the fans for helping Download sell out, at the end of System Of A Down's set on the last night, I had mixed emotions. On one hand I was immensely proud and grateful for having the opportunity to be part of all this. On the other, I was a bit sad, as I knew a large part of this incredible journey was now behind us, our work largely complete.

I also remember the morning of Sunday 12 June, '05 was a pleasant, sunny one. A perfect day, you might say, for breaking the world record for performing for the longest amount of time whilst suspended from the rafters by meat hooks through your own flesh. I bet you just read that again. Well, that's what Society 1 singer Matt Zane must have thought when he woke up that day and he duly got on-stage and accomplished his goal. When you set your mind on something, kids. . .

Of course VF was on hand to capture the gory spectacle up close (trapped on stage next to the freak) for the full 45 blood-dripping minutes. Whilst it did not do much for my hangover, it gave me some images I will never get out of my head again ever. Thanks and well done."

Steve Jenner (Founder of Virtual Festivals.com & UK Festival Awards)

"Carrie, being the experienced camper, always comes fully loaded to these events. As such, we were the last people to leave the campsite. As we packed the last couple of things into the car, Vanessa from the Live Experience (who organise the RIP side of Download) came with a bribe of beer for feedback and an apology for things not going too well. Not that we'd noticed - but we accepted and told her I was a moderator on the forums and that we'd organise some feedback from there. We took her email, got feedback and emailed it to her a week or so later. And then forgot about it.
Carrie had also been emailing Steve Jenner from Virtual Festivals quite a bit - they'd run a competition through the boards to get boardies to review the festival and she'd come close to getting picked. Steve as I've already mentioned was at the time the main go-between for the boards and the organisers...
So - Middle of January 2005. The boards are at fever pitch in anticipation of headliners being announced. Carrie and I gather together all the feedback we'd got after the festival, and update it with what's going on the boards. We send it in to Vanessa. Carrie gets a call from Vanessa. "We're doing a launch for the festival next Tuesday in London; we'd like you and Phil to come down." This is followed up by an email from Steve at Virtual saying he'll meet us with tickets. We book our trains and a hotel, arrange time off work and meet Steve outside the Marquee in Leicester Square. Up we go for our free beers and Snickers bars...
Stuart Galbraith comes on stage and intro's a short video which announces Black Sabbath, System Of A Down, HIM, Billy Idol, Velvet Revolver et al. Ozzy and Sharon come on stage, saying how much they're looking forward to bringing Ozzfest to Download. We meet Sophie and a few other people, have our photo taken on the media stand and Carrie hyperventilates as she sees Billy Idol wafting through the crowd. A trip to a bar round the corner and we're talking to

Stuart, Sophie, and Mark Yovich for a couple of hours about Donington pasts, present and future. We leave feeling that Doningtons future is in good hands.

By the time the festival came round, we'd organised a few events to keep those who'd come on the Wednesday & Thursday occupied. Five a side football, plus a Twister tournament! The festival had expanded to three days/four stages this year, though there'd been a bit of a hoo-haa about the Indie bands (JJ72/Dinosaur Jr/Garbage/Feeder). It was quite a sight after Megadeth left the stage seeing a full arena shrink down to a crowd of about 500 people. And given the uproar a couple of years later, it was interesting to note that a steady stream of people were crossing the arena during Dinosaur Jr's set heading over to the second stage to catch My Chemical Romance...

The Friday was rounded off with a rousing set from Billy Idol. Saturday saw a couple of our friends bands play - Panic Cell (who have ever since insisted that it was us bleating on to the organisers about them at the launch party that got them on the bill) and Breed 77 again.

First band of that day for us were American Head Charge, who Panic Cell had been touring a lot with. AHC had just lost one of their guitarists to a prescription drugs overdose, and their set was particularly poignant (some of the footage made it onto their "Can't Stop The Machine" DVD), especially when the 10,000 strong crowd started to chant for Bryan.

There was then a 15 minute gap between the end of their set and the start of Panic Cell at the Third stage. Five minutes before Panic Cell were due on; it looked like they were going to be playing to the Donington equivalent of 2 men and a dog! A stream of people pouring in from the AHC set soon filled the tent to capacity for a stormer of a set. Later a reunited original lineup of Black Sabbath (with the exception of Bill Ward, who wasn't well enough to play but came on only to get de-bagged by Ozzy!) bring that days events to a satisfying conclusion.

A dreary Sunday morning saw a full tent for the Henry Rollins "Sunday Sermon" on the third stage, with Henry's colorful spoken word/stand up style show setting everyone off for another Donington day.

Society 1 played a record breaking set, with front man (and porn star/producer) Matt Zane setting the "suspension" record. Basically he was hung up on meat hooks through his back and spent the whole 30 minutes swinging back and forth dodging the odd bottle. Ouch...

2005 was one of the best years for performance artists and arena entertainment. Returning to the arena from the bar to catch Slipknot on their gradual climb up the bill we were caught up in a "SWAT" team stalking along the edges of the arena, waving semi-automatic water pistols. During the hailstones that accompanied Slipknot, I caught a glimpse of the SWAT team hut-hut-hutting in silhouette along the crest of the hill to the left of the stage.

System Of A Down delivered a career defining set to close the festival - many have complained that they seemed detached, but what I saw was a band that had moved beyond the common crowd and raised their game to headlining status. A few years earlier they had seemed like just another great band but that year at Donington they transcended that. I've only ever seen two bands perform sets of that caliber - NIN at Leeds in 07 and FNM at Download 09 (but we'll get to that later).

One other notable thing about Download 05 was a little thing called Damnation Festival, which was actually kick started when Bowling For Soup were announced. "We need more metal" said Gavin McInally, a long time forum member. He gathered a team of like minded individuals from the forums and got going with that. But there lies a story for another book!"

Phil Hull (Download Forum Administrator)

"I've been a fan of Garbage and Shirley Manson since before seeing them perform at the Reading Festival 1998, and did enjoy watching their performance on Friday.
Billy Idol was good in the Snickers tent along with MCR and Flogging Molly, but one of the funniest and best thing I saw over the weekend (apart from Bowling For Soup, on Saturday, who are

genius) was seeing Lordi play in their full horror make-up in the Snickers tent, prior to them going on to win the Eurovision song contest the next year."
Mike Horton (Plymouth)

"<u>Friday:</u> Queen Adreena on the main stage who get things off to a good start. They rock hard enough, with a bit of groove provided by the band and a touch of mentalness from their singer whom at times seems as fragile as her clothes. For some reason she performs a lot of the set standing on top of a chair. Anyway, they put on a good performance which sets nicely with this early start. That is until they appear to have the plug pulled on them.   Next up is Fozzy and there's pretty much no chance in hell of getting into the Snickers Second Stage. The Y2J chants have already started. Though I wonder how many people here can actually name even one of their songs. Jericho is clearly a great performer and keeps the crowd entertained throughout their set. The music itself is just big dumb rock which makes them a rather good festival band to coincide with the alcohol. But it also means the band will probably never really amount to much. But fuck it man, sink some brewskies and rock your ass off! Hell even Chucky is doing so it appears. Lordi are interesting to say the least, mostly visually. I'm not too sure what to think because at this moment of time my head just cant really deal with seeing what looks like a collection of the evillest baddies from Power Rangers rocking out on stage. Add to that the fact that some guy is wearing a hat which appears to have been a pair of jeans in a former life. There is comedy in seeing a 'mummyesque' bassist lamping a Druid roadie with his bass. But add the sounds of babies crying and this is all starting to get too freakish. This could very easily give me the 'fear'.

And thus we come to Underoath. Do we really need another band like this? Call it screamo or whatever you want it doesn't matter its all poor. Yes we get it you can jump around like the Duracell bunny and scream you lungs off. Seems almost every new band can do that. Whatever happened to singers? It seems there just no good metal singers emerging anymore so everyone is just trying to compensate by screaming as loud as they can and to be honest it sucks.

The crowd is going pretty crazy for Apocalyptica. Of course they are playing Master Of Puppets, which is being entirely sung by the crowd. To an extent though it just makes you wish Metallica were here themselves. But it is rather cool hearing Master played on a cello. Their own songs are not bad but they're always going to look a bit weak next to Metallica songs. I didn't stay for long though as Megadeth would soon be playing their final UK show and I needed a decent space.

It seems Megadeth are the band most people want to see today judging by the t-shirts and the huge crowd gathered at the main stage. They don't disappoint. They're on fire from the word go. Although it would have been better if they had been given a longer timeslot. Many classic songs are absent because of this and it all seems to come to an end too soon with Dave Mustaine remaining onstage alone addressing the crowd, taking a bow and departing as Sid Vicious cover of My Way plays over the speakers. The crowd at the main stage (which had been packed) now rapidly disappears and as Dinosaur Jr comes on stage unannounced the crowd is very thin. Hold on somebody has ballsed up. Dinosaur Jr has just finished their 2nd song and as the sound quiets down you can hear that the main stage speaker is still playing the radio channel. In the end the band aren't half bad, I've never really been able to get into them, but at the moment they're good to just listen to and chill out.

Now its time for Garbage, the band I was most looking forward to seeing today and my excitement was justified. They were absolutely amazing despite some technical problems and wardrobe problems (Shirley's dress just doesn't seem to want to stay on). But both problems are dealt with as Shirley jokes with the crowd and manages to laugh the problems off. Musically they are even better live than on record. Shirley's sultry vocals verge on intoxicating. Again though it seems to come to and end all too soon, they should have been headlining instead of Feeder.

Now its time to dance my ass off to some Billy Idol. Twelve years since you last played the UK? Throwing signed paper

plates into the crowd?
Well tonight I'm gonna dance the night away! He plays on for 30 minutes more than scheduled including an awesome cover of Van Halens 'Jump' and a cover of the Who's 'Who Are You?' That was one hell of a show, groove on!
<u>*Saturday:*</u> *There are bands to be seen but I just feel like having a few pints of the black stuff and checking out some crazy shit. God dammit man let it settle! You call this Guinness!? It's meant to be thick! I've had thicker water! Well, time for the first band. Arrive in the Napster 3rd stage for the last few minutes of Diamond night. They seem to play just straight up balls out rock. And I wanna rock so fuck yeah! Hey is that a beer token!? Pounce! Free booze! Wayhey the best of all kinds.* Crucified *Barbara, these 4 Swedish girls bring to mind a much heavier more rocking version of the Donnas. The heavier backed up by a cover of Motorheads Killed By Death.*
Panic Cell is up next. They're just a pure heavy fuckin' metal band. This kicks ass. Definitely a band to keep an eye on. EA getting hassled by a penguin!? Did you hear that!? What?.. Nevermind. Orifice free
sheep? Bowling For Soup are on the main stage. Their music probably isn't really up to much but they are a good fun festival band. Alter Bridge just seem a bit average to be honest. Open their eyes grabs my attention a bit more as does their cover of Zeppelins Kashmir but perhaps for the wrong reasons. It's a nice touch to see the organizers playing video footage of last years Damage Plan main stage performance as a tribute to Dimebag Darrell.
Now for some old school Anthrax. Which bloody rocks! There's no point comparing Joey Belladonna era with John Bush era as there's pluses for both parties e.g. some great songs won't get played because they were done with Bush but there are old classics played instead which you wouldn't have got. And there's the sight of Joey running around in his headdress during an awesome 'Indians'.
I've tried to give HIM a chance but this just isn't very good. Their fanbase appears to be mostly girls and kids. All of which are screaming their lungs out at every silence which is rather

painful. Just like the awful muffled sound that is HIM themselves. Okay so maybe they have 1 or 2 songs I could listen to and maybe even enjoy if in the right mood. But the rest are a bit samey and become tedious.

Thankfully things soon pick up again when on comes Velvet Revolver who tear the place a new arsehole. Rock N Fuckin Roll indeed! During 'Sex-Type Thing' Scott comes racing along the barrier splitting the crowd, where I happen to be standing and he shakes my hand on his way past. He proceeds to the sound desk and climbs right into the middle of the crowd and then proceeds to perform the rest of the song while in the middle of 60,000 people. Then out comes Slash complete with double-neck guitar for an incredible cover of Pink Floyds 'Wish You Where Here'.

They finish with an awesome 'Slither' and depart to the wailing sound of sirens. Now that rocked!

The question is now how do you top that? How about with Black fuckin Sabbath. These guys have still got it. Ozzy looks healthy, energetic and is clearly loving it. They're on great form. The crowd is going mad for it. During the first notes of 'Black Sabbath' you find yourself just asking for the skies to open and pour with rain, but the sea of flames stretching all the way to the back is just as good. The generals have indeed gathered in their masses. This is just simply amazing! Now no more words its time to go feckin crazy. And I did.

<u>Sunday:</u> Tried to catch some of Henry Rollins spoken word set but by the time we get there the Napster stage is absolutely packed and you can't hear shit outside. So time for some more booze and prepare for Society 1s world record attempt. I'm not entirely awake at this point of time but the sight of a guy hanging 25/30ft above the stage suspended from 4 fishhooks in his back will sober you up rightly. Musically they seem decent enough and when he screams you believe he means it. But it's hard to pay attention to the music. The thing is he looks like he may actually be enjoying it as he swings from side to side, front to back and around in circles. Many faces in the crowd are either grimacing or just cant look at the sight at all. But sure enough he remains suspended for the full 30 minute set and thus breaks his own world record.

Many years ago I liked Papa Roach a little bit so I figured I'd check them out and they were pretty alright and seemed to go over with the crowd quite well. However I'm starting to get the feeling that today is going to have problems trying to follow yesterday. It should pick up more soon though but I doubt it can surpass last night unbelievable ending of Velvet and Sabbath. Roach pick up a bit towards the end of their set with some older songs and a short cover of QOTSAs 'Feel Good Hit Of The Summer'. Now stumbling around for a beer I somehow end up meeting Lacuna Coil who seemed pretty cool. Christina is cuter in real life. Nightwish are apparently stuck on the motorway and will be 30 minutes late for their set. One hour later and still no sign of Nightwish, so I've missed Nightwish and Mastodon. At least Lacuna Coil are good enough to make up for it. Christina Scabbias voice is as amazing live as on record. At times it's almost breathtaking. The new song played sounds very promising for the new record.

Funeral For a Friend are the secret band!?!?!? Funeral For a Friend my arse! Fuck this shit! Now to head back to round up the troops hold up! Do I hear Slayer!?! Dead skin Mask!! Charge!!! Circle pit galore! [I wasn't going to see them because I've seen them several times before and I'd never seen Lacuna Coil.] Now it would appear that in a case of serendipity Nightwishs balls-up has meant Slayer are on a good bit later than scheduled and I've just caught them just moments into their set. However their set has been cut short to about 35 minutes. But a feckin sweet 35 minutes they are. Now for some grub and somehow end up meeting Nightwish completely unintentionally and without knowing anything really about them. They all looked quite confused when I asked them how's the craic? Considered thanking them for allowing me to see Slayer but was advised against it by my attorney. Kick out the jams muthafucka. MC5 are finishing off. But wait! On comes Lemmy and there's a cover of Johnny B. Goode. Are Slipknot still playing!? Hailstones in summer!? The crowds going mental, I'm still bored of Slipknot.

Almost an hour has passed since System was due on stage and still no sign. The crowds agitated, they're trying to

entertain themselves by 2 ways: Bottle war or flashing for the camera. Just about on the hour late mark on comes System with a Daron Malakian who appears to have lost a fight with a lawnmower. But who cares because System rock! They're schizophrenically good and bring the proceedings to a fine end.   Thus comes to an end quite probably the greatest festival I've ever been to yet. I've rocked like a bastard all weekend. Too much perhaps for this mortal body to cope with lol, but I'm still fighting on, rocking on! Rock till I drop! But I can now leave easily saying that I've definitely bought the ticket and taken the ride."
Jason Kennedy (Belfast)

"One moment from Download 2005 that will stick with me forever is a certain point during Slipknot's performance of 'Duality'.   The vibe around the crowd was amazing. It felt like one massive unit, all one and the same, here for the same reason... let's do this!
I remember being down the front, probably jumping about like a loon in one of the pits and the last big chorus hit and throughout the song the crowd had been singing along to every word but when this chorus hit, it felt like something special happened.
The clouds opened up and it started pouring down with rain onto us as everyone sang... well, roared!! In unity to the last chorus. We all came together and it was amazing. The only word I can use is epic! A truly 'goosebumpy' moment.
That is just one moment for me, but there are many, many other things from all the Download Festivals over the years that will stick with me, long live Download!"
Charley Olsen (Brighton)

"I think it was Download '05, we were all back at the campsite having a drink
and getting ready to go back to the arena when one of my mates Sam Stocker
was having a bit of a play fight with a girl.
They both fell down and one of them groaned, they both got up and we noticed that stocker had a fork impaling his hand

and it had noodles from a crushed pot noodle hanging from inside his hand. He quickly said "to the medical tent" and ran off to have it removed." **Andre Jenkin (St Austell, Cornwall)**

"So I went camping. For 3 days. At Castle Donington rock festival. Age 33. I had been going to the Reading festival just for the day since 1999. I had always cringed at the thought of camping. Especially when you walked through the campsite and saw all the piles of rubbish and all the bewildered faces staring at you from graffiti covered tents. You can't wash, the toilets are disgusting and the whole place resembles a refugee camp. "I'm never doing that" thought I.
I went to the Castle Donington rock festival to see the really heavy bands (Reading is more trendy/ flavour of the month band orientated). It was great but still the idea of camping filled me with the horrors.
Then I saw the Donington line-up! Black Sabbath with Ozzy, Motorhead, Slayer, Slipknot and hordes of other bands that would have a pussy like you wetting the bed. THIS was the festival to bite the bullet and break my festival camping duck at. Also, it was in June so that considerably reduced my permission problem. Gerard didn't want to go (as he now hates METAL) and Ed would die in a tent due to multiple hygiene issues. So it was me and Bruce that booked up to join the 45,000 other campers for the 3- day festival. I wondered what I'd done. I was actually doing this, the toilets, the discomfort THE METAL!
I have got James, the bloke I sit next to at work into metal and the pre-Donington excitement was contagious enough for him to book up to join us for the Saturday + camping.
Louise packed my stuff and with PLENTY of trepidation I waited for Bruce to pick me up early Friday morning. This was a bone of contention because when we attended the festival last year we had to queue for an hour to get in and (wait for it) 4 f**king hours to get out of the car park!! My Idea was to go up Thursday night and also stay Sunday night. But it was beer festival week and Bruce works there, so going Thursday night

was a no go and the little fartknocker hadn't booked Monday off so we had travel back Sunday night!?!
(In hindsight this turned out to be a godsend).
The first band I wanted to see (Flogging Molly) were due on stage at 1pm and I didn't think we would get there and pitch the tent in time to see them.
Bruce picked me up and things got off to a bad start as the little arsehole was hung-over and irritable. I pointed out that he wasn't listening to a word I was saying and he started shouting "Do you want us to crash?" at me!
We got up there in good time and to my surprise there was no queue to get in (I began to think it had been cancelled but it was just that the Friday was least attended, the next day Black Sabbath played and the crowd doubled). We parked easily and got our shit out of the car. We had plenty of gear, especially Bruce who even had a cool bag with butter, bread and cold cuts of meat in it which he made sandwiches each day. We hauled ass to the campsite, the first two were full and we were directed to the yellow campsite that boasted showers. We pitched the tent close to the aforementioned showers in a tiny space next to a youth with an acoustic guitar. I pleaded with Bruce to put it somewhere else as we would want to smash that guitar before the weekend was over but he was already feeding the fishing rod like supports through the tent canvas.
We queued to get in and it occurred to me that most people were fat, ugly and wearing black. The festival site is located at the end of the runway of East Midlands airport. The planes roar over so low that you can see the passengers looking at all the Metal kids giving them the finger and throwing beer cans at them.
We saw Flogging Molly on time, who were great. The rest of the day was spent watching other bands you've never heard of. At one point I returned to the tent alone. Even though I was having a fantastic time, I felt really homesick. I got into my sleeping bag and cuddled up to my rucksack like a bitch as thousands of teenagers talked shit though clouds of weed in the tents around me.

After a hard day's rocking we returned to the tent ready to sleep like logs. Unfortunately, it was like trying to sleep through a riot. Out of their heads and away from mummy 44,998 teenagers were now screaming their heads off. Sleep was impossible. I eventually dropped off awaking at 5:30am to total silence. I seized my chance and headed over to the shower block for a lovely hot shower. I didn't wake Bruce because he'd get the arse ache . The showers were empty! I needed a shit and played portaloo Russian roulette, eventually finding one that didn't have vomit and brownjack splattered all over it. I had been building up my thigh muscles so that I didn't have to sit on the seat. As I tucked into a breakfast baguette I enjoyed the sight of the first plane booming into land waking all these bastards up! I noticed that people were drinking and smoking weed at 7am!?

By the time Bruce surfaced and went over for a shower there was a massive queue AND the hot water was off! He didn't bother to wash and we went to the campsite entrance and waited for James to arrive.

He was difficult to spot as he was wearing black and is ugly. He has a conifer hairstyle and this was the only place on earth that it wouldn't look out of place. He was horrified by the size of our tent (a 2 man tent masquerading as a 3-man tent!) we went into the arena and as I'm an only child I was in charge of picking which bands we saw.

As the first band were all female 21 year olds from Sweden I didn't hear a peep of dissent as we raced toward the Napster tent. Another day of seeing multiple bands ensued but there was a lot more drinking as James was with us. We took him to the Guinness tent where all the barmaids were stunning. "I don't even like Guinness" said the great mullet gulping it down like he was drinking piss. He liked the barmaids. You could not take booze into the arena so James and I kept running back to our tent, he to take a massive hit from his vodka and lemonade and me from my bottle of bourbon and coke. This resulted in our attendance in the Anthrax mosh pit. From the chaos of the pit you can't actually see the band!?

We were all separated during Sabbath and at the end I retired to the tent absolutely knackered. I lay there waiting for the

others, my back hurt, my legs hurt and my feet were killing me. Eventually James arrived. "You took your time?" I asked "I was watching the pole dancers in the Napster tent" Replied Chewbacca grinning
"WELL DON'T JUST STAND THERE, PASS MY SHOES!" shouted I heroically summoning the last of my strength.
"It's finished" he said disappearing into his sleeping bag.
Bruce entered the tent soon after
"You never guess what I've just seen in the Napster tent?"
"F**k you!"
We had another sleepless night. I awoke again at 5:30am and I took advantage of the empty showers and shithouse. I looked at the two wretches in my tent. Bruce was a little irritable bundle that farted in his sleep and James looked like a plastic Christmas tree when it's in its box. They surfaced in time to see the shower queue snaking through the campsite. We said farewell to James and had another day of ROCK. 5 hours later I turned on my phone to see two texts from James: 'Legg, I can't find my car, are you still there?"
Then
"I found it, 5 hours later!"
Apparently they had put him in the day parking instead of the camping car park and he had been going round in circles in the wrong car park.
We had a plan to leave just before Motorhead finished so that we could get out a good hour before the band on the main stage finished. This we achieved and got out of the car park no problem.
In conclusion I loved going for 3 days but the camping was pretty hardcore. Funnily enough I have realised that I quite like camping but not surrounded by drunken teenagers! I would like to go on a camping holiday with Louise but you wouldn't get the Metal bands in the new Forest!!"
Simon Legg (Grays, Essex)

2006
Tool, Metallica & Guns N' Roses

This year saw the return of two metal titans to Donington; Download regulars Metallica were back for their 3rd headline show on the Saturday and returning for the first time since their show in 1988, eighteen years before, Guns N' Roses finished the festival off on the Sunday evening.
Friday night was headlined by Tool, coming back to Donington at an elevated level after their appearance at Ozzfest four years before.
The Metallica set on the Saturday featured the 'Master Of Puppets' album, played track by track plus some classic other tracks played afterwards; for the encore, members of other bands including Trivium came up and sang along with Metallica on some cover versions.
The most controversial set of the weekend was the GNR headline slot on Sunday night, with Axl spending more time off the stage than he did on, at some points. Guns were a shadow of their former selves and even the special guest appearances of Izzy Stradlin and Sebastian Bach (ex- Skid Row), did little to alleviate the problems or raise the crowd's spirits. Axl, early in the set, slipped on the

stage and went off for ages whilst his band performed jams until he came back on, seemingly more relaxed and went through to complete the rest of the set without a hitch; after the set, the weekend was marred by the riots in the campsite, a once off occurrence in the history of festivals at Donington.

Elsewhere on the mainstage were a host of 'usual suspects', popular Download regulars in the shape of Bullet For My Valentine (gradually climbing the bill), Trivium (also scaling the bill to an equal 3rd place slot on the Saturday), Korn (again in the 'special guest' slot) and Funeral For A Friend playing just before GNR. The Korn set was very different to usual as Jonathan Davis had been rushed to hospital, so they played with special guests on vocal duties; vocals were carried out by Matt Heafy from Trivium, Benji from Skindred, M Shadows from Avenged Sevenfold and Jesse Hasek from the virtually unknown Ten Years.

Another extremely controversial choice was when The Prodigy were chosen to headline the 2nd stage. 'Dance Music' at Donington? Would it work? Would people attend the stage? The answer to all these questions was answered in the positive, with a huge crowd, a 'banging' set and the most popular show in the tent for the whole weekend.

Sick Of It All had the task of playing against the GNR slot on the 3rd stage and Lordi made a triumphant return to Download playing before SOIA, after having won the Eurovision song contest the same year with 'Hard Rock Hallelujah' and the tent was packed.

The Snickers Bowl, featuring skateboarders and performances from smaller artists such as Betty Curse and Get Cape, Wear Cape, Fly; the Bowl was very popular all weekend, as were the free Snickers bars, which were in abundance.

Another great weekend and the festival would return for its 5th time the following year.

"We obviously headlined Download in '06, which was probably the best gig that we have ever done on the Donington ground and I would say that it even eclipsed the '95 appearance. We played 'Master Of Puppets' in its entirety and I just remember all other bands were crowded around the stage; I remember watching Phil Anselmo over at the side, banging along to every not of 'Master Of Puppets'.
We played a 'blinder' that day, as the English say and we played a new song, I believe at the time it was called 'The New Song'; I think the intro and the middle part morphed and ended up in the song 'The End of the Line' which is on 'Death Magnetic'.
We played 'Puppets' in it's entirety and then a Misfits cover for the first encore and a bunch of the other bands came out and sang with us; that was definitely the best Donington appearance, it was a good one."
Lars Ulrich (Metallica – Drums)

"The last time we played was in support to Guns N' Roses, just before they made their return and it was one of those things that you wish you could scrub from your memory really. I would have rather been watching Sick Of It All."
Matt Davies (Funeral For A Friend – Vocals)

"The most difficult show was the one where we were main support for Guns N' Roses. It was still enjoyable, but there were a lot of people who were just there just to see Guns N' Roses, who were probably immensely disappointed, as I was. I had set myself up for disappointment to be honest as I couldn't really see it being that great and it wasn't. I wish that they would just leave GNR alone, unless Slash would come back, but then it would still just be Axl, Slash & Friends."
Ryan Richards (Funeral For A Friend – Drums)

"The first time we played was 2006 and we were all really excited to play the festival especially because of the history of it because it was always Monsters Of Rock when I was growing up, but it's still the same festival, with a great variety of rock bands.

What happened on that trip was that we had a big falling out with our drummer; he had decided that he couldn't come on the trip due to his own reasons and that was 2 hours before we got on the plane. So we were at the airport trying to figure out what we were going to do. We didn't have many dates on that tour, we had to cancel a bunch of them in the end, but that's a long story to get to that; but there weren't many festivals and one of the biggest ones was Donington and we really wanted to get there and do it. We felt that playing at Donington was very important and we also wanted to see some of the bands that were going to be there; it was just a great opportunity and it's beautiful there too.

We decided that if the worse came to the worst and our drummer decided not to fly out, we would rehearse with our drum tech because he knew all the songs and had been around with us for so long. We arrived at Donington the day before and immediately started rehearsing and he learned all the songs or whatever he could at the time to fit in to his mind. We had about 5 hours to get all this shit together and he was a really great drummer. His name was MP (Michael Petrak) and he got together whatever he could to pull it off, if our drummer Josh wasn't able to fly out and he didn't.

We had a great slot at around three or four in the afternoon, which is kinda prefect.

It came down to showtime and we were all scared shitless, but we got up there and in front of that huge crowd we pulled it off. I guess that the positive part of the whole story was that in front of that crowd we realised that we were going to be ok; things got shittier as that tour went on, but that was a big part of being able to turn around a say 'we did that show, in front of that huge crowd and it worked out'. We were still able to do it even though all that bullshit was going on, especially for Claudio and I at that point as we were given a good example of how it would be to go on if shit really hit the fan, which it did. Beyond that, it was a pity that we never got to see more bands because of all the bullshit going on; Deftones played the same day as us and I am a big fan of their music and a couple of other bands. We were only there for the day, which I was a bit annoyed at, as Metallica were playing the next day and I was

really dissapointed; I heard that they did all of 'Master Of Puppets' and that was something that we all had wanted to see.
So, not only did we get to share the stage with other bands that we respect and are fans of, but at the same time we got to play in front of this crowd and realised that either way we were going to be ok and even in the worst of times and in the shittiest situation, we could still make the best of it and make this music.
But, it was a good experience in the end, it just started off pretty crazy."
Travis Stever (Coheed and Cambria – Guitar)

"We played the mainstage very early in the afternoon and I don't think I had ever seen so many people in my life. It was the first time that I had seen such a huge amount of people. We came with a tour bus that time though. The variety of bands impressed me a lot because there is something for everyone; you could almost have a family coming here, from the young 16 year old who wants to listen to the extreme metal bands, to the parents who would like to listen to the old school or mainstream bands like Slipknot, so there is literally everything for a 'rocker', all kinds of rocker.
It's the variety on offer that makes it the best festival in Europe."
Andrea Ferro (Lacuna Coil –Vocals)

"We played the year that Guns N' Roses played.
We just go up onstage and have a good time. All of these festivals are like a 'high school reunion party', because you meet all these bands that you've toured with and you meet new friends; it's just about hanging out.
What I like most about festivals is the part where you can go anywhere, meet your friends and have a laugh; what I really hate about festivals is that they seclude the headliner and put them alone with gates and security outside and if you are the headliner, like we have been, you sit there alone and it's fucking boring.

*The festivals in Europe are a little differently organised and us being from Europe, I guess it's what we are used to.
But we have fun on everyone, especially if we have a good show and get to see our friends."*
Peter Iwers (In Flames – Bass)

*"The last time that we came to Download me and Aaron got a lift down a day early, because we wanted to see Tool.
So we arrived a day early and it was such an awesome show; to see them at night with a massive crowd and the planes flying over, it was an amazing experience like no other. It's just a cool experience; you wouldn't see planes that low anywhere else.
There was an after party and the guys in Alexisonfire were there, so we all hung out backstage and it was pretty cool. We got to meet Phil Anselmo and he was singing songs to me and George from Alexisonfire; he was like 'hey guys I've got a new song, check it out'. He would just start signing and five minutes went by and me and George were thinking 'this is so surreal right now', it was great.
It was such a cool experience."*
Ian D'Sa (Billy Talent – Guitar)

"One of the great things about being at Download was that I got to meet a couple of the Metallica guys and I got to watch all of Metallica's set when they played 'Master Of Puppets', which was really cool. It was amazing to be so close to the band and then to look out at the crowd and realise the importance of Download, especially for metal."
Jon Gallant (Billy Talent – Bass)

"So here I found myself backstage in the VIP "free drinks" section. I didn't have the appropriate wrist band to be back there but Aaron from Billy Talent headed to bed early for the night and gave me his. I used a paper clip to secure it on my wrist and it was free drinks for me! (Sorry Download! But the exchange rate is pretty hefty for us Canadians and we ain't rich!)

So I'm standing around with some of the Billy Talent boys chatting and shooting the shit, when who walks in??? Ex-Pantera frontman Phil Anselmo. He was completely smashed, which was exactly how I expected him to be. The second he got a drink, he bee lined it over to this chap wearing a Minor Threat t-shirt, pointed at his chest and said "1st album only...FUCK Fugazi." That alone was probably the best thing I could have possibly witnessed that weekend. But the story didn't end there. Later that evening when Phil got within earshot of me, I told him I thought he was going to perform with Alice In Chains, as I had heard several rumours. He quickly responded, "I was too wasted. They would have never let me on stage." A fitting answer from the man who has died three times. More time passes. My friend Ben and I are hanging out when who strolls over but Phil yet again. "Hey, where are you guys from?" "Toronto, Canada," we respond. "Ahh...a couple of Canadians! I'm Phil from Louisiana. You guys wanna hear me sing something?" You are damn straight we wanted to hear Phil Anselmo sing something. A personal concert just for me and Ben. I was totally jazzed. Phil puts his arms around us and begins his tune, "...happy birthday to you, happy birthday to you, happy birthday dear...worst song ever. Take it easy guys." I probably don't need to tell you it wasn't my birthday. Phil then let us go and was wrangled by one of his crew. And that's the story of the night. Phil Anselmo sang me "Happy Birthday". You just can't make this shit up. Totally true story."
George Pettit (Alexisonfire – Vocals)

"The buses were about 5 miles away from the stage and we had to get someone to drive us over. To get to 'our stage' it was about 7 miles away from the bus.
We arrived a 2am and so we didn't get to see Metallica do their 3 hour show; you wouldn't get to see us do that."
Pete Koller (Sick Of It All – Guitar)

"It was awesome; we played the small tent and it was the defining moment of our career up until then. It was the first festival that we did and the tent was absolutely rammed and

just to look out and see that many heads was pretty incredible."
Roughton "Rou" Reynolds (Enter Shikari – Vocals / Synthesizer)

"We had gone to the festival the year before and it was pretty weird to be playing it the year after, but it's always awesome and pretty scary, because there are always a few bottles. That first year we played was our first 'big show', apart from that we had been playing lots of club gigs; it was I think also our first festival.
It was so scary, but it was pretty fucking cool. We had a massive pit and a 'wall of death'."
Oli Sykes (Bring Me The Horizon – Vocals)

"I had never been to Download or Donington when I've not been in a band, so the first year I went to Download was pretty cool; first time at Donington and I was pretty stoked on it."
Matt Nicholls (Bring Me The Horizon – Drums)

"We were booked to play the tent and we had a blast, but I am friends with Robert in Metallica and he said 'dude, Jonathan Davis and they are looking for someone to sing and I have put your name forward'. I just went up there and spoke to a couple of the guys in Korn, they said that they had wanted me to sing two songs, but I said that I would do one, because if it all went horribly wrong I could end up getting covered in piss. They then said to me to sing one song.
Of all the metal bands in the 90's I was a massive Korn fan, I'd even paid money and bought tickets to go and see Korn and now I've got Fieldy asking me to sing a Korn song, it was like a dream. I had Robert Trujillo saying 'dude, you can do it' and I'd got Fieldy saying 'will you do it?' and I'm just an asshole from Newport, with these two hug 'rock monsters' asking me to do it.
I went up there and I thought that I would just give it my best shot and I know that the British heavy metal fans love my band, so I went up there and gave it all I'd got. I sang

'A.D.I.D.A.S.' and to this day I think 'my god it's just a dream!' It was incredible!!
I met Corey from Slipknot; I hadn't really known him before, but he was really trying to bring it all together. So there was Corey, Dez from Devildriver and the guy from Avenged Sevenfold and he was like 'c'mon guys this is not about us, we're representing Jonathan Davis here and we've really got to get this together'. He gave us a pep talk before we went on and cheered us up. He made us feel like a team and made us all feel comfortable. I wish that I had really done another song as the entire crowd sang along; you either get covered in piss or kisses, I guess we got covered in kisses!"
Benji Webbe (Skindred – Vocals / Synthesizer)

"We played in 2006 and I think our story is pretty cool.
We were actually slotted to play first on the 2nd stage, we had done some big shows like Ozzfest before, but we were slotted in to play at 11am and we were wondering if anyone was going to be there and it was on the Sunday too and people had been rocking out for the whole weekend.
So the doors opened at 10am and we got there at about 10:30am and there were hardly any people out there, so we started freaking out. We were fired up and pissed off and shouting 'this is bullshit'. We got ready to play and the intro goes off and we got out there and it was completely packed and we couldn't believe it; we were like 'holy shit'.
Being that we were so early, we were speaking to other people about it and they said that they hadn't seen that many people that early in the day before, so they were coming to see our band!
The show was insane, the crowd went nuts and we actually used some of the footage for a music video.
It was a pleasant surprise and I think it was still probably the biggest show that we have played, even bigger than the Ozzfest shows that we'd done."
Doc Coyle (God Forbid – Guitar)

"It's a tough call to really sum up our experience at Download in just a few words.
It was like all the fuckin planets lined up for us that day...Everything was perfect...and having the crowd respond to us in that way was just over the top. It made us feel like kings for the day...well...for our set anyway!
Watching the footage from the show is almost as good as being there again...I just keep watching it, ha-ha! It was a good day for us, and made us feel 'valid', ya know? Very cool...very memorable...and something that I will never forget, and always cherish.
Thanks to all at Download...the fans, the crews, everyone that made us feel right at home there...you're all gods. Metal Hailz!"
Jed Simon (Strapping Young Lad – Guitar/Backing Vocals)

"It was awesome.
We were really happy that we made it, after 2004, when our bus broke down and we missed the show and felt really bad.
I think that the band right now is stronger and better than ever, with AJ Cavalier as our frontman now, we are a lot more in your face. We are still heavy, but we're still melodic and I think True Self (Album) shows that.
We played a good mixture from Scars, Re.De.Fine and the new album.
Thirty minutes of blistering intensity and then a good friend of ours Jada Pinkett Smith of Wicked Wisdom came on stage and she helped out with Halo.
It's good to be on a big stage again. But it's hard to feel how hard the crowd is into the gig, when they are a shitload of feet away from you. But from the reaction I think that they were having a good time, and it was beautiful weather"
Shaun Glass (Soil – Guitar)

"We played on the mainstage and went on at noon, Guns N' Roses was the headliner that day. It was set up a little bit different to now, because the stage was in a different area.

One thing that I do remember about that show was that the weather was also great and it was sunny and the temperature was perfect; we really 'lucked out' there!"
Frank Novinec (Hatebreed – Guitar)

"I guess for any metal kid its classic grounds; I grew up with a lot of classic British heavy metal and also through the Guns N' Roses era and obviously most of these bands had classic gigs when they played at the Monsters Of Rock at Donington. So without us getting to play there when it ended, it was a bit sad. When it reappeared as Download a few years ago, we got to play it and it was amazing.
I remember being very fucked up, it was very hot and our bus had some real problems. I was sleeping in our 'Nightliner' because we were there for two days and I suddenly woke up in a garage, because the driver had driven off to get the bus repaired, not knowing that I was in the bus. He couldn't just turn around and take me back, as we were at the garage; so I spent most of one of the days at the garage far from away from Download; not that fun.
But I do remember that it was a good gig. The only downside is that you have so little time to do linecheck and soundcheck, both the crew and the band and the promoters get a bit stressed out about that."
Nicke Borg (Backyard Babies – Vocals/Guitar)

"It was absolutely unbelievable and the one that I was really looking forward to. I was really nervous before going on stage and there were a lot of people there and the crowd were really, really responsive.
I was a bit worried because my act isn't as heavy as some of the other ones, because it's a very heavy festival and some of the acts are REALLY HEAVY.
But everyone was really brilliant and everyone was clapping and it was probably one of the best responses I have had and I'd just done a 2 week tour including Rock AM Ring and Rock IM Park and this was definitely the best response.

I came down in my dads campervan and caught Metallica and we were right at the back and couldn't even see them because I'm so small"
Lauren Harris (Lauren Harris – Vocals)

"Our next visit to Download was in 2006 and this time we played the Prestigious Main Stage, bigger Crowd and bigger nerves go along with this honor.
This time was not the best of luck for me as I had blown out my voice in Sheffield a night earlier, but as they say the show must go on, it did. I survived it but it wasn't pretty.
 It seems a little vague to my memory of all the happenings due to me being a bit under the weather, but never the less we were stoked to be asked back for our 2nd time."
Brock Lindow (36 Crazyfists – Vocals)

"We played at Download in the tent. We hadn't been playing or touring much as we had been writing songs for a new album.
I had really bad cramp; it was a horrible gig for me. My left hand completely froze up during the first song, all my tendons right up my wrist; it's the first time that it had ever happened to me, they went like concrete, so I couldn't move my hand. So, I did the whole set in utter agony, as it really hurt as well; it just went like rock and went solid.
All I could do was use one finger and follow what the bassist was doing, so I was just making some sort of noise, but no one seemed to notice.
I went to the St John's Ambulance after to see what they could do, but it eventually just went.
Then we went to see Guns 'n' Roses and left in disgust."
Larry Hibbitt (Hundred Reasons – Guitar)

"Lot's of interesting things have happened to me at Donington/Download. When I played there with Ginger And The Sonic Circus in 2006 we had the Psycho Cyborgs appear with us who proceeded to impale my arms, five insertions per limb. All was well until they pulled out the rods and for the next 45 minutes the stage was filled with my blood. It was great fun

seeing the band skidding around in my plasma."
Ginger (Ginger And The Sonic Circus – Vocals/Guitar)

"I think our first experience of Download was probably the most nerve wracking of our lives in 2006.
We came on to a wall of bottles, but it was probable one of our most triumphant shows, as we overcame it."
Omar Abidi (Fightstar - Drums)

"I was really nervous because Download is a predominantly metal festival and I remember from when we walked out, to the moment the crowd changed and a massive mosh pit opened up."
Charlie Simpson (Fightstar – Guitar/Vocals)

"Download was significantly important for me, as a kid growing up in the mid-'90's. I remember seeing Sepultura on their 'Chaos AD' tour at Monsters of Rock, must have been '94 and the footage that 'Headbangers Ball' had put together was probably what pushed me into being in bands.
So it was a dream come true to play there and it's different from other festivals as it's such an exclusively metal festival. You get a great sense of belonging and everyone there is like 'part of a tribe' an therefore there is goodwill that extends beyond what you experience in day to day life, because everyone realises they are in it together, everybody's into the same shit and it's all about unity and belonging and that's why it's special. Download and Donington epitomises that."
Dan Haigh (Fightstar – Bass)

"*Download was like everything we'd ever dreamed of, it was amazing, huge crowd and a big stage.*
I think the crowd at Download is better than the crowd at Reading, but both festivals are amazing."
Angel Ibarra (Aiden - Guitar)

"My friends in As I Lay Dying said that our show in 2006 would be the best show that Bleeding Through had ever played,

because they thought that it was the best show that they had ever played in 2005.

We were really nervous about coming over as we had no idea what to really expect. We got up on the stage and it was one of those shows where it made us feel like Metallica. It was the closest that I had ever felt to what it must be like to be in a 'big band'; it felt like being a God on that stage and that we could have got away with saying anything up there.

It was to just have that experience and I think I walked off the stage that day feeling very fortunate for doing it.

I do feel fortunate because this is my life, I get to hang out with all these bands and Download was the pinnacle of that year."
Brandan Schieppati (Bleeding Through - Vocals)

"It was an honour to play Download. Everybody stills views Download as being Castle Donington, that's how I still view it anyway.

Tried to play it many times before, but we never got on it. Our old manager, who was a guy called Paul Loadsby, was the guy that started Donington, it was his original idea in 1980 to get it all together. I wouldn't say he was bitter, but he was annoyed that when he managed us and wanted to get us on Donington, we could never get on it.

But eventually we've done it. I think it was a good gig, I think we did alright and the crowds were into it.

I can now sit back in my rocking chair years later and say that I've done it!

I watched Bullets & Octane and they were very energetic, enthusiastic and got the crowd going with a good set. Then one of them came up to us afterwards and said we were pretty cool!"
Gary Jennings (Cathedral – Guitar)

"I went once before at the old site, inside the racetrack; the year 'Guns N' Roses' played, in inverted commas."
James Davies (The Blackout – Guitar)

"It was great, a lot of energy, it was wonderful. I would like to see a few bands, if only we get the chance to do it, there's so much going on at the same time."
Rocky George (Fishbone – Guitar)

"I'm glad to be here."
John McKnight (Fishbone – Keyboards/<u>Trombone</u>/Guitar/Vocals)

"What the hell's going on here? Too damn much and I want to see all of it!!
I want to see Tool and the Deftones. Ours set was too short. The energy of the crowd was good though, really helped out. It was cool."
John Steward (Fishbone – Drums)

"I'm loving it and having a good time, but you can't really cover Fishbone in thirty minutes. But I'm enjoying the festival with all the beautiful women.
But we're only here today and then off to Hungary, Budapest, Holland and French gigs"
Curtis Storey (Fishbone – Trumpet/Vocals)

"Download rocks. Knock some heads, ripped some shirts, and inhaled some dirt. The crowd was great, we love the UK. We're gonna keep on rockin' y'all, you better come back. Later!!"
Dre Gipson (Fishbone – <u>Keyboards</u>/Vocals)

"One thing I remember about the Download Festival is that I went into the performance and did some poetry.
I shaved my hair that day after growing it for about a month or so.
I can't remember too much of what happened as far as the crowd's reaction it was top of the line Fishbone Moshpit skank-n-hoffin chaos.
I liked it and thirty minutes wasn't enough and we never really got to get started.

But from the way the crowd was reacting it looked like they let us know they were enjoying it."
Angelo Moore (Fishbone – Vocals/Saxophone/Theramin/Percussion)

"I had a good time at the Download Festival, but there oughta to be more bitches up in this mutha fucker for Norwood his damn self. Know what I'm saying?
It turns out to be a family affair, there's a lot of people here that we have toured with over the years."
John Norwood Fisher (Fishbone – Bass/Vocals)

"It was fucking great; I was kind of excited of the turn out and the kids that were into it considering that it's a metal fest. I was really fully happy. We're more like Megadeth meets Winger metal, with some Run DMC thrown in the mix."
Matty Lewis (Zebrahead – Vocals/Guitar)

"We didn't know what the turnout would be, be it was really good. What made me smile was when I asked 'how many of you guys are drunk?' at least like 30% of them shouted yeah and it wasn't even noon yet!!!!
Ali Tabatabaee (Zebrahead - Vocals)

"We played Download this year with Mondo Generator and got thrown out for breaking a chair or something. It wasn't something serious; it is always for something silly."
Ben Thomas (Mondo Generator - Drums)

"Download this year wasn't very eventful, we got thrown out."
Ben Perrier (Mondo Generator - Guitar/Vocals)

"It was one of the most frightening experiences of my life, but at the same time quite fun and so I enjoyed going on.
But, before I didn't know whether to vomit or shit? But I didn't do either!
I was considering shitting myself on stage, because I thought it's very rare that people do that, but it takes a lot of effort and

*I don't face those toilets; so I thought I would go up and lower the whole tone.
I went to check out Aiden, Cradle of Filth, Prodigy and Guns N' Roses"*
Betty Curse (Betty Curse – Vocals)

*"We played the Snickers Bowl which was very hot with a great atmosphere. We were on around 2:30pm and before the show we were quite anxious to get on there and 'rock out'!
I used to skate, so watching the people skating was fun and distracting at the same time, but it went down really well, we enjoyed it, Meg (Betty Curse) enjoyed it."*
Adam Curse (Betty Curse – Bass)

*"This year the celebrations were cut short. We opened the mainstage and we were chucked out of the VIP area at about 2 or 3am in the morning as there was a fire in the campsite. There's always something happening at Donington, this year Jonathan was missing from Korn and Axel Rose was the talk of the town for all the wrong reasons. It reminded us all about everything that you always wanted to forget about the rock industry and a very helpful reminder to keep you feet on the floor, unlike Axel 'fly with the fairies' Rose.
They cleared the whole backstage area for him to get into his dressing room enclosure, which is really weird because it's only artist's back there and no one is going to go and kiss his ass!!!! There's been enough of that done for a whole lifetime. I bumped into him backstage and we didn't even exchange words, he looked like Axel Rose's dad. He looked like a low budget movie and they had fast forwarded twenty or thirty years to when the main characters are old and they look like they have splashed some flour on and really, really naff makeup and they look really 'un-human' because they look all 'plasticky', that's what Axel Rose looks like. I saw him about three inches away from my face, weird as fuck!!!
Another thing to colour the festival experience at Donington, is that there is so much going on, BMX and skateboarders and performers, the whole cast of Star Wars, there is so much stuff going on all the time, it makes for the full rounded festival*

experience and you've got a sense of accomplishment at the end of the day, you have survived another day at Download. You walk around and there are people sleeping in puddles of their own piss, people suffering from heatstroke and you don't quite see it at other festivals now. All the other festivals seem very 'state run', very much for the masses, homogenised and diluted."
Paul Isola (Breed 77 – Vocals)

"The first time we got to play was in 2006, when there was an incredible line-up. It was really exciting for me on a personal level as I got to see to Tool for the first time, who are one of my favourite bands. We got to watch Metallica the following day; the whole experience was just great. It was just like the 'who's who' of rock and metal, which I think is the theme of Download in general, bringing these bands from all over the planet to the biggest festival."
Dave Peters (Throwdown - Vocals)

"*Well*, Download was many things.
We have never played a fest that big before. There were a lot of people in black with more hair than I have ever seen in one place. But what I remember most was when we were playing and started getting bottled. We played in a switched timeslot with Darkest Hour. So people were confused, then pissed. So as they threw bottles at us I kind of liked it...so much that I told the crowd that they can throw what they want, I am just glad they stuck around at all.
Our fourth song was a slower song. One that may not be choice to play since we were at a metal fest. But I realized we had won over the crowd when they stopped throwing bottles for that song.
Most bands would get bummed having bottles thrown at them...us we thought it was great.
Not even half full bottles of water can bring us down at a metal fest."
Kenny Bridges (Moneen - Vocals/Guitar)

"This was our first time in England, first time in Europe, our drummers Italian, so he's been to Italy, but other than that it's everyones first time in Europe and we had an amazing time. The stage we played on was absolutely fantastic. The crowd from the kids in the front to the people in the back, all the way through it was just fucking brilliant. By the end of our set we had five burlesque dancers on stilts behind us for the last two songs!! They were quite randy!

We had a blast, the weather doesn't get any better. The highlight of the show, for me, was Alice In Chains, Tool and Deftones were fantastic. It finished very early, in Canada the festivals go on into the night.

We were absolutely astounded with England, Donington especially. The one thing that is the best about Download is watching your favourite band on the mainstage and having a plane come fucking flying over your face, it's awsome."

Jonny Hetherington (The Art Of Dying – Vocals)

"Playing Download was by far the coolest experience that I have ever had.

This was our first time in England and to play a show of this size was just fucking unbelievable.

To see that many kids come out and actually stay and watch us and be interested in what we were doing, it was just unreal. Especially being 4000 miles from home and having people actually care in what we were doing, when they could have been doing anything else at all, it's just a real surreal amazing feeling.

We've watched All American Rejects, Aiden and Metallica, it was a long show but it was good"

Danny Stevens (The Audition - Vocals)

"Playing Download was such a surreal experience. We're still a really new band, even when we're back home in the States for anyone to know us so far away from home it's still a thrill. But when you fly over an entire ocean and you go to a completely different country and there are kids who know your band and want to meet you, it's even more insane than being in your own country, because you are 4000 miles away!

You take a band like us and we were put on a stage in front of 3000 people, the biggest show we've ever played and we did our thing and did the best we could.

We were really nervous coming in to this, because this is the biggest metal festival, we like metal, but we're not a metal band.

The band that played before (Enter Shikari) us on our stage was crazy. They had techno beats and they would then go into these crazy breakdowns.
They all wore soccer uniforms on stage and all of them looked like friends I had at home, so I thought they were going to be a 'pop rock' band, but they were definitely not.
Seth Johnson (The Audition – Guitar)

"Obviously it wasn't one of the greatest stages, but we were on classic ground and it is of course a cool thing for us to be able to come here. It has been a childhood dream ever since we started playing, of course we want to play something bigger next time, but we ended up here (Snickers Bowl) because we came in so late. I don't think that Evergrey is much preferred in the skateboard world, but it doesn't matter and we were honoured to play here."
Tom S. Englund (Evergrey – Vocals/Guitar)

"However our second experience totally blew the first one away. I think our performance at Download 2006 will be one of the most important memories in our bands lifetime if not, The most important. It was certainly a moment in my life that I can always look back on and my hairs stand on end.
For me playing there is like 5 years hard work and touring all condensed into a 30-minute moment. This time around we couldn't have hoped for anything better, we had an incredible time, the crowd were amazing and the booze flowed for 24 hours.
We saw some amazing performances over the weekend too; Alexisonfire, Alice and Chains and Strapping Young Lad were all sets that the five of us enjoyed. Other than that Download was one giant haze of booze, cocktails and bulldozer headaches.
I hope every band in their lifetime gets to have a moment like we did, we'll never forget it."
Olly Mitchell (Johnny Truant – Vocals)

"Download, wow, what a weekend! It was great to be part of something that
means so much to so many rock bands and fans alike.
Our own show went really well and it was a fantastic and privileged feeling to perform on such a great stage.
Being local to the area and achieving a dream of playing to a packed out audience at The Charlotte, Leicester and then to perform at Donington is something else. Man, I loved every minute!
The chicks' walking around in bikinis and stilts was also a highlight for me!"
Andy Driver (My Awesome Compilation- Drums)

"The sun beat down on the smooth racetrack tarmac, thick black skidmarks wound across the track. We sped out of the pits and crossed the finish line, and that was it. We were there. We weren't racing though, merely walking out of the artists' paddock and into the festival grounds for getAmped's very first Download festival at Donington Park racetrack. But for all intents and purposes it could have been a race - it turned out to be one hell of a high speed, adrenaline-fuelled ride.
Our trusty, stalwart manager, Carl, and I arrived in Nottingham late on the Thursday night, so we could be at the festival early the next day. Although getAmped would not be playing until Saturday afternoon, I had been recruited by the editor of a national rock magazine, Burn, to interview some of the other Download artists, and I would need to be at the festival for the whole long weekend. The interviews I conducted would be transcribed in a 'Download special' for the magazine, and also aired on the getAmped podcasts for the next few weeks (so look out for them here!). I was a ball of nerves, wired on excitement and expectation that night, and coupled with it being one of the first hot, and humid summer nights this country sometimes spews out, I didn't get much sleep. Nevertheless, I was full of energy on Friday morning, bouncing around like a kid on Christmas morning, much to Carl's annoyance.
After visits to both the artist accreditation cabin and the press

reception to collect our multitude of wristbands and passes, we wandered into the festival ground itself, before it was open to the public. I was blown away by the vastness of the place, and most of all, the black and red metal behemoth that was the main stage. The crew for one of the first bands were tuning the PA, and massive booms echoed around the track as some roady relished in banging a kick drum. I felt my pulse race, my stomach drop, and palms tingle a little as I contemplated playing on the main stage. I couldn't help but feel that I was staring our destiny, as a band, in the face as I took in the enormity of the view. 'Maybe next year," I mused to myself, "it'll be our turn up there." I snapped quickly out of my daydream as we reached the Snickers Bowl, where we were due to play on Saturday. It was dwarfed by the Death Star-like proportions of the main stage, but was still impressive with its mad structure which was centred around a 15 foot skate bowl, with rows of staged seating set up around it, stadium stylee. I couldn't wait to get up there and rock out. Behind the bowl was a colourful sea of tents, as many of the 73,000 people who would attend the festival had already arrived and were setting up their pitches. After leaving Carl to schmooze with other industry execs in the press tent, I sped off back into Nottingham to pick up Jackamo and James, our film crew for the weekend. As I drove out of the festival gates, a slight car accident had already caused a couple of miles worth of tailback back to the M1 - this was going to be one mad weekend!

My first taste of the balls out, high energy, high wattage craziness that embodies the Download Festival was 'Strapping Young Lad'. As I walked from the car with the film crew over to the press room, I paused on the hill in the centre of the track and stood aghast at the sea of frothy moshed-up bodies pulsing to the angry kick drum-ridden throb of these mentalists. The front man was a crazy dude that looked like a cross between a mad monk and a hillbilly, but boy could he scream, and more importantly, boy could he work a crowd. But I couldn't stay for long - I had work to do. Download is the pinnacle of the rock and metal scene in this country, and nowhere was this more obvious than in the press area. The *place was a hive of activity full of internet hook-ups, photo backdrops, body guards, press agents, photographers, A&R men, and of course...rock stars! This was like a bloody 'Who's Who' of rock for 2006. I didn't really have time to be starstruck, as before I new it I was interviewing crazy space-rockers Amplifier, who'd just come off a cooking main stage set. I hadn't heard a note of their music before the interview, but will be sure to check some out, as they were absolutely top lads. They were still positively effervescing after their show and we soon got deep into band related-chat, covering topics as varied as why people fancied their roadies more than them, and their favourite types of sausages in Germany. This was to set the trend for the weekend really, in that most of the guys I interviewed were just really cool down-to-earth people who were a pleasure to chat with. There was none of the rock 'n' roll bullshit arrogance that I had been half-expecting.*

Next in front of the mic were 'InMe' and we chatted away about the differences between playing a festival and a club, what they liked to eat best on tour, and more weird and wacky stuff that was coming off the top of my head. I was getting quite into my role as journo for the weekend, and was starting to get a feel for it. One thing that struck me was how well organised the weekend was by the media - InMe arrived, were straight into the press tent for a whole heap of interviews, including mine, and then whizzed straight out to hit the Snickers stage and play their first show in 6 months. The pace was relentless.

All-American Rejects have been a fave band of mine for a while, so I was really stoked to get to meet Mike and Tyson from the band for the interviews. I was even more stoked to discover that not only are they an ace band, but they are extremely friendly, candid and grounded people. We got on really well, and joked about the so-called 'hardships' of life on the road in a band, before they wished me luck for our set, and disappeared off to get ready for their set. They were headlining the Snickers stage that night.

After a few hours in the press area, I was done with band interviews for the day, so Carl and I strolled out into the park and met a few people in the park and interviewed them for our

'Download special' podcast. We also hooked up with our legend tech and roadie, 'Mustard', who emerged, unfazed and gnarly-looking, as only roadies can emerge, from the seething masses of the main stage. After dolling out a truckload of getAmped shoelaces, we finally took in our first bands of the day. We watched 'InMe' at the Snickers stage, and then checked out the All-American Rejects. AAR were really great live, with Tyson working the crowd up into a frenzy like a dervish. The place went off for their song 'Swing Swing' and they deservedly got an encore from the appreciative crowd. The energy and buzz of the place made me even more excited to play the next day. As the crowd swept over to the vast fields of the main stage to watch 'Tool', I decided to head back to the hotel for an early night and some rest. I would need all my energy for the performance on Saturday.

Another hot, sticky, restless night was interspersed with crazy, non-sensical, skittish dreams about rock lineups, soundchecks and interviews. Before I knew it, the big day had arrived. getAmped would play the biggest hard rock and metal festival in the UK before the sun was down. We got on the road early, so we could meet up with Tim who was bringing up the wolfshark with all our gear, and Jase. We plonked our tiny van amongst the macking great tour buses with their power hook-ups, satellite dishes and blacked-out windows, and started to unload our gear. I wandered around the bus paddock taking in the names of the bands that were stuck in the official parking passes in the bus windows: 'Trivium', 'Atreyu', 'Soil', 'Clutch'. We were mixing it with the big names and I felt really proud to be there. We piled our gear into the special shuttle bus that would take us to the Snickers Bowl, and were whisked in true rock-star style to the stage.

At the gates to the bowl, I was mistaken by one of the security ladies there as being one of the guys from Motorhead. I wasn't sure I was entirely flattered by this, especially given that Motorhead weren't on the bill for the weekend, but hey, at least she thought I was a rock star! We were welcomed to the Bowl by our stage manager and quickly settled in to the VIP area, which was really cool - a decked out area with garden furniture, water coolers, sun loungers, a great view of the bowl and most importantly, a freezer full of free Snickers Ice Cream! We watched Scottish all-girl punkers, 'the Hedrons', rock out before it was our turn to hit the stage. We set up our gear, and got everything ready for our set. We would have no soundcheck, so it was really important to make sure everything was working and sounding like it should. With Channel 4 filming the action in the bowl, and indeed our set, we would need to hit the ground running. After hurriedly scribbling some set lists down backstage (it's amazing the stupid things you forget to do when the pressure's on) it was 1pm, time for getAmped to rock the place out. I took a deep breath and...Bang, we were away blasting into the first angry chords of 'Down To Us' our opening number. It was really hot in the midday sun, and I could feel my throat drying up almost instantly as I belted the vocals out, but we play our first 2 songs of every show back to back, so there would be no chance to grab water before we were straight in to 'Phoney Society'. We played fast and furiously, trying extra hard to compensate for the distance between us and the audience that the bowl was imposing. I finally got my much-needed glug of water before we burnt into T-Rex, which went down a storm. By now I could see a crowd gathering outside the bowl gazing in at us which was a really nice feeling. With so much to look at - TV cameras pointing at us, photographers on stage, media types in the front, skaters ripping up the bowl, the crowd in the stands, and then mayhem going on outside the bowl - it felt like a dream up there and before I knew what had hit me we were playing our single 'Reject & Sterilise'. In spite of the distance between us and the crowd I could see people mouthing the words back! I was loving it and it was going to be over in 1 song! We stormed through our final track 'Black Clouds' and that was it, our first Download performance was over. 30 minutes has never gone so quickly. I was hot, sweaty, gasping for air and water, but I felt proud, exhilarated, relieved and sad all at the same time - it was all over too soon and it will be a whole year before we get to play it again. There were loads of familiar faces in the bowl from all over the country and I really would like to say a massive thanks to all the fans who showed up at Download to support us - it was a huge day for us and it really meant the world to see you there. Carl and the team gave out getAmped shoelaces and bags to people in the audience, so everyone left amped up to the max! But in many ways the weekend had only just started for us. Tim managed to collar skate legends, and long time heroes of his, Bucky Lasek and Tony Alva, for a quick chat for the podcast. I sat listening to these legends chat away to Tim, glugging ice cold water and stuffing ice cream down my face in the VIP area in gorgeous sunshine with my first Download performance under my belt. Life couldn't get better...or could it? As soon as Tim had wrapped up his chat with Bucky, it was back to the press area for interviews, but this time the mic was pointing the other way! We caught a few of the unmistakably dirty riffs of a re-issued 'Alice In Chains' blasting out of the main stage PA, but again couldn't stay to watch more - our lovely PR team at Hero had scheduled in a string of interviews for TV, press and radio as long as your arm. We were there for 3 hours talking to everyone about our show and the new record. We bumped in to Emma Scott, the ex-Power FM DJ who played our records ages ago on her 'Incoming' show and did an interview with her for Kerrang! Radio. We also talked to Maximum FM, Juice FM, and Total Rock. We also did a stint on the Redemption TV couch with the lovely Julia, and some comedy 'You're watching Scuzz TV' one liners which you'll have to keep an eye and an ear out for! If any of you see or hear them, let us know.

It was then back to my interviewing and podcasting duties, so Tim and I had a quick chat with Matt from 'Bullet For My Valentine' and the guys from 'Reuben' who are both Download veterans. We talked about how they'd worked their way up the stages and how much of blast it was for them to come back play it again and see the audiences getting bigger and bigger. I found it really inspiring, and vowed I'd work as hard as possible with the band to make sure that would happen for getAmped. The press area was mad, and absolutely buzzing again - Metallica had just arrived for their evening set, and I was just turning round to get my stuff and go and watch Jase play in 'This Is Menace' when Lars Ulrich walks in munching a bowl of fruit salad, minders hustling people out of his way. This was a full-on rock daydream!

Jase absolutely killed it with 'Menace', and I was amazed at how much energy he had given he had already played a full set with us! He was bashing the drums like a man possessed, and it was great seeing all the vocalists in action. They are starting work on their next album soon and I'll be helping Jase with the production duties, so I can't wait! When I was backstage on the Myspace stage talking to Jase, I clocked the Lordi dressing room, and all their monster gear was lined up outside. It was mad - a full on thick rubber construction supported by mad metal struts - I had a new found respect for how they perform live in that gear, especially in the heat. I'd have passed out!

After 'Menace', we chilled for the first time in ages, grabbed a few beers and burger and settled in to watch Korn, minus frontman Jonathan Davies who was ill, and then the mighty Metallica. The sun went down and Metallica echoed out over the biggest crowd of the festival yet. It was a massively impressive sight, reminding me of the CGI scenes of the Coliseum in the film Gladiator. Again the mosh pit frothed away, spewing dust and plastic bottles - people were going nuts. But in spite of the awesome grandeur of the setting and the vastness of the crowd I couldn't help but feel a little flat. As impressive and fun as festivals are, I felt that the gig was so impersonal, so disconnected, that I might as well have been watching them on TV. Sure I wasn't in the bowels of the mosh pit but thousands and thousands of people weren't, and I couldn't help but feel that you lost a bit of the atmosphere of the other, smaller stages. Nevertheless, I was watching Metallica headline a bill that my band's name was on (we're even on the official T-Shirts for heaven's sake!), and I was seriously happy and immensely satisfied! It was back to the hotel for the first good night's sleep of the weekend.

The weather was still glorious on Sunday, and I woke feeling happy and relaxed and ready to enjoy my final day of the festival. The pace was quick from the off, though - I had loads of interviews lined up. I caught the end of the 'Breed 77' set on the main stage, which I thoroughly enjoyed, and then trundled back to the press area to interview them. They were super laid back guys, and were really fun to talk to. I could hardly believe they'd been thrashing the shit out of their instruments on stage a few minutes earlier! I had my photo taken for the official Download 2006 press release, and signed the massive poster alongside the other artists - I was really getting in to this rock star malarkey! Carl, the crew and I went down to the Snickers Bowl again to catch up with weird and wonderful goth punk 'Betty Curse', who was warming up for her set. She was a really lovely girl, has an amazing image and it was a heap of fun chatting to her. Her music rocks too, but we could only catch the beginning of her set, as we wanted to catch 'Fightstar', meet some fans and get them on the podcast and give out some free getAmped stuff after the 'Fightstar' show. People outside the tent were hurling abuse about Charlie, and he got bottles thrown at him on stage, which I thought was really off. I really respect the guy for having the guts to follow his heart and pursue a career making the kind of music that he loves in spite of the haters and doubters. To turn up at a show with the sole purpose of throwing things at the band is just really low. People lapped up the shoelaces after the show, and we had a real scrum around us giving them out, we also talked to some really nice people for the podcast, so subscribe to it and check all that out!

It was about this time that I got a text message saying I had just co-produced my first number one album. The 'Sandi Thom' record I recorded in January was this week's number one album and my very first gold disc is on its way! Could the day get better? Hell yeah!

Back up to the press tent, and I did a quick interview about getAmped for Canadian extreme sports lifestyle channel Much Music, before settling in for a mad bout of interviews with other bands. I met Peter from 'Winterville', Kieran from 'The Prodigy', chatted to Chris and Gareth from 'Funeral For A Friend' outside the Kerrang! tent, before questioning legendary 'Skid Row' singer Sebastian Bach, the 'Hundred Reasons' dudes, old touring buddies, 'The Zico Chain', and Swedish metallers 'In Flames'. These interviews will all appear in 'Burn' and feature on the getAmped podcast very soon. Right now,

I'm almost home from a fantastic and magical weekend, I'm tired and sunburnt, and I have a LOT of editing to do for the podcast, but by god what a fun weekend! I can't wait until next year!"
Rick Parkhouse (getAmped – Vocals/Bass)

"We were travelling from Oslo, Norway and as we were a quite small band were playing quite early and we had to drive from the airport directly.
There was an accident on the 'freeway', so we had to travel around, which was a three hour longer drive.
I was for the first time driving on the wrong side of the road; so we had a rental car and we had to drive SO fast, about 150 mph, on the road side of the road for me!
We got there and didn't know where to come off the highway and we had ten minutes until we had to come on.
So I phoned a guy and said that we could take a left turn or a right turn and if we took the wrong one, we wouldn't have been able to be on; so we tried left and it was the right one. When we got there, we were thrown into a cab and Agnete was doing her make-up in there and we had some passes thrown in the window on the way. When we got on stage five minutes late and had to throw all the gear up there; it was a really tough gig."
Christian Wibe (Animal Alpha – Guitar)

"Our first experience of performing at the Download Festival was at 11.45am at the Snickers Bowl Stage on Saturday 10th June 2006.
It was the warmest day of the year so far, and the seating area was packed out. We found out after the gig that lots of our Myspace fans couldn't even get in!!!! In The Hedrons short life, it has to be our best gig to date.
We opened with 'Stop, look and Listen', which is a real punk 2min 10sec song, and the place was jumping. We played nine songs in total, which really wasn't enough; we would have played all day if we'd been allowed!
Highlights of the gig have got to be seeing the audience in the arena getting into our music, watching all the people standing

outside the arena trying to get in, and putting on a great show and playing a real rocking set! Every one of us had a ball!!
My personal highlight was when I bravely jumped off the stage into the audience. I did rip my t-shirt and hurt my back, but it was worth it. I decided to run around the bowl, which I soon found out is actually a very BIG bowl, and then jumped up to the seating area to sing to audience, it was such a buzz. When I came off stage I felt as if I had run a marathon!!
The best story of the weekend was when Soup – drummer Hedron, was back stage at the warm up area. She was playing around on the kit when Jerry Cantrell from Alice in Chains put his guitar on, plugged in and started jamming with her! What a great pre-gig warm up! Until next year…"
Tippi (The Hedrons – Vocals)

"Playing Download probably meant the most to me out of the band because I'm into a lot of the 'heavier' type of music; I feel that's what I bring to the music.
It was unfortunate that we didn't get to see as many bands as we would've liked, with the way things were working out. But, we did manage to catch Korn with the multiple singers; they were doing a 'Metallica', if you want, with the 'Korn Karaoke'. But seeing Corey was great as I'm a big Slipknot fan which was fantastic. We a caught a wee bit of Alice In Chains as we had supported them at the Astoria.
I wanted to go and see Guns 'n' Roses on the Sunday, because I had ticket years ago when they had Buckethead, but he fell ill and then they cancelled on me. But when I read the review it was disappointing, but it still is Axel Rose. Sometimes I think he should just do something else.
I'd love to go back and do one of the bigger stages, but just to be a part of it was great."
Chi (The Hedrons – Bass)

"My memories of Download are very good memories actually. It was quite an achievement to be invited along and to play in amongst so many well established rock acts; it was quite something for us.

The Snickers Bowl stage was brilliant and the crowd was all up for it and we actually had guys on BMX's and skateboards doing tricks in front of us.
It was a strange set up but we've made some new friends through Download, it was brilliant"
Soup (The Hedrons – Drums)

"Thinking back to Download, it was a great day for us, to be in amongst so many great bands, Donington is the home of rock! Considering we have only been together for just over a year. We saw a bit of Alice And Chains, who we had supported at the Astoria and we got to jam backstage with Jerry Cantrell"
Rosie (The Hedrons – Guitar)

"Playing Download was a dream I'd always had, but I never thought that I would actually do it. It was great fun and the crowd loved it. We'd had a few fans come down to the Underworld gigs and I could see them in the crowd in their Voodoo Six shirts."
Henry (Voodoo Six – Vocals)

"It was a dream come true, it is the place for rock bands, a year ago I would never have thought that I would have played here in this band, but now it's happened. Me and Henry are the new boys, the other three had been together for a couple of years writing the songs and we came in last summer and finished the album and then started gigging, it's all just come together.
I watched Metallica and it was just amazing, it was just lovely to see that many people, loving that kind of music and apparently there's a Gun 'N' Roses Tribute band playing later that we might watch"
Matt (Voodoo Six - Guitar)

"The stage and set-up was amazing and so un believably professional to
point that I was slightly intimidated by it all, having 4 techs on stage when
usually with only one was a bit over whelming.

The performance was the best we have ever done as a band, it sucked
that we had to play our first 3 songs to a handful of people due to the gates being closed, but as soon as they opened it was such a rush to people running in to see us, we filled up the tent with people still trying to cram in by the time we started our last song.
The crowd reaction was amazing, so many people screaming and just enjoying our music!
I met my idol, the bassist for A7X backstage which was pretty mind blowing
because he's been my idol since I started playing.
The sound of the main stage could have been better because it was swaying from side to side because of the wind. The sound on our stage (Snickers Bowl) was fantastic and by far the best of all the stages (maybe due to the fact that it isn't as big as the others); we sounded as though it was cd quality.
Carl Dawkins (Sintuition – Bass)

"Download's online community was now a virtual juggernaught steaming ahead on its own momentum, lovingly cared-for by its more-than-capable new foster parents Phil and Carrie, both motivated by passion over money, as it should be. The organisers decided, quite sensibly, that the festival had grown to such an extent that they felt more comfortable bringing the website's content and communications in-house. They did still keep us on-board for a couple more years, however, to produce the official coverage ("The Dog's Blogs") of the event and we had some really great times doing it. As our role at Download was diminishing, Virtual Festivals was expanding rapidly as a business (undoubtedly boosted by experience I picked up from my Download days) and commanding more and more of my time and energy. Where one adventure comes to an end, I find you don't usually have to look far for the next one. But that's a book (or two) for another day. What's important here is the rich legacy that those three incredible, pioneering years have left behind. The fantastic spirit of open co-operation between promoters and fans that we helped to nurture back then is still prevalent today with the

promoters now communicating directly via forum posts and twitter messages, and even meeting up with groups of boardies at regular 'fan forum' events (life imitating web). Beyond that, though, the seeds we planted together have since blossomed and spread out into the wider marketplace to revolutionise the way all festivals market to and interact with their fans. It's not a complete coincidence that once our template started to get replicated and the process propagated the whole festival marketplace underwent an explosive growth spurt. In the case of the boutique events that started sprouting up all over the country, innovative audience engagement would go so far as to overtake line-up as the main draw. Download has a lot more to answer for than just the rock.

Axl Rose's unpredictability on and off-stage is the stuff of legend, and one of the characteristics that has made him such a popular and enduring star. Yet one thing you can pretty much always rely on is that he will take to the stage late. Sometimes, as in his most recent (at the time) performance at the Hammersmith Apollo in London, two hours late. Don't ever plan to catch the last train home after a GNR show. So, there was a 'degree' of anxiety backstage at Download before the show. Festival licenses being as delicate and restrictive as they are (god forbid Doris next door should be disturbed by any noise after 10.30pm other than aircraft landing every two minutes), a late show would be a no-show which could be (and has been before) a riot. I heard an unsubstantiated claim that the promoters had arranged a contingency, in such an eventuality, whereby the Second Stage headliners (The Prodigy) would step up to the main stage if Axl missed his cue.

Suffice to say it came as a great surprise to the crowd and much relief backstage when the opening chimes of 'Welcome To The Jungle' erupted from the PA, 5 minutes ahead of the scheduled start time. Like I said, nothing but unpredictable, that man.

In fact, the set got off to a storming start and I managed to secure the best seat in the house, right next to the mixing desk operator who, I discovered, had one of the most stressful jobs in the world. He had a kind of intercom device on his desk, which appeared to be a hotlink to Adolf Hitler. A demented voice would frequently bark abusive orders out of it, like "Turn the f**king drums up, asshole!" and I realised that these coincided with the singer's regular jaunts off to the side of the stage. It was his voice, controlling the sound like a maniac! Amazing. Although there was a set-list taped to the wall, Rose seemed utterly oblivious to it, announcing each new upcoming song through the intercom, forcing the poor sound guy to frantically re-set all the levels for the eight piece band in the few seconds before it kicked off.

Four songs in, however, during Sweet Child Of Mine, it all went tits up at the front-end, literally, as Axl Rose's leather-soled shoes slipped on the water/ piss/beer-soaked stage and he fell on his bum. He then stormed off the stage, to the promoters' horror. Backstage, it was chaos, as Wild West style showdown kicked off between the promoters (threatening that Axl would never get a gig on this planet ever again if he didn't get back out there) - I may have embellished that - and Guns' management demanding the entire stage be carpeted first (that was true). While all this was taking place, new guitarist Bumblefoot was despatched to the lions to 'entertain' the crowd. His choice of delivery was inspired – an instrumental rendition of 'Don't Cry'. But the tears were flowing behind the scenes for a good, tense twenty minutes until a compromise was eventually settled on which met with Axl's approval – he would have to borrow a pair of rubber-soled trainers for the rest of the set. In a bizarre Cinderella-style ritual, every member of the festival and stage crew in the vicinity was asked to remove their shoes until Rose selected a pair that met with his approval (and fitted his demure size 5 ½ feet). One shoeless stage-hand then went back to work, as did Guns N' Roses. It's fair to say that the set did not go down as one of their best, but it was certainly one of their most memorable – especially from my vantage point."

Steve Jenner (Founder of Virtual Festivals.com & UK Festival Awards)

"Another year and more innovations. This year saw the Boardie BBQ follow the five-a-side matches. Held in the third stage tent, 400 board members got to chit-chat with Live Nation before the festival got going. OOFA Hill, home of the Official Old Farts Alliance was firmly planted on the slopes and the sheer number of people that I knew by now made it a part supreme. The hospitality bar was now in the Exhibition Centre, and this was the main entrance for those of us RIP'ers. A pint on the way into the arena, and the first thing you got when you walked into the Arena was that "Donington moment".

A friend of mine was doing the sound for Soil on the mainstage, so I got my first taste of watching a band from the sound desk this year. As I was led up the gap in the T-Barrier from the front I was recognised by a few boardies who started yelling out to me. Mark Yovich seemed quite amused that I was getting my own cheer from the Donington masses!

Later on I watched Tool from OOFA hill, which was a bit distracting - Tool are one of those bands you need to listen too, having young boardies (aka HOOFA's - Honarary Official Old Farts) running around all giddy doesn't help! But it's all part of the festival atmosphere.

Metallica headlined the Saturday night, playing 'Master Of Puppets' in its entirety. I never got to see this as Killing Joke were headlining the third stage. I love Metallica, but I love Killing Joke too, and I figured Metallica would be back one day, whereas Killing Joke might not.

The booking of The Prodigy in the tent on the Saturday night was quite controversial. That a non-rock band managed to pack it out (and in fact 25,000 people tried to cram into a 15,000 capacity tent) showed a broadening of horizons. Despite headlining the second stage, they finished in time to catch Guns 'N' Roses. A bit of a funny one this, with Axl Rose threatening to strop off the stage for the first half of the show (due to slippery leather soled hand made shoes - fixed by a pair of £5 trainers and matting!). I gave up when the guitarist was noodling through Christine Aguilera's "Beautiful" to cover for one of Mr Roses off stage excursions, though by all accounts the rest of the show was good once his shoes were sorted.

This was also the year of the "riots" - can't really say much

about that due to being over in RIP having a nice chill-out."
Phil Hull (Download Forum Administrator)

"Guns N' Roses played a really good set but what ruined it for me was seeing Axl's almost unrecognisable plastic face amongst his entourage of a about a dozen people who hurried him through an almost empty backstage area earlier in the day."
Mike Horton (Plymouth)

"My first Download experience was the Saturday of 2006, I was 15 at the time and I went along with 5 of my friends as well as my dad and my friends dad who drove us up there. The reason I wanted to go so badly was to see Metallica for the first time so I persuaded my dad to take us. I was so excited. I'd been to a few gigs before but nothing anywhere near as big as the Download Festival.
I woke up early in the morning and couldn't wait to leave. I remember arriving at the Donington services, walking in and seeing it completely packed with rockers and metalheads everywhere. It was strange to see but just got me all the more psyched up about actually getting to the festival.
When we got there and walked in to see right in front of us all of the stalls of the market I couldn't believe how awesome this place was, it was a dream come true.
I saw quite a lot of the bands playing the main stage during the day including Stone Sour and Korn.
Korn was a really memorable performance due to all the different vocalists helping them out in Jonathon Davis' absence but by this time I was so excited about Metallica that that was all I could think about.
When the 'Ecstasy Of Gold' started playing I just started beaming, I couldn't stop myself. My friends and I had made our way right to the front of the crowd and it was one of the best moments of my life. What made it even better was seeing Metallica play 'Master of Puppets' in its entirety. I will never forget that day."
Matt Percy (Hemel Hempstead)

"I've been to Download for 3 years and I've not experienced a festival like it! The classic surroundings of Donington Park and being absolutely 'Muller Cornered' with about 80000 fans who share a similar taste in music coming together in a scene of unity I love it.
My fondest memory would be seeing Alice in Chains in '06; they absolutely blew the stage apart. Brilliant!"
Matthew Alexander (Shipston On Stour)

"What a weekend.
Most memorable moment for me was on the Saturday night. After watching an amazing set by Metallica, me and my mate Presh headed to the Aftershock Tent for a few more beers. Anyhow, after having an amazing time in there we stumble out of the tent about 2 in the morning. On our drunken way back to our tent we spotted a game of rugby going on, on the 5 aside footie pitch. In my drunken stupor it looked like a fantastic idea to join in and have a laugh.
Presh tried to talk me out of it saying "You'll get battered ya daft cunt, don't do it Fozzy",
 "Nah, I'll be alright, I used to play rugby,"
 "Yeah when you was sober and you're 20 years older now daft lad"
"Ahh bollocks, Fuck it", I thought, "I'm havin' a go"
And with that I ran onto the pitch. There was pissed up blokes staggering all over the place with everyone barging into each other and running around like headless chickens I couldn't even see who had the ball.
Then suddenly I saw him, the lad with the ball, "He's mine" I thought as I charged towards him ready to take him out good 'n proper.
As I drunkenly launched myself at him things didn't really go to plan. I got my arms around his waist ready to bring him down but he basically shrugged me off like a fly, straight into the path of some other lad's knee, straight on the end of my nose "Crack"
Well fuck me; I didn't know what had hit me.
Meanwhile Presh was pissing himself on the touchline; unable to speak he was laughing that much.

"I told ya you'd get battered, but I didn't think it'd be in less than 10 seconds after going on" He took great delight in telling me.

By then blood was pouring out of my smashed nose and my face just felt numb, but I couldn't feel nowt, thankfully. I even thought it was quite funny at first.

As we made our way back to the tent I started feeling sorry for myself with blood going everywhere, and I began to think maybe it wasn't such a great idea after all.

The next day, Jesus Christ, was I suffering.

Not only did I have the mother of all hangovers but my head felt like a brick and my face felt I'd been hit by a truck.

Never again!

I ain't touched a rugby ball since."

Gary 'Fozzy' Forrester (Hull)

2006 Monsters of Rock Deep Purple

Alice Cooper, Journey, Thunder, Queensryche, Ted Nugent, Roadstar

Returning after a 10 year break with a move to a new location, Monsters Of Rock was back. The festival was now based at Milton Keynes Bowl, the site of other massive rock gigs such as Metallica's 'Big Day Out' and the Bon Jovi 'New Jersey' gig.

Blessed with a beautiful sunny day with temperatures in the high 80's, the Gods Of Rock were certainly shining down on the festival; an abundance of red faces were in attendance all day.

First band on were Roadstar (now Heavens Basement), managed by Laurie Mansfield one time guitarist of the band More who had played in 1981 at Donington, they fitted the 'Classic Rock' style perfectly and went down well with the early afternoon crowd.

Next up, making a rare UK appearance was the 'Motor City Madman', the man who brought us 'Wango Tango', the Nuge himself, Ted Nugent. Trail blazing his way through his extensive back catalogue, Nugent was a big success on the day, with more guitar licks than you could shake a hunting rifle at. The applause was well deserved and Nugent could have played much higher on the bill, perhaps another time at Download?

Queensryche played next and as with their previous appearance at Donington, some of their atmosphere and grandiose stylings were lost in the open air, in the middle of a hot and sunny afternoon. Definitely better in a hot and sweaty club, Queensryche put in a career spanning set with many tracks from the classic 'Operation Mindcrime' album, which has always been a crowd pleaser.

British classic rock on a sunny afternoon in late June, what could be better? And Thunder was the band to fill that gap. Always a good band live and Danny Bowes had a voice that could belt them out with the best. A band that also featured two amazing rock guitarists in Ben Matthews and Luke Morley, a great bass player in Chris Childs and Harry James, a drummer who was splitting his career between Thunder and Magnum, keeping time at the back; what a perfect combination and a winning formula. This was the 3rd appearance at Monsters Of Rock for Thunder and on the day it was only them and Queensryche that had actually played at Donington before; Thunder would return to Donington for their final appearance at Download 2009 as part of their final tour.

Next on the line-up was the much anticipated return to the UK for Journey, the 'Kings Of AOR'. Having rarely performed in the UK, in recent years, it was great to see a band as polished as Journey, with Steve Augeri on lead vocals, playing one of his final shows with the band. Journey would search on Youtube and find their next singer Arnel Pineda, in a Journey tribute band in the Philippines; this would be the line-up that would make their Donington debut at Download 2009.

Having never, surprisingly, played at Monsters Of Rock before, Alice Cooper was always going to be a very popular choice for the 'special guest' slot. Featuring all the stage props, from guillotines, to straight jackets, to swords and Alice Cooper Dollar bills, entertainment was the name of the game and Alice was at the top of his. Having played live for nearly 40 years, his show was perfectly executed, as was Alice with the
guillotine. His daughter also took part in the stage show and was stabbed through with a sword, a befitting way for Alice to treat his offspring.

After the theatrical performance of Mr Cooper anything that followed had a lot to live up to, but with classic tunes and a superstar band, Deep Purple filled the headline slot with plenty of energy, passion and great
entertainment.

The crowd did 'thin out' a bit after Alice Cooper's set, but that was understandable due to the young crowd in attendance, but what could beat classics like 'Black Knight' and of course 'Smoke On The Water'
playing in a field on a balmy summers evening.

Monsters Of Rock was back and with a vengeance, less of a capacity than in previous years at Donington, but popular all the same. MOR would come back amalgamated into the Download bill on the Sunday.

"Monsters of Rock at Milton Keynes, the atmosphere was exciting, I felt this 'buzz' all day long and it was one of the best vibes; EVER."
Ian Gillan (Deep Purple - Vocals)

"The good thing about playing these festivals is you're always getting to play with old friends. When you've been round for thirty five to forty years, everybody on the bill is someone you know or someone you've played with before. Whether it's Deep Purple or some of the older bands it's fun for us.
We never change our show ever; it's always going to be the same show. So we get up and look at the bill and say 'Who's on tonight'. I remember one night we played with Arthur Brown

who I hadn't seen since 1968 and he came back and he looked better than he did in '68!! It's great to see bands like that, bands that we learned from and that is the coolest thing, playing with old friends.
We do have total respect for any band that we play with, but it's kinda unfair for the band that comes on after us, because of all the production. We went out on a twin bill with Deep Purple, in Europe and I wasn't sure how they were going to fare after the guillotines and the confetti, but I have to say that they are better now than they were then."
Alice Cooper (Alice Cooper - Vocals)

"It was a message from God himself, he turned the lights on and this was the first nice day of the year really.
I thought about a week before, no it's not going to happen, but it's terrific and I think you need good weather for a festival and I think that it went well."
Luke Morley (Thunder - Guitar)

"We played at Milton Keynes Bowl with Deep Purple and the weather on that day was spectacular and it just makes everybody happy.
There were quite a few lobsters on the way home, people getting caught in the field and going bright red."
Ben Matthews (Thunder - Guitar)

"The weather was good; I don't remember anything that stood out about the day, but I guess nothing went horribly wrong, it's hard to remember details.
It's not the best situation, like your own show. In the States we don't have festivals like that, or the longevity, going on for years and years."
Geoff Tate (Queensrÿche – Vocals)

"The energy and piss and vinegar factors were off the charts, and I heard joyful tales of appreciation for our 1976 Reading rockout every year I return, including when we rocked their brains out again in 2006. The human and musical bond is timeless."

Ted Nugent (Ted Nugent – Guitar / Vocals)

"Well, an interesting thing about our show at M.O.R was that it was only the
2nd show for Syd (our new guitarist).
He made his debut the night before at the Pitz when we opened for Diamond
Head in a warm up show for the festival. Now the rest of the guys (myself,
Jonny, Rob and Richie) had some big stage experience from our supports to
Meat Loaf, The Darkness, and Nickelback etc...But Syd had none!
The warm up gig playing to around 300 people was actually the biggest gig he had ever done, until the day after of course when we opened the festival to around 10,000 ha-ha!
We were very happy with our performance, we had a few onstage problems but I guess that's to be expected at a festival! The crowd was great before we went on and the response as we left the stage, we couldn't have asked for better!
The day in a whole was something we will never forget, we have joined an
elite club of bands that have played 'Monsters of Rock' unfortunately we
couldn't stick around for 'Purples' set as we had to head up to Manchester to
open for Queensryche the following night..
As for Crazyness, hangin' around with the likes of Ted Nugent, Alice Cooper
etc was pretty crazy ha-ha!

Chris Rivers (Roadstar – Drums)

"This was our first Monsters Of Rock event and what a line up?
Travelled from Plymouth to Milton Keynes, straight to the hotel then taxi to the venue. Arrived at the Bowl and the music had already started by Roadstar.

After checking out the merchandise and sinking a few beers it was on with the music. Waiting to see the great man himself Ted Nugent and he did not let us or the crowd down, with classics like 'Cat Scratch Fever' and 'Wango Tango'. Followed by Queensrÿche, then Thunder......what great sounds from groups that we never had in our record collection. A top up of more beer then some noodles and we were then ready for Journey.

Journey played all the classic tracks like 'Don't Stop Believin', 'Any Way You Want It' and 'Separate Ways' with singer Steve Augeri. Not the same vocal range as Steve Perry, but a great show.

Alice Cooper followed, with all the great on stage show antics. He still rocks!

After some late supper, it was on to Deep Purple. This was the second time of seeing Deep Purple and they still rocked, with classic songs like 'Smoke On The Water' and songs from 'Rapture Of The Deep' album. The crowd had reached about 20,000 and the bowl was shaking.

Deep Purple was a great finale to a great event and venue. We were hoping for a follow up seeing this was the first Monsters of Rock for 10 years but this never followed at Milton Keynes Bowl."

Mark & Jane Jewitt (Plymouth)

2007
My Chemical Romance, Linkin Park & Iron Maiden

With the announcement that My Chemical Romance were to headline the first day of the festival, the uproar on the boards was rife; you would have thought that Girls Aloud playing the hits of Metallica had been announced, as the anger and hatred at the choice of headliner was on an unbelievably furious level.
The least favourite headliner in Donington history, if the forums were anything to go by, came to the festival and played a set which consisted mostly of their recent album 'Welcome To The Black Parade' and all the people who weren't interested drifted off to watch Korn headline the 2nd stage.
Linkin Park returned to headline the Saturday and Iron Maiden made their record breaking 4th headline appearance at Donington (twice at MOR and Twice at Download) on the mainstage on the Sunday.
Motley Crue headlined the Saturday on the 2nd stage, making there 3rd appearance at Donington and proving that they were as popular as ever.
Billy Talent, huge in Canada and now making inroads into Europe with the release of their album 'Billy Talent II',

closed the 2nd stage on the Sunday and had the unenviable task of competing with Iron Maiden who were performing on the mainstage.

The line-up was questioned as many of the bands were returning to play the festival quite soon after they had previously played, these included Bowling For Soup, Machine Head, Slayer, Marilyn Manson and Lamb Of God; the return of many of these artists was due to increased tour revenue/popularity and so their profiles had been raised considerably since their last appearance, warranting an appearance at the festival.

Mastodon made a big impression with their mainstage debut on the Sunday and due to their increased fan base would play as one of the support bands to Metallica at Wembley Stadium a month later.

The weather for the 5th year in a row was good and very unlike the Monsters Of Rock mud baths from previous years; the last bad weather had been Ozzfest in 2002, since the start of Download, the Gods Of Metal had been shining down on Donington Park and all was good. With June being an unpredictable month weather-wise, Glastonbury, 2 weeks later, still continued to receive torrential rain, flooding and mud slides; Donington was just lucky.

This would be the last time that Download would be held within the Donington racetrack with it moving outside the track in the following year, due to the bid to hold the British Grand Prix at Donington; in 2009 it would be revealed that the bid to hold the GP at Donington had failed and that the company had gone into receivership, but by then the festival site would have moved again to an even better, more permanent site also outside the track. The future of Download Festival at Donington Park was safe.

"It's an amazing festival. I've seen the look of elation on kids' faces and this is what they've been waiting for all year, saved their money up. It's huge."   **Duff McKagan (Velvet Revolver – Bass)**

"I was here was with Stonesour and Iron Maiden headlined so I went out in the audience and watched. It was incredible – moment after moment after moment and it was incredible. I was 14 again."
Corey Taylor (Stonesour – Vocals)

"We did the tent as we chose to do that. I didn't like the way the press was going and they were trying to make it more of an alternative festival; I think My Chemical Romance were headlining the mainstage when we were on.
I saw it in a lot of the metal magazines that they were bringing in so many alternative bands to the mainstage that we thought we'd prove a point and play the tent. I'm all for change but why change things when they are 'pure'? I talked to a lot of kids and they were pissed off about it.
I should have played the year before, but I got sick, so we thought that we would play the 2nd and then all the hardcore Korn fans would come and it kind of proved a point; everyone came to see us. The tent almost collapsed, we had to stop the show a few times.
The people know what they are doing, but I had been coming here for 15 years and I just lost it. Just drifting away from the original festival, it's sad. I don't know if it's lack of bands or not, I don't know. What do you do?
Things get lost in the cracks; I enjoyed coming here, not that I think Korn is a traditional metal band, but there are so many metal bands that played here that I love; Sepultura, Ozzy, Slayer, Iron Maiden, Machine Head, those are the bands that I look forward to seeing every year."
Jonathan Davis (Korn - Vocals)

"We always like playing Donington, it's a good time. I liked the tent that we played in and all the bands that were on."
Nikki Sixx (Motley Crue – Bass)

"Donington was magic. We (Evanescence) were playing in front of Iron Maiden. IRON MAIDEN! I knew about the European Festivals from when I was a kid dreaming of being Eddie Van Halen playing the Monsters of Rock Festival. This was my first trip to England, or Europe for that matter. Tens of thousands of people all there to listen to the music that they love, that we, the musicians in the bands, make and want to share with them. It was an amazing experience, although, I narrowly escaped being blasted in the face with a plastic bottle...that being the only ego-threatening incident during the set. The crowd was good to us that day.

We arrived a day early and Will Hunt, our drummer, knows Tommy Lee from Motley Crue. So, we went to see them Saturday. We watched from behind Tommy's kit. It was awesome! After their show I went back to the dressing room area and it was just a big party. I met up with my friends in Bloodsimple and we drank some beers and watched the spectacle. People were getting tattoos; there was a disco and bars everywhere and celebrities wherever you looked. It is definitely something that I will never forget and every serious musician should experience.

I was floored by some of the things that I saw backstage but it's like Las Vegas. What happens there stays there!!!!"
Troy McLawhorn (Evanescence – Guitar)

"It's really strange because we were 'super young', I don't know if there were any other bands of our age at the show? I don't think we could even fathom how much history there was behind this festival, but we feel honoured to have been a part of it and to have been asked is just such a great opportunity.

Even if we had nothing to do with the other bands, it was just great to be a part of Download."
Hayley Williams (Paramore – Vocals)

"There are so many bands that we really don't sound like and we were the 'poppy' band of the day, but it's all good as we love rock music and we were just there to rock"
Zac Farro (Paramore – Drums)

"It was an amazing show! To be honest we didn't expect to have much of a crowd there, because there was more metal

bands than we've ever played with. Not to mention the fact that we played right before Korn.
The crowd was really accepting and it was a great show. I'm glad they liked us; because we thought we were going to get bottled.
We were so stoked to see DragonForce play. They are an amazing band. We definitely had to watch them play coz we didn't know if we were ever going to get to play with them again.
There were 2 bands in particular that we both watched and got to hang out with at the download festival. My Chemical Romance are an amazing band and they are always really nice to us. Lost Alone is one of our favourite UK bands. We really spent a lot of time hanging out with those guys.
It's really an honour to play with all of those bands, because we really look up to them and love metal music A LOT! Plus, I saw Slash and I said 'Hey', it was amazing."
Jeremy Davis (Paramore – Bass)

"Then we headline the tent and it was wild, we didn't know what to expect. We thought that we were going to play in front of 800 people, or something like that, but it was completely packed. We killed it and it was awesome.
We played after Wicked Wisdom, Will Smith's wife's band and he was standing at the side of the stage watching, which was cool."
Jon Gallant (Billy Talent – Bass)

"Dream Theater had the honor of playing Download twice so far...2007 and 2009.
In 2007 we played on one of the side stages and it was an awesome experience...however a bit of a cock tease if I'm being honest....it was like being with a really hot chick but not getting to close the deal...."   **Mike Portnoy (Dream Theater - Drums)**

"The crowd was chanting and going crazy, but we were told 'nope it's over'. People then started booing and going crazy and throwing stuff at the stage. We went out there on stage

with our hands out and we pointed at the side of the stage, as if to say 'they won't let us' and everyone started going 'booooooo!!' Maybe they were booing at the authorities and not us?

But people tend to think 'the band doesn't want to play anymore, what a bunch of fuckin' assholes', they've got their million dollars and are taking off in their limos to their mansions; that's what people think.

I felt so bad; because the crowd were so amazing and I wanted to go out and play some more and they wanted it SO bad. It was kind of a bummer ending for such an amazing night, day and a show."

Aaron Barrett (Reel Big Fish – Vocals / Guitar)

"I remember the Donington festival for a couple of reasons, part of it's because it's on that world famous race track and I am a motorcycle fan and I love super bikes and we got to cruise around the track in the Spritzer van, which was totally awesome; the other thing was that we did an autograph signing right after Dimmu Borgir. We got to hang out with some of those guys and for a band who play music like they do, they are the sweetest bunch of guys that you could ever meet, they were really, really cool.

We played our show and the crowd were spilling outside our tent and we had to play at the same time as Iron Maiden played; it was overflowing, a fountain of people. Not only were the crowd electric, but they were absolutely fabulous.

The festival wouldn't let us play an encore. We had a set amount of time and we thought that we would get to do an encore, because we were the last on. So we went off the stage and wanted to come back on.

I think that it was one of the favourite shows that I had ever played. They also had a free tattoo booth backstage."

Johnny Christmas (Reel Big Fish – Trumpet)

"I was technically still a 'fill in' and I was wondering what I was going to do when I got home as I had quit my job to 'fill in' on that month long tour. But I got a new job though, lucky me! The day before flying home it all became official."

Derek Gibbs (Reel Big Fish – Bass)

"We played the second stage and we were the main support to Korn, which was interesting.
It was absolutely rammed again and another 'step up' for us. I think that Download has been a very good indication of where we are, always stepping up; it's been great every time.
For me as a kid Reading and Download were my two festivals that I went to, so every time we play we try to stick around for the weekend as well. We watched the Prodigy in the tent and there were people climbing the stanchions and it was all kicking off."

Roughton "Rou" Reynolds (Enter Shikari – Vocals / Synthesizer)

"We were lucky enough to be asked to play the mainstage in a very good timeslot and in the company of some amazing bands. I watched several of the bands before us and it was amazing to see the crowd and the massive amount of talent that was coming to the stage.
Something magic happened when we took the stage and not to take anything away from the bands that played before us, but there was an energy, some kind of connection that happened where the place erupted. The amount of shared energy and power that was coming from both the stage and the fans, I know will be something that I will never forget.
I know now that this was the biggest and most memorable show that Lamb Of God has ever played."

Chris Adler (Lamb Of God – Drums)

"Once I looked out and saw the crowd, I was in awe of how many people we were going to be playing to. Once I saw the banners go up and heard the Lamb Of God chant, the hairs were raising on my body and it was the most memorable event in our career, as far as Lamb Of God goes. To have played to that many people and to get the response that we did, to be welcome there, it's unbelievable.
Everyone was waiting to see Iron Maiden, I had wanted to see Stone Sour but we were doing press at the same time."

Willie Adler (Lamb Of God – Guitar)

"I thought it went really well, we had a great response, it was my second time at Donington and it was friggin' awesome. I couldn't have asked for a better friggin' show, with a better bunch of guys.
We had a great response and I was watching the faces and they were really into it. We had a couple of 'pits' going during our set and it was awesome.
When we played with Damageplan we played a lot later, but this time I think we had more. I was really shocked to see how many people there were out there at noon.
I looked forward to seeing Slayer and I wish I could have stayed another day to see Iron Maiden, as I am a massive Iron Maiden fan; Steve Harris is a god."

Bob Zilla (Hellyeah – Bass)

"We were second on the mainstage and I was so surprised how many people showed up for our set; there had to be 40,000 people out there, as far back as I could see anyway. It was good to see the turn out and the fans were into it. On my side of the stage I could see kids singing the words, so some of them had the record anyway and hoepfully we got some new fans out of it.
I looked forward to seeing Machine Head, Slayer and Motley Crue.
It was a great day and a great festival; we travelled 23 hours to get there, but it was worth it."

Greg Tribbett (Hellyeah – Guitar)

"This year we came fully equipped with two eight foot blow up sheep, they were massive.
I don't know what it is, but I think that we have found an audience over here that appreciates us and a lot of it crosses into that metal genre and that we are a happy fun band and we are what we are.
I had got really intoxicated the night before and we watched My Chemical Romance. We had actually missed a whole day

of press because we were late getting on the ferry, but it all worked out.
But we rolled in and hung out with the Dragonforce guys had a great night, and then played a great show.
I also played an acoustic show at the Nokia tent with Eric, which went really well."
Jaret Reddick (Bowling For Soup – Vocals/Guitar)

"This year was really cool because we invited back to play on the mainstage and we got to play in front of the largest crowd that we have ever played for.
It was remarkable the numbers that were there. You don't realise it as you are concentrating on what's going on, on stage. That day they gave us a DVD and the crowd started at one side and went right over to the other and there were people as far as you could see.
It's just such a great opportunity to come from Wichita Falls, Texas and then 13 years later to be able to play to something like that, it's absolutely amazing. It's one of those moments that you go back home and tell your friends about it, but they wouldn't be able to understand it unless they were there.
We try to watch as many bands as you can. My biggest moment this year was watching Damone, so it was a real thrill to get to see them. The night before Kai from Army of Freshmen and I went to see Suicidal Tendancies.
It was an amazing experience to be on the mainstage again, very few people get to do the things that we do, so it was very cool."
Eric Chandler (Bowling For Soup – Bass)

"We had the best stage prop ever. Blow up sheep that were 15 feet tall, you can't beat that ever in the history of stage props; that beat the hell out of Spinal Tap's 2 foot tall Stonehenge.
Just being there was so cool.
We also got stuck on a ferry, but that sometimes happens, you get stuck on a ferry in life!"
Chris Burney (Bowling For Soup – Guitar)

"It was a strange one because it was the first time that we realised that our band meant something to people. Further to the few tours that we had done prior to Download nothing had really 'kicked off'. We were still trying to tell people that we were here and we had an important message to say.

We got to Download and it fucking really freaked me out to be honest with you; playing a tent, close to 10,000 people, that had just come to check you out, but the first 150 rows of people all knew the words and were all singing along.

I was looking out over a sea of people and I couldn't even see the end of the tent. It was really shocking for us because you can't comprehend how it's going to be until you get up there on the stage and look out and all you can see are people singing back at you, expecting so much from you.

It was the first gig that I had really been hounded by people for photos and autographs; I couldn't walk around without being spotted by people which was really strange and messed my head up a bit, but it comes with the territory if you're in a band and that's what you're going to get eventually.

It was a great show, everyone had a blast and I called my mum and got everyone to say hello to her. I called her when we had just finished and she was still crying; it was wicked. It was the first time that we realised that things were really going to happen with our band. Playing a show for about 9,000 people at four in the afternoon really blows your mind, it's crazy; especially when we come from the backrooms of pubs where there are about 20 hard core kids all smashing each other faces in and then you come and see that and it's like 'what the fuck is going on???'

I'm not going to complain though, it's amazing.

I watched Cancer Bats, who were wicked and Turbonegro, who are one of my favourite bands. I got to sing with Kid In Glass Houses on the last day. We stood up on the hill and watched My Chemical Romance and there were hundreds of people walking off to see Korn.

I also got to see Iron Maiden, which of course is what people go to Donington for really. You got to Donington to see new bands but you GO for Maiden and it was just unbelievable, everyone there was just there for them! A few bands got big

crowds, but everyone went to see Maiden, where does that happen? How many other bands could do that? I would not want to a band up against that at Donington."
Frank Carter (Gallows – Vocals)

"The first time we played we were completely in awe. We came into the track in a van and we couldn't believe how expansive just the sheer 'real estate' of the place was. Being an American band, Donington has such mythic properties over their for us and knowing that the G'N'R video for 'Paradise City' was shot there and listening to stuff like that as a kid, it just made Donington even more legendary. Actually being there the first time it came and went so fast; our heads were spinning the whole time that we were there and we didn't really get to take it all in. We played at 11 o'clock and we got a half an hour, it just went so fast and then we had to get out of there and fly back to the States for a gig, as we had to be in Kansas City the next night."
Keith Nelson (Buckcherry – Guitar)

*"I had been building up to this since seeing it on MTV when I was a little kid in Norway. I saw all the bands like Motorhead and Ozzy and I would have loved to have come, but England was a long way to travel from Norway.
When I grew up we did Rosklide, but it's nothing compared to what this has been, total fuckin' rock 'n' roll hardcore all the way.
It is a great honour to be a part of rock 'n' roll history here now!
I watched Slayer and had hoped to see Devildriver.
I also loved Iron Maiden as a kid, I had posters all over the walls of my room and I looked forward to seeing them."*
I.C.S. Vortex (Dimmu Borgir – Bass)

*"It was our first time on the mainstage and it was pretty scary! I'm not going to lie; it was definitely the biggest crowd that we have ever played in front of.
It was a bit nerve wracking getting up on stage; you plan what to do your whole life when playing a show like that and it I*

went over it a million times in my head the night before, but nothing ever works out.

It took about two songs to find my stride, in my 'comfort zone' where I wanted to be I guess.

It was hard to utilise all the space, we're just not used to it; the 'warm up' show the night before, we had about 2 inches of space.

But I heard afterwards, that they were still chanting our name at the mainstage, a couple of bands after us."

Mark Hunter (Chimaira – Vocals)

"My experience of Donington was the not the best experience in the world, I was a little disappointed; we had a bad equipment day. But, I was absolutely astounded by the size of the venue, the amount of people and organisation that had to go into it. It was the first time that I had actually driven in a van to a stage.

The crowd were very good, because Fastway a more 'blues based' band and the crowd are there mostly for the hard-core heavy metal, so we were a little worried about our reception, but I have to say that they were a great fucking crowd. I think that the Donington crowd is a good crowd and they were really good to us.

So all I have really are fond memories of Donington. As I never played it with Motorhead, I'm glad that I've played it now and crossed it off my list of things to do before I die!"

Fast Eddie Clarke (Fastway - Guitar)

"It was awesome! The crowd was really big; there were quite a few people there and all of our friends said that it went over really well.

The food was amazing, lots of beer and lots of Jagermeister. It is so organised which rules and I got to see Billy Talent later, which I was happy with."

Jason Bailey (Cancer Bats – Bass)

"Download was amazing for us; I had been hearing about Donington and Monsters of Rock since I was a kid, bands like Metallica, Panter and Guns 'n' Roses, reading about all these

amazing bands playing here and then getting our own chance to play is something else.
I kicked off the jet lag and threw up in the toilet and then felt a lot better and was ready to play. A small band from Canada getting to play there to thousands of people is always an incredible time and I had a lot of fun.
We checked out Napalm Death, Billy Talent and Iron Maiden, it's an amazing experience. I would be happy to play anywhere again."
Scott Middleton (Cancer Bats – Guitar)

"Our return to Download was in 2007 on the now named "Dimebag Darrell Stage" and the show actually topped the fan reaction and amount of people watching us from the last time we played the same stage. Again that same adrenaline rushed through our bodies and created another timeless memory.
Unfortunately we had to leave almost immediately after our set because we had to go to another show in a different country, so the enjoying of the other bands and consumption of good times and alcohol failed to happen for us on that go around.
We do hope to have many more chances to hit the stages at Download and be sure to never book a show far away directly after it again."
Trevor Phipps (Unearth – Vocals)

"Donington festival was amazing; as always when we do a big festival like that usually we don't have crew. We just roll off a plane, show up, put it together the best we can and just go out there and do it.
I remember slugging back a couple beers fairly quickly to take the edge off of getting off the plane and trying to get in the 'game'.
It was an awesome show, half hung-over and half jetlagged, but it was a great time."
John "Slo" Maggard (Unearth – Bass)

"We had never played such a huge event before, especially the mainstage it was very busy!

We were in the backstage area because all the make-up takes a lot of time, so we were there at 8 o'clock and it was quite quiet there, Motley Crue or Slayer weren't there I can tell you! We played at 11 o'clock, really, really early and it was the second day so people had been out partying and drinking all night, so we were a bit worried about how many would show up at that hour, because in Finland nobody would be up before 2pm to see any band.

There were a lot of people there at 11 o'clock and I was really amazed and it was very cool.

We came the night before, so we didn't see anything on the Friday, but we stayed until Sunday evening to check out Maiden and then left right after, as we were playing the Metal Hammer Golden Gods show on the Monday.

Playing at 11am on the Saturday and being finished by 11:30am, we had a lot of press going on; we were very busy, but it was good to spend the Sunday just doing nothing.

There were a lot of people who had never heard of this band before and as the opening band, I think the reaction we got was really, really good.

We've been playing in the UK a lot since and there are always people who come up to us now and say "I saw you at Download, I'd never heard of you before, but I love you now."

Mathias "Warlord" Nygård – (Turisas - Vocals/Percussion)

"In '07 we were very drunk because it was the first year we had played Download and we were quite young, walking around getting quite star struck; it was the biggest show we'd ever done.

So we were hanging around in the backstage area and I could see Tommy Lee's dressing room and there was a queue outside of it and all this music coming out, so I thought 'I've got to go and try to get in there'. So I walked up to the door and a security guard opened it and came outside and stood there. I said 'I'm here for Tommy Lee's thing, I should be on the list', the security guard said 'No you're not on the list', so I said 'get Tommy he'll remember me'; so the guard opened the door, Tommy looked out and said 'no' and I was then asked to leave. So, I can happily say that I got denied entry to Tommy

Lee's party, by Tommy Lee; it was probably awful anyway, tiny little room, didn't want to be there.
Dan our drummer sat on Hayley from Paramore's lap.
Everyone was walking around trying to talk to Korn. I got my hair cut with Jacoby Shaddix from Papa Roach."
It was fun, a lot of people didn't know who we were, but we played to a lot of people and they seemed to enjoy it.
I had a good time, I felt nervous, it was only about my 8th show with Architects. But it was a lot of fun and we stayed all weekend."
Sam Carter (Architects – Vocals)

"When played Download it was an honour as it has so much history going back to Monsters Of Rock.
We had an amazing time and we drank a lot of alcohol; probably too much.
It wasn't just amazing playing, it was amazing being there and we had such a great time; probably one of the best times that we have ever had as a band.
We stayed all weekend partying; we camped up and did it the way you're supposed to do it, I guess.
An awesome experience."
Dan Searle (Architects – Drums)

"Download was fun; 50% getting drunk and pissing off people, let's call them 'rock celebrities', we gave some respect to Iron Maiden, but I'm not sure I take it very seriously.
We walked around and saw bands like Korn walking around; we felt like kids in a playground, you don't think that those people are real.
Playing the show was awesome.
We missed a lot of our friends bands, Gallows, Bring Me The Horizon and Enter Shikari, because of our stage times, it would have been good to see how they went down; but I'm sure it was insane."
Tom Searle (Architects – Guitar)

"Mastodon on the mainstage were good as were Lamb Of God, but I wish that they were playing smaller stages, because I prefer watching them there.
I even watched bands like Linkin Park and Marilyn Manson, who I would normally not bother going to see."
Alex "Ali Dino" Dean (Architects – Bass)

"We may have been the first band to have played the Cambridge Folk Festival and Download; we have that distinct honour.
Why it took is so long to get booked at Download I'm not sure, because we'd wanted to do it every year, but I think that when we changed booking agents, he had a little more clout.
When we first got there we wondered why we were playing the 3rd stage? Not because we think we are the 'Mack daddies' of all rock 'n' roll or anything, but we just thought that we were going to have a big crowd at this thing and sure enough we did.
The whole tent was completely packed out and I think that it was one of the best crowds we'd play to all year. I think that people really misjudge us sometimes, because we really are a rock 'n' roll band, we're just playing instruments that people think of as 'Hillbilly instruments', but the attitude, the energy behind it, is very much of a rock 'n' roll band.
Me and Jake and come more from a rock 'n' roll background and Don and Dale, who play the banjo and the mandolin are more from the bluegrass side of things. But, that again is just a slight slant, as we all grew up listening to everything and they're quite rock 'n' roll at heart really, especially Dale; anyone with 'Keep on rockin' in the free world' tattooed on his shoulder, really means it.
It really was one of the best crowd responses that we had all year. I didn't really get to see that much of the festival proper, but apparently I was the only one who showed up on a motorbike, the security told me that.
We saw Slash and his stripper lookin' wife pull the baby carriage out and she was yellin' at him. She was bitchin' at him incessantly and he was just looking 'hen pecked'.

I didn't see any other bands actually. We got there, got something to eat, did the soundcheck, played the gig and then had to leave to get to Europe the next day on the ferry.
We played like six festivals in a row and we were all travelling together, which is kind of comforting.
I did see one band, I saw Turbonegro between the soundcheck and our set and they were a lot better than I expected them to be.
The guy from Suicidal Tendencies walked out on stage and got a lack lustre response. He started yelling at them 'Is this how you fuckin' do it? Is this how you fuckin' do it?'
Me and Jake were saying to each other that contempt for the audience is not really the kind of thing you want to have! Me personally, I'm darned glad they gave me a job!
Download was a very well laid out festival, Glastonbury though was probably the worst festival that we have done from a purely logistical point of view, possibly because we had to play 3 shows on the same day."
Barley Scotch (Hayseed Dixie - Vocals/Acoustic Guitar/Violin)

"It's like doing a travelling circus when you do these festivals as you keep seeing the same acts at every one.
They had free tattoos as well.
I remember that the band after us didn't have the quite invitational welcome that we did. But, maybe after that many years you become quite jaded.
We are a tribute to drinkin', cheatin' and killin'."
Jake "Bakesnake" Byers – (Hayseed Dixie - Acoustic Bass Guitar)

"It was one of those final pieces in the jigsaw of my career playing at Download, because when I was in Little Angels we never got to play; we always wanted to do Donington but never did; we did Milton Keynes, Wembley Stadium and most of the big rock venues but we never got to Monsters of Rock. It was fucking ridiculous, we always wanted to, but it was just one of those 'wrong place, wrong time'.

When I got the call to take part in Fastway and found out that we would be doing Download, it was absolutely great.
We stayed for the day, caught some of Maiden. It's not the Donington that I remember, it's huge and sprawling, but it's on THE site!
I was really surprised how our performance went, as we were in a bill of very young bands and it was good to see how Download is very 'inclusive' of many different types of rock and metal and the band that played before us in the tent were very extreme, with guitars down to 'C' or something like that, chugging around ad I thought 'what the hell are we going to do?' But, Lauren Harris had been on previously, so there were some bands playing of a similar ilk. But the tent filled up and there was a great reaction and we all a bit nervous as it was Donington and only the 2nd show out of the blocks after 18 years away, but I don't think that we could have wanted it any better.
I think Donington Park is one of those 'iconic' festival sites that every band, particularly of the period mid '80's to mid '90's, had a desire to play there. When you saw the videos of the interviews backstage every year, you could guarantee that there would be a band who'd say 'well it's Donington and we had to play it', it's just great to take part in it and be part of the history. An old mate of mine Andy Copping runs it and he was instrumental in helping Little Angels in their early career."
Toby Jepson (Fastway - Vocals)

"Cut to 11 years later. We are back at Donington, but this time for the Download Festival; the successor to the Monsters of Rock Festival, whilst still feeling very honoured to be asked to be there, seems a much less cosy affair in the backstage area. Possibly down to the fact that there are an insane amount of bands playing.
This is also a much more commercial festival.
None of the bands backstage seem to want to see any of the bands onstage. Everyone seems more concerned with networking.
On the plus side this is a much more musically diverse festival.

Rock and metal music has splintered into thousands of variations and its all here.
The show went very well. It amazed me that rock and metal music still has such a fervent following in the UK. For some reason metal music seems to be a dirty word amongst the UK media but Download proves that people can think for themselves."

Gregor Mackintosh (Paradise Lost - Guitar)

"What do you do but say, fucking yes, when asked if you want to be a part of one of Rock / Metals biggest festivals? Download! Or to us "old moshers" as I'm sometimes referred to, Monsters Of Rock, Castle Donington.
It is where I cut my teeth as a festival goer, seeing the likes of Metallica, Kiss, Slayer, Megadeth, Anthrax, Paradise Lost and AC/DC over a number of years.
It is the epitome of what a rock festival should be, bringing the best of all genres together in one giant cauldron. It is the Promised Land but without the virgins.
We, as My Dying Bride, felt honoured to have been asked to play The Dimebag stage. We felt this especially so as this was the first time for us to perform there and also as the stage we would be on was named in the memory of one of metals greats. So again just a truly humbling experience getting to play in England at our biggest metal festival. Something I will never forget".

Andrew Craighan (My Dying Bride – Guitarist)

"It was our first time; I think we were one of the only bands that camped, that was the way that we wanted to do it and to be honest I had never been there before.
We went up in two parties and one van broke down. So we got there that night had a few beers, set the tents up and then went to sleep, to be woken up at 11am the next day by some rock 'n' roll music; which was a good start to the day in my eyes.
We grabbed a couple of cans and went around the arenas. It was awesome the bill, with the big guns like Maiden and Motley Crue."

Tom Lacey (The Ghost Of A Thousand – Vocals)

"We got about 15 minutes outside of Brighton before the car broke down. We had all the camping gear in the car, so we got it all out and sat on the camping chairs on the hard shoulder waiting for the recovery truck to arrive. They then towed us all the way to North London, which took about 3 hours because they had go at 60 mph or even less than that; we stayed in North London that night.
The next day we woke up, pushed the car for a mile and a half to the garage and then spent the day in London milling around waiting for the car to be fixed.
We made it to Donington in the afternoon on the Friday, we got there just as Velvet Revolver were playing, I think; I arrived to the sounds of Slash 'ripping a solo', which was awesome. It was our first big festival and it's such a big name in rock and metal these days that it was a real honour to play it. I went and checked Motley Crue play the 2nd stage instead of the mainstage, Biffy Clyro and Suicidal Tendencies and basically had just an awesome weekend. I went on the fairground rides, just trying to experience the whole thing and it was a good time.
I really enjoyed the gig, we were really 'buzzed up' and then after the gig, we spent the rest of the day having a party and had a really good weekend.
It was definitely one of the gigs that sticks in my mind as it started a lot of things really. That summer for us, we played Download and then the touring never stopped. So I look at it as the springboard that propelled us to where we've got to now; so it meant a lot and that was where it all started."

Andy Blyth (The Ghost Of A Thousand – Guitar)

"It was legitimately a dream come true for me and Army Of Freshmen.
I remember being a kid in America and watching MTV and every summer for one weekend they would do a live broadcast from a place called Castle Donington. As a kid I was led to believe that there was a castle there and it was like

a magical place where King Arthur lives and now he has heavy metal concerts there. Being a little kid in New Jersey, your perception of England is pretty skewed and you think that people are still in 'knight uniforms'!

You'd see those pompous MTV DJs, back when they had perms saying 'it's the greatest rock concert of all time' and as a little kid I just wanted to be part of that world, half because I thought there were knights there and half because it was a big rock show. It was just such as mystical thing, but as I grew up I got the rock magazines and the heavy metal magazines in the States and they would have reviews of the Donington festivals and it was just such a big deal.

It was something that I never thought Army Of Freshmen would ever get the chance to play because we are predominantly a 'pop band' / 'pop punk' band and Donington and Download were still a metal festival.

Then we became friends with Bowling For Soup and they told us that they were getting ready to play the Download Festival which used to be Castle Donington and I was like 'Oh my god, that festival is still happening, but it's under a different name'. So they told me all about it and described it as the most incredible experience and the backstage is full of big time rock stars, everyone is mingling and the crowd are just psychotically amazing. I thought we would never have the chance, because Bowling For Soup had success in England and the metal crowd really accepts Bowling For Soup for some reason because they take the piss out of it and they don't take themselves too seriously.

Bowling For Soup then played a second year and told us all about it and I was incredibly jealous. So we did the 'Get Happy' tour and we were playing in Birmingham and one of the Live Nation guys was there by the name of Steve Homer who is just an utter genius and a wonderful person and he caught our set and he was talking to us backstage and he said 'I think I may have just found out that you are going to get an offer to play Download' but it wasn't 100% and I was freaking out and bouncing off the walls. I spoke to the guys and told them that it might not happen and we were at the hotel waiting to get picked up to go to the airport to fly back home and I checked my emails on one of those pay terminals where you put a pound in and we'd had an offer from Live Nation to play Download.

We hadn't left England yet and none of the guys knew and they'll hate me for this when the book comes out, but I didn't tell them and I kept it to myself the whole plane flight. I was in a joyous rage the whole flight and they were wondering why I was so happy, but I waited until we got home to tell everybody as I wanted to give them a nice surprise, because when you get home after a big tour like that you do get depressed for a few days, so then I got to drop that on them. So the joy of the tour continued.

Our biggest fear was 'we're not a metal act' and our names not out there yet, we are going to get bottled. We were inventing crazy skits in our head, like we'd come out dressed like My Chemical Romance, rip our faces off Scooby Doo style and it's us and everybody likes it!

We got to the festival and saw everybody camped out and we'd already decided that we were going to make a weekend of it. A lot of bands we know come in for the one day and then they leave. But this was our first UK festival, so we thought that we were going to suck this up!

It was a real dream come true. Just to be there to check out the backstage and we turned into real autograph stalkers. We had cancelled a show just to get down there early, because we didn't want to come in, never having played the festival, not knowing what was up. So we got in day one and hung out and then I woke up next day with no sleep and a ton of drinks in me. I packed my bags and will never forget the walk that I had to do, because we I woke up it was so early that the trolleys weren't running yet from where the buses were, so I took my suitcase and I had to walk that entire track; walked all the way from the backstage, walked all the way to my stage, I walked about 2 miles at six in the morning, just to take a cold shower, because I wanted to be completely ready for the show.

We were the second band on the stage and we were convinced that no one would be there. But I will never forget walking around that 'big top' and taking a look at the crowd

and the place was 75% full and we were ecstatic; we could have went home, we didn't have to play one note that day, 'we'd drew a crowd at Download!!!' we were just freaking out. So we proceeded to go on that stage and the energy level and the excitement and the emotion that we had was such a high that I feel it was one of the better shows that Army Of Freshmen had ever played. The energy level of the crowd was nuts, everybody was into it, there were no bottles; it was just a dream. It was like being on cloud nine, to see a tent like that and everybody's happy.
My most intense memory of being there at Download was of Marilyn Manson. He's really exciting, but the security made everybody backstage, even legitimate rock stars, made everyone go to the sides and stay in their room, so that he could make the walk from his backstage to a van!
I thought it was really pretentious, because I really believe that you create the scene around yourself that you want to create. OK, if you are famous, people are going to stop you, but its how much attention you bring upon on yourself and if you make everybody stop and bow down for ten minutes, so you can pass by, you are going to create an air and energy about yourself. So of course I was kind of transfixed and I went to see the set and I thought he was incredibly lacklustre, seeing Marilyn Manson in the daylight and watching his make-up dry off! I had to be crammed in a hallway for 15 minutes so this idiot could walk by to play a bad set!
From that nine year old kid watching MTV and hearing about the festival, to literally 15 years later being an artist there. The aftershow party was amazing, getting our pictures taken with the guys from Maiden and Pantera; one of the greatest days in Army Of Freshmen's history was when we played Download."
Chris Jay (Army Of Freshmen – Vocals)

"Download was one of the best weekends of my life. I grew up as a 'metal head' so to be walking around backstage and bumping into Bruce Dickinson, Vinnie Paul and all the guys from Slayer, I was literally 8 years old again and googly eyed. When I spoke to Vinnie Paul I was literally shaking and the picture I took came out blurry, because I was so intimidated.

I tried to see as many bands as possible and there wasn't one band who wasn't 'beyond nice' and didn't put on a great show. I thought Lamb Of God were amazing, I was a casual fan before that, but now I'm sold. Mastodon were also SO good and it was the third time that I'd seen Machine Head and they were brilliant.

One day I was in one of the shuttle buses to the stage and there were two of the guys from Machine Head, Jeff Hanneman and his guitar tech. I was just sat in the back of the shuttle and these four guys got in and I was just listening to them talk. Then I was just staring at one of Jeff Hanneman's custom guitars and all I wanted to do was to sit down and play one Slayer song on it.

The cool thing is the access you have, because all the bands walk around and watch every other band and everybody just wants to have a good time.

We were on pretty early in the morning; we were the second band on that stage, at the same time as Hell Yeah, which were Vinnie Paul's new band. We thought that we were going to go out and play to nobody, but it was packed. It went off swimmingly and we were on cloud nine the rest of the day.

I was the first one up and the last one to sleep every single day. Half of the guys like metal, half don't. So they were like 'I'm just going to go and have a wander around', but I was running frantically from stage to stage; I even typed up a schedule for every day, of all the bands that I wanted to see. I like to watch the bands from the crowd, because watching from the stage, the sound isn't so good and you can only see half the band, but when you go out with the crowd, that's where you really get the energy.

There were some kids at the mainstage, waiting all day just for Marilyn Manson, which was a little weird and I thought he had one of the worst sets of the day and I like his music a lot, but I just thought his song choices were weird.

One of the big intrigues that spread round the whole festival was that people were going to see My Chemical Romance, because of what happened to them at Reading & Leeds. People were really angry about that band. I saw people tearing down posters and making signs! There were so many haters throwing bottles, but none of them hit the stage, maybe one or two, but it was cool.

The whole atmosphere and the fact that they can bring so many people to the festival and keep it all under control, with the exception of a few fires at the end, is just so great. We can't do festivals like that in the States. Woodstock was the last one and a bunch of dumb American tough guys turn up and try to hit on girls and do a bunch o' crap; but Donington is the biggest metal festival in the world, with a load of nice people just there to enjoy the day. Beautiful countryside, movies at night and the camping grounds! I walked around the campsite one night and there were some people there who just camp and hardly step foot near the music!

And everyone is SO nice. To be at Donington as a metal head, it is THE Festival, so I'd dreamt my whole life of going, let alone being a part of it; when I was a kid it was Donington, which is what it will always be to me. It was just incredible."

Kai Dodson (Army Of Freshmen – Bass)

"Over the years I've been there as a PR for Bowling For Soup, Art of Dying, DV8, Zebrahead and Army Of Freshmen and worked with Tool in the torrential rain at Ozzfest's visit to the site in 2002.

Download is a brilliant opportunity to new and mid-size bands to meet key media all in one place, as well as perform to a broader rock/metal audience than they would usually get at their own shows. A successful Download performance can really help a band breakthrough in the UK. It's been really rewarding for me to see Army Of Freshmen prove so successful at the festival as it was always a big ambition of theirs' to play at such a legendary event. They performed to a packed third stage tent in 2007 and 2008, even though they're unsigned, and it has definitely helped to significantly increase their British fan-base and media presence.

The festival always has an incredible line-up, mixing upcoming artists with rock legends and every band playing will be excited to see at least five other acts, so working as a band's publicist can be like trying to hold mercury. I always ask my artists to tell me in advance which bands they want to watch so I can schedule their press around it, but you can guarantee that a band member will suddenly disappear just when he's needed. I'll find him having his photo taken with Nikki Sixx or Slash, or over at the third stage catching that years' Next Big Thing!

The rock/metal world is pretty small so every time I go to the festival I'll bump into bands and crew that I've worked with, or toured with, and it can be like a family reunion."

Emma Watson (PR – Bowling For Soup/MC Lars/Zebrahead)

"And so to my third Donington.... Different band, different stage, different day. Would it be as good after the past two experiences? In a word 'yes'.

We played early in the day and weren't expecting much more than a 'front row' to greet us. We were wrong. The marquee was packed for that time of day and we (Malpractice) played probably our best gig to date. The gig took on a life of its own, and by the end of the set the smiles and sweat weren't just onstage. Not bad for the 'early slot'... too bad it had to end so soon. Thanks Adam, Benny, Spreader and Paddy for that one. Hopefully it will be back to the main stage at some point in the (not too distant) future... who knows. One day."

Mark Chapman (Malpractice – Guitar)

"It went really well, I think that the turnout of the crowd was much better than anything we could have expected; we were expecting a couple of hundred people to turn up at the front, but the tent was absolutely rammed from the front of the stage, right to the back and some people standing outside of the tent as well. They were just cheering before we started, it was ace! It was definitely the best show that I have ever done. The day was way beyond all of our expectations really.

We watched Motley Crue on the Saturday night, we were quite a way back but they just sounded phenomenal.

We camped in the normal campsite with all our friends and girlfriends; it's just part of the whole festival experience really, with the added bonus that we got to play it."

Venno (Beyond All Reason – Vocals/Guitar)

"It was an amazing gig, I really enjoyed it and I couldn't believe how many people were in the tent, I didn't really expect it.
It was just really, really good just to be part of the festival; just seeing the amazing bands that were playing and then getting to play at the same festival.
We hadn't actually been to this festival before, but it was one that I had always wanted to go to because of all the good bands that are always playing, everything I'm into really. So to actually play the festival as well, it's an absolute bonus, the whole thing has just been incredible really and a great experience."
Russ (Beyond All Reason – Guitar)

"It was absolutely phenomenal. It was the first time that we had played a tent as well and it's mad that your playing somewhere in the middle of a field, that shouldn't usually be there.
I wanted to see Iron Maiden and Dream Theater.
Hayseed Dixie on the first day were great on the first day; I can't believe that they get SO wrecked and still play in time without a drummer!"
Mark (Beyond All Reason – Drums)

"We had a fucking awesome time. To get such a good crowd, we weren't expecting it, amazing!
We went down to the tent the previous day and there were only about 100-200 people in there, so we didn't expect the crowd we got.
Then we did lots of interviews and had a laugh."
Nick (Beyond All Reason – Bass)

"The first time we played at Download we played the 3rd stage. I remember we were standing on the side of the stage and we were just in awe; we just couldn't believe it. There was a sea of people and we were honoured and grateful and in the moment."

Maria Brink – (In This Moment - Vocals/Piano)

"We really didn't know what to expect, we had just released our first album, we'd done a run of festivals in Europe and it was definitely an awakening for us.
We had confirmed to do Ozzfest in the States, but we did all these shows including Download before that and it really opened our eyes to playing shows in front of a lot of people."
Chris Howorth (In This Moment – Guitar)

"Download was amazing for me, growing up as a metalhead, and now I was getting to play in the same festival with Slayer, Motley Crue, Megadeth & Maiden. I can't even explain the honor it was, cuz to me I have never been a part of something like that. It seemed to everyone else it was business as usual, no one was really impressed, but to me, I was like a little kid. I guess that's how it is when you see ya heroes in the flesh, or just close enough to touch.
I was the only rapper on this festival and I felt a bit out of place, because it isn't like people in the metal world have their arms wide open to a rapper. People are rather close-minded, but me and my boys made the room ours backstage, harassing every fine little metal chick that would walk by, in true old school metal fashion. I'm old school, the metal I listen to is not new shit, so when I think of metal, and metal gods, and metal legends, I think of perverts, debaucherous motherfuckers looking to fuck every hot girl in the room. Well it was a rapper/hip hop/metal head pervert such as myself that was playing that role, and enjoying it. I actually brought some sluts to the gig, my own English whores, who got on stage during my set and got raunchy, then got choked backstage in front of everyone to see.
At one point backstage, I wanted to pay homage to Motley Crue, who I felt were the kings of groupies, so I made this girl take her bra off, showing her tits through her fishnet shirt, and tight booty shorts on barefoot, with a leesh around her neck, and I walked her over to Nikki Sixx's backstage room. Everyone was out there partying so I know they saw this hip hop fuck walk over with this whorebag on a leesh. I offered her

to Nikki as respect and homage for what Motley Crue did in the 80's, and he looked at me like I had 2 heads on my shoulders. I was a little surprised, considering I just supported him and bought his book, which detailed fucking tons of hoes, some on drugs, some off, but neverless, a lot of fucking. Anyway, he was with a girl, and she didn't look too impressed either, and they both were pretty shady and just walked away from me, showing me no respect. So I thought to myself, fuck it, let me bring this peace offering to Tommy Lee, he was a few feet away, getting crazy with some hoes in his room, I walked over with my slave offering and his bouncer was being a dick. I screamed out, 'Tommy!!!, Tommy!!!! I got a gift for you', he looks out his door, stares for a second at us, and boom goes right back in his room, no respect!!!

His faggot bouncer was not being cool, and then his tour manager who knew me walked over, and didn't do anything to help or accept my slave offering

So now, I'm thinking, where the fuck is Vince Neil, he won't front on me

Anyway, after not finding Vince, I said fuck this shit, and fuck them, they aren't worthy of my efforts, keep in mind, this was backstage, so if you weren't important you couldn't be there

So I'm thinking I can't even get respect backstage when showing love and paying homage

So much for "rockstars"

Now on a better note, I saw Tom Araya, walking by me the day before, and I thought, shit, that's Tom Araya, now he is different, I'm not looking to bring groupies to him, he is a brutal legend, he doesn't need to be bothered, so I had to think quick, how do I pay homage to this thrash god, so as he walked by me, I screamed out just loud enough that he heard, "Reign in Blood!!!", that said it all, I didn't need to say anything more, anyone that truly knows Slayer, and was ever truly a fan, knows what that album means, he responded with a friendly and cool, "Thank you", and a little smile, I felt good, because I knew I paid homage and I didn't need to ass kiss or get played out.

Now don't let me tell you about the after party where I took a shit right next to Kerry King, he was in the other stall,

hahahahaha, I said out loud, " Oh shit, Kerry King is taking a shit right next to me", he goes, "No, I'm not" and I said ok, then 5 minutes later, he is still there, and I said, "that's a long piss" and he laughed, he was mad cool, showing all the fans love, so thumbs up to Slayer for being awesome!!!
Besides, that I played to a tent of 3500 kids, and they showed me a lot of love, and over all it was a good experience, and I hope to play Download again sometime in my life."
Necro (Rapper)

"In 2007 I worked there in the bar, because I was skint and needed the money. So I saw a different side of it; but it was a great laugh as well, because I was around beer all the time and was just getting drunk and then rolling off and watching bands and then coming back and doing the same thing."
Casino Brown (Ted Maul - Keyboards)

"It was our third show in England and we didn't expect that much from it as there were so many awesome bands playing there that day and we played really early so we weren't sure how many people we would get.
We played on stage 2 and the entire tent was packed! There were so many people and they were very enthusiastic and we got a huge response. We saw a lot of people singing along and for a band that hadn't played here so much, it was amazing to see.
The first two shows here were amazing as well, but being able to play at the Download Festival which is so big, with great bands, it's a huge opportunity and for us it was amazing to see how the reaction was.
We had to leave for the airport at four so we didn't get to see many bands; it was shitty as I had seen the line-up!"
Floor Jansen (After Forever – Vocals)

"We played at the Mean Fiddler (London) in March and the promoters of Download saw us at the Mean Fiddler and they made us an offer to play Download, so we were pretty happy. It was a very nice impression to be in the UK and to have a big crowd, the biggest crowd we'd ever had and we were very

*nervous for the first time, but it was amazing. The crowd made us feel very welcome.
We were there for all three days and we watched Marilyn Manson, Korn and Dream Theater, to see if they are still all good on stage."*
Anatoly (aka ANJ) (ANJ – Vocals/Guitar)

*"It was our first time in the UK. We saw Motley Crue and it was absolutely packed, they closed off the backstage area to everyone as well!
We play on stage three and it was an incredible experience and as we had never been to the UK before we didn't really know how the response would turn out, so having a good size crowd at the show was really amazing."*
Ryan Kirkland (Between The Trees – Vocals/Guitar)

*"Coming over here we were really nervous as to what was going to happen, as we are still on a small indie label, so financially it was a big jump for us. We never say no to an opportunity and every time we say yes, something bigger has happened.
So we got here and we watched Paramore, who we are really good friends with; they are really great guys and a great girl! The festival is like a different breed out here and completely different than the US. I wasn't sure how they were going to react to us, being a 'poppier', rock/pop kind of band. But back home if people don't like you they will just walk away, but here if they don't like you they throw stuff at you; I was really, really nervous that I was going to get smacked in the head with a water bottle, but the show went well."*
Jeremy Butler (Between The Trees – Bass)

*"We played just before Kids In Glass Houses and they had a really sing-along crowd, so we looked forward to touring with them after Download. I was very surprised how well everything went though.
We didn't really check out a lot of bands."*
Josh Butler (Between The Trees – Drums)

*"It was fun coming out to the UK, I'd only come here once before to London.
It was fun hanging out and meeting with other bands. It was a once in a lifetime moment to see Motley Crue."*
Wes Anderson (Between The Trees – Keyboards)

*"We didn't know what to expect coming over to Download as there were a lot of metal bands and a few from our genre, but it was great.
The weather was good, all the kids were awesome to us and no one came up and hit us in the face; so that was cool. We were in a pub and we told some kids that we were from America and were in a band and we were treated like royalty. It was cool to play our first show in the UK and it grew throughout the set and we sold a lot of merch, which was great. There were a few people singing along which was cool as they knew who we were."*
Brad Kriebel (Between The Trees – Guitar)

*"I honestly think that it's really an honour to have the stage named after him and to think that people loved him as much as they do; it feels good.
I remember waking up and Vinnie had sent me a link to where they had posted it and it was a great thing to wake up to for the day, with a big smile on my face."*
Rita Haney (Dimebag Darrell's widow)

*"Loads of people didn't want to see My Chemical Romance, so we gave them Suicidal Tendencies up the hill or Korn on the Tuborg stage.
People always as why do you put certain bands on certain stages? Korn wanted to play the Tuborg stage and it worked, it was absolutely fantastic; as it was when Billy Idol played in there and Metallica.
I like the way that the festival has shaped now and that we have three stages and that we can programme them differently.*

We will always get criticised for clashes; like when people wanted to see Korn and Suicidal Tendencies, but it's just unfortunate and bound to happen.

We are also open to different stages, as we were in 2003 with the Deconstruction stage and 2005 with the Ozzfest stage; so be it a Bamboozle stage or a New Band stage, which would feature new British bands and we can't see anything wrong with that, so we may start looking at that for 2008.

I don't have so much to do with booking the talent as I used to, Andy Copping in the office does most of that now, but I have to say I like his work, he does a good job!

It's nice to see that the festival started out in 1980 with a show that was seven bands. Then towards the end of Monsters life we did a second stage for the last two or three years; we broke bands out of that stage like Korn, Type O Negative and Biohazard and that was fantastic. But to sit here now and look at a line-up that is one hundred bands over three days is fantastic.

Download as a brand is now rolling out with four Download festivals in America, though they are more indie in America. The ambition is to make Download a 'global brand' and to roll out into two more territories next year and then just do it progressively.

People still insist on calling it Donington, but Bruce Dickinson, has now taken to calling it Download."

Stuart Galbraith (ex – Donington Organiser)

"My Chemical Romance. Oh my giddy aunt. People had been upset enough about The Prodigy, but judging by the reaction to My Chemical Romance as headliners you'd think Live Nation had posted a fresh turd to each and every Download goer in the land. Linkin Park didn't help, but no one seemed to take stock of Iron Maiden as a headliner...

2007 was also the year of the first Fan Forum meeting in April, where we took a group of board members down to London to meet Live Nation and chat about the festival.

It also saw the first band at the Boardie BBQ - Scumface - and we can't really take any credit for that as Mike Hyslop (1 half of Scumface) was at the meeting and managed to talk his way

into it.
On the Friday night we went to see Hayseed Dixie & Suicidal Tendencies on the 3rd Stage. The tent was packed (well, they were up against MCR!) but we were lucky enough to catch Sophie on the way round, who took us side of stage. I also got to meet DJ Krusher back there, and had a bit of a Fan Boy moment!
Saturday was Motley Crue - and again Sophie tried to get us side of stage, but unfortunately the stage manager wouldn't let us! She did manage to sneak us into the Nikki Sixx press conference however, and I guess that made up for it.
We watched Crue from outside the tent (packed again!) and I saw Mastodon chatting with a group of fans, take a fancy to one of the fans t-shirts, do a swap and wear the lucky fans shirt onstage the next day!
Sunday was "Flat Spit" day. Flat Spit was a cardboard cut out of a forum member - SpitItOut - who couldn't make it that year. So friends made a life-size cardboard cut out... Spit's girlfriend, WebWitch is one of the moderation team so we decided to take it out and about.
It's amazing where a life-size cut-out will get you... Live Nation let us take him into a meet n greet with Killswitch Engage who were great, and who signed and posed with Flat Spit. We also got to take him side of stage for Stone Sour, not to mention serving burgers and crowd surfing.
Maiden brought the festival to a suitable finish - in fact, of all the Download Festivals I've been to, Maiden gave the most Monsters Of Rock atmosphere to the place. It could have been the 80's - good natured old school bottle fights and all. There couldn't have been a better finish to the festival, which given the (unknown at the time) fact that this was the last time the infield would ever be used to host a gig. But it wasn't the end of Donington as a festival."
Phil Hull (Download Forum Administrator)

"Linkin Park headlining the main stage on Saturday was incredible. I loved Wolfmother and Paramore on Friday, but all I can say is we are all not worthy of the awesome talent that is Hayseed Dixie.

All hail to the gods of Hillbilly!!"
Mike Horton (Plymouth)

"Well, roll on a few years and Monsters of Rock became Download. A personal high point has to be, being there for Bruce belting out, "Scream for me Donington!" in '07, well Bruce I fuckin' screamed myself hoarse... Bring it on Download!"
Matt Allison (Plymouth)

"A cloud of hairspray seemed to loom over the historical Donington site all day, scattered amongst it were zebra print clad, leather wearing, eyeliner rocking glam rock fans; their 'ready to rock' pre-dyed manes of hair fierce and on display, like a violent peacock on Halloween. It's amazing that so many people (boys, girls & a few in-betweeners) managed to look so glamorous despite living in a field for the past couple of days.
Come sun down, you could pretty much follow the cloud of hairspray over to the second stage, where it seemed to gather together to create one big glam cloud of fun. The Jack bottles were out, the tops were off and without sounding too cliché… it was time to party.
The tent was well and truly packed, it almost seemed like an insanely overheated, over hyper and over intoxicated circus had rolled into town with all guns blazing. You can't help but wonder what main stage headliners Linkin Park were thinking before they hit the stage; considering the amount of people that swarmed off to watch the Crue.
The band were due on stage at 20.45, but no real fan expected them at that time, they arrived about 10 minutes late in true Crue fashion, hair teased to the max, leathers & guyliner on, but more importantly ready to rock the shit out of "Donnnnnnnington". With the crowd of 15 year old girls gathered around us, screaming "NIKKKI" & ready to flash their tits the very second they thought he cast a glance our way, it's almost easy to forget that's a 50 year old father they're screeching at, in a band that's been going for well over 20 years.

They delivered a perfect set, featuring all the hits and classic Crue songs as expected, however it's not just the songs that the Crue deliver so perfectly for me, as many bands over the weekend did that. It's they're ability to create an atmosphere, where the person at the side of you feels like your best friend, despite never knowing or possibly having anything in common with them. It's they're ability to take a sweaty 50 year old truck driver, a 30 year old uptight female office worker and an unemployed 17 year old glam rock girl, throw them all into the same environment and make it feel like a party.
During the set; my friend got pissed on, another was threatened to have her hair set alight and I was punched in the mouth, but we wouldn't have had it any other way, it's a Crue concert!
And from the very opening cord of 'Dr. Feelgood' to the last yelp of "When I say Motley, you say Crue" from Tommy Lee, that's exactly where they kept it; a Crue show. They might well be in Donington tonight, but Motley Crue showed the crowd that they weren't about to be intimidated or overshadowed by any of the historic bands that have played this venue and in the process proving why they're the perfect band to play at this festival; reflecting the fact that both band and festival only appear to be rocking even harder as they get older.
For me it was by far the best set I've ever seen any band do and for that I salute both Donington & Motley Crue for this match made in heaven hell… "When I say Motley, you say…"

Robert Southwell (Shirebrook)

The summer story begins with Scuba Steve running through arrivals at Terminal 3 and throwing up the metal horns before a solid 2 minute embrace. England, Amsterdam, Belgium, Paris and Scotland will never be the same. Seeing Kat and Steve was a blast and certainly three weeks I won't forget in a hurry.
The obvious highlight was Steve and I trekking to the Download festival, the ultimate experience in rock/metal. Three days of camping in a field, Jägermeister for breakfast and rocking out with 99,998 other like minded metal heads to the world's best riff masters. Key bands were Motley Crue,

Slayer, Megadeth, Iron Maiden, Lamb of God, Killswitch Engage and countless others and although the hangover lasted two weeks and required Penicillin it was one of the best experiences of my (and definitely Steve's) life. I could go on and on for days about the adventures of Download. And I will. The fun didn't end when the bands finished, the night time entertainment was immense. Highlights included sleeping bag wrestling, random tent crashing, drinking with the police, camp sing alongs and just generally engaging in the dumbest activities known to man.
This was all fuelled not by shots of Sambuca, but by sculling straight out of the bottle. Fun times.
Daniel Steffe (Gold Coast, Australia)

"At the Download Festival of 2007 I was stood against the rail in front of the sound stage waiting for Marilyn Manson to perform. As I was waiting and looking over the crowd, I saw stood behind me a long haired very well build man who stereotypically looked like a rock star and the tattoo on his chin was very individual.
I began talking to him as a normal person, very casual conversation the 'hi how are you? Having a good weekend' just basic small talk before Marilyn Manson came on.
When the show started I turned my back on the very rock n roll man and thought nothing of him until about two weeks after the festival and I picked up a music magazine.
Low and behold there on the front cover was the man I'd met at the festival, long hair, very well built and the unique tattoo on his chin. I had no idea what so ever I'd been talking to Dez Fafara the lead singer of Devildriver! Who have now come to be one of my favourite bands and I met the lead singer and passed him off as just some other guy!"
Gary Killelay (Doncaster)

"Back in 2007, Bowling For Soup, on the mainstage, were having the greatest gig ever, performing along side 2 giant sheep and one which had been thrown up in reference to a previous gig.

As a plane passed by the mainstage, the band stopped, point reference at the plane and the Donington tyre which made the festival different from others, when a guy from the back goes crowd surfing in a blow up dingy.

'White water rafting' the band sang and laughed at the stunt and hit straight where they left off."

Lawrence Taylor (Hull)

"Download is the most established festival around in my opinion it always has an awesome atmosphere and there's always something to do; if you don't like any band there at the time you will always be able to find something to keep you busy.

My best memory of Download is from 2007 when Iron Maiden played with the Iron Maiden tank and Bruce Dickinson falling onstage and not messing up the song that made my festival. As for Cup Man, nobody seems to know who he is but he's always as Download collecting cups, some people say he does it to make enough money to go to the next festival but whatever reason he does it for he become a legend at the festival.

Everyone who has been Download will know who Cup Man is."

William Bell (Darwen)

"It was the Sunday of Download 2007. I was standing to the right hand side of the stage near the food vans.

The smell of cooking burgers filled my nostrils. I began to feel a mixture of excitement and panic as Iron Maiden made their way onto the stage. The atmosphere was amazing and as the songs kept coming I felt the energy coming off the crowd powering me up.

The next thing I knew my view was blocked by a tall man with long dreadlocks. I turned to my friend as I was incredibly annoyed.

"Why do people always choose to stand in front of me? Is it just 'cos I'm tall?" I said. "Dude do you not realise who that is?" My mate said.

Then it dawned on me. In my mind I thought that's Brian Fair from Shadows Fall. Then next to him I also saw Jim Lamarca from Chimaira. I went over and said hi and they were some of the nicest guys I've ever met.
Turns out even rock stars have heroes similar to rock fans and they were there rocking out to Iron Maiden with the best of us."
Mike Barnett (Dunfermline)

"Being packed into the Dimebag Darrell tent to see Mötley Crüe, singing along to Iron Maiden's 'Fear of the Dark' with thousands of others... such moments just can't be described! I'll never forget the feeling of walking through the gates of the festival for the first time, and it's an occasion I look forward to like no other, every year."
Andy McDonald (Clydebank)

"One of my best memories was waiting for Linkin Park to start in 2007.
This was when Download of course was on the actual track. There was a massive bottle fight between the people in the crowd and the people who were sitting on the hill just off of the track. It was massive. I remember being covered in liquid (and trying not to think what liquid).
As soon as the band started it was amazing the bottle throwing stopped and everyone went crazy for Linkin Park."
Emma Bucknall (Nottingham)

"Me and my group were pitched up behind the speaker stand at the main stage during Iron Maiden's set on the Sunday in 07. Right in the middle of 'Fear Of The Dark', my two good buddies Pauly G and his twin brother Craigyluvspudz were getting a bit pissed off with some geezer in front, He was so out of it and falling backwards all the time.
So the twins decided to play "lightsabers" Basically they got their truncheons out in front of everyone and pissed all over the backs of this geezers legs while he was dancing. They were pissed themselves but no where near as mullered as this fella. Anyway after getting me to hold their drinks, they

slashed away making all the sound effects from Star Wars. This poor bloke didn't have a clue what they were doing. When they finished they were cheering for themselves etc and the guy turned round and started cheering with them and gave them both a big hug! He obviously thought that were cheering for Maiden.
 Classic moment!"
Danny Ramsay (Swindon)

"My First real festival experience was Download Festival 2007, and what a year it was.
The one thing that struck me the most about it all was the amount of different and diverse people you could meet there just by saying 'hello'.
I fell down a pot hole the day I got there and hurt my knee and stumbling back from the first aid tent I needed to sit down and just as it happened at the entrance of the campsite was an inflatable sofa, so I asked these random Scottish people if I could sit down and I introduced myself and they did the same they were Neil, Danny and Bobby and they were really nice to me, we all struck up a conversation about all the bands we wanted to see over a bottle of JD and I ended up spending the whole weekend with them, if it wasn't for Download I probably wouldn't have met one of my best friends Neil nor would I have been able to meet up with him at every Download Festival since then!
The best band of that year was Iron Maiden, I went to download not really liking them and I left a die hard fan! The atmosphere that Sunday evening gave me the goosebumps!"
Charlotte 'Coxy' Cox (Portsmouth)

"My Uncle Nik, He used to go to Monsters of Rock back in the 80's, when it finished. He was gutted. Literally devastated. Anyway, when it was back as Download, he went ballistic so I am told. Back when it was '03 and '04, he used to go for the day. Then in '05 he went for the weekend. I went on the Saturday in 2005 and met up with my uncle. He, that day gave me the biggest gift ever, my love for Download.

In 2006 we spent all weekend there, together. My Uncle was the one who got me into "this sort of music" back when I was around 7/8. Anyway, in 2006, I had realised I was in love with the festival. The weekend soon passed and we were already planning for 2007 the week after! But my uncle had a huge heroin addiction, and owed money to dealers, now I am not going into details, as I would like to keep that part private. But before 2006 ended, he was dead. I was mortified, as expected, and depression sunk in.
And from that day, I vowed I would never miss a Download again. But in 2007, when the announcements were being made, the words MOTLEY CRUE came up. That hurt. As they were my Uncles fave band, and he had never been to see them. But I had vowed that I would see them, for my uncle Nik.
So I took well in excess of 100 photos (All on an old computer, sorry I don't have them.) and put them on my uncles grave. Now, coming into 2010. I am still going to download. Not just for me. But for the both of us."
Dan 'DivaDan' Brain (Wellingborough)

"It was coming up to Download 2007 (my second year) and to my luck, I'd just developed a chest infection. But that didn't stop me. Neither did the thought of the dust and dirt getting kicked up and lining my lungs. I still went to Download despite this, and had an awesome time.
Met Darth Vader and the Stormtroopers, even managed to cough up a few words to Corey Taylor in the signing tent with Stone Sour. Managed to get a hug from him too! Score! Don't know what he would have thought of me as I was as pale as a ghost, coughing and spluttering. Although I was made to take medicine 3 times a day I still managed to have the best time of my life. To top it off, I was only fifteen years old."
Casey Fudge (Gloucester)

"My first Download Festival was 2007; I've been every year since without fail. Since 2007 I've been trying to get to Donington as early as possible and leaving as late as possible. I just cannot get enough of Download!"

Graham Simmonds (London)

2008
KISS,
The Offspring,
&
Lostprophets

This year was the first time that any of the festivals at Donington had been held outside the track and also the first time that the 2nd stage was in the open and not within the confines of a tent.

The capacity was slightly smaller this year and there were nothing but complaints on the Forums about the mainstage headliners, Kiss, The Offspring and Lostprophets, but all three put on great shows and Kiss made their 3rd appearance and their 2nd headline slot in full make-up at the festival.

The second stage was built on a tarmac car park which did cause some problems for 'moshing', but the size of the stage was much bigger than usual, now being outside. The headliners on the second stage were Simple Plan, HIM and Cavalera Conspiracy.

Biggest crowd of the weekend, on the 2nd stage, had to go to Pendulum who were making their Donington debut;

the amount of people wanting to see the 'Drum & Bass crossover' band was phenomenal and it seemed like most of the festival were at the 2nd stage for their show.

The crowd were treated to a double dose of their painted idols over the weekend. Kiss played on Friday and the crowd was treated to a full 'Kiss show' with flames, fireworks and blood and Saturday Ace Frehley played a rare UK performance on the second stage with a mix of his own and classic Kiss songs.

Elsewhere there were many other 'classic rock' bands playing over the weekend. Friday on the mainstage saw the return of Judas Priest after a 28 year gap, Motorhead also played the Friday mainstage, Rose Tattoo made their Donington debut and Saxon played as special guests in the tent, 26 years after they had last played, on the Saturday.

The weather all weekend was good except for a ten minute shower on the Saturday morning during the Skindred set, with half the crowd running and taking shelter in the 3rd stage tent, packing it out for GO:Audio. The 'cup collecting' which had began a few years before, in line with the green issues of the festival reached new heights with people making serious amounts of money and keeping the rubbish down to a minimum on the site; 'Cup Man' was spotted all over the festival again, dressed in 'Viking like' attire and collecting cups like there was no tomorrow; whether Cup Man actually watches any bands is unknown.

Some of the site was on a gravel slope so was not the ideal place for the festival, but all would change the following year, new site, still at Donington, outside the track and weather that was close to tropical, Download was to find its new and permanent home.

"We're back and we are celebrating 35 years. We'll be playing 'Kiss Alive' and a whole bunch of other stuff.
Trends come, fashion come, but we just don't go away; we're like herpes I guess?

We don't live within the boundaries of other bands, they wish they could be Kiss, we don't wish we could be them."
Paul Stanley (Kiss – Vocals / Guitar)

"In all seriousness, it's unfortunate but the record industry is dead, six feet underground and unfortunately the fans have done this. They have decided to download and file share; there's no record industry around. We are going to wait until everyone settles down and becomes civilised and as soon as the record industry 'pops up its head' we will record some new material.
But honestly we have the time of our lives. We get to wear more make-up and higher heels than your mommy does, we get to go up on stage and blow up shit, we don't have to explain what our lyrics mean and we have the best time in the world.
If I was given an Aladdin's lamp and was told 'rub this and you can become a member of any band', guess which band I want to be in, right here baby,
THE HOTTEST BAND IN THE WORLD; KISS."
Gene Simmons (Kiss – Vocals / Bass)

"What was really cool that day was that the venue has so much history to it. To be perfectly honest we had a tough schedule and we were in and out that day and I didn't really the chance to see many other bands; we played our show and then took off.
Judas Priest and Kiss headlined the day before and whenever they put bills together like that it makes me chuckle. I grew up listening to Kiss and 'Kiss Alive' was my very first record, so to be on the same bill, in the same headlining slots it's almost so ridiculous that it's hilarious; it was like 'wow, we shouldn't be here!'
We did watch some of Incubus, who we had played some shows with them in Australia, when we had played Soundwave, so we had got to know them a bit.
There was quite a bit of press, we did it all in the backstage area in our little portable dressing room.

It sounded like a cool thing to do; we'd played the Reading Festival, but with Download we decided to play and mix it up a bit. It was definitely a bit of a change, but it was really cool. People had told us that the crowd would be a different crowd, more of a metal crowd and that it may not be the same reception for us, but that was not the case. I thought it was a great show."
Dexter Holland (The Offspring – Vocals / Guitar)

"Download 2008 was incredible and out metal maniac fans went mental, as did the rest of the 50 thousand strong crowd!"
Rob Halford (Judas Priest – Vocals)

"When we first started to tour the States we toured with a lot of bands, REO Speedwagon, Foghat, you name them, some were appropriate to have Priest on the bill, but some weren't. Back in those days we were lucky to get one spotlight and that didn't always work, so we had to jockey about on stage to be seen. But when we played with Kiss they were already a well established band and they were pretty good to us. They weren't stingy with the lights and it was the first time that we were able to get any production going in the States. It was great to play with Kiss.
So it was very poignant to do the Download show with them, as we go back a long way. I've got a lot of time for Kiss; I think they are a professional band, but a show business band. They've got great songs, they're great showmen and people want entertaining and they do it well.
We had already done a lot of shows with Motorhead and they're great.
It was very symbolic to come back, 29 years on and it shows the sustaining power of Priest and I think that the one thing, a compliment that has been paid to us many times throughout the years and it is something that we are proud of and that is that Priests music is fairly timeless. It's something very satisfying to know, that something we did 29 years ago still carries through today."
Glenn Tipton (Judas Priest – Guitar)

"I had wanted to see Children Of Bodom, but I was doing press so I missed them, but it's work and it's unglamorous."
Jonathan Davis (Jonathan Davis - Vocals)

"The first thing that hit me was that it was freezing fucking cold. We went onstage and I think someone told me it was either 3 or 4 degrees so it was really cold. I think I went on in a sweatshirt where I had cut the sleeves off. It was raining, I think that it stopped when we went onstage, but the crowd had been there forever and it did put a dampener on things; no matter how much you twist and turn it's not as happening as it would have been on a nice sunny day and dry.
But still it's a good festival and we had a great time. I watched the end of Judas Priest and saw the end of Kiss; I didn't see anything else as I flew in that same afternoon and then flew out that evening for another show."
Mikkey Dee (Motörhead – Drums)

"This year was cool we had a good show, every year is good. I didn't like the new layout and I got lost. But Donington is always a cool place to play.
We never get to watch many bands, because we turn up, do interviews, and rehearse for 30 minutes and then play. Lots of friends and family turned up, so we had to see them and then go to an airport and fly to another country."
Jason "Jay" James (Bullet For My Valentine – Bass)

"I just love Donington. There's not a lot to say apart from I love being a part of it. It's a prestigious festival; it's Download now, but it used to be Monsters of Rock, it's a kind of 'holy' field for rock and metal, it's notoriously famous.
We don't care where we play. In the tent you get a bit better atmosphere and the sound tends to be better, but being on the mainstage is pretty big deal with huge crowds."
Matt Tuck (Bullet For My Valentine - Vocals / Guitar)

"It was one of several shows in the festival season, but one of THE shows that we were all looking forward to, because it's the Download Festival and the biggest one that we were on. At some festivals, especially with the amount of acts, everyone gets about 25 minutes, but at Download we had 50 minutes; which is great for a festival.

Metal festivals can go either way for us, we have some appeal to some of the metal crowd, but we tend to do alright. The crowds in the UK in general have been pretty warm to us and at least they give us the time of day and both times we played Download we had huge crowds.

The line-up was quite interesting this year as well; In Flames went on before us and Jimmy Eat World went on after us, so we were kind of transitional between the two.

There really were some vibes on stage, because Download is a festival where we really want to shine when we come out. We had the two backing singers and our keyboardist Wes and it fills up the sound, especially for the arena shows that we were doing in the States opening up for Linkin Park and for something of the magnitude of Donington, it just adds a new dimension to the music.

I think that it went well; we walked off and people seemed happy.

I hope that we get more Downloads as we'd love to come back and rock harder and harder each year."

Michael Todd (Coheed and Cambria – Bass)

"The last time we played was two years ago; it's a cool festival and it always has a great line-up. This time we came a couple of hours before we had to play and we had a lot of press, so I didn't get to see many bands. Coheed and Cambria played a couple of hours after us on the Sunday afternoon; I had really wanted to see them but missed out.

Peter Iwers (In Flames – Bass)

"When we played it was called Download and it was our first experience of playing at the festival and had been our aim for a long time.

It was pretty cool, to get the opportunity to play there as it was legendary and it was still as big as it used to be.

I thought our performance was great because we were fired up and ready to go, we had a good time. It was everything that we expected and hopefully we got our foot in the door for next time.
I got to have a wander around the festival grounds, after I had done some press and it was great.
It is THE big festival of Europe."
Chuck Billy (Testament – Vocals)

"My memories are of technical difficulties; my guitar had a fault with the wireless system, so it was just squealing all the way through the gig, it was really annoying.
It was interesting because being a 'metal festival' we were worrying about it beforehand, but it went down great actually. It was cool because we had already done Donington with the Stereophonics, but we had all grown up listening to Radio One's broadcasts from the Monsters Of Rock back in the day. We came just for the day; I was pretty pissed off because we got to miss Judas Priest and Kiss."
Tim Wheeler (Ash – Vocals / Guitar)

"I do remember that we were hanging out backstage before Pendulum and they got a really crazy crowd. We were up in the car park and all the Pendulum fans kind of disappeared after their set and it was like 'WOW'.
A lot of people turned up, which was a bit of a relief. That was our biggest concern, because we were one of the more melodic pop bands on the bill; beforehand I was anxious that we were going to get loads of piss thrown on us, but there wasn't any which was really good."
Mark Hamilton (Ash – Bass)

"It was one of our best gigs and one of our most memorable as well. We're really into rock & metal, so just to be asked to be at that festival and not as punters was just fucking amazing.
We turned up for the whole weekend to see In Flames and a couple of other bands. There are very few bands that we

actually get impressed by sound wise, usually you get the CD and it's great and then you go to the live show and it's crap, but In Flames completely pulled it off.
In Flames seem to be one of those bands that play the tiniest little sweatboxes and then the biggest festivals and they seem to be one of those bands that can do both.
We were just recently playing the States and we played this tiny little rock club called I-Rock in Detroit and In Flames had been there a few weeks before and it was hard to think how they fitted on the stage, it's tough for us to fit on small stages. We didn't really know where we were playing, we knew that we were at Download, but that was about as much as we knew.
I remember when we were in the van driving up to the stage, it was quite a while away and I thought we were going to be in one of the tents, as they were quite close to our dressing rooms. But as we were driving up there was this massive fucking stage and a massive audience in front of it. I was going 'what the fuck?? We can't play here man, it's a metal & rock festival and we're coming with a load of synths; we're going to get drenched in piss'.
We were on after Ace Frehley and before Ash
For us backstage, it wasn't a case of 'if' we were going to get bottled or not, we were just planning for 'when' we get bottled! It was just going to be an inevitability, with a crowd like that, but we didn't get a single thing onstage!
I remember on the Download website they had a bunch of quotes from different bands and my quote, which I must have said in an interview was 'bring on the bottles of piss….just kidding, please have mercy'.
Just looking out over the crowd and seeing people as far as we could see and about 9 circle pits, it was just crazy. In the distance I could see where the fairground was, way past the mixing desk and the crowd was still thick out there. Next to the fairground rides there were circle pits going off it was crazy."
Rob Swire (Pendulum - _Vocals/Synthesizer_)
Gareth McGrillen (Pendulum - _Bass/Secondary Vocals_)

"Download was quite nerve wracking for me the first year we played it as it was a big 'cross-over' gig for us and we weren't too sure how the crowd was actually going to take to it. But as soon as the bass kicked in on the first track, we just destroyed them; we all looked at each other and we all felt very at home on that stage.
Coming from drum & bass which is primarily heavy, for me it always sounded like a form of rock music with that beat, but an electronic rock beat, so it worked."
Kodish (Pendulum – Drums)

"I played with Apocalyptica and that proved to me that whatever you do, you just have to be up there, be honest and be yourself and people will go crazy.
Download is definitely one of our favourite festivals."
Cristina Scabbia (Apocalyptica – Guest Vocals)

"It was the first major festival that we had played in the UK and a pretty big festival, so it was a good opportunity for us to present our band to a lot of new fans.
Donington Park is definitely the classic metal ground and I remember reading about it as a kid in magazines back in Sweden, when it was Monsters Of Rock and now this is as close to it as we can get nowadays.
We had a good show, it felt great. I did feel that we were a bit rusty as we had just come out of the studio to play the show, but the crowd seemed to be into it and that's the most important thing.
We had a lot of stuff to do in London, so we didn't get to see much. At the festival I was going to watch Saxon play but I drank too much and we also had a lot of interviews to do. Children Of Bodom came by the dressing room and then Kerry King came by and it was just a big party there; everything went into oblivion."
Johan Hegg (Amon Amarth – Vocals)

"Well for Madina it was a bit of a nightmare lol. We discovered 1 minute before we had to play to 50K people that the bass rig

was completely out, the vocal mic out, Mateo's wireless system, out. Hah!
So aside from playing to the biggest crowd we'd ever played to, we had all that to deal with. Mateo ended up using a 6 foot guitar cable meaning on that gigantic stage he had to stay within 3 feet of his rig. Matthew's bass rig simply didn't work the entire show etc. However, we decided we didn't give a shit and we were just gonna go have a blast. And we did.
The best part, however, was when Matthew got hit in the balls with a plastic yogurt bottle and upon lurching in pain he slipped on the splattered yogurt and ended up on his ass. The backstage, after show party was the best; most fun we'd ever had.
The crowd reaction was mixed, based mostly on the fact that our equipment didn't work and that we aren't a metal band so our "slot" was a bit difficult. However, we did have our solid crew of Madina kids representing and making it awesome for us. Backstage we saw some cool shit too. We shared a bus with the Dillinger Escape Plan and those dudes are hilarious and amazing. As for shenanigans, I've gotten in way too much trouble for opening my mouth so if it's all the same, just wait for the tell all expose book we're writing!
Hope to hear from them soon."
Nathan Leone (Madina Lake – Vocals)

"This past summer was our 3rd time at Download and definitely my favorite, we once again played the Main Stage and it was just an amazing day all around.
We played our set and for me personally after having a dismal previous Download due to my voice, I felt vindicated after the set, crowd was absolutely amazing and we couldn't of been more thankful for them...
We partyied pretty hard after the gig, I met One of my all time favorite singers ever, Chuck Billy, And later Phil Demmel (Machine Head) and the rest of the boys drank everything in sight at the after party. I may have talked Chuck Billy's ear off that night as well but I have some great pictures to last a lifetime. All in all Download is an incredible honor to be a part of and if you think of the grand scheme of things and how

many bands there are in the world, to be asked to play three times is utterly mind blowing....Can't wait to be asked again............."

Brock Lindow (36 Crazyfists – Vocals)

"Download is a heritage festival and its values are heavily weighted in the metal scene. It's one of the only festivals that is predominantly rock & metal, most other festivals have a big Indie side to them now; so for us playing the mainstage it was a big honour for us walking out and feeling that we had got this far.
It was an amazing experience and a great festival to do. People know it the world over; it's a very famous place for a band to play. You grow up and think that one day you will play that stage and then when you do it's amazing.
The site had changed apparently because a racing car had slipped on a hot dog!"

Charlie Simpson (Fightstar – Guitar/Vocals)

"We were booked to play Donington and I was really excited, but I wasn't sure because I looked on the bill and we were booked 2nd at 11:45am. I love playing in England but we always play at ridiculous o'clock. I said to my kid 'go and check how people are out there', walked out and then said 'there's hardly anybody there'.
I want to be ones of those bands from Britain that gets a big following; I went into the dressing room, sluggishly got changed, put my jacket and hat on and thought 'ok, let's go out there' and by the time we walked to the stage there were about 40,000 people in front of us.
It was one of those gigs that just turned around. We went on stage and using the Star Wars intro, we played and I had a blast. I had always watched Donington as a kid on TV, when it was Monsters Of Rock and I had always wanted to play there. I was so buzzed to think that all these guys from all over the UK had just come to see us and it was like 'YEAH'.
Being a black guy from Wales I'm not supposed to be into rock, but I've always liked going out there and representing British metal all over the world.

That day at Donington showed me that Skindred has a foundation, maybe not to break through in the media, but I was just blown away."
Benji Webbe (Skindred – Vocals / Synthesizer)

"This was the second Download that I had been to and I have to say that as much as all the branding has changed and that it's not Monsters Of Rock anymore, I do think that it has retained a certain amount of what made it special and what made it special was a load of people who loved heavy metal and rock music used to gather here every year and watch a lot of great bands and it was awesome.
Twenty years ago I stood out there as a punter watching Helloween, David Lee Roth, Megadeth and Guns 'n' Roses, Kiss and Iron Maiden and twenty years later I am on stage playing the thing. I couldn't resist, in the last song, saying 'scream for me Donington' à la Bruce Dickinson, it was a lot of fun.
It's Donington and there's so much history and to walk out on stage and say 'I am playing Donington', which to me will always be Monsters Of Rock, is just awesome."
Richie Edwards (Stone Gods – Vocals/Guitar)

"This time was great; for a start I can remember this time. It was good and for two in the afternoon there were a lot of people there. It's always a danger at festivals that you could play to two or three rows of people, you don't know how it's going to go. But we could see people as far as the control tower, so it was really good; I was really chuffed actually."
Dan Hawkins (Stone Gods – Guitar)

"I always heard of the Donington rock festival and that it was THE rock thing to do. Listening to the Radio One Rock Show, Tommy Vance was always banging on about the Donington rock festivals.
It was the rock festival to do and now we've done it and I'm over the moon. I came from a more indie background, but it was great to play Donington and seeing a bunch of 'metal maniacs' out there."

Toby MacFarlaine (Stone Gods – Bass)

"It was one of those typical shows. What made it palatable, driving in a bus for 30 hours to play 35 minutes, was that it was Donington and it is an historical event. But a couple of years ago we did fly from Australia to Russia to play an hour and a half for Harley-Davidson and we worked out that by the time we got home, we had spent more time in the air travelling than we had on the ground; but because the vodka is so good over there, we hardly suffered jet lag, until about a week afterwards, when it caught up with us.
One of the things about being involved in these festivals is that at least you are 'doing it' and committing yourself to history, which is nice.
After a few hours we then got a ferry and drove back to Hamburg, but I feel that the 'moments' that we have are always worth it as you may get run over by a bus tomorrow; you've got to live your 'moments' as they are given to you.
I don't remember the last time I was at Donington, but then again I don't remember a lot of those days, it blurs into one. Then there is that wonderful phrase 'if you can remember it, you weren't doing it well enough' or something; a bit like the 50's 'if you can remember it, you weren't really there'. It's like some of the other great moments that we've had, if it wasn't for the photographs and other folks tales, we wouldn't know that we had been there.
We watched Airbourne; they are a bit more 'edged' than AC/DC, maybe the way the they used to be, but it's so long ago I can't remember, but they haven't played at Donington for years. AC/DC are in the position at the moment where they could do things 'not for money'.
You go full circle in life, you start out in life doing things 'not for money' because there's no money to be had, then you go to this middle period where you do command money so you play for money, not just for money, as there are very few bands that play just for money and then when you make SO much money you can play wherever you fucking like and it doesn't matter how much they pay you. I can only imagine that if you

were that big and didn't need the money, you could go and play the corner pub!
But it's that middle section where you are ruled by economics, record company and band management, so you need to 'make hay whilst the sun shines'. There's always that old saying 'money doesn't make you happy' BULLSHIT, it's your state of mind; if money is the only thing in your life, it probably won't make you happy."
Angry Anderson (Rose Tattoo – Vocals)

"It was great, Disturbed, Judas Priest, Kiss, it's a pretty classic rock line up there and we were kind of the 'new kids' in the business.
We had nerves backstage and I was literally shaking.
We were going to set up this thing where one of our crew threw a bottle from the front of the stage of apple juice and I would pick it up and go 'oh yeah PEE' and start drinking it!
But, the highlight of this tour and my career has been playing this festival; I've played some great shows with some great bands, but this is just legendary!
The British crowd is discerning and definitely a more difficult crowd to impress. I walked to the side of the stage and peered around the corner and everyone was going crazy.
I'm not sure what we set out to achieve originally but I think all our expectations were met and raised and then superseded, it was a good time."
Shaun Morgan (Seether – Vocals/Guitar)

"This year was a surprise for me, coming into this as a new member of Seether. They hadn't played here before, but by some chance I had, so I felt like I had some information, 'Hey guys, check this out, they are going to throw shit everywhere'.
We went onstage and it was amazing. We played at 2:35pm, which was early in the day and I thought that it was going to be one of those situations where we go onstage and there would obviously be a lot of people by default, but the crowd was 'way' into it!
It's an iconic festival and it's HUGE!

It feels good to walk away from the show at Donington without egg on your face, that's the bottom line. I saw Maiden get hit with eggs in 2007!"
Troy McLawhorn (Seether - Guitar)

"I used to be all about festivals. I loved to get fucked up in a tent, so much in fact that I used to drag people to any field on the way home, put up the tent and continue the fun. Sometimes, of course, the weather was so bad that we'd just leave the tent standing at the festival. That's what UK festivals mean to me, get so fucked up that it doesn't matter about the shitty weather.   The Wildhearts appearance in 2008 was a magic moment for me. I had a feeling that we were gonna play great, something that I don't normally associate with the variable sound problems at festivals shows, go down great with the crowd and leave a lasting impression. I didn't think we'd go down SO well that a mini-riot would ensue, forcing the organisers to cut our sound in a bid to calm the crowd down. I was so proud of every single person watching that show. They showed me that The Wildhearts are still very loved in the UK and gave us more than enough reason to stick around and continue making music." **Ginger (The Wildhearts – Vocals/Guitar)**

"The show was really, really cool; really eventful! Probably one of the 'funnest' shows I've ever done.
It was kind of shakey at the start, I didn't know what the fuck was going on when I saw all the bottles flying and stuff, but I blocked that out of my mind and I came to do what I got paid to do and that was rock the crowd and I think that I did that at the end of the 35 minutes!
It was really fun, I really enjoyed it.
I wanted to check out BFMV and Fightstar, but they played a different day, but I checked out Lostprophets.
I really find watching bands is really inspirational for me, especially live. I take tips and nick a few things and then put them into my hip-hop show and that makes it kind of unique from everyone else.

It was an eventful week for me, with load of controversy about me doing the show; I don't think I am ever going to forget that day."
Lethal Bizzle (Lethal Bizzle – Vocals)

"Playing Download felt like a massive achievement for us. We were actually meant to be playing one of the smaller stages and for some reason one of the bands pulled out or got taken off the mainstage. I can't remember basically how it happened, but our agent called us up and offered us the slot. I remember I was on the phone to all the lads and we were going through the idea that people might not like us as we're not a metal band.
So we'd got the opportunity to play the mainstage, it would be the same money and we were trying to weigh up if it was going to be a better gig or a worse gig. We could have played the mainstage and the 'vibe' wouldn't be there or people wouldn't know us, as we were a new band trying to make our name and we weren't big or anything. The main conclusion that we came to when we were given the offer was, if we pass it up there's a million bands who'd say 'well we'll do it then, if Beat Union don't we will'.
So we thought that we'd be dick-heads to pass the opportunity up, so we ended up playing it.
It was a tough show; we were on early in the day, but we got up there. There were a few hecklers in the front who wanted some metal, but 70% of the people towards the back were just listening, their day just started and probably half enjoying our set and thinking this is alright.
So even the hecklers didn't bother me; you've just got to have a laugh about it. I think that if I was a metalhead and I went to a festival and I'm getting pissed off early in the morning, it doesn't mean that you hate the band and you want to send them 'death threats', you just want to have a laugh and some lads get a bit lairy and have a few beers, they're probably having a wicked time; if they're getting a bit drunk and a bit loony to our show, you can't really blame them.

We left that evening as we had another show the next day, so it was drive in, play the show watch Kiss and then we left that night."
Dave Warsop (Beat Union – Vocals/Guitar)

"We didn't know what to expect as we had never played there and we had heard it was quite a big festival.
We were on tour at the time and had played a few headline shows around the UK, the shows went really good.
When started it was three times bigger a crowd than we'd ever played to before.
We were there two days before we played and the bus was parked about three kilometres away and it sucked, but after the show we had a really good feeling and a good vibe."
Jaska Raatikainen (Children of Bodom – Drums)

"We were here to see Kiss for the first time and we were very excited.
We a very extreme band, sometimes going at 2000 miles an hour, so I like the opportunity to scare the normal people in the crowd and this opportunity is the best thing to ask for.
Music of the pariah; skeletons, death metal, horror; bad people like us!! But a lot of people like it out there, so it's a good opportunity for us to speak for 'Extreme Metal'."
Trevor Strnad (The Black Dahlia Murder – Vocals)

"It was awesome.
We played early in the day and I was very stoked at the amount of people who came to see us, even though there were thousands of people still coming in.
We did a signing at the Kerrang! tent afterwards and a lot of people were complaining that they didn't get to see us.
We left for Switzerland ten minutes after as we were playing the Greenfield Festival, so it was a bummer that I didn't get to see any bands at all.
I loved the amount of kids walking around in Kiss face paint as it made me feel like I did, when I was a kid."
Ben Osmundson (Zebrahead - Bass)

"Download 2008 was fucking incredible.
We were all really stoked to have an opportunity to play 2 years in a row. So to the people that made that possible, THANK YOU!
Both years that we have played Download have been some of my favorite weekends I've had on tour. The vibe of the fest is fucking awesome and everyone's there to rage and have fun. I spent a lot of time drinking ridiculous amounts of beer and liquor over the weekend. I also spent a lot of time hung-over, which isn't that big of a deal because there were plenty of kickass bands to watch as I stumbled trying to find someone to buy me the first beer of the day.
We had the pleasure of playing on the main stage which honestly was rather intimidating. We had never played for a crowd of that size and I was a bit uneasy. But as soon as we started playing it was pretty badass.
The crowd was awesome and a lot of fun to play in front of. Despite a couple technical difficulties I felt pretty good about it. After we played we got to party with our good friends in High On Fire and Children Of Bodom.
The performance that absolutely stood out to me was Dillinger Escape Plan. Every time I've seen them they've been fucking intense.
So all in all, Download is the shit. I hope that we get another chance to play as soon as possible."
Bobby Thompson (Job For A Cowboy – Guitar)

"I watched 2008 from computer I remember watching Kiss and it was just like 'I wish we could be there'. Download is just one of those festivals that you want to play every year, it's like 'I wish I could play it again'."
Chris Howorth (In This Moment – Guitar)

"When I was told that we were going to go to the UK to do Download, it was like 'awesome another festival'. It sounded familiar and then everyone said 'that is THE Festival' and it was like wow!!
It is definitely an insane festival and we got to watch Judas Priest and Kiss and hang out.

We were all nervous and we are not a mainstream metal band, we are more of a younger 'metal-core' band, so we weren't sure how we were going to be viewed, but it was awesome.
People were respectful and people came to our stage, it was good."
Mike Hranica (The Devil Wears Prada – Vocals)

"Download was awesome and the show went a million times better than we expected it go.
We really had a blast and watched the Offspring, because I grew up listening to them and have all their cd's.
I really can't wait to come back to the UK."
Daniel Williams (The Devil Wears Prada – Drums)

"We went this year, as fans and watched some bands and hung out, it was great."
Tom Searle (Architects – Guitar)

"The vibe of the festival was a little different in 2008. Everyone seemed a little discombobulated, everyone didn't seem to know where everything was.
We got up on that stage and it was the most people who had watched us ever and the stage seemed bigger than the mainstage! The amount of people that were there, they were right back past the amusement arcade rides.
It was cool. I think this show had a different feeling. We got up on stage did our thing and we got a great response. We got a circle pit to go round the soundboard.
When I got off the stage I felt that it was the most humbling thing we had done as a band; I think it was because we were so pleased how that many people had come out to see Bleeding Through. We never had aspirations about being a 'mega rockstar band' ever, but we know where we sit with kids and fans and so I thought that the performance was one of the pinnacles of the band.
I stayed there all weekend, arriving just before Kiss played and they were awesome! I had also wanted to see Municipal

*Waste, but I woke up at 2:20pm; I was so bummed that I missed them.
The weekend was just as magical as the other year we played, great bands and meeting up with good friends."*
Brandan Schieppati (Bleeding Through - Vocals)

*"We played the second stage; it was a big outdoor stage, we would have been happier to play the second stage like we did before, when it was in a tent. The tent was more fun and it pushes the crowd in to the stage and gives you a much better live show.
But it was crazy, we came out with Throwdown and played back to back (I believe), it was a lot of fun.
I thought it was cool to play. Festivals tend to be a bit of a rush and kind of a mess for the bands, but it was awesome, it's one of the biggest crowds that we get to play in front of.
One of the highlights for me was Cavalera Conspiracy, that was awesome; I watched Kiss a little bit, I'm not a great fan of Kiss, I kind of enjoy them, sort of?
One of the best shows that I saw there though was The Dillinger Escape Plan and also Testament were great.
The whole trip out we saw Testament a few times and seeing them was one of the highlights of our trip.
The layout was kind of bizarre, with the second stage being so far from the rest of the show, you really had to walk to get the second one."*
Derek Youngsma (Bleeding Through – Drums)

*"I was super excited the first time I got to play download festival! It was with one of my former bands, Bleeding Through and it was the first show on my first European tour with the band.
We arrived quite early on the first day (one day before we were scheduled to play) and we were sharing a bus with Throwdown. Everyone was starving but we were all broke, the food at the festival was too expensive and we weren't allowed to have any meal tickets as it wasn't our show day. Everyone on the bus emptied out their backpacks and between about 13 people we had one Clif Bar, a Belgian waffle and a few*

assorted candies. I remember all laughing with hunger pains as we watched Dave Peters (Throwdown) trying to cut a tiny Belgian waffle into 9 pieces so it could be shared around! The next day we raced to the catering tent and made our one meal ticket stretch over the next two days by piling up spare plates full of food to keep on the bus.
The show itself was amazing and one I'll remember forever! After a few first show technical difficulties we ripped into an awesome set and the crowd loved it. Brandan (Schieppati/Bleeding Through) commanded that the whole audience run a circle pit around the sound tent and they did it! It was insane watching what must have been 1000 fans running in this huge 100 meter radius circle. It was also one of the first times I took advantage of the 'ladder like' stage rigging and climbed to the top to give the fans something to remember.
The only real downsides to the festival (aside from trekking through mud and rubbish) were starving half the time and having to walk around the entire outer perimeter of the festival to get backstage due to Kiss's security not allowing anybody anywhere near the main stage."
Jona Weinhofen (Bleeding Through – Guitar)

"Our set was incredible this year, I have zero complaints and the kids were awesome.
The way that everything was set up this year was a little bit different and I heard that from a lot of people, but we still had a great time.
But, I was a little disappointed in the lack of metal on this years line-up in general.
For a band that has travelled thousands of miles to get here, we really couldn't ask for anything more because of all the people here with a positive attitude. You play big clubs in New York City or LA, but what comes with that is the sense of people becoming a little jaded; but the whole thing about Download is that it's not just another show but a great experience and someone in five years will remember the whole weekend of Download and I appreciate that too.

I like being at a festival as a fan as well; I like to get all our business out of the way so that we can watch bands. There were some bands that I was excited to see this year, especially HIM, I am a massive fan and love their songs.
The cool thing about festivals in general, especially Download, is that there's no pretension in the festival crowd; everyone is just there to watch all these bands and they are very receptive and very excited."
Dave Peters (Throwdown - Vocals)

"I love the UK and the weather was really nice. I walked around a bit and the stages were really huge.
I am really into new Metal, so I hoped to see Simple Plan.
We played on the second stage. We had hoped to draw more that Kiss; we should probably have headlined all three stages as the kids can't get enough of us.
We got like a million dollars to play, it was crazy!! But we don't care about money……."
Neil Westfall (A Day To Remember – Guitar)

"We should have played three times on each stage; but we're really here just to do it for the kids."
Alex Shelnutt (A Day To Remember – Drums)

"It was chaotic! From getting the right entrance, to getting the right passes, the usual conundrums, but it was really good fun. The three of us had been in a band (The Ga Ga's) for three years prior to the 2008 festival and we'd played there, but it was a long road to get back. It really felt good to be back on that stage again, but the crowd were fantastic and they really warmed to us.
It's always 'hit or miss' as to how you are going to go down, whether people are going to judge you to be 'heavy enough', but they were really responsive and we had a fucking good time!
What threw us was the new layout and we got lost a bit, but the vibe there was really great and the family friendly vibe was amazing. To have such a massive festival that the rock

community can come to; hopefully next time we will be on a bigger stage.
We had a gig the next day so we had to split, but we saw Kiss."
Tommy Gleeson (Slaves To Gravity – Vocals/Guitar)

"We didn't really know what to expect, but we were really happy with the way it went.
We got there in the morning, we were third on and when we began to play it started raining so everyone came into the tent which was a bit of luck for us because everyone stayed in there to watch. Even when the rain stopped, a lot of people still stayed on. There were people who really wouldn't like our music, being a metal festival, but I think we went down really well and the crowd gave a great response; if I told them to put their hands in the air, they did it, so they were quite receptive in that respect.
At one point when we were playing I could see a stall called 'Weed World' and just for a laugh I said 'if you want to come and say hi, you will probably find us in Weed World' later on and everyone started cheering. When I got off stage this guy came up to me and said 'you mentioned Weed World' onstage mate, come with me I'll sort you out' and he gave me a big bag, which as I don't smoke I gave it to Johnny Truant!
We've got some mates in a metal band called Johnny Truant and they were there, they were playing that night and we were going to camp with them and watch them, but we got offered another gig in Yeovil so we had to 'up and leave' straight after. But Johnny Truant watched us from the side of the stage and it was a great experience and we can't wait to do it again.
So next year we would like to hang out and get hammered."
James Matthews (Go:Audio - Vocals)

"Download was really good fun. We'd wanted to watch Kids In Glass Houses as we had just done a tour with them, but we had to leave to go to a show in Yeovil.
Our sound was good and we had a great time
We hung out and ate some chicken curry baguettes."
Joshua Wilkinson (Go:Audio - Keyboards)

"When we got to Download we were all a bit scared, because we were a bit more 'pop' than most of the bands on that stage. We arrived and there was some really heavy music going on and we were all getting a bit worried about that. I think Trigger The Bloodshed were going to be on after us and we were on after Rise To Remain, so with all these bands names we were like 'oh dear, what are we doing??'
I did a couple of shots of vodka before I went on. We got there about nine in the morning so I had a few tipples, but luckily it didn't knock me out for the gig.
But it was a good experience playing on that stage, in front of that crowd. We played it with no bottles thrown, which we were expecting. But it went smoothly and was a great gig in the end. The rain helped us, because everyone pile in the tent. I think that it rained during one of the most 'pop' songs in our set and everyone came in and we thought 'oh no, this is a bad point to come in', but it all went really well and we were happy with it.

Andy Booth (Go:Audio – Drums)

"We had an absolute blast playing the show, there was an ungodly amount of people out there, and it was definitely a massive crowd.
It was a total blur because everything went by so fast. Our songs are only 2 minutes long so we played about twenty songs, but it seemed so short, but it was fun; a once in a lifetime experience.
The crowd was absolutely going wild for us and we had a giant 'circle pit' and a 'wall of death', it was a typical Waste show, but on a massive scale.
The great thing about playing these kinds of shows are that there are little hermes who will see us for the first time and get stoked; but I'm not sure if we are a great role model!
Onstage it's a different atmosphere playing, but I hope that the sound was good. Its such fast music and we just come right out of the gates and sometimes sound guys just don't get it.
It's cool to play a festival like Download, because there are so many types of music and fans and hopefully they all came and

got exposed to us, people that wouldn't normally see us and if one of those kids bought a cd then it's a bonus, keep on expanding!
I didn't get to see much, a bit of Animal Alpha. She was furious backstage in 'clown make-up', stomping around like she had lost something and we were like, 'it's kinda scary'. Maybe she was doing that just to get hyped up for the show, or something."
Landphil (Municipal Waste – Bass)

"We played the Tuborg Stage, which was the 3rd stage. It was very cool and exciting for us because we were a fairly new band and we'd only just put out our first record and so we were very lucky to get a slot on the 3rd stage.
We played on the Friday around 4pm and we had no expectations of what it was going to be like; although we had been to Download when we were a bit younger, hanging around the mainstage, we hadn't really ventured into the 3rd stage, so we didn't really know what to expect from playing there and if anyone was going to turn up to watch us.
So we turned up and set all of our stuff up and we had a lot of people helping us out and it was a real cool day up until we played and then it was crazy!
The tent was absolutely packed and there were circle pits, crazy moshing everywhere and it surpassed all of our expectations; it was honestly the best day of my life.
I couldn't have enjoyed anything more. We were in a band for writing and then performing our music and to get to perform it to about 3,000 people, who really enjoy your stuff it's amazing. We didn't play to anywhere near that amount of people on tour, so for all of them to turn up and watch us, when there was such a great bill, it was incredible."
Rob Purnell (Trigger The Bloodshed – Guitar)

"It was an absolutely pleasure to play Download, as it was a festival, to be honest, that I wasn't wholly aware of, having grown up listening to Nirvana whereas our guitarist James had grown up listening to Sepultura and Machine Head. He came

down to Monsters Of Rock, with his dad and saw Pantera and had a great time, but to me it was all about Reading Festival. Later in life, as my taste in metal has progressed, I actually now love the bands who love to riff that hard and so I can appreciate how Download has risen and become THE festival for rock and metal music.
 We had tried for 3 years to get on at Download, so it was great to finally get to be there."
Will Simpson (Brigade – Vocals/Guitar)

"It was pretty amazing doing Download as I had never played a festival before with Johnny Truant, or anyone. The crowd massive and I shit myself before I went on, obviously.
I saw Comeback Kid and Fall of Troy. I kept saying to people that I was going to see a band and they were always telling me 'they're on now' and it was always the farthest stag away. I missed Biffy Clyro and I was fucking pissed off."
Alan Booth (Johnny Truant - Bass)

"We were third from the top below Testament and Saxon and I remember that while we were setting up the tent was really empty and there were loads of people there who work for us and with us because we had been getting a lot of press in the lead up to the festival.
It suddenly dawned on me that if no one was in the tent to watch us it was all going to be over and we might as well fucking chuck it in, so I really started shitting myself 5 minutes before we were due to go on. But the tent then really packed out and it was amazing.
I couldn't hear a thing on stage, the sound was rough as shit and I almost fell off the monitors into the photo pit as well, which was good.
We turned up on the Friday really late; we'd wanted to see Beat Union and Rolo Tomassi, but we missed them both. We went to bed early and some fucking bitch tried to break into our van. Me and Olly were asleep at about 5:30am in the van and some one was trying to open the side door of the van. So, I jumped out of the van to give them a kicking and it was some

15 year old girl, totally off her face, she didn't know what was going on, which was a good laugh.
We played Saturday and got really hammered. We waited until we had played to start drinking. So when we got chucked out of the VIP area at 3am and everyone else was in bed sleeping, we drank half our body weight in alcohol and went on a mission to go to the normal camping area and bothered people until 10 in the morning.
I bought a tent just to ignore it all weekend; it was just a place to keep our beer.
Dillinger was amazing, Biffy Clyro were amazing; I've never seen either band play a bad set ever.
The problem with it being the main metal event of the year in the UK is that when you get backstage, everyone you have ever had a beer with in band are there, so when you try to go to see a band, by the time you have walked 10 metres you've had about 15 beers with people and you miss everything. It's cool, but it's bad when you see your mates and they say 'did you see us play' you have to tell them 'no I was having a few beers'. We spent the first 24 hours trying to stay sober before the show and then we spent the next 24 hours trying to get better."
Reuben Gotto (Johnny Truant - Guitar)

"There were only a handful of bands that I had wanted to see, Rival Schools, Biffy Clyro and Kiss, there were too many of those fucking generic Emo bands that sound the same and they really bore the fuck out of me.
So I spent most of the time getting really 'lashed' in the backstage area on the Friday, complaining about the shit music and basically making a fool of myself. I think I took a running leap at a gigantic woman at one point, she was about fucking 9 foot!
I was kinda hanging on her going 'Your massive' and she said 'Get the fuck off me' and at I think she called me bitch one point, which I was really shocked about, but I took it really well being Irish n'all.
The next day I had the worst hangover ever imaginable; it was just so bad it was like my whole face had melted and I had to

go have a shower. I couldn't even eat and when we had to go and have photos done, it looked like someone had sprayed me with AIDS, I was really, really fucked!

I felt better when we got on stage and then my guitar cut out which really angered me. I tried to turn around to somebody, anybody onstage, but there was smoke everywhere and it was just me a big massive cloud; I was like 'where the fucks the band??'

That's the thing about being in a three piece on a massive stage, 'where the fuck did everybody go?'

So, I had a bit of a nightmare for the first few songs, but then it was grand and the crowd really got into our band, so it was great exposure for us and we played a good show and I thought we were tight.

I really enjoyed my Download experience. I spent the rest of the day checking out various bands and hanging out with some friends in In Case Of Fire and Biffy Clyro.

It was an easy run, but a good 1st Download experience and I hope they have us back."

Cahir O'Doherty (Fighting With Wire – Vocals/Guitar)

"It was our first time there and a great experience. We'd always known it from the Monsters of Rock, so to get the chance to play, we were honoured.

We arrived the night before and camped. We saw Kiss, so that really set the scene for us, it was just spectacular. The ultimate moment for me was when I went to the toilet backstage and as I was walking out, Tony Iommi was walking in! That was pretty fucking amazing; that was my ultimate 'rock moment' of all time. It was one of those moments when you see someone you recognize and say hello, but it was a couple seconds later that I thought FUCK; but it would have been a bit creepy for me to have run back into the toilet where Toni Iommi was taking a piss and have a chat.

We unfortunately had some technical difficulties with Cahir's guitar, but from my side of things it was all good. We had a good turnout, considering it was our first time there and we it one of the biggest stages that we had been on; we had a lot of smoke machines as well. I remember turning to look at the

guys and all I could see was smoke, I was trying to make them out! I knew they were on the stage somewhere, I couldn't see them, but I could hear them!'
Jamie King (Fighting With Wire - Bass)

"We got to Download a day early, went and set up in 'Artists Camping' and proceeded to get absolutely 'bombed'- steaming drunk.
We went to see Kiss and they were absolutely amazing, they blew me away, it was good fun.
The day of the gig, me and Jamie weren't too bad, but Cahir suffered the most because he's a cryer when it comes to hangovers, whinging away 'I don't feel too good', 'I'm so nervous'!
Then his guitar cut out on the first song, which just set us up for the rest of the gig; made him play with anger which was good.
But I really enjoyed the gig, with a great onstage sound."
Craig McKean (Fighting With Wire – Drums)

"Download was great for us. We arrived actually a few days earlier in Stockholm, from the States. It had been about six months since we had been on tour, which was rare for us because we'd been on tour for four years with only a break of three weeks in between.
We made a new record in February; we finished writing in California in January and then recorded in Seattle. Then we were about to come over here for five weeks on tour with Turbonegro, but Euroboy got cancer; so instead of coming over and doing some of the dates that we had booked, I went ahead with giving my father, who had been really sick, one of my kidneys.
I should have had about six weeks recovery time, but I only had four weeks, as we had lots of shows booked. Three weeks in I felt 'up to it' and we left for Europe.
We watched Municipal Waste and Airbourne. We really like the guys in MW, Nitewolf used to work in a skatepark in North Carolina and we knew them from other bands as well. It's just

awesome to see us touring and them touring and growing into this!
They came over and partied with us.
We were busy doing interviews during the rest of the day and then it came down to the show.
Some of our buddies, who we'd met on tour with Motorhead in Germany were there helping us and a couple of other guys that we had met in Wolverhampton were also working on the stage.
We did also get to see some of Between The Buried and Me, who are also from North Carolina.
It was one of the bigger crowds that we had played to and in Kerrang! we got five K's and there were only about five bands that got that; I hope that some people come and check us out after that."
Valient Himself (Valient Thorr – Vocals)

"Sweden was sick and then the whole whirlwind of Download was intense!
We had a lot of good dudes helping us out, we don't really have a full set-up crew or anything like that, but we know a lot of crews from other bands and we 'scooped' them up and they all helped us out."
Dr. Professor Nitewolf Strangees (Valient Thorr – Bass)

"It was a big dream coming true for me and for us, it was a childhood dream you have wanting to play Donington as we all grew up with Maiden recordings and stuff like that.
It was just fantastic, but there was a lot of stress before the actual show, with getting the gear set up and we had some problems that the keyboards weren't working properly, they weren't working at all actually!
But we finally made it and got a good response. A lot of our fans were there and we also got exposed to a lot of people who didn't know Firewind; I think that it was really worth coming over to do Download.
We just came off a 30 date US tour and we then went back to Greece. We watched Judas Priest and Kiss; and Kiss had

never played in Greece before until 2 weeks before Download, but I was away on tour so I missed them."
Gus G. (Firewind – Guitar)

"We played on the first of the three days, in an afternoon slot, up against Kid Rock.
A little bit before Kid Rock was due to come on he cancelled, so that helped us out a lot. We had a pretty decent crowd there and then all of a sudden a lot more people came over from the mainstage, as they had nothing better to do and thought that they would check out this other 'Kid' that was playing at the other end of the festival grounds.
We ended up having an incredible time, we were there for Saturday and Sunday as well, we got to meet some people from Atticus, promoters, the guy who booked us at the Underworld (Camden, London) and met lots of new friends. We also watched some bands and hung out with bands like Bleeding Through.
I watched some bands, but I must admit that a lot of the festival was in an 'alcoholic haze', but I did watch Kiss and Judas Priest; I'm not a Kiss 'fan' but I watched them out of curiosity. I also watched Jimmy Eat World and In Flames on the last day and we saw Dillinger who 'killed it' as usual.
Some of the food was good from the vendors; I usually have a bit of a diet issue, but not there. Also everyone who worked at the festival were very helpful and on the ball, it seemed very well organised."
Jeremy Hiebert (Comeback Kid – Guitar)

"It was absolutely amazing; we had only been to the UK four times previously.
I really enjoyed myself. I did this thing where we asked people if they knew who we were and I couldn't believe the amount of response that came back; the hands in the air, the screaming! When I looked out, I saw everybody singing along and I was really blown away.
We are on an independent record label and we had turned down some majors; what I'm trying to say is you couldn't find

our record if you tried, so to see the internet 'word of mouth' it was beautiful. It was a blessing and I had a great time.
I really wanted to see Children of Bodom. I went for a pee earlier and Alexi was waiting to take a shit. I walked over and I asked 'are you waiting to take a pee or a shit' and then I did that quick double-take and I said 'I'm a big fan', that was all that I could say, all that I could splutter out!"
Craig Owens (Chiodos - Vocals)

"We played two years in a row and 2008 was our first festival experience and we were really expecting the best show we'd ever played, to thousands of people and for it to be an incredible experience. We got there and we played to 1,500 people which was amazing, but in a tent that holds 8,000, it was a bit 'hit and miss'.
So the first year was good it was an amazing experience. I went to see Kiss and then came back and watched The Dillinger Escape Plan and I thought that this was what a live band needs to be like; we were standing at the side of the stage in awe. They went out and the way that they were moving and swinging their guitars, I was amazed that they didn't kill themselves."
Richard Carter (Blackhole – Vocals)

"We played the festival first in 2008 and we were about midway up on the 3rd stage. We were really pumped beforehand and thought that it was going to be a really good show, but it didn't live up to our expectations; I think we set our expectations a little too high."
Nick Mitchell (Blackhole – Guitar)

"My first experience of Download was last year and that was the first ever festival that I had personally been to. It was pretty crazy and I was really nervous, I think because I expected too much; it was definitely a good learning curve. The festival gives lots of young bands a good opportunity to play there."
Andreas Yiasoumi (Blackhole – Guitar)

"We played the Gibson stage at 11:35am on the Saturday. Playing was unbelievable, it was a 'step up' from what we usually do. The crowd was fantastic, a lot of people were dancing and headbanging; they were literally doing what we intended to make them do! The crowds at Download are absolute fantastic, amazing!

I think that the line-up was great, it had something for everyone, with bands like Pendulum and Lethal Bizzle catering for the more mainstream needs and bands like Job For A Cowboy, who have a niche audience, but they never fail to impress.

I came to the first one in 2003, came back in 2007 and now came back and it's a step up, as we're playing it! We were incredibly honoured and excited and could only hope for the best and we can't wait to come back in 2009 to headline the mainstage!"
Austin Dickinson (Rise To Remain – Vocals)

I was 'bowled over' to be playing the festival, after years of having the posters on my walls since I was about 12 years old, to be finally playing it is just a great honour.

We had been listening to a lot of Trivium and Shadows Fall and a lot of American influences, as well as the grandad stuff like Maiden and Priest, but just to be part of the 'young generation' of this tradition of Metal, everyone just feels as one.

Getting on that stage and seeing everyone headbanging, just coming together to see a new band and make them feel good. It was nicely filled out."   **Ben Tovey (Rise To Remain – Guitar)**

"Download Festival was possibly the highlight of my life! Stepping up from playing bass in one band to playing rhythm guitar in this band, it's just the best band that I have ever been in.   I've only known Ben for about 2 years and now we've played Download together, it's just such an honour; Metal forever!"
Will Homer (Rise To Remain – Guitar)

"It's just a big thank for everyone that made this happen, it's been the day of my life, absolutely awesome. Can't wait to come back! Keep the metal running!"
Joe Copcutt (Rise To Remain – Bass)

"Download for us was a great experience, we'd been partying hard since the Thursday night and checking out all the fuckin' awesome bands that were on offer.
Then Saturday night came and our hearts were pounding with excitement like a 7yr old on Xmas eve. The feeling being out on a stage that big in front of that many people can only be described as "fuckin mint"!
We just went out there, did what we do and had good fun; the crowd seemed to as well which is what matters most.
For most of us we've been coming to Download for years and it was great to be on the other side of the barrier. For Chris it was his first time at Download and I don't think many people can say on their first time there, they stepped out on mainstage.
All this said and done, Download is, and hopefully will continue to be, the best metal festival in the world."
Davey Death (Glamour Of The Kill – Vocals/Bass)

"It was one of those shows that started off as a 'stand off', like any good duel does, but as the intensity grew and grew, by the end of the show it was incredible, awesome, with a great vibe. People were very supportive, but I think that they were a little freaked out by the concrete underneath them.
But is was fun, people were very loud and responsive, with horns in the air! I wish that I had seen Rolo Tomassi, the line up is very diverse and very cool." **Andrew Forsman (Fall Of Troy – Drums)**

"We have been coming since Download was Donington and this year we got to play and it was just phenomenal.
The crowd was huge; we opened the second stage at eleven o'clock and we had thousands and thousands and thousands

of people there and as soon as we 'cracked in' they went absolutely berserk!
For me, that's what Donington is all about, its people who have come out and they want to see bands; they're not just worried about the headliners, they want to check out the other stages.
The fact that we are British is a really big thing to me, I am really proud of the heritage of the music scene in this country and I think that it's growing and growing and growing. There were so many British bands on the bill that were getting really good turnouts, which is really healthy for the country and for our music scene."
Dale Butler (Malefice – Vocals)

"To me it's the pinnacle of everything that we had worked at over the last couple of years. It's a bit surreal from when you start out in someones bedroom, just jamming and playing some covers, to going to play at THE biggest metal festival in England.
You can't really describe it. It's like a birthday and Christmas for ten years, all rolled into one; it's just phenomenal.
We thought that it would be tough, being the first band on, having to work to get the crowd going, but as soon as it kicked in they went fuckin' mental!
Basically, it's five English guys, no bullshit, who like Heavy Metal, no gimmicks, in front of a crowd of people who felt the same."
Alex Vuskans (Malefice – Guitar)

"This year was cool and very fun to play. We had a really good monitor guy and he gave us a very good sound.
The Download Festival is one of the best festivals that we have been to and not many of them have such a nice backstage area."
Christian Wibe (Animal Alpha – Guitar)

"Just looking forward to look at the **Smörgåsbord***."*
Agnete Maria Kjølsrud (Animal Alpha – Vocals)

"We played the Gibson stage at 3:35pm on the Sunday afternoon. It was amazing and we had an excellent time. We managed to get the lovely ladies from Area 51 to do a little boogie to one of our remix songs as an intro and we got our good friend Nick Barker who was in Dimmu Borgir, Testament and Cradle of Filth to introduce us, which was another really exciting moment.

We were so excited that there were so many people in the tent to watch us and the fact that there was a big circle pit, we were really 'over the moon' and well happy!

We just had a crazy time, arrived on the Friday and got mangled for two days. We had all our crew and we camped, all our friends were on our crew, so it was really like a family event. We had a ten man tent so we all stayed together, drinking all hours and going crazy; to have our boys with us was the best.

I've been going to the festival since '95, since I was a kid I had wanted to go from '93, it's just amazing.

I used to go every year and the first year was Metallica, White Zombie, Skid Row and Corrosion Of Conformity, it was wicked, so it's a pretty big deal; we never thought that we would get to play there.

I prefer the tent, so I was so pleased that we played in the tent. We spoke to Biff from Saxon who gave us a lot of inspiration. He was saying that when he wrote that song about Donington (And the Bands Played On) it was because they were so excited to play Donington.

They layout was a lot different this year and quite intense, I preferred it in the racetrack.

We were so lucky that we got a chance to play there, especially for such a relatively small band as us."

Luca Grandi (Ted Maul – Guitar)

"This year was brilliant because I was it was my group, rather than with someone else's that did it.

I only turned up on the Sunday and left about four or five hours after we'd played, so I didn't have a massive Download experience.

I remember thinking the layout was a bit weird, but it was good."
Casino Brown (Ted Maul - Keyboards)

"Download for me is different as I come from a different country, I lived in Gibraltar and I used to read in the magazines thought 'shit I want to go', seeing the bands that were playing.
I finally came over to England and with my cousin Stuart Cavilla the bass player in Breed 77, they played three years in a row so I went with them. I had the best time of my life.
This year has been a bit different getting used to it, this year wasn't so much like a festival, more like you were in a car park.
The gig was amazing, we were so excited to see such a big crowd, it was the best for us, the best day of my life."
Solomon J. Lucifer Christ (Ted Maul – Vocals)

"I remember seeing Pendulum and they were absolutely banging. Everyone was there. It was the end of Bullet For My Valentine and everyone was leaving the mainstage to go and see them."
Mikey Serpico (Serpico – Vocals)

"I remember we played the Gibson stage and it was the first proper festival we'd ever played. It was quite something to walk out onto a massive stage, with proper big monitors and side fills; it was quite something at the time.
Even though we were the first ones on there, there were quite a few people there and the gig went pretty well considering it was our first at a festival.
I then remember a couple of bands later, there were all these chicks with bikinis on, like lap dancing on the stage; of the course the tent was then flooded with hundreds and hundreds of guys and whoever came out after that, it was a good fucking ploy!
We went to a bar afterwards and it was a good party atmosphere."
Logan (Sons Of Albion – Vocals)

"The great thing about the Gibson stage was that behind Gibson had loads of amps and stuff so you could try them out and guitars and shit and a drum kit set up there as well and a bass. So we could plug in there and have a warm up before we went on, which was cool."
Gones (Sons Of Albion – Bass)

"The merch just got misplaced, I guess, with all the excitement of being our first festival. We were gathering everything up to leave after we had been to the backstage bar and we got back to the tent too late and we lost about 50 t-shirts; but it was our managers fault.
So that was our first experience at a festival, look after the merch."
Nuno Miguel (Sons Of Albion – Guitar)

"Download, WOW…! The day just blew us all away. No matter how many gigs you play, you always strive for a slot on the bill at the "Mecca of Metal" & we snatched it up with open arms. From the minute we were in through the gates until we went on stage everything seemed a blur and when our time finally came the adrenalin was at fever pitch. The atmosphere back stage was totally electric as our intro kicked in, each of us straining at the leash to be let free to rip the stage up, hearing our anthem fire up in such an awesome rig!
I doubt we'll ever forget the moment when each of us proudly marched on stage to the roar of the crowd. It made us all stand a foot taller & set fire to our souls.
Playing the set was very surreal, the 30 minutes was over in a flash & the left us walking round in a daze for the rest of the day. Each of us has now taken a sip from the Holy Grail…"
Ade Carloss (Hostile – Vocals)

"We played our first festival, in the thousands; we were really pleased to be there and the sun came out!
There were lots of massive acts there and they all looked so pleased, from the looks on their faces, to be there.

We played the Gibson tent and we were sandwiched in between two quite heavy bands. We are a rock band, but not a metal band, so we felt that we had to win over quite a difficult crowd, but we did and we aren't signed, but we put a lot into the music and we feel that it is starting to pay off."
Leo (Caimbo – Vocals)

"When started playing there was a full tent and the crowd just got bigger. We were expecting cups being thrown or anything; it's Download anything could have happened!!
But everyone was really nice and it was great."
Piers (Caimbo – Guitar)

"Download is the playground of Rock. It covers all aspects from metal right through to more indie. They have huge mainstream bands playing right next to smaller upcoming bands, yet they are both treated the same from the crowd, with great respect! In fact I would have to say that Download is the most respectful festival out there, everyone looks out for each other, and you don't get any drunken lads trying to ruin it for others. Year after year they continue to have one of the strongest line ups in the world.
To be honest we were all a bit anxious to see how we would be received by the audience, as we were one of the lighter rock bands playing at the festival. Although all nerves vanished as soon as we stepped on stage. The crowd were brilliant and made us feel right at home. Download has definitely earned its place as one of our favorite festivals. There was a lot of alcohol at the festival. So combine vast quantities of that with some of the backstage facilities, mainly the tattoo parlour, you can imagine it was a very eventful day. Although at the end of the night, a couple of random fans wanted to party on, so they hopped on our bus and came back to our hotel... which was 50 miles away. After 1 minute of being there and panic starting to set in, they jumped in a cab back to the festival. And what a party they missed!"
James Cairns (The Haze – Vocals)

"Download is an amazing festival for seeing musicians who can genuinely play. The heavy nature of the music that's being presented always brings out the best in the guitarists and drummers. It's extremely humbling to be on a bill where the best of the best play.
I think two bands had already been bottled off by the time we hit the stage. Not being the heaviest or most well known band on the bill I was slightly concerned what would eventuate. Shouldn't have worried, the gig was awesome; we won a lot of new fans and were wrapped to be part of a great day.
Our guitar tech, Bozza, is the biggest metal fan on the planet and was totally in his element. He saw his hero, max Cavalera, back stage and cautiously approached him. "Max, we need a photo," "sure" Max replied. Bozza turned to him and said "Now look more metal than you've ever looked before!!!" Max did, Bozza did. End result a classic pic."

Johnny Galvatron (The Galvatrons – Vocals/Guitar)

"It was great to see Simple Plan headlining the second stage in 2008 as I remember them opening for Bowling For Soup when they released their debut album. Bowling For Soup's bus is always the party bus and is usually the scene of some surreal sights like their drum tech serenading a perplexed Dimebag with a Michael MacDonald/Aaron Neville/Meatloaf medley! Each year I know I'm going to head home on Monday morning exhausted, but with some great memories."

Emma Watson (PR – Bowling For Soup/MC Lars/Zebrahead)

"A new site. The Infield had been redeveloped as a motocross course, so it wasn't available to use. A new site had been located to the west of the circuit where the Sunday Markets are held.
Kiss were announced as headliners, which was ok. But the other two headliners were The Offspring and Lostprophets, and that didn't go down well. Not quite as bad as MCR the year before. Metallica & Slipknot had been expected on the bill, but Reading/Leeds had snagged them.

For us in RIP, the new site was well located, as the entrance was 2 minutes away. From the main campsites on the east of the circuit, it was about a mile. Quite a hike. I found the layout ok, but it was just missing that sense of 'epicness' that had always been in the air.
2008 was probably one of the least successful years - not as good a layout, headliners not what people really wanted. But it was still a good weekend, and still had plenty of gems tucked away on the bill. Saxon had a triumphant return, KISS put on their best Donington show ever. But I'll not linger here."
Phil Hull (Download Forum Administrator)

"This was the year Kiss went for the world record for the most Kiss face painted people in one place world record. I didn't play. Kiss played a great set, the highlight being when Gene Simmons was winched up into the rigging and played 'I Love It Loud'.
The Offspring were good on Saturday along with Biffy and Bullet on the main stage, but Sunday was a better day when I saw Coheed and Cambria for the first time live and Claudio Sanchez's massive hair.
I became a fan of two other bands that day Municipal Waste and Airbourne. "Municipal Waste are going to fuck you up" was the random chant of guys I went with (who included my mate's 10 year old son) for the rest of the day."
Mike Horton (Plymouth)

"Well, I am 18. From the age of about 14 I was dying to experience download festival in all its glory. When I hit 17 I was finally granted this by my parents, my exams finished early and all was clear. That year I received the best birthday present ever. A ticket to my first festival, Download 2008.
I couldn't stop talking about it until the time came, my best friend at the time also had a ticket and a few of my other friends managed to get some. First festival for us all and boy did we learn a lot!
We over packed on random things, under packed on alcohol. We brought too much food. Sensible packing didn't help much when we got there! Luckily, as is the way of Download, we met some people as silly as us in Red Camp who had over

packed beer, but under packed food so trading was at hand! Between the 2 camps we managed to get by well. Me and my friend Savage decided we would stay out all night, every night, and not return until morning. It amazed us how easy it was to find people to talk to and things to do there, everyone was friendly and we sat down with many campsites for a 'chill session'.
Overall I'll never forget Download 08, been back 09 and returning in 10 again. The bands were amazing, but it's the community and people who make the place so brilliant, a holiday you'll never forget, a home away from home. Download Festival, Donington Park, THE wildest party you'll ever go to."
Craig How (Milton Keynes)

Quiet, comfortable, sensible, light-hearted and enlightening. These are just a few words that don't describe the Download Festival. Hardcore, psycho, wild, extreme and outrageous on the other hand are words you could use. My brother in metal, Scuba Steve, describes it as "the world's biggest party, with 100,000 of your best mates."
Our festival team seems to expand every year. Kat and Steve flew all the way from Australia again and also brought two legendary mates, Shannon and Evan. Our friend Lisa also joined us, plus we met up with some of the crazy cats from last year, including Neil, the god of Download. He has been every year since 1984 and that is something us mere mortals can only aspire to. As word spreads of the levels of fun that is had, more and more people seem to join. So ALL my friends that are into rock and metal, next year, it's on like Donkey Kong.
It's difficult to describe the festival in words. It's basically a week of camping in the biggest field you have ever seen, with three days of the biggest bands in rock and heavy metal at the end.
We saw bands such as Kiss, Judas Priest, Disturbed, Children of Bodom, Cavalera Conspiracy, Saxon and Testament. Plus, Aussie legends, Rose Tattoo and Airbourne. The band line up

was not as strong as last year but that didn't stop us going mental when the opportunities arose.

Front row for CC was a clear highlight for Steve and me, with chairs and two litre milk bottles narrowly missing our heads, and then Steve getting the set list off the stage at the end. It was pretty crazy and is certainly up there with some of the more special gig moments we've had.

On the Sunday of the festival our whole group wore Aussie flags as capes, superman style, and in a fit of much awesomeness, when Airbourne were playing; the lead singer jumped down off the stage and took Lisa's flag off her. He then climbed back on stage and hung it over his monstrous Marshall stack. Now that, as a story, would have been pretty cool, but what happened next was legendary.

After a very short, non-existent, chat with health and safety, the singer, with his guitar over his shoulder, took the flag off the amp, took a swig from his bottle of Jack Daniel's and proceeded to scale the side of the stage. He then tied our flag to the roof of the arena before breaking out into a guitar solo hanging by his legs from the scaffolding. I'd like to see Justin Timberlake do that!

Earlier in the week we had met a guy named Joel, who was by himself but offered us beer at a time when we did not have access to our own. This, at Download, is seen in the same light as laying down your life and so we took him in and repaid our debt. Joel was good fun all weekend but on the last night, Joel realised that he had too much left over alcohol. Some would share it, some would give it to strangers and some would just try and lug it all home. Not Joel. He drank it. All of it. And landed about three feet from where he took his last sip. We really felt sorry for him and so we did the only honourable thing we could do. We buried him under all the camp site rubbish.

Watching the bands during the day is damn good fun. But it's the camp site parties that really make the festival. After the last riff is played, everyone heads back to their tents. And not for cocoa and a sing song but for JD through a funnel, food fights, drunken badminton and then a sing song. With people you don't know and with songs you've just made up.

Now they say it's not over till the fat lady sings. Well at Download, it's not over till you start a crash tackle initiated stacks on right at the feet of the police. Shortly followed by pushing over a porta loo with someone in it.
Daniel Steffe (Gold Coast, Australia)

"I asked my girlfriend (Charlie) to marry me, on bended knee at the end of Judas Priest in 2008. Nothing major in that, except her response was:
"You've got to be f*****g kidding me". Nothing in life is guaranteed.
She eventually said yes and we are got married 31st October 2009."
Jon Flannagan (Broxburn, West Lothian)

"It was the last day of Download 2008, the year full of bands from my teens. It had just been a great weekend, the sun had been baking everyone for most of the festival, had been awesome for music and everyone seemed to be in a really chilled out, Woodstock kind of atmosphere.
Anyways, I had spent the whole day lounging around with my close mates from back home, I never get to see them most of the year but Download has become a sort of tradition where we can all meet up again and let loose, I think we've done it for the past four years now?
So, we're sitting on the top of the hill, each of us slowly passing out from too much sun and vodka and whisky and beer and whatever else we'd managed to get in past security, and it was the last few bands of the main stage. Coheed &Cambria had just lightened every ones spirits, but I think it was Jimmy Eat World up next that did it.
The next few hours were just one of those great moments in life where your sitting in the sun with your mates, just enjoying each others company and having a great time, the music really taking us back 5 years or so, all of us pissed and hugging each other, "I love you man" speeches and the rest, my girlfriend at the time just finding the whole deal amusing, taking photos of us all...
Anyways, while Lostprophets are on me and my mate Aaron

start the first big circle pit of the set, right over on of the gravel pathways. I got smashed sideways by some massive bloke and ended up with a two inch scar on my elbow and a concussion, but that afternoon will always stand out as one of the happiest of any summer."
Joel Minter (Peckham)

"Watching Lostprophets on the Sunday evening, I was right near the front and during "Rooftops" (My favourite song) I turned round and all I could see were people, as far as I could see, all singing my favourite lyrics of my favourite band.
I'll never forget that moment, it really was the best part of the festival and a great introduction to Download!"
Emma Taylor (Carlisle)

"It was a long 6hr train journey for us.
After being hassled by an old woman trying to steal alcohol off us, we finally arrived and waited to get into the festival.
We finally got a camp set up. By this point the drink was starting to take major effect and two of our friends started a friendly wrestling match; but we hadn't yet cleared the camp properly.
After about 5 mins of wrestling you could see them starting to get tired, the next thing we knew one of them, Jimbo (also known as the Shitting Man) went flying into a metal trolley which we had used to haul our stuff in with and had a big cut above his eyebrow.
So, being sensible, Captain Zara (his sister) took him to the First Aid tent but because it was only 2pm on the Wednesday the paramedics hadn't even set up there tent yet and ended up having to deal with it out in the open while there tent was laid out on the ground.
But they took it all in good fun, though Jimbo could hardly see out of his eye all weekend."
Brian Dunn (Stenhousemuir)

"My best experience was at Download 2008, this was my first ever Download festival. I had wanted to go to the festival for so long and when I got the ticket as a present I couldn't wait for June to roll around.

Out of all the bands that played over that weekend the one I was looking forward to the most was the one and only...KISS. Seeing Kiss on stage was going to be even more amazing, as it would be the first time that my Dad would have seen them live in full make-up, which for us was a big deal, anyway waiting for Kiss to come on stage seemed to take forever the anticipation was killing me, then all of a sudden a voice came over the microphone saying the sentence we were all waiting to hear "Alright Download, you wanted the best, you got the best, the hottest band in the world.....KISS", then the curtain came down and they were being lowered down from the ceiling all I could think was 'Oh my god that's actually them, on stage'. WOW.

The ultimate point in the show for me was during 'Rock 'n' Roll All Night'; the confetti cannons went off, and at that moment I apparently turned to my Dad with the most amazed look on my face, at that point I was nearly in tears, and I have never been like that for any band I have went to see live.

KISS were the best band on the lineup that weekend, it completely made my year."

Christine Dickson (Belfast)

"In 2008 I was living in Spain and made the trek from Alicante to Derbyshire for that year's Download Festival.

I met up with a friend of a friend that I didn't know particularly well but within about half an hour I was cooking up sausage butties for everyone in the surrounding area and became great friends with all the people we were camped with.

On the Friday I met a nice guy who lent me his shoes and coat because I was so cold and on the Saturday I danced with a load of crazy guys in sailor's hats! Over a year and a half later I'm back living in the UK; I spent my first New Year over here with the friends I had met and camped with at Download and am still great friends with all of them, frequently popping down to Derbyshire to see them; with them sometimes coming up to see me in Manchester too.

I've been dating the guy who lent me his shoes pretty much since the festival and had a fantastic long weekend in Birmingham with the guys in Sailor hats in February (and again in Norwich last summer).
Having been unable to go to DL09, I can't wait for 2010 where I'll be camped in a giant circle with all the different people I met in 2008, my boyfriend and his friends, and a few people that I'll be dragging with me."
Jade Holden (Glasgow)

"It was Download 2008 and it was the first time I went with a largish group of my close friends. Myself and my mate Joe were giving each other beer showers, I poured two cans of beer all over Joe he jumped up and ran straight for the beer cans. I ran off as fast as I could. I looked over to my left and I could see him chuck a can in the air, I ducked as I thought the can was going to hit me. Stupidly I ducked down thinking it was going to miss me but in fact I ducked enough so the beer can smashed me in the side of the head and knocked me out for a few seconds, I had a massive lump for the rest of the weekend but it was awesome!
In 2008 I went with a group of 6 very close friends of mine and whilst I was there I met loads of great people especially one in particular; Eve, my girlfriend of 2 years since Download 2008, so Download 2010 will be our Anniversary of being together for 2 years and it's all thanks to the best place on earth... Download!"
Graham Simmonds (London)

2009
Faith No More, Slipknot & Def Leppard

Q. The final year before the 30th Anniversary and what do we get at the festival?

A. The best line-up of any of the Download Festivals so far, the most glorious weather so far – high up in the 80's and the most popular site since moving out of the race track; no make that the best site ever, even better than in the race track, due to the actual layout and the room for festival expansion.

The mainstage headliners this year were Faith No More, Slipknot and Def Leppard. Def Leppard were returning to the Donington stage after an absence of 23 years and this time in the well deserved top spot, Slipknot had earned their place at the top of the bill on the Saturday night after gradually building their fan-base, year upon year and Faith No More were playing their first date since reforming; FNM did play a warm up show at the Brixton Academy a few days before, but Donington was their first 'major show'.

The second stage had the return of Motley Crue playing at Donington for the 4th time, The Prodigy coming back with their latest album 'Invaders Must Die' and Trivium headlining their first Donington stage.

Over the weekend there were many 'old school rock bands', which proved extremely popular, including Journey, ZZ Top, Whitesnake, Tesla and the reformed Skin; classic rock was here to stay and was a hit with all ages of attendees, from 'Download Virgins' to 'MOR Oldies'.

The addition of the 4th stage gave many bands, some unsigned, a chance to play at Donington, when they would never have had a chance in years gone by; remember the MOR days when there was only one stage and only six bands!

Friday on the mainstage had a 'nu-metal' vibe with the return of Korn in the special guest slot yet again and the Donington debuts of Limp Bizkit and Staind, all had massive crowds on the day, especially the reformed Limp Bizkit, who came back to a heroes return.

Anvil also sailed back into Donington to headline the 3rd stage, all on the wave of success created by their movie 'Anvil: The Story Of Anvil'; this was their first appearance at Donington since 1981, 29 years before. Following Download Anvil went on to open on some of the AC/DC 'Black Ice' tour dates in the USA.

So, probably the best year *EVER* at Donington! Great weather, great bands and a great new layout, things couldn't have been better.

"If I remember correctly, we decided to play Download about 2 months before the actual event. We hadn't seen each other, much less played together in a very long time, we had some work to do as far as getting back to speed, and I don't think any of us had any idea as to what to expect. When it came down to show time, we did a warm up show at Brixton

Academy which was both fantastic and surreal at the same time.

Download was the big one, but honestly I think we were so focused on what we needed to do, that the scope and size of the event went a bit over our heads; that is, until we played. For our second show in 13+ years, I thought that we'd already ironed out a few kinks from the earlier one, and we performed the set well and with confidence (of course, the incredible enthusiasm from the crowd itself had a lot to do with this too). I knew that the show was being filmed, but didn't pay much attention to the cameras during the performance. This turned out to be for the better, because I was to learn later that the web broadcast from the show went everywhere; to my surprise, I received a TON of emails from all over the world, all within less than an hour after playing the set.

So looking back, I can say that, though I was a bit single-minded at the time, this was probably one of the more critical shows in our history as a band. It was a landmark in that it proved that we were able to overcome our own personal obstacles and rise to the occasion, but I also think that the success of this show also did a lot to set the tone for the shows we ended up doing over the next year and a half."

Bill Gould (Faith No More – Bass)

"Headlining here is huge; it's like in high school reading Ripped magazine or borrowing copies of Kerrang! – This is insane for me, I can't believe its happening but at the same time I balance it with the fact that for ten years we've worked toward this. With every album it's got better and stronger and no matter what's been going on with the band we came together and we made this happen together. I'm really proud. It wasn't just handed to us – this was years of toil and bleeding and just getting out playing in front of everyone. It's a dream come true, man.

This is the King Daddy, this is the one you talk about – the one you make your own or it makes you something that you're not so you've just got to do it and mean it. Bands here [that I remember] were Maiden, the historic AC/DC night, it's incredible.

You read about the crowds, you see the pictures of Bruce Dickinson with his foot up on the monitor: "Scream For Me Donington" – what more do you want? That is rock.
Our setlist is one of my favourites, it has so many great elements that we pride ourselves on. It's got the deep cuts, the heavy stuff that people always look forward to but at the same time it's got all the singles that I can't believe we have. Radio singles and hits! And crowds are really responding to it so I'm excited."
Corey Taylor (Slipknot – Vocals)

"Download this year was really spectacular and when we got out there with Def Leppard it was beautiful weather and a big show, picture perfect actually and the line-up was pretty cool. I made a point of going out and watching ZZ Top; I had really wanted to watch Journey as we had toured with them in the States, they are a fantastic band with their new singer."
Phil Collen (Def Leppard – Guitar)

"This is my fourth time playing here and I've known John Jackson the promoter here for 22 years. Just walking through people maybe saw the band dressing room and there's a generational skip now to the younger bands. They get real quiet and you hear them whispering and little do they know I'm just a fucking dork like I always have been!
Being included with my new band – people are going out their way to help us. Whether it's karma or whatever, I'll take it."
Duff McKagan (Duff McKagan's Loaded – Vocals/Guitar)

"Wow! Donington was the most outrageous festival I've ever played! The anticipation of going on stage was immense, as I knew this crowd was going to rock!
The mosh pit was swirling around creating so much dust, like a whirlwind was about to form! I loved every minute of it!
I missed Slipknot as they where on at the same time as us. I would like to have seen them as I know they put on a good show."
Maxim Reality (The Prodigy – MC / Vocals / Beatbox)

*"We arrived and played our set and then had to leave. We weren't even at Donington for 5 hours, because we had to play Switzerland the next day. So, unfortunately we finally got to the mainstage and we never even got to enjoy it; it was a bummer!!
We were really bummed about not seeing Faith No More, but we saw them in Switzerland the next day."*
Jon Gallant (Billy Talent – Bass)

*"We were up on the mainstage, 3rd from top, before Marilyn Manson and Slipknot. But to see it all kick off at Download is amazing and when onstage I have the best seat in the house. I don't know how many people there were, but it must have been about 70,000. When the bass kicks in the waves went all the way to the back and it was a great feeling.
Manson's band weren't too happy when we came off stage, they were shitting themselves and they should have turned the bass down, but they didn't and it just distorted.
I am an admirer of Slipknot and I think that they are fantastic musicians. I think that if you put all the show business stuff aside, underneath what they do, they are amazing musicians. Joey Jordison is one of my favourite drummers; he actually nearly broke my hand when he shook my hand, he's so strong, but a little guy. I'm not huge, but he was quite a short guy. But they were really all cool dudes, the Slipknot guys and it was a really good experience to meet them.
I also met the drummer from Korn, Ray Luzier; he was a really big influence on me. I was absolutely blown away, Korn were the Zeppelin of the weekend for me they had that 'groove'. We missed Limp Bizkit, but they've got an awesome rhythm section as well.
I have also noticed how the crowd have changed from Monsters Of Rock to Download, simply because rock music has morphed into so many different styles of music now, which has basically created this new audience.
I like Download Festival for many reasons. It's so well organised and Andy Copping is a brilliant guy and anything you want he'll help you out with, whatever, nothings a problem*

for him. The whole backstage area is nicely organised and it's really friendly with a good vibe."
Kodish (Pendulum – Drums)

"We really looked forward to seeing what would happen.
I have my Donington plaque, that I was give last time, it's hanging outside the bog."
Lips (Anvil – Vocals/Guitar)

"The last time I went to Download was 27 years ago and when I arrived this time, I could see that it was a whole 'another generation' of stuff; it was a long overdue return.
The successful movie opened the doors to Anvil and I am happy with it all. We built an amazing band and we are now getting recognised for it.
I still have my most memorable Donington plaque hanging on my wall."
Robb Reiner (Anvil – Drums)

"The amount of bands, the different diversity between the bands makes it special. That's what I like about Download, because they put together bands from rock to extreme metal, without any problem and people come to the show with a totally different attitude than those going to a specific festival with just metal bands or black metal bands and that's it. The attitude of the people is going to be different because the crowd will just want to have fun, because they already know the all the bands are doing their own stuff and they appreciate that; that's what I love about Download."
Cristina Scabbia (Lacuna Coil – Vocals)

"It was our 3rd time at Download Festival in 2009. Every time that we come back to the festival it is growing and doubling the quantity of people."
Andrea Ferro (Lacuna Coil –Vocals)

"In 2009 we played on the main stage and that was indeed the full penetration with the full climax! 80,000 people is an unbelievable sight to behold...wow! DT has played thousands

of shows and dozens of festivals throughout the years, but I must admit Download is absolutely hands-down one of the coolest highlights of them all!"
Mike Portnoy (Dream Theater - Drums)

"This year's bill, especially the Sunday, really did hark back to the Monsters Of Rock days. If they carry that on for the next few years, or the foreseeable future, it will be a great success."
Ryan Richards (Funeral For A Friend – Drums)

"The line-up is always stellar, with great bands and we had a good energetic set, like we always do and the UK fans are amazing. We had some technical difficulties up there, but you work through those and give it your best.
I watched a little bit of Devildriver and I had wanted to see some of ZZ Top and Def Leppard, as I am a fan of old school rock, but our hotel was very far from Donington and our singer (Jamey Jasta) was hosting the Metal Hammer awards on the Monday."
Frank Novinec (Hatebreed – Guitar)

"The second time we played Download it was a lot more relaxed. We were actually in the middle of a European tour and we got to see some of the other bands and hang out with some people that we knew.
I remember driving out in the van around the racetrack and it was crazy.
Nothing compared to the first experience of Donington though, that was unreal."
Keith Nelson (Buckcherry – Guitar)

"For us it was our second visit to Europe and it was pretty cool to be invited and to play on the mainstage, which is huge, so it was a good start.
We were second on the mainstage and the second day, so people are hung-over and hanging around in their tents, so we didn't know what to expect.

We got close to the stage and the people were chanting 'Five Finger Death Punch' and when we hit the stage there were about 20,000 people already and there were signs everywhere.
It was like 'WOW' because they all knew the lyrics, so people had been downloading alright!! They were chanting the name of our band between every song, so that was really, really welcoming. We felt that if you were approved by this crowd, then we must be doing alright; so that meant a lot to us, we must have been doing pretty good.
These festivals tend to be like 'family reunions' because we know most of the people here, because one way or another we had toured with them. We have met friends from other bands and even the crew, it's a small world really; somebody who was our roadie last year was somebody else's this year. We met Dragonforce and we are really good friends with them, they are a lot of fun and it's always good to see them. It was awesome to be invited; Donington is the 'hot bed' of rock and metal."
Zoltán Báthory (Five Finger Death Punch – Guitar)

"It was my first time at Download and it can't be any better than to play the mainstage, with my first solo record out.
It was a great experience. The day before we did a lot of press and bumping into other bands; it was like a family reunion.
To hang out backstage there were bands at the 'top of their game', from Staind and Motley Crue to Limp Bizkit. Just sitting out in the courtyard was amazing."
Tim "Ripper" Owens (Ripper Owens – Vocals)

"On the way over here Tim was kind of 'sheepish' because we were going to be on so early in the morning and I said 'Dude, it's the mainstage! Nowhere else can you play on a mainstage at 11am to 20,000 people'. Usually when you are on early in the day you're not doing very well, but to be at Download on the mainstage, I told Ripper 'you got walked right to the front of the line'.

*Most bands who had played here had been out working for years, so for me personally, I was proud of Ripper to come in for the first time and to play the mainstage, even the line-up on the second stage was as impressive as the first stage.
For Tim it was a cool badge of honour to walk onto the mainstage for your first Donington Festival."
For me it was a personal triumph to come back and play Donington, as it will always be Donington to me. To stand on that stage and to cherish a new life and to play at 11am; I would never have been up at 11am before!
Donington for me, the last time, was 'bitter sweet' because it was that moment that I had previously made a mess of my life and couldn't really enjoy it for what it was; so this one I think I will remember a little better, for many years to come."*
Dave Ellefson (Ripper Owens – Bass)

"When we played we 'underlined'; a bit of metal in the morning."
Simon Wright (Ripper Owens – Drums)

*"It was my first time at Donington and I had the Donington LP and always made me want to play here, being that Judas Priest was one of my favourite bands.
It was a great time playing there, a lot of fun."*
Chris Caffery (Ripper Owens – Guitar)

*"We were totally stoked to open the festival. It's legendary, we don't have stuff like this in the US and to play on the day Faith No More reunited was awesome. When I grew up I was 13 when they broke up so I never thought I'd see them. What more could you want?
Music attracts normal people but also people who are attracted to the lifestyle – or the one they think we lead. When you bring someone backstage they're always like, 'is that it?!' cause it's not nearly as cool as they think it is. I actually think it's bad for them. It's fun, I can't ask for a better life cause I get to travel and do what I do artistically for a living but there's not girls in booty shorts dancing around on poles. Some places you'll run into some whacky shit but not here yet. I'm more*

interested in what's happening in the camp grounds than being backstage.
Johnny 3 Tears (Hollywood Undead – Vocals)

"It was our first ever Download experience playing; we played the mainstage and it was awesome.
We had a sizeable crowd, I'm normally good with numbers, but there was at least 15 people watching us.
It was good to play, we did a medley of songs; we did one of our songs and went into a Korn song, a Limp Bizkit song and then into Faith No More song.
We had a blast and it was good fun and we hope that we come back, because it was one of the best festival line-ups that I have ever seen. If they could beat the line-up in 2010, then fair play to them.
It was a year of the reunion, with Faith No More and Limp Bizkit; I remember seeing Wes backstage all painted up! Completely painted black, with a big feather Mohawk, like a horse; like you do.
Our dressing room was next to Motley Crue. Our drummer is a big Motley Crue fan, with a tattoo and when he found out where our dressing room was he shit himself.
We were probably 'too gay' to have played the festival before, but it was good to be asked to do it. I met Andy Copping and he was dressed as a cowboy; I'm not sure if he does that everyday or just for the festival? No jeans and 'buttless chaps' for him next year?"
Sean Smith (The Blackout – Vocals)

"It was the first time that we were actually lucky enough to participate.
It's such an historical place, in the world of rock; you'd had so many things like Monsters Of Rock in the same sort of area or compound.
The line-up covered all sorts of music. You had Slipknot, probably one of the most successful rock acts of the last 10 years. Then Def Leppard, Whitesnake and ZZ Top who were proper classic rock bands. I was also very excited to see 'Journey Idol', who were on before Dream Theater.

It was a good show, a lot of fun. Our monitor mix was a bit slap-dash, I had some strange noises; I had a burger van from down the road in my wedge.
Hopefully, we will come back and play again. We are thinking about having another day and instead of calling it Download we're thinking of calling it Blackout and we will play for 12 hours, so you wouldn't have to go to work; but we may play for as long as we want, which may be 10 minutes or 12 hours."
James Davies (The Blackout – Guitar)

"It was the first time that I had been to Download and it was awesome; I was usually a 'Reading Festival boy'. In a way rock has come back into fashion again.
When we turned up it was a field, pretty big; but when we saw all the people fill it it was like wow, I didn't think it was that big! I loved all the bands, but the one I really wanted to see was Faith No More, a big influence on our band."
Rhys Lewis (The Blackout – Bass)

"We played this year and it was awesome as usual, it's always good. It's Donington Park, so it's good to be a part of it."
Oliver Sykes (Bring Me The Horizon – Vocals)

"It's always fun playing Download. We always have the odd heckler, but we always go out and have a good time at Download and it's a good laugh. The same goes for the rest of the weekend, if we stick around, we always have a good time and see people we know there; it's guaranteed to be a good time.
I watched Meshuggah; they were 'super tight' and they sound like machines. I also saw a bit of Korn, Limp Bizkit and Sylosis.
I enjoy it; every time we play it it's good, so hopefully we'll get to do it again."
Matt Nicholls (Bring Me The Horizon – Drums)

"I've since returned to play Download with my current band, Bring Me The Horizon which was another amazing show for me.
From a bands perspective, Download is like a big annual party; you get to catch up with heaps of friends and bands you haven't seen or toured with in ages, there's always something going down in the backstage bar, those who drink can get pissed up and hang out and those who don't can hang out, watch and laugh at those getting pissed up. From a fan's perspective (myself included) it's a great opportunity to see a handful of your favourite bands all at once. I saw Meshuggah, one of my favourite bands, for the first time at 2009 Download, got to see and hang out with my long time friends from back home in Australia - Parkway Drive, and met idol's such as Tony Iommi all in the same day!!
I don't like to make fun of our fans because I'm always grateful that they're the main reason I get to live this amazing lifestyle and play these insane concerts such as Download; but I will say this, there are some freaks in the crowd at that fest and one of my favourite pass-times is just walking around and people watching!
I'm greatly looking forward to the next time I get to rock Download!"
Jona Weinhofen (Bring Me The Horizon – Guitar)

"There were a lot of people in the crowd who I bet had never seen or heard of us before, but it was great to see that there were some of them who were really watching our show intently.
It has been a great honour to play this prestigious festival, and my sincerest thanks go out to all the people who brought us here. We definitely hope to come back again to Download in the future!
Being backstage was a blast; I bumped into Motley Crue's Nicky Sixx and met with Jonathan Davis who I've not seen since Family Values 2006 when we toured together. I also got to meet so many other bands and it was just as
fun backstage as it was watching the bands play all day long.

*The weather was also simply terrific that day. I was under the blazing sun
while we were doing press. It's been 3 years since I had sunburn which was bad as it hurt a lot in the shower for the next few days!"*

Die (Dir En Grey – Guitar)

"I didn't have much time to check around as we had many interviews, but the day was amazing. It's a huge festival, very exciting and it had been 10 years since we had been in England; I think that the last time was in '99, if I remember well. But I promised that we wouldn't take another 10 years to come back though!

There are always a lot of metal bands and there are always bands that you want to see. So you come to the festival and realise that they are on the line-up, like Meshuggah, so it's great for the bands also and not just for the public.

Our friends Faith No More played; we toured with them and Soundgarden in 1990, so I was really excited to see those guys again for sure.

We had to leave the day after we played to go to another festival, but we arrived the day before we played, straight from Montreal, a little jet-lagged. We had played Sweden Rocks the week before and then flew back to Montreal and then came back to Download, so it was a lot of flying.

It's often the case when you agree to do the 'festival circuit'; but it's better for Voivod that we do the 'festival circuit' rather than do our own tour in clubs because we are pretty underground, but to play festivals you get to play in front of so many people and we sell a bit of merch, it's a very good scenario. The pay is also very good at festivals and better than playing in little clubs. Quite often we tour and we come back, but we don't make much money; but if we spend the summer playing festivals we are actually making a pretty good pay. We tend to get paid between 5,000 and 15,000 Euros per festival, so if we bring along one tech, we make pretty good money.

You try to have about 20-25 festivals, but now that people know that Voivod are back on the scene we are getting lots of

calls from promoters; so next year (2010) we are hoping to book 50 festivals.
We were told the camping sold out in 2009, so people are really going for it. It's a very amazing festival and I didn't think that we would ever get to play there, so I was pretty proud."
Michel "Away" Langevin (Voivod – Drums)

"Being from the states I had only heard references to Download Festival but the Monsters of Rock title travelled pretty far and was something I had always hoped I would get to be a part of.
Download '09 was my first Real Rock festival where all the bands were heavy and good. A lot of festivals in Europe are such a mix of styles so it was fun to be a part of something that was so exclusively heavy.
I'm a huge fan of Corrosion of Conformity, Pantera and Down so this was the first festival where I actually went out into the trenches and checked out all of Down's set. It was at around 2pm so I fried in the sun and fought off the hammered punters to do it! They were fucking great, the way it's supposed to be done. Phil and Pepper came to hang with Chris Cornell before our set at our dressing room so it was rad to get to hang with those dudes.
We also hung with Anvil, whose show I also caught, and they slayed. Anselmo even sang back-ups on a few jams as he's a fan as well! Great to see those guys still rocking as they were at it before most of us! Caught a bit of Slipknot as well and hung side stage for some of Manson but he was throwing his mike more than singing into it so we bailed!
It's great to play such a momentous festival and know you rocked and did your part. It was rad to look out and know the crowd was totally with us during our show, to have the best photographers documenting and have some of your metal heroes watching you from side stage!"
Jason Sutter (Chris Cornell Band – Drums)

"I went this year as a punter to hang out for a couple of days and watched some Faith No More, which was great. They

have the greatest up there; I went to 2 festivals in 2009 and it was much better at Donington than 'P In The Bin'."
Rick McMurray (Ash – Drums)

"A lot of women in America shave their vaginas on a regular basis and we hadn't had any oportunity to see any vagina yet, because we arrived the night before and had been partying; so we were looking forward to the aftershow party.
I ran into David Coverdale, I actually ran into him and he fell, it was weird; I tried to help him up. Heavy Metal is killer, David Coverdale and Whitsnake are a pretty sexy band.
This was our first time taking the jump over the pond and we were so excited to be there."
Michael Starr (Steel Panther – Vocals)

"American Audiences, since we live in LA, are able to see our shows, as they are a lot closer than people that live in England."
Lexxi Foxxx (Steel Panther – Bass)

"I think that Steel Panther fits in anywhere that we can, it make just take a little while."
Stix Zadinia (Steel Panther – Drums)

"We appreciate what Whitesnake have done for music and what we are trying to do here is bring the style of heavy metal that those guys made popular 25, 26, 35 years ago, we're gonna make it popular again. Those guys look killer still, they've got bitchin' hair, bitchin' pants and that's what we do. We focus on the look first, we pride ourselves as a band on how we look more than anything; the music is always secondary with us.
All the fucking record labels are a bunch of fucking pussies, even our label and I will fight anybody at Universal and I will kick their fuckin' asses; I'm just kidding, I like our label and they are awesome. I love Universal and they are my favourite label."
Satchel (Steel Panther – Guitar)

"Hanging out with Slipknot and being friends with them and being able to kick it; it was awesome. We did a summer tour with them in the States and at one point in my life I didn't like that band, but now they're one of my favourite bands; as far as their onstage presence and their music goes.
We landed Thursday night and got to Donington Friday morning. We hung out all Friday and Saturday and played on Sunday. We did a few interviews on Saturday and we did 'walkarounds', where we went out and talked to people in the audience.
I was smoking a joint and Tommy Lee walked by with six 'hot ass bitches'; dude that's fucking rock 'n' roll right there."
Mitch Lucker (Suicide Silence – Vocals)

"I was there all weekend long and watched all kinds of 'bad ass bands', some that I hadn't seen for years and some that I thought I would never get to see again, like Limp Bizkit; that was fucking crazy.
We played at 12:30pm on the Sunday on the 2nd stage; there was a good breeze, so it wasn't too hot and everybody was just having a good time.
The stage was really big, the stage sound was really good and everyone that was working the stage was really cool.
I have known about Download for a while; we were going to do it in '06 but something happened and we couldn't come over, so we were really pleased to play it in '09 and it was awesome and I'd love to do it again.
We had to watch Whitesnake, ZZ Top and Journey. I was surprised that Motley Crue were headlining on the second stage that seemed like a bit of a step down. I was star struck as hell when Nikki Sixx walked by.
On the Saturday I had been at the Jagermeister area all day long and I swear, I probably drank about 60 shots of Jager, but I didn't pay for a shot; Tom was really cool and he just kept giving us wristbands with 5 free shots on it and it every time we finished, it was like 'hey, can we get another wristband?'.
I was so drunk that I didn't get into a conversation with anyone for about 5 minutes and then said 'bye' and went down the front to watch Slipknot."

Mark Heylmun (Suicide Silence – Guitar)

"The best day of my life, ever.
Mum, if you are reading this, I have taken some drugs and it was nowhere as good as the day at Download was; the best high I've ever had."
Baron Kev Von Thresh Meister Silo Stench Chisel Marbels (Lawnmower Deth- guitar)

"Mum, you know that I've done drugs and the magic mushrooms, that was why I destroyed the house; but it was unbelievable, it really was THE best thing that I have ever done. It was like 'from work' to 'that', it was phenominal, absolutely phenominal. I was absolutely buzzing."
Concorde Faceripper (Lawnmower Deth- guitar)

"I was absolutely knackered after playing Download and we'd love to come back again; it was absolutely amazing, thoroughly enjoyed it."
Explodin' Dr Jaggers Flymo (Lawnmower Deth- Drums)

"Everything was brilliant and Mr Flymo could hear for once what we were doing and I kept nodding to him, but I could hear absolutely 'jack'."
Mightymo Destructimo (Lawnmower Deth- Bass)

"It was an honour. I enjoyed every second, the only thing that made it better was that Rainbow were headlining??!!
It was the bollocks, it was absolutely brilliant."
Qualcast Mutilator (Lawnmower Deth- Vocals)

"The UK is definitely its own kind of world in terms of the history, enthusiasm, the press and media; there's a lot of hype, so to be a band that's not necessarily the flavour of the week, it's still gratifying.
I was excited; if you have a good performance at Download it reverberates beyond the day. Some bands have 'exploded' just because they had a good performance at Download; you

play in front of 20-30,000, that's a whole 'metal community', it's just insane."
Doc Coyle (God Forbid – Guitar)

"I played in the tent with Manraze, in the Tuborg tent, which was cool; I think I was the only artist to play it twice this year. The tent was massive, big for camping in.
With Manraze we can go off on a tangent, but Def Leppard is very structured. As a three piece, we can do what we want, but I do get to 'groove' more in Def Leppard.
In Manraze I don't get a second break, it's either singing, solos or changing guitars; I'm just getting into that and I'm really enjoying it. I learnt how to sing properly when we were rehearsing for Download. We'd be rehearsing twice a day in Dublin; I'd be rehearsing with Manraze in the morning, then Def Leppard at night and then vice versa, zooming across town to a little rehearsal place and then going up to Joe's house to rehearse. I was trying not to put my voice out, so I learnt how to pull it back a bit, which was interesting."
Phil Collen (Manraze – Guitar)

"Last summer one of our dreams came true and that was to play the Download Festival at Donington.
We played on the Red Bull stage, which was one of the smaller stages, but we were just thrilled to be there and be part of it; part of the whole event of Download.
What's really great about Download, is that we thought we weren't 'metal' enough or of a certain style, because we are one of those crossover bands; we use electronics, we use a rock sound, use a bit of metal sound and merge it together and that's what's become great about Download, people coming to the festival are open minded enough to enjoy the way that music has evolved.
It dicked on 'T In The Park'; we were on a smaller stage, but it's good to compare it to other festivals that we've done and Download was just leagues ahead in the reaction and the whole vibe of the festival.
I just love the way that the festival has evolved and the whole atmosphere of the festival."

Laurence René (My Passion – Vocals)

"Playing Donington festival was a great experience.
Since my childhood we grew up with it being THE big festival to play, the only one basically; when I was little it was the only one I wanted to go to and you'd watch the bands and you be like 'god that's what I want to do'.
It was unbelievable, we were sat backstage and we had our own dressing room and for us that was like 'WOW'; we saw our name on the door and it was crazy, we were there! Chris Cornell had his dressing room next to ours and it was unbelievable.
After we had done our press we had 15 minutes before we were due to go on stage and we were sitting there in our dressing room saying 'we're just about to play Download' and it was just the biggest thing for us.
We had only just started getting press and we walked on stage to do line checks and the tent was pretty empty, to be fair, apart from a few die hard fans down the front. So we went off and then when we came back on ten minutes later the tent was packed and we couldn't believe it.
We watched Slipknot, I'm a huge fan and their stageshow was out of this world."

John Be (My Passion – Guitar)

"Download was one of those things where we couldn't believe we were there. It was like a military operation, we just had so much adrenaline that we were going so mad; the shame was it seemed like it only lasted 30 seconds for me, it was so quick and we did have half an hour.
It was to be able to show other people that we could play Download and that we can play to people who like metal and people who like rock and they can still get into it."

Jonathan Gaskin (My Passion – Drums / Synthesizer)

"I am a big fan of festivals; I cannot remember when we first made our business contacts at festivals, made friends with people from other bands and how many people we played in front of, but all in all to be back at Download was great.

It's the best opportunity for a small unsigned band to get a gig at a sponsored stage. You may think that people wouldn't give a shit, but they are drunk and happy and curious about stuff; maybe it's me getting old, but I can't imagine why people are curious about anything at eleven in the morning, but it's a very good sign and it makes me happy.
But I remember what it was like 20 years ago and we would play gigs at 11am for a sandwich to 100 people and we would be so happy."
Nicke Borg (Backyard Babies – Vocals/Guitar)

"We headlined the Red Bull stage on the Sunday.
It was our first ever Download Festival experience and I had never been to the festival before, let alone played it, so it was a wicked experience for me to just go and see what it was like; then on top of it that, to play it as well was amazing. We played on the Sunday, so we played as the last band on the last day.
We arrived on the Friday morning; we camped, hung around all weekend and watched a lot of bands. At first I thought that I would prefer to have played on the first day, get it over with and then hang out, but I quite like the 'hype'. While we were there we hyped it up throughout the weekend and the last thing we did was play it, which was really cool.
I saw a lot of bands; Limp Bizkit were wicked and Faith No More were awesome. The Saturday was the best day in my opinion; got to see Hatebreed who were amazing, Slipknot were incredible, Architects were really good and You Me At Six were really good on the massive 2nd stage.
It was so hot; we got back to camp not realising how hot I was. When I got up in the morning I was completely red and had to play that night, burning up on stage.
We had a lot of press to do on the day on the Sunday and then we had to load in and get ready at our stage. We watched a bit of Twin Atlantic who are our good friends.
It was awesome."
Dan Brown (We Are The Ocean – Vocals)

"I had been to 2 or 3 Readings, but this was my first Download experience. It was pretty similar, but the bands were a lot heavier, which has its advantages and disadvantages.

I party a bit too hard and missed a lot of bands that I wanted to see. I woke up on the Saturday night at midnight having missed both Slipknot and Architects.

I actually got dumped at Download, but I don't think I can really blame the organisers of Download festival for that, but it's just a warning; if you are in a relationship and got to Download Festival, 'just beware'. But I have also been dumped at Reading, so maybe it's just me.

I thought the Red Bull stage was a great addition and there are some really good bands coming through, so I spent a lot of time there; Fall From Grace I discovered there. When a lot of bands play Download they are playing big stages and the sound gets lost, so to play a small tent, where it's much more intimate is good and the sound in there was awesome. Crowd wise, we couldn't have gone on the 2nd or 3rd stage, but the tent was great and a good opportunity for smaller bands.

Friday and Saturday, when I was sober I spent a lot of time at the mainstage and also saw Journey on the mainstage on the Sunday.

If I had to compare it with Reading; I have a much softer taste in music, but Reading doesn't have enough heavy music, but Download doesn't have much 'softer' music in case you want to chill, so I'd say combine them! It would be called Redload or Downing."

Jack Spence (We Are The Ocean – Bass)

"We set ourselves up for a rubbish show, as it wasn't the reception we were after last year, so we thought we'll tell ourselves that no one is going to be there, so whatever happens is going to be good. We were on at the same as Meshuggah, Faith No More and Motley Crue and we still got a good crowd, which was awesome as that meant that people who go to Download are there for everything, they're not just there for the headliners.

For such a small band to play the 'brand new' 4th stage, it was just so amazing that so many people came to see us. So my

main overall experiences of Download are amazing, apart from camping, I'm just not a fan. Camping aside, Download is a great festival; I love it."
Richard Carter (Blackhole – Vocals)

"We headlined the 4th stage and it was just a great show. We were a bit nervous beforehand because of the year before and we were clashing with Faith No More and Motley Crue; I was pretty bummed out because I wanted to watch them.
We thought that we were playing against these big bands and no one would come to see us, but we filled up the tent and it was really just a good show.
WE stayed all weekend and left at about midday on Sunday; we caught Slipknot on Saturday might, Bring Me The Horizon, Youmeatsix; we saw a lot of bands, it was a really good festival."
Nick Mitchell (Blackhole – Guitar)

"This years Download was a highlight of our summer. We played Friday night because we had the chance to enjoy the rest of the festival and to check out loads of other bands over the whole weekend. One of the best bands I saw was Slipknot, they were quality and at one point they managed to get everybody to sit down that was epic. We also had a lot of our friends playing the same stage on the Friday, so it was a great experience."
Andreas Yiasoumi (Blackhole – Guitar)

"We played at Download before in 2006 & 2007, so this was our third time and yet again the response was amazing. The tent was really packed out.
You always worry before you go on stage if there are going to be as many people there as before and will they be 'into it' and sometimes with an English audience they can be slightly reserved, but at Download you always get a good response. Everyone was happy, it was the first day and the weather was really good, everything was on our side and we had a great

time; the crowd were great and we stayed around all weekend.
We watched Faith No More, Leppard and Journey, all these 'old school' bands that we all look up to."
Lauren Harris (Lauren Harris – Vocals)

"There were a lot of great bands at Download 2009 and we had a lot to live up to. It almost makes you more focused and driven, as we want to fill those shoes; you just want to go out there and give it your best shot because of those amazing bands that were playing.
The people were great, the weather was great and the first day is always the best in my opinion, because everyone had just got there and they were all ready to get mashed off their faces.
I think that 2009 was different from the last two times that we had played there, as we had a new album to come out, so we were showcasing what was to come and it was a bit more personal."
Richie Faulkner (Lauren Harris – Guitar)

"It was an early show, but there were about 5,000 people in the audience, so it was good. Considering that everyone is really drunk in the evenings and had to get their ass up that early, RESPECT!!
It was really good for my first time at Download, as I am a new member of the band, since Thomas Silver left and it's been awesome all the way.
We came on the Friday in the afternoon and checked out bands all day. I watched Faith No More & Backyard Babies. Then I went around eating really expensive food that didn't taste of much, but I'm not complaining!
Download is everything I expected and more."
Vic Zino (Hardcore Superstar – Guitar)

"We were lucky enough to play the 2nd stage, I heard that a couple of years ago it was used as the mainstage. We were honoured to be playing that 2nd stage, regardless of how big it was and that it had TV screens either side of the stage. We

had played Hammerfest and a few shows in Europe, which were big shows, but nothing on the scale of that stage.
We were all a bit nervous, but full of anticipation for what was going to happen. We were playing the Sunday and everyone was very hung-over. We played very early, we were the second band on, so we on at 11:45am and we were a bit dubious about anyone turning up to see us that early, but it was packed! You couldn't see the end of the crowd and I guess that there were about 6-7,000 people there, I couldn't believe it.
Everything that we get we're blown away by because we're not one of those bands that are in it for the 'scene', we're in it for nothing else but the music. So when people actually turn up to appreciate what we are doing, especially as we are so extreme, it's an HONOUR, because when you have bands like Slipknot, Limp Bizkit and like 'girly' Def Leppard and all the really big bands, the fact that people take the time out of their day when they could be watching Tesla, who were on at the same time as us, to check out what we're doing is incredible. So we were overwhelmed by the response we got and it was a great experience for us."
Rob Purnell (Trigger The Bloodshed – Guitar)

"I had butterflies all week until we got there. I was nervous because it's 'THE' metal, epic, rock 'n' roll festival in the entire world; it really is.
To be called back for a second time is just epic. You could see people as far back as you could see and the energy was out of friggin' control!
This time that we played it was a bigger stage and a bigger crowd.
We stayed until the end of Friday, then left and came back on Sunday.
There is such a different calibre of bands and nowhere else in the world would you get so many epic bands together."
Maria Brink – (In This Moment - Vocals/Piano)

"To get invited back in 2009 was huge and we were so excited to get the news that we were playing it, it was amazing. The second stage was bigger and had more people and it filled out completely when we played. It was nearly as big as the mainstage; it was killer.
We were the second band on. We threw out balloons and we tried to make an impact and make it something that people would remember; it was really cool.
You even get small bands playing the small stages that no one really knows about and that was us in 2007."
Chris Howorth (In This Moment – Guitar)

"We were really excited to come to Download as we are an 'independent band' and it was a lot of work and lot of people helped to make it happen.
We are signed to Corey Taylor's independent imprint 'Great Big Mouth Records' and he was obviously a great supporter; being able to play on the same day as Slipknot, two Des Moines in one day at Download was a pretty unique thing to happen and we were certainly very honoured and proud to be a part of that for sure.
Everything was fun and the crowd was great.
We stayed the whole time and Faith No More! They are a main vein in the band; we'd all loved them since we were teenagers."
Fred Missouri (Facecage – Bass)

"I was just really excited to be there and to see Faith No More obviously, but I wasn't able to see Meshuggah my 2nd favourite band of all time, I had to watch Faith No More as it was a once in a lifetime opportunity, but I hope that it wasn't. We played probably the best that we had ever played, thanks to the energy that we felt from the crowd. It was really positive and it was just a great, great experience. We pulled the crowd in, they just kept coming in.
It was just great to be at Download with my friends; to be there was just an honour."
Jim Stockham (Facecage – Guitar)

"It was an absolute dream come true; everyone has a list of things that they want to accomplish in their life and no BS Download was one of them. I had always wanted to come to England and play the Download Festival without a doubt and I can cross that off the list now; but now I have a new one to add and that was playing Donington a 2nd time and a 3rd time and a 4th time. Anytime that we are able to come back we will be coming back for sure.

We always considered Donington to be the pinnacle of musical success whether you are a small band or big band; getting the chance to play at the place where rock 'n' roll was born and showcase your talent is unparalleled.

This was the culmination of so much hard work, it took us eight years to get there and it was a dream come true. Being put on the same poster and the same t-shirt as some of our idols, it was just an unbelievable experience.

Faith No More was just unbelievable; when we found out they were on the bill, we were just flipping out.

It was our first show ever out of the country and it was at Donington, we couldn't have kicked it off with more of a bang; crowd was awesome, show was awesome, and can't wait to come back."

Matt Nyberg (Facecage – Vocals)

"Dream come true, lots of people, it was fun and I thought we played great. We had a really big circle pit on the 3rd stage, pillar to pillar; I don't think it could have got any bigger. It was a big tent, I could see a circus in there no problem.

It was our first time out of the country and it was just an overwhelming experience."

Ryan Berrier (Facecage – Drums)

"Donington was amazing. It was amazing to be able play where all the rock legends had played before; you here all the stories from AC/DC to Def Leppard playing at there, it's the mecca for every rock musician and it was amazing to get to play it. The first ever tape I bought when I was 10 was 'AC/DC

Live At Donington' and I learned to play guitar from that tape and then we played there!!
We were on 2nd stage, which was a big band stage, so it was a massive step for us, it was huge. We had a great following and a really good day; we opened the stage, but lots of people came to watch us and it was a good show.
We watched Faith No More and Shinedown as we had toured with them."
Carlos Garcia (The Crave – Guitar)

"The last band to play on the stage before us was Motley Crue, as we were the first band to play on Saturday morning; we were just freaking out saying 'what is going on?' You could say that we went on after Motley Crue.
It was absolutely amazing.
It was absolutely insane as no one had really known us. We have been in this band for 7 years, so to open the 2nd stage was insane, we would have played in the fucking car park, it was unreal; hopefully if we get to play in 2010, we will be higher up the bill.
We had full passes for the Saturday, so we could go wherever we wanted in the artist area, but we couldn't use the artist area on the Sunday. We thought 'fuck it', we are the 'Kings Of Blag'; so we figured out where the kitchen door was in the artist area, put our biggest set of bollocks on and just walked in. We walked straight through the kitchen and into the artist area, because Shinedown were playing on the Sunday and we wanted to go and see those boys; we met up with Shinedown and had a few drinks and then just blagged our way through. We watched Limp Bizkit; we saw Limp Bizkit four times in two months, as we had also played Rock Am Ring and Rock IM Park.
It was just awesome."
Ryan Burnett (The Crave – Vocals / Guitar)

"It was really great.
I went there when I was 16 when Metallica played, so to be back there again to play was wicked.

*I didn't recognise the place because they'd changed it all around.
I was sober for the whole time, so I didn't do any crazy things.
I just wish that I had got one of the free tattoos backstage!"*
C.J. Evans (The Crave – Drums)

*"The highlights really for me were Limp Bizkit, Korn and beer backstage.
Two tents, three men; me and C.J. got our tent up really quick, it was a quick erection! Then we looked over at Ryan and he was just there kicking his tent and going 'ohhhh hay fever'. We decided to help him, but he did look very sorry for himself and it was very funny."*
Tom Swann (The Crave – Bass)

*"It was a good gig, we had some technical difficulties, which is something that I guess you kind of get used to, but on the whole we had fun and everyone who saw us seemed to have fun.
As far as playing Donington goes, I have been a 'metal kid' as long as I can remember. I remember listening to the Monsters Of Rock festivals on the radio, wishing that I could go but being far too young. It's the quintessential metal festival and bands from all over the world, know that if you are going to play Donington it's gotta be fucking metal. That's what I grew up on, listening to bands that played it and wishing I was there.
To play it??? MY brain doesn't manage it that well; it's completely dis-related from my memory, the fact that we did play it was amazing."*
Lee Vincent – (Pulled Apart By Horses – Drums)

"I had a Download voice, to get in with the crowd more; it was more of a shout to get rid of my weak Birmingham accent. It was amazing, I hadn't actually been to Download before, so be there for the first time 'to play it' was incredible."
Tom Hudson (Pulled Apart By Horses – Vocals / Guitar)

"It was amazing. The first band that I ever fell in love with as a kid was Def Leppard, so I'd gone through a few years of shame having to admit that but I still love them a lot and the played on the night that we played, so it was all good."
Robert Lee (Pulled Apart By Horses – Bass)

"When I found out that we were doing Download I was quite overwhelmed. I'd never been before, cardinal sin, but to actually be there and to play alongside so many great bands, it was the greatest line-up not only for Download but for any festival. There was pretty much every type of heavy rock genre covered. But even compared to the line-up for Reading and Leeds, it was just incredible.
We missed the first few days as we were playing gigs, then we turned up and played and we were then free to go and watch Whitesnake, Def Leppard and ZZ Top; it might be the only time that we'd get to see them, so we didn't want to miss it.
It's an institution Download and 2009 was it's pinnacle, especially compared to the line-ups in previous years."
James Brown (Pulled Apart By Horses – Guitar)

"It was fuckin' awesome.
We had a great time, the weather was brilliant and there were great bands on; there were some really great reformed bands, which everyone in our group were really looking forward to seeing. We had all the guilty pleasures like Korn, Limp Bizkit and Faith No More on Friday and on Sunday the mighty Whitesnake, Def Leppard and ZZ Top, we just couldn't wait to see them, for all the right reasons; I'd never seen them before. I'm a big Coverdale fan and I was more of a Purple than Whitesnake, but the same with Def Leppard, I couldn't wait to see them; a guilty pleasure.
It was a big revival in '09, it was like they picked up Download and took it back to '85; it was really good.
It's a great festival, because you can go to a nice quiet tent if you're chilling out and not interested in Pendulum or whatever, wander off and see something a bit more underground and a

bit more unheard of. There were a few of our mate's bands on the bill as well, so it was pretty cool.
It's a dream come true really, because everyone wants to play Donington."
Darrin South (Sacred Mother Tongue – Vocals)

"We were really nervous as it was the biggest gig we'd ever done and we thought we'd try and 'step it up' and make it look like we're a really good band; hopefully that came across as there were a lot of people cheering.
No bottles of piss were thrown, so that was good!
I think that there were about 4,000 people, but they all looked small from the stage. But, even then we could see people we know, from little pockets, from all around the country.
There wasn't a lot of grass, so when I got up there and there wasn't much grass to be seen, I was happy."
Andy James (Sacred Mother Tongue - Guitar)

"When we played Donington it was quite a shock really because it was the biggest thing that any of us had ever done. We had all been in other bands and been friends for such a long time, but not all of us in the same band before. The band had only been going since summer 2008, it was quite a shock to be asked to play Donington as it's pretty a big gig.
We had done some shows with Airbourne in Europe, but people over here still didn't know much about us and then we played with the Datsuns, which was slightly 'left field' of the Donington stuff, but it was kinda good. We then did some shows with Stone Gods which were amazingly good and we'd got the right crowd in there and then some shows with Danko Jones and that was good too and I think from there things kind of grew a little bit and then Download was just amazing.
We were nervous and very wary; more pessimistic than anything else, thinking that it was going to be really shit and that there would be nobody there. When we got there we hadn't played for a while, we'd toured a little bit a the beginning of the year, but then we hadn't done any shows since April; we didn't even do a 'warm up' show before Download, so it was like 'shit what are we going to do?'

The band before us finished and we went out and set up our own gear and it was pretty dead. But we thought that we would go out there and give it our all, it might be our only chance because might not do anything like this again and in six months time we might have been next months chip paper. We went back into our portakabin and had a whole lot of beer and thought 'fuck it, let's go for it', this could be the biggest chance we had of making an impression on anyone. When we walked out we were all so shocked and just so surprised that the tent was packed. I think everyone got really excited about it, which was quite good and I think that we ended up playing the songs a bit faster than usual, because our adrenaline was going and it was just amazing. I don't think I have felt anything like it before really, it was just such a weird feeling. I never usually get stage fright or anything like that, sometimes after gigs I get a bit ill because we're the sort of band who really 'go for it' and we mean what we do; I just make myself ill because I really go for it, like it's maybe the last gig we ever do. Download did us a lot of favours; we did a great gig, great set, lot of people in there and having that amount of people shouting 'FUCK YOU' back at you it was amazing! It was just so bizarre.

I was so nervous and at times you just don't know what to say. Sometimes I am quite witty, but at the end I said 'Donington put your noses in the air, take a deep breath and smell the victory of the show'; it was amazing and everyone was just loving it and the band were falling about laughing, they thought that I had learnt that, but it was just an off the cuff comment.

This year was a good mix of bands. We came down on the Saturday afternoon and got to watch Anvil after we played, because they headlined our tent. The Sunday was great as we were looking forward to the bands as lots of them had influenced us. We were looking forward to Def Leppard, Journey and ZZ Top was just the best, they were awesome. It wasn't the original singer in Journey, but he was ok. Whitesnake were amazing; David Coverdale is worth the money just for his inter song banter, he's almost like the James Bond of rock, he has so many bits of banter and he's

such a gentleman and so suave that it's quite funny. All the weekend we had been thinking about what Coverdale was going to say and he said something about 'The English Riviera' which had us in tears."
Pete Spiby **(Black Spiders – Vocals / Guitar)**

"It was amazing! It was our first time at Download and we didn't expect to have even nearly a full tent. We walked out on stage and it was packed; we were over the moon about it. We had an amazing time, the crowd went mental and we couldn't have asked for a better crowd response it was awesome. We tore the crowd apart at the end with a 'Wall of Death' with a twist; me, Jay and Rob jumped the middle and when you jump in the middle, it just ignites the crowd that little bit more. We done it before with just me in the middle, but for Download we thought that we would make it stand out a little bit, it was good fun.
We watched Architects who were incredible and so good, as were Meshuggah. We watched a bit of Steel Panther, but you could hardly get in the tent though; it was packed all around the tent, you could hardly see them. I'm a huge Billy Talent fan and they were awesome.
Overall Download Festival 2009, sweet."
Marc Halls (Fei Comodo – Vocals)

"We were on the Red Bull stage at 2:30pm on the Sunday afternoon; pretty packed, pretty damn good.
Me, Jay and Marc all got in the 'Wall of Love' or 'Wall of Death' (or whatever you want to call it) at the end and it was pretty mental."
Rob Clemson (Fei Comodo – Drums)

"We were really chuffed to be there, because festival crowds are really 'up for it'. It was really cool. Everyone is usually drunk by midday, so when we played everyone was really into it and it was a great experience."
Jamie Graham (Sylosis – Vocals)

"It was pretty hilarious, there were a couple of thousand people there and we had an insane circle pit. It was probably the best thing that I have ever seen and done in my life."
Carl Parnell (Sylosis – Bass)

"I looked forward to seeing Opeth and Faith No More; I would have liked to have seen Motley Crue do 'Doctor Feelgood', but they were on the same time as Faith No More and it had to be them."
Josh Middleton (Sylosis – Guitar)

"I wanted to see Trivium, God Forbid and You Me At Six mainly. I thought that our set was hilarious and great fun. The crowd was much bigger than I thought it would be and we got a massive circle pit. I can't wait to do another festival really."
Alex Bailey (Sylosis – Guitar)

"It was an amazing atmosphere and totally different to any other show that we had played.
I then got the drink in and I just got shitfaced for the rest of the day!"
Rob Callard (Sylosis – Drums)

"I was so excited. I had obviously been to festival before as a fan but hadn't the chance to play before, so this was the most surreal experience of my life and it was absolutely amazing.
It was so good we had a full tent and there were people outside. It was the biggest crowd that we had ever played to and people were all singing along to the words.
We were so excited to see Limp Bizkit, a total party band."
Scott Kennedy (Bleed From Within – Vocals)

"Download is like a big platform gig and every time you play, you just go up and up and up. To go from the small clubs that we play to this is amazing; we could sometimes play to 20 people and then 100 people the next day, it's just so 'hit and miss'. But when I was growing up and I formed a band, people

would always say where do you want to play and you would always say 'Download'."
Craig Cowans (Bleed From Within – Guitar)

"It was an honour. I only joined the band a couple of months ago and did a couple of tours and Download was the highlight of it. It's been the best turn out and the crowd was phenomenal."
Davie Provan (Bleed From Within – Bass)

"Everything was made quite easy for us to get from the van, to the gear, to the stage, so thumbs up to the organisers.
I wouldn't come to Download had we not been paid, not that I don't like the festival; it's just that we are not metal fans.
We shared a shuttle bus with the singer of Down, who used to be in Pantera; he didn't say anything, but that was cool.
There wasn't enough beer for us so we went to Asda to stock up on beer, not that we are promoting Asda, but it is good at what it does."
Alex Kershaw (The Computers – Vocals / Guitar)

"It felt a little bit rushed, getting everything to the stage, but to all the people who were organising and directing us I would like to say that they were very helpful, which helps a lot at these events because the last thing you want is some 'douche bag' being annoying.
We had about 15 minute's downtime, while the friends that we had brought along with us set up our kit, whilst we were able to go and get changed into our slacks.
We played and it was fucking great fun; we'd been to Reading before but never Download and we had certainly never played anything that big before.
The sound was awesome, we did have a sound guy but he had to go and do something with Fightstar, so we had the 'in house' or 'in tent' sound engineer. We had a load of friends at the side of the stage run on every time a pedal got unplugged. We had an awesome time and the tent was packed. We could see a bunch of our friends from Exeter; Alex our singer said that we were from Devon and then we saw a big Devon flag

appear and we could see various friends of ours, faces around, so that was very nice.
Couldn't wait to see ZZ Top and Journey and we were a bit gutted that The Ghost Of A Thousand didn't play.
It was really fun."
Nic Heron (The Computers – Bass)

"It was absolutely incredible! We were there the year before, just to watch bands and we were saying 'imagine if we played here, imagine next year!' We obviously didn't expect it and then suddenly we were playing it and it was one of the best things, to this day, that we have done.
It was the first big gig that we had done and to share such a major festival, with such big bands, it was just incredible, as was the gig itself.
On the day that we played, we didn't have too much promo, but we were obviously setting up, but we got to watch Architects, who were are big fans of and they blew us away and Faith No More. We also caught our friends band Jett Black.
We were walking around Donington when it was empty, before we soundchecked, which was before the 80,000 people turned up.
It was just incredible; it's the best festival."
Ben Jolliffe (Young Guns – Drums)

"It was absolutely awesome; it was amazing.
First of all, when we played the tent, it wasn't that full, but by the second song there were quite a few rows there, a load of 'metal horns' in the air and everyone was loving it. There were quite a lot of people singing along to all the words, which was quite weird and I didn't expect that at all; MySpace is helping us out 'big time'!
I really wanted to see Motley Crue and Duff McKagan, but our sets clashed with theirs, but I did get to see Faith No More and they were amazing when they played 'Epic'."
Robb Wybrow (New Device – Guitar)

"I had come to the Download Festival for the last 4 years and seen all my favourite bands, including Motley Crue and Buckcherry. It's got an amazing atmosphere, way better than other festivals because everyone seems to be on the same page.

It's quite diverse in sense of style; Friday they had Hollywood Undead rapping, Slipknot on Saturday and then Def Leppard playing on Sunday, complete opposites.

I think that everyone gets something out of everyone band as well, it's one of the most diverse audiences and there doesn't appear to be any 'slagging off' of bands or empty stages; it's a wicked place.

We played the Red Bull stage and it was wicked. It was awesome to be a part of it."

Rozzy Ison (New Device – Drums)

"Certainly I'm a bit younger; at only 23 I am part of the Download generation, however our guitarist Stevie had been coming to Monsters Of Rock since before our drummer was born, so we have a lot of Donington history.

I came for the past 5 years. The first time I came my friend won tickets in a bar and he asked if I wanted to go, I said yes and have been hooked since then, coming every year.

We came in 2007 with a few guys from the band. Some people knew who we were and asked 'are you going to be playing next year?' and we said 'I hope so', but then we didn't. So we came last year and people again asked 'are you going to be playing next year?' and again we said 'I hope so'. So then we started pasting on the boards and then it all fell into place.

Our drummer is our booking agent; we don't have a manager or a big fancy agent or a label; so it's just hard work and persistence really. We just kept getting on Andy Copping's back and saying 'Andy, Andy, Andy, come and let us play? Andy, Andy, Andy, Andy, Andrew, Andrew, Andrew, come and let us play?'

To be fair our drummer pulled a bit of a fast one on us really, because he came to us and said 'we've been offered this gig in Margate, some mini festival in September or something, are you up for it' and of course we said yes. Then he said 'we've also got an email from a guy about a gig on 13th June' and I was like 'dude don't be stupid, that's Download' then he came back with 'yeah that's what the guy called it Download', so there was plenty of excitement then. We were one of the last bands to get announced, so we had waited a while to get the nod finally.

But it was really good with the times and nobody really clashed with us and we got a really good crowd and we were really pleased. The doors had opened at 10am and we were on at 1:30pm, so there was plenty of time for everybody to get in and get involved, shaking off the drunken haze of the Friday night. It was the first big festival show that we had done and there were people from all over the place that had come to see us on some of the tours that we had done with bands like Black Stone Cherry. There were people from Ireland, Scotland and down south; so we have fans from all over the country and it was good just to get them all together.

We stayed the whole weekend, trying to see as many bands as we could. All our friends were here and people from friends bands and it was a good way to see lots of bands that you would not normally see."

Mikey Serpico (Serpico – Vocals)

"It was one of the highlights of the bands and one of the concerts that we have always wanted to play since the band has been together. It was the smallest stage at the festival that we were playing on, so we had gone in at the start of the day to check it out. We had noticed that the crowd was a bit sparse for some of the early bands, so we were a bit concerned that we weren't going to get much of an attendance.

We were well rehearsed for it and we treated it like we do with any other gig. Then it was 'show time' and the guys that we have working with us put all our stuff on the stage, then we get the call and we walked onto the stage and the place was absolutely full. It was a fantastic response even before we'd played a note, just an explosion of noise.

I got quite emotional; I could see all these faces that I recognised from all over the country, from Birmingham, Manchester and Scotland, who had come to see us before; we had a relatively short set, about ½ an hour.

It was a great honour to play Download in the first place, but to have all these people supporting us and considering we don't really have a record label, it was amazing.

So that was it, we came off the show and we were on an absolute high, bumping into these amazing people who you'd had posters of, up on your wall for all these years; Def Leppard, Journey, Brian May and Anita Dobson!"

Kenny Collins (Logan – Vocals)

"The one thing that I have to mention was that we had not soundcheck, sound engineers that we hadn't met before and we weren't using our own gear and we walked onstage worrying about it, but the sound was absolutely fantastic; the best sound we've ever had. Both the front of house sound and the onstage sound was phenomenal. So I have to 'shout out' to the Download tech guys because the sound was incredible."

Mick Coll (Logan – Guitar)

"I thought it went really well.

We had played an acoustic set with Black Stone Cherry earlier that week in the Gibson Showroom and I think on the day at Download our sets overlapped by about a quarter of an hour, so I thought 'Oh my god, people are going to watch them over us'.

So I didn't look onstage until we went on, so I ran out there and it was full right to the edge of the tent.

We didn't get a soundcheck, just a line check, but the sound was really good and it was amazing.

I think Journey was playing after we played and we were watching that guy who they found off You Tube, he must have been stoked!

We filmed a music video the weekend before, played the Isle Of Mann TT on the Tuesday, had one day off and then came down to Download, stayed all weekend and played on

Sunday, staying to watch Def Leppard; it was the best week that I've had for many a year."
Will Stapleton (JETTBLACK – Vocals / Guitar)

"We got told that we were playing about a month before it happened. We had grown up on the music of Monsters of Rock, so we were just so happy to be playing there. We played on one of the smaller stages and we were up against some big names, Black Stone Cherry were playing the same time as us on the Sunday afternoon and they are very popular; so we just thought that we would see how it goes.
When we turned up it was amazing weather and the other guys had been there all weekend; there were Tesla, Skin and Journey playing that day. But when we came out the tent was pretty much packed; to say that we 'won them over' may seem a bit arrogant, but I think we did. The tent was packed right to the back.
We came onstage and said that we didn't want to call it Download, today was going to be Monsters of Rock and it was wicked. An amazing day.
It was one of the best gigs that we have ever played and definitely the best gig that we played that year. Everything was perfect, the weather, all the bands that were playing were great, and it was fucking amazing."
Tom Wright (JETTBLACK – Bass)

"I was quite disappointed with the line-up in 2008, but I went this year as a punter and it was quite funny watching Limp Bizkit, Korn and Faith No More; it brought me back to '97 and it was like 'fuck I'm old now'."
Nuno Miguel (Sons Of Albion – Guitar)

"I returned to Download for the first time in 21 years in 2009. We shot some shows there for my 'VH1 Classic' program.
It was great to be back and see how much the festival has grown and changed. One of the things I always loved was the diverse rock lineup and how the fans are so open to all kinds of music on the same bill.

Had the chance to introduce Tesla on the main stage in 2009 and we accidentally walked off stage with singer Jeff Keith's vocal mic, leaving him essentially naked on stage as his band played!
It's a remarkably well run event for its size and I also love the community vibe backstage in the artist village."
Eddie Trunk (VH1 Classic DJ)

"Another new site. More competition - Sonisphere, being run by former Download head honcho Stuart Galbraith.
This year the site was much better - to the south, plenty big and with that sense of Donington 'epicness'.
Andy Copping had done good this year - brokering a Faith No More reunion, snagging Slipknot and putting on a classic rock Sunday that featured no less than two former Monsters Of Rock headliners on the main stage."
Phil Hull (Download Forum Administrator)

"I think Staind are a cool band but was a bit disappointed they didn't play 'It's Been A While' it was still a good set. Being in a crowd of people who knew the words to 'Outside' was just something.
The Faith No More set again on Friday mainstage was very good and they played almost everything I wanted them to play including the classic Commodores number 'Easy' another crowd pleasing sing-a-long song.
On Saturday I was pleased to see The Prodigy were back on top. Their set was cracking. I have seen The Prodigy play a few pretty bad gigs at festivals in the past but this was not one of them.
On Sunday I pretty much stayed at the main stage to watch Def Leppard Whitesnake, ZZ Top and Journey. The ZZ Top set was superb as was Journey.
The best band I saw though had to be Steel Panther in the Turborg Tent. I saw their posters around the site during the day and at first thought they were advertising a new Will Ferrell film. But how great are they!? Awesome!! With songs like 'Asian Hooker' and 'Party All Day'!
I was still a little disappointed that Will couldn't make it though, but may be next year."

Mike Horton (Plymouth)

"So, I go to a club in Plymouth every week and listen to my favourite bands and know a lot of people.
Download released the confirmed bands for Download Festival and I got very excited. Faith No More and Slipknot as headliners 'hell yes I'm going to be there!'
So I come up with the idea of all going up in convoy. A big group of us met up at the start place (local superstore at the beginning of the journey). We all went in and bought our booze and alcohol I made up two cd's one of which has a song from bands that are playing at the festival and one that will generally get everyone in the mood for a long journey and get the heads banging so of course I had to put 'Bohemian Rhapsody' on. Then we agreed to meet up halfway for a stretch, so we did.
We got to Download and set up camp.
There are a few main highlights of the festival first of all; all the people we came up with in convoy met up everyday and we stayed in one big group, then one scary moment was the day we moved over to the second stage to see Static X. The whole crowd ducked for cover and ran like hell because a swarm of bees had decided to swarm through the crowd. Later we heard that there was a nest before the stage was built up and they had smoked them away but the bees had decided to return which was pretty scary!
Second highlight had to be everyone trying to build a human pyramid next to us on the last day it was amazing, it got to eight people high.
The experience and feeling I get from Download Festival is a feeling of people coming together sharing a passion for music meeting new people from all sides of the globe."

Tish Crutchley (Plymouth)

"The day I met...Dimebag Darrell. the look alike
I was heavily drunk on Thursday 11th June, walking around with Gaymers Cider in one hand a camera in the other, till I shouted really loud 'OMG DIMEBAG DARREL CAME BACK FROM THE DEAD, OMFG!!'!

*The sheer momentum of bliss wept my mind, the guitar messiah had been resurrected.
I took a photo and bragged it to everyone in the village saying how he was alive. Lol I have no idea who's the dude with him was...probably the sound technician."*
Kira Concept09girl (London)

"Download 2009 was for me my first ever festival experience and has to be one of the best moments of my life and I'm only 18. I went with my 3 friends Callum, Josh and Starkie and there we just made so many more, everyone there was so friendly and was always up for a laugh, as long as there was alcohol involved of course.
The days just became so random and you never knew what was going to happen, I remember one time this guy casually walked into our area where we were camped tied to a camping chair, he couldn't even speak because someone had taped his mouth shut, it was hilarious, we had to run round and scavenge to find something to cut him loose and all we could find at the time was a plastic knife so we just had to rip through it, the marks he had on him afterwards were crazy.
The lineup for this year I thought was amazing, I still can't pick which my favourite day out of the weekend was with my personal favourite performance of Korn on the Friday which I thought was the best of the weekend, they just got the crowd moving so well, I knew every song, we all just loved it.
Not to mention bands like Killswitch, Billy Talent and Bizkit just sweetened the deal so much more.
The Saturday on the other hand was just as good, with an early 'ish start to the day for us with Five Finger Death Punch, who being one of my favourite bands made my day straight away and it was barely midday then to move on straight after to Devildriver who's meet the wretched circle pit was immense, the sheer size of it blew everyone away, so much we had to take a break for a while. We watched Hatebreed and Down from a distance instead of being in the middle of it, to then appear back in the crowd for Manson and Slipknot. Slipknot were also quite an amazing band this year, with already seeing them once before I knew what was coming but

it was even better than I expected especially for the 'Spit It Out' ending, for the whole crowd of thousands to kneel down and "jump the fuck up", it was amazing to even see it, never mind being a part of it, it took so much out of us.
My friend had to buy about 5 bottles of coke to survive afterwards, not caring about the prices for once.
 Sunday was more of a relaxed day for us, with me and Josh waking up somehow at 7 in the morning after going to sleep at 5 and finding that someone was asleep in one of our left out camping chairs so that was quite a funny start to the day. We then managed to walk over to the cafeteria and actually have a proper meal for once to keep us going although the constant cooking of noodles kept me happy most of the time.
Sunday I thought wasn't as good for me with the bands, I mean Shinedown put on a great show, Roach were really good too and Trivium were amazing
It was unfortunate we had to leave half way through Trivium's set to go home but only seeing half of it made our day.
So overall I thought it was a great life experience and we're definitely coming back. Roll on Download 2010."
Simon James Ward (Garforth, Leeds)

"First time at Download was in 2009 and what a great venue and atmosphere.   My early images of this festival were Monster's of Rock, when I got myself a copy of Whitesnake, Live in concert 1983, Monsters of Rock, Castle Donington on Video.
My son Alex and I left at 4.20 am to get on the road and arrived at our sleepover for 9.30am. We shared a Taxi with other first timers to Download, who had travelled from Cumbria.
We were looking forward to see Journey, ZZ Top and Whitesnake. It was worth the travel and great sunshine, to enjoy the classics of Rock.   Can't wait for 2010."
Mark (the Redrocker) Jewitt & Alexander (the Pear Cider) Jewitt (Plymouth)

"During Download 2009, I think one of the highlights for me was inside the village, on the Sunday night.
Just bought a Dominos Pizza to share with a friend. As we sat down to eat, some guy literally just in his Y-Fronts and wasted, was being dragged out from the Fairground by two guys. To top this all of, he had the skids! Was really unexpected and pretty hilarious, then I thought to my self, 'Only at Download!"
Ben Calloway (Wolverhampton)

"2009 was my first year, so I thought I'd be prepared, packed a hex stove and some super noodles.
Thursday morning we woke up at 5 am (no idea why!) and the guys went back to bed, but I sat in the sun to read. Before long I started to get hungry so, thinking it was lunch time, started to cook up some noodles on the little fuel block... Wondering why I'm getting all these strange looks, my fiancé came out of the tent coz he could smell chicken, and wondered who the hell was cooking lunch at 9 in the morning! I honestly didn't realise that Donington had a different time zone when you've been drinking and was so 'jet lagged' I thought it was lunch time!"
Alley Payne (Farnham)

"The highlight of 2009 however was Def Leppard and how surprisingly great they were live and everyone shouting 'Buttscratcher!'"
Charlotte 'Coxy' Cox (Portsmouth)

"Download 2009 was my first ever festival and one of the best times I've ever had. By Sunday the camp site was like a beer can grave yard. The chaotic mess of download stands out to me.
5 days of no washing, no hair brushing the lack of rules and hygiene."
Shellie Allport (Isle of Sheppey)

"I literally had the BEST 4 DAYS OF MY LIFE at Download 2009.

To some this may sound a little absurd, but I felt entirely in my element surrounded by similar minded souls, beautiful sunshine, and a constant run of happiness and excitement. During Slipknot's headline set my mind went to another planet, I was in awe, and filled with a simple content that I haven't ever experienced before. Fantastic metal-ling times, all nighters, warm wine, new friends and mosh pit comradeship, I'm psyched I've got my 2010 ticket!"
Lauren Marina Greaves (Norwich)

"2009 was my first time coming to Download from the sunny island of Jersey and it was one I'd never forget.
It was the first time I'd ever had the chance to be in the front to watch a band. I was with my friend and since I am in a wheel chair I normally don't get the chance to get to the front but when Forever Never played the Red Bull Jam stage I finally had the chance.
It was nuts to see the band up close; nothing compared to that the whole weekend (apart from Faith No More) it may have been short set but I will never forget seeing Forever Never."
Dan Dicker (Jersey)

"I always meet a ridiculous amount of new people at Download, and always stay in touch with a fair few afterwards. It has got to be the friendliest place I've ever been, and I can't wait for 2010!"
Lucinda 17 (Cheltenham)

"I was walking around wearing nothing but a pair of shorts, a Mexican wrestling mask and a woman's bra (to this day we still don't know whose it was) in the arena in 2009.
Slipknot was rockin' the mainstage and I was making my way closer and closer to the front. As I was going I got numerous calls to pose for a picture and plenty of fine gents attempted to remove my bra, all of them failing.
I had to say it was the best of performance of Slipknot I had ever seen.
The whole festival vibe lent a hand to that. We were all brothers. Maggots. Brotherly maggots.

I only wish that I could see those pictures people had taken. All my ones sucked."
Henry Melville (London)

"Our friend Grum is a big bloke, so he can handle a lot of drink, but after getting there and setting up on Thursday afternoon, we decide to go into Donington Village to the pubs. An all day drinking binge occurred. £1 a shot, DOUBLE Jack Daniel's + Coke for £2.50, and Cigars for 60p. We somehow get back to camp (apparently by bus) about 10pm, Grum not feeling too great.
He opens up his tent and spews all over all of his stuff, and the stuff of the guy he was sharing a tent with. Thankfully we only heard the sickness. To top off this unfortunate occurrence, Scott (the guy who he shared a tent with) never realised what had happened, went to the tent to get something, opened it up.....Yes, he spewed too!
Limp Bizkit - a performance I will NEVER forget. 30 degree sunshine, lots of alcohol, and 85,000 people crammed up at the Mainstage. Opening with 'Break Stuff', I have never felt such intense crowd. Constant bouncing, if you didn't keep up, you'd go under and have to stay on the floor until someone picked you up.
Anyway, by the time 'Eat You Alive' was on, I couldn't take anymore, needed a drink, or I'd pass out. So, I got the attention of the guy beside me to boost me out, and I crowd surfed the 3 or 4 metres to the barrier, where Fred Durst was. As soon as I got to Fred, the security were on me, it was actually quite scary. About 4 stewards grabbed me and pulled me over the barrier.
"SHIT! Where's my camera?!"
I told the steward I dropped my camera, and tried to go back in, but they wouldn't let me. That camera cost me £70, and for someone just left school, that's a lot of cash.
"1, 2, 3.....Send him away!" is a little bit too long to explain in one line, so I'll do it here.
I was at Dragonforce, no idea why, think I was just too tired to bother getting out of the crowd of Down. Throughout the first few songs, I heard these guys shouting "1, 2, 3.....Send him

away!", but at this point had no idea what was going on. 6ft tall and I still couldn't see over.

Anyway, a few songs in, don't know the name, (all Dragonforce songs sound the same) I saw these 4 guys, and with there chant, they were going up to random people and throwing them up in the air, to be crowd surfed out. When they were beside me, the 4 became 3. They did this to one of their mates, when not looking. I saw it, so I looked at the guys and laughed; they laughed back, and said something along the lines of "got 'em there, eh?" Well I turn away and look at the stage, next thing I know.....

"1, 2, 3.....Send him away!"

Oh shit, they got me, ach well. Just this time I kept my hands tight in my pockets until I got out of the crowd.

And for this, sorry to the bloke I ACCIDENTALLY kicked in the face."

David Muir (Montrose)

"Download 09 was my first ever Download and first ever festival but it was possibly the best time of my life, I had been having a bad time and needed a break and I saw the line up to the festival and bought my ticket and my mates ticket as well. The fun started from the beginning when we got there at 5am and were at the front of the cue to get in, drinking Kopparberg and suddenly we were dodging a flying fish that was being thrown which was a random event but was an example of the weekend ahead as it went from random event to random event with a load of amazing performances around it (Slipknot stood out for me). on the Wednesday the weather turned horrible in the evening but me and my mate were well drunk by then and there we were, walking round the camp with no tops on, with a massive keg of beer in our hands dancing like idiots to the fair music; it was awesome.

Then on Thursday we went to the Tuborg tent and there was a massive circle pit with a mix of anything from Slipknot masks to skinny colour jeans and it went on all night and I ended up meeting sum lovely ladies as well.

Then the music started and the chaos of Download ensued and the atmosphere was electric. But the best bit was when *me and my mate as well as a mate with a day pass went to see Killswitch Engage and ended up crowd surfing and then as we were watching them they called for 2 'Walls of Death' and suddenly everyone separated behind us and we were stuck in the middle of a rather long Wall of Death, so we used it to get to the front but got caught up in it half way which was painful but absolutely hilarious and by this time everyone's voice was shot we all sounded like Darth Vader, without his mask on.*

Then on Saturday it was Slipknot day, so we both bought masks, me a green soldier mask and my mate a ninja mask and headed to the arena for the day that would change our lives forever.

First up was Static X, a band I had wanted to see since I was young and they were amazing; the pits were brilliant. Then we did the Brutal Legend World record attempt air guitar to 'Ace of Spades'. It was a great laugh.

We headed to main stage for Pendulum and had a massive rave with some rather attractive ladies in the middle, then I got separated from my mate getting through to the front but he wasn't far away I found out that night. Manson came on by which time I was at the front to see one of the heroes of my life and I was able to see him literally in the flesh and I have never been so excited in my life and although it wasn't the best performance it was exhilarating to see him so close.

He was just the starter before the main course of Slipknot. the atmosphere was rising as we waited and watched the stage take shape and all of a sudden about 10 bottles land all around me and on me and one hell of a bottle fight started and it wasn't just bottles of water there was sun cream, beer, a boot, a deck chair and random other objects then it stopped and all was silent as the stage went dark and the 'Iowa' intro came through the PA (speakers) and a roar of the crowd greeted the 9 legends as they each arrived on stage one by one and kicked into live with 'Sic' and the crowd all moved as one in a perfect imitation of waves.

Circle pits broke out all over the place getting bigger and bigger like a tornado of bodies and this was the response to most songs but the best part of it (and the festival as a whole) was the zero bullshit during 'Spit It Out' where Corey Taylor asked the crowd to get down on the ground and then made us wait till the famous "Jump the f*** up" line and as he built up with Joey the atmosphere built with every hit of the tom and kick and on cue the entire crowd erupted into chaos circle pits and mosh pits everywhere, it was the most adrenaline filled moment of my life.

When the set ended hardly anyone moved as they watched Slipknot wave and take pictures in front of the crowd sharing group hugs and then as everyone headed home they all agreed it was one of the best they have seen. Also they broke into a chorus of Queen on the way back to campsite which was again another random moment of the weekend.

Sunday was a chill out day after the night before and we spent most time at second stage as most the bands we wanted to see were on there and we managed to see the all bands from the front, as I was still wearing my mask and ended up being quite popular with the stewards, photographers and a few artists who came to the crowd.

The highlight of the Sunday was Shinedown when the lead singer made a speech on how music crosses all boundaries of race, sex and lifestyle it was so emotional every guy had a lump in his throat and the girls had tears in there eyes it was a special moment an something I will remember forever. It summed up my weekend really as it was the first time I had no worries on my mind and I could just have fun and me and my mate still talk about it and how we can't wait to return to the hallowed grounds of Donington Park."

Gary Whittick (Ellesmere Port)

"Download. The greatest five days in the calendar year. Five days of partying, shouting a lot and amazing live bands.
I say five days- you really are missing out if you don't go for the whole camping experience. I have been attending Download since 2007 and had a blast every year since then.
I have many favourite memories, but the one that sticks out the most is our 3 person circle pit outside the DJ tent at around 4 in the morning in 2009. Or it could be the memory of three of us squeezing into a two man non-waterproof tent with

all our luggage, or when I got adopted by around 20 welsh people singing Pantera's 'Walk' a lot in 2007. There aren't many other places where you could start singing The Fresh Prince Of Bel-Air theme and have 20 people join you. I often find myself having to refrain from yelling things in public for the week after Download. I hope to return to the festival every year...every year it gets better and better.
Thanks for the brilliant times Download!"
Matt Rabong (Norwich)

"I remember just as we arrived, waiting for entry into the campsite, just having a nice conversation with a random soldier on shore leave. This went on for what seems like an eternity (thank you, security being thorough mind), and so, in the spirit of fun, I shouted "I LOST THE GAME!!!" I may have proved upsetting as virtually everyone in the queue moaned, but no one lynched me. That was the best start to any festival."
Joshua Stewart (Castleford)

"The greatest thing about Download is that the atmosphere is so electric, I've been to many festivals and none have the same friendly vibe that Download has. Every single second spent in Donington is like being in Heaven. The bands are so passionate about their music and the fans are really enthusiastic. The whole weekend is aimed at people enjoying themselves... it's rock 'n' roll chaotic mayhem in its purest and loveliest form.
The absolute highlight of Download 2009 for me was getting to see Whitesnake and Def Leppard. I was utterly shattered (having basically not slept for the whole weekend) but the moment David Coverdale walked out on stage and the Whitesnake guitarists had an almighty guitar duel, I was stood there thinking "God... this is the life!".
'd been on my feet all day, in 3 inch high heeled boots nonetheless, and they were really hurting me but about 30 minutes before Def Leppard came on, I dragged my friends right to the front of the main stage. I stood there singing my heart out and dancing like a total lunatic throughout the whole

of Def Leppard's set, and screamed myself hoarse. I also almost cried when Rick Allen got a standing ovation... the whole of the crowd went absolutely wild for him, and you could see he was touched. It was a perfect moment in history and everybody remembers it, it was definitely one of the stand out moments of DL'09.
When their set was over I realised I actually could not walk... my feet were basically dead from the boots I was wearing, so my friends had to carry me all the way back to our tent, cue lots of giggling as they repeatedly almost dropped me in the dark!".
Claire Fitzmaurice (Classic Rock Fan)

"Donington is just... my home.
The times I've had there have given me what can only be described as a spiritual connection with the festival.
From wandering around the campsites drinking beer with friends old and new, through seeing some of my all-time favourite bands deliver stunning sets, to getting to DJ in the entertainments tent myself; they are all memories that will never fade.
Seeing Kiss being lowered to the stage on a giant platform!!!!"
Andy McDonald (Clydebank)

"I have been into rock 'n' metal for years; for as long as I can remember. I have a brother that's ten years older than me, so I was brought up on likes of Deep Purple, Thin Lizzy, Yes, Black Sabbath etc.
I am forty now, still rocking hard, my beer belly is bigger and my hair is now shaved off, I am still taking the journey to Castle Donington when the congregation of the metal rockers meet for the festival, I will attend as long as it's on or I will die first.
I still went to '90, '94, '96, but the events of '88 made me more aware of safety for myself and to others. R.I.P. fellow rockers. There were a few years after when I thought Donington was over, 'til my brother phoned me in excitement, this was in 2003 and that Donington the domicile of metal was back on! Download what kind of bloody name is that for our festival we

want MONSTERS OF ROCK!!!
I have been to '03, '04, '05 and '09 and I am 'made up' that it went from a one day festival, to a two and now a three."
Paul Townsend (Widnes)

"I was walking through Blue Camp with my mate at like 1 o'clock in the morning, and walked past these big guys that kept stopping people for high fives, I stopped to high five them all but little did I know that one of them was gonna catch me out with a question, (must add at this point I was well out of it by now).
He asked "what's the first rule of fight club." and I responded "I dunno, what is the first rule of fight club? What's fight club like?" (and many more questions about fight club) for about 5 minutes I was oblivious that everyone had a proper stern face aimed at me, so after I realised I became slightly scared.
I walked away with said mate as quick as I could, only for him to explain to me the first rule of fight club, I know it sounds trivial now but I felt like the biggest idiot ever at that time..."
Daniel Stromberg (Newark)

"There was a crazy woman directing us where to park being very overly hyper and joyful, sitting in the boot with friends and having the first few beers of the festival, then making your way through the campsite, with the atmosphere from all the people just being electric.
Getting to the campsite, having a few beers, trying to put the tent up and failing, being slightly tipsy, having a few more beers, trying to put the tent up and succeeding, followed by a well done beer.
That's the _I've arrived moment_."
(Steve Brodowski Bradford)

"Me and my mate Hunter decided to re-enact the Family Guy Chicken Fight across the Festival. I was dressed as the chicken and Hunter was dressed as Peter.
We started in the campsite and beat the living shit out of each other. We even ended up on Youtube when we were fighting by the lockers!

At this point we were sore as hell; both had injured legs and the worst for wear. The best part had to be when we held the fight in the middle of the pits during Devildriver's performance where I was knocked unconscious when my attempt to RKO Hunter was blocked and I was sent crashing to the floor head first knocking myself unconscious. I was apparently knocked unconscious twice!
I saw Devildriver on their UK tour months after and the guitarist Jeff remembers seeing us fight from the stage!
That was a Festival highlight for me, and possibly many others who I've gotten in touch with from the festival."
Jay Norris (Birkenhead)

"Well to start off, this is a story of the general kindness of the patrons of this magical festival.
It was Sunday; our group 12 (or so) were getting hyped for journey. Just next to us were a group from Yorkshire who were packing up planning to leave after the bands that night and were left with some spare alcohol so one of them kindly offered it to us .Being Scottish we happily agreed to receive some free drink .
As we were waiting maybe at most expecting a few beers they all started walking over all three of them with arms full; they even had to do two runs each .
By this time we were all flabbergasted and couldn't stop thanking them while they just shrugged it off and said 'We can't be bothered taking it home'.
In all they gave us around 60 mixed cans of lager and cider and around 3litres of various Sourz, 2 double inflatable mattresses and a duvet. All of the drink was consumed that day we nearly missed our journey due to being drunk. Most of us then fell asleep in the sun in front of the main stage .I was awoken by the epic ZZ Top of who I'd missed half the set. But I ask you this, what other festival in the world would you find strangers who are so generous?"
Brian Dunn (Stenhousemuir)

"2009 was my first Download festival as I have spent the last 10 years living in Australia but, you can guarantee I'll be back

in 2010 the flights are booked, the early birds are on sale tomorrow, happy birthday Donington here's to another 30 years of rocking hard."
Neil & Maria Bees (Perth, Australia)

*"There are many stories in recent years of amazing bands such as Lostprophet's pulling off the headline set in 2008, The Blackout's two stand out sets to moderate crowds and Limp Bizkit's stomping comeback in 2009 but one of the more interesting events that I was witness to was the bees.
It was a day of random occurrences. It started with a story from a mate that they'd been stung by a bee on the way to Derby that Saturday morning in 2009 and ended with My Passion's electro-rock stylings in a song about bee's (Day of the Bees).
They couldn't have played on a more appropriate day or at a more appropriate time for while they were playing in the Red Bull Jam tent, the second stage was being closed down due to a swarm of, you guessed it, bees!"*
Jenni Wallace (London)

*"A first favourite memory of mine is when I woke up at like 5 in the morning and could hear someone snoring really really loud, my friends then woke up and were like "is that what I think it is?". We got out of the tent to see where it was coming from and a group of other campers were creeping around the tents going "We're getting closer to the snoring beast!", We actually still don't know to this day who was snoring! But oh my it was louder than the planes flying over our heads! I really wished I had filmed it!
Another memory is our tent! We had put it up wrong it was barely standing, it had a blow up cock tied to it and a Slipknot flag. Lying in the tent of a night and people going past saying "Okay there's the slipCOCK tent, so our tent must be over there!" It's nice to know our tent helped a lot off people back to theirs!
My Last favourite memory is when I was watching Trivium and my friends decided to go in the mosh pit. I couldn't because I had bad sunburn and just got a piercing! (How cool am I?) Ha-*

ha, and I was just standing there and heard someone shout Titanic Is coming!
I looked around and there were two dudes in a Rubber Dingy! (Blow up boat for the sea!) crowd surfing in it, the effort it took them to get to the barriers and then watching the Stewards pulling the boat down from the people heads! And one guy falling out! was the most hilarious thing I have ever seen. I can honestly say I couldn't breathe after seeing that. Pure genius!"
Laura Philipson (East London)

"For the past few years it has been me and my best mate "Thelma and Louising" it, we make a point of dropping everything just to make sure we go as we have both always been the core of the group who have slowly filtered, got married, had families and found things more important than this festival but to us two girls its one of our highlights of the year.   I must admit we do RIP it nowadays but believe me I think we deserve it after this long!! Anyway in 2010 our fella's are coming with us as we felt a bit mean leaving them behind for AC/DC so this will be a nice new experience for all of us!"
Jude Wright (Wallasey, Merseyside)

"Friday night at Download '09; Limp Bizkit as the sun was going down, police helicopter hovering overhead watching too! Pretty sure I didn't imagine it. Awesome."
Rose Mills (Derby local)

"Download '09 was my first ever Download, and didn't really know what to expect...
However, the first thing I saw as I walked into the first campsite on Thursday afternoon while looking for a place to pitch my tent, was a man passed out with a tent pitched on top of him.
Obviously, he had had a little bit too much to drink and passed out. His mates then thought it funny to pitch his tent for him, on top of him. Poor guy...
That was my first impression of a Download experience, and

one that pretty much sums up Download '09 for me..."
Timmy Cochrane (Guilford)

"One of my friends was a 19 year old virgin at Download 2009, he is a large guy but everyone in our group decided it was our mission to get him laid!
This one girl liked the look of him and said that she might be up for taking his virginity until he shouted "I'll cum in 5 seconds!" She then moved on very quickly. Later the same day, another girl was up for it but once again he ruined his second chance by running away scared!
He then had another chance the very same day. The girl told him to wait where he was and she would get everyone out of her tent and then they would go back but he ran off once again even though my mates tried to keep him there!
Hopefully Download 2010 will be his time!"
Graham Simmonds (London)

Epilogue

Well, that just about ties it all up, as far as 1980-2009 that is.

There will be another volume that I shall release when I have enough chapters, 2010 to 2020 maybe – to celebrate the full 40 years since the first MOR way back in 1980, who knows it might be out sooner? The addition of more bands means more interviews, a bigger book, a wider fan base etc...

I must say that I love the festival very much from the beginning and forward into the future, though my camping days are gone, I'm still there at the front drinking beers, signing along and watching some awesome bands, long may the festival continue!!

Thanks Section

Andy Copping, John Probyn & Stuart Galbraith from Live Nation

Steve Jenner from Virtual Festivals

Tom Ames – Reel Big Fish TM

Emma Watson – Fifteen To One PR

Kas Mercer – Mercenary Publicity

Adam Lawrence – He likes the ladies & benches with plaques on

Laura McCartney – Full of good ideas and my #1 promoter

Phil & Carrie Hull – Download Forum Gurus

Mike Horton, Karl Woodcock & Mark Jewitt for drinking too much

And all those people that I have forgotten……you know who you are and if you don't, you shouldn't drink so much?

Finally my biggest thanks to Raine & Nathan Carroll for putting up with me all the time, love you both (and Rex)

Printed in Great Britain
by Amazon